Equity Hybrid Derivatives

MARCUS OVERHAUS

ANA BERMÚDEZ

HANS BUEHLER

ANDREW FERRARIS

CHRISTOPHER JORDINSON

AZIZ LAMNOUAR

T0368016

BICENTENNIAL
1807
WILEY
2007
BICENTENNIAL

John Wiley & Sons, Inc.

Published by John Wiley & Sons, Inc., Hoboken, New Jersey.
Published simultaneously in Canada.

For general information on our other products and services or for technical support, please contact our Customer Care Department within the United States at (800) 762-2974, outside the United States at (317) 572-3993 or fax (317) 572-4002.

Wiley publishes in a variety of print and electronic formats and by print-on-demand. Some material included with standard print versions of this book may not be included in e-books or in print-on-demand. If this book refers to media such as a CD or DVD that is not included in the version you purchased, you may download this material at http://booksupport.wiley.com. For more information about Wiley products, visit www.wiley.com.

Library of Congress Cataloging-in-Publication Data:

Equity hybrid derivatives / Marcus Overhaus ... [et al.].
        p. cm. — (Wiley finance series)
    Includes bibliographical references and index.
    ISBN-13: 978-0-471-77058-9 (cloth)
    ISBN-10: 0-471-77058-2 (cloth)
    1. Derivative securities. 2. Convertible securities. I. Overhaus, Marcus. II. Title. III. Series.
HG6024.A3E684 2006
332.64′57—dc22
                                            2006005369

10 9 8 7 6 5 4 3 2 1

Contents

PART TWO
Equity Interest Rate Hybrids

Preface

Equity hybrid derivatives are a very young class of structures which have drawn a lot of attention over the past two years for many different reasons. Equity hybrid derivatives combine all existing, and therefore established, asset classes like equity, credit, interest rate, foreign exchange, and commodity derivatives. Hence, they present a very interesting challenge to combining different modeling techniques and thereby forming a solid hybrid model framework. This is why we have again decided to publish a book entirely concerned with this very interesting topic. Hybrid derivatives are a strategic and profitable business that every serious top-tier investment bank needs to offer to its client base and are therefore an integral part of its derivatives business.

In this volume, we have not tried to write an introductory text: we have assumed some prior familiarity with mathematics and finance. Part One of this book gives insight into different volatility models (Heston, SABR etc) and their applications to equity markets. It also contains some very recent developments such as variance swap market models. Part Two gives a brief review of short rate models and their incorporation into equity-interest rate hybrid structures. Important examples are discussed, such as the conditional trigger swap (CTS), convertible bonds, and the very popular CPPI structures. Part Three contains a thorough introduction to credit modeling and its importance to equity-credit hybrid derivative structures. Pricing and calibration techniques are also discussed in detail, and important examples like the EDS (equity default swap) are given. Part Four is dedicated to advanced pricing techniques applied to various hybrid and callable structures. We start with copulas applied to equity and credit derivatives (Altiplanos and default baskets), then discuss forward PDEs and local volatility calibration techniques and their application to equity-rate hybrids. This is followed by a thorough presentation of numerical solutions for multi-factor pricing problems, including an important example, the convertible bond. Finally, we conclude with an exposition of American Monte Carlo techniques for derivative pricing.

We would like to offer our special thanks to Professor Alexander Schied for careful reading of the manuscript and valuable comments. We would also like to express our gratitude to Kenji Felgenhauer, Eric Bensoussan, Peter Carr, and Maria Noguieras.

The Authors

London
February 2006

PART One

Modeling Volatility

CHAPTER 1

Theory

In this chapter, we will introduce some basic concepts of equity modeling. We will discuss how the stock price can be modeled in a framework with deterministic interest rates, dividends, and default probabilities and how a given implied volatility surface can be matched with Dupire's "implied local volatility." We also mention alternatives and how European payoffs whose value depends only on the stock price on a single maturity can be priced independent of further model assumptions by hedging with European options. We also make a few remarks on theoretical aspects of replication. This chapter is the foundation of chapter 2, where we will discuss applications: various stochastic volatility models, pricing of Cliquets, variance swaps, and related products and models to price options on variance. The assumptions of deterministic interest rates and default risk probabilities are then subsequently relaxed in the later chapters of this book.

1.1   CONCEPTS OF EQUITY MODELING

Since the main focus of this chapter is the modeling of the pure equity risk, we will work with a framework where interest rates, dividends, and default risk are deterministic. We will model the stock price on a stochastic base $\mathbb{W} = (\Omega, \mathcal{F}_\infty, \mathbb{F} = (\mathcal{F}_t)_{t \geq 0}, \mathbb{Q})$. The measure $\mathbb{Q}$ is the "historic" measure. We denote by $r = (r_t)_{t \geq 0}$ the deterministic interest rates and we use $\mu = (\mu_t)_{t \geq 0}$ to refer to a deterministic repo rate (it represents the gains we make from lending out a share). We will also use B for the cash bond (or "money market account"), that is,

$$B_t := e^{\int_0^t r_u \, du}$$

and

$$P(t, T) := e^{-\int_t^T r_s \, ds}$$

for the price at time t of a zero bond with maturity T (see chapter 3 for the case of stochastic interest rates). We also assume that the stock can default: In the event of default, whose time we denote by τ, we stipulate that the value of the share drops to zero. We also assume that corporate zero bonds of the company we want to model are traded for all maturities, and that the value of any outstanding bonds will also drop to zero in the event of default (in practice, this rarely happens: usually, a bond will have some "recovery value," which represents the fraction of the notional that the defaulted company is still able to pay).[1] Since the "risky" corporate zero bond can default, its price at any time prior to τ must be less than the price of the "riskless" government zero bond with same maturity and notional: the zero bond is trading at a spread. We will assume that this spread, or *hazard rate*, $h = (h_t)_{t\geq 0}$, of the risky bond interest rate over the riskless rate r, is deterministic, such that the price of the risky zero bond with maturity T at time t is given as

$$P^S(t,T) := 1_{\tau > t}\, e^{-\int_t^T (r_u + h_u)\, du}.$$

(Our restriction to deterministic hazard rates will be lifted in chapter 6, where we discuss approaches to model h as a stochastic process.) The default event τ itself is then modeled as an inaccessible exponentially distributed stopping time with intensity h, which is assumed to be independent from the filtration $\mathbb{F}$ (i.e., of stock price, interest rates, volatility, etc.).[2] Inaccessibility means that the default cannot be foretold by observations of the stock price: It excludes, for example, stopping times that are the result of the stock price crossing some barrier.[3] In this setting, we assume, under any pricing measure $\mathbb{P}$ equivalent to $\mathbb{Q}$ that

$$\mathbb{P}\left[\tau > T\,|\,\mathcal{F}_t\right] = 1_{\tau > t}\, e^{-\int_t^T h_s\, ds}\,, \tag{1.1}$$

which implies the intuitive relation $P^S(t,T) = \mathbb{P}[\tau > T | \tau > t]\, P(t,T)$ (i.e., the price of the risky bond is the price of the riskless bond times the probability of default). Moreover, our assumptions that zero bonds are available for all maturities, implies that we can *roll over* a capital investment of 1 into the risky zero bonds and thereby generate a risky cash bond,

$$B^S_t := 1_{\tau > t}\, e^{\int_0^t (r_u + h_u)\, du},$$

which will also drop to zero in the event of default.

As mentioned above, the availability of both the risky and the riskless bond allows us to synthesize a payoff of 1 if the company has defaulted up to some maturity T. As a consequence, we can hedge out the risk of default when pricing an option. A put written on the stock $S = (S_t)_{t\geq 0}$, for example, can be decomposed into

$$(K - S_T)^+ = (K - S_T)^+ 1_{\tau > T} + K 1_{\tau \leq T}.$$

Hence, we can split its value in the "default value" $K 1_{\tau \leq T}$, which we can hedge by entering into a long position in a risky zero bond and a short position in a riskless zero bond, and the "survival value" $(K - S_T)^+ 1_{\tau > T}$, whose hedge we can approach using standard replication theory, as explained in section 1.4.

---

[1] Section 9.6 on page 279 covers the pricing of convertible bonds under various more detailed assumptions.

[2] Blanchet-Scalliet/Jeanblanc [1] provide a good introduction into intensity models.

[3] Mathematically speaking, an accessible stopping time can be approximated by an increasing sequence of stopping times $(\tau_n)_n$ with $\tau_n \uparrow \tau$ for $n \uparrow \infty$.

1.1.1 The Forward

We also assume that the stock pays dividends. On each of the dividend dates $0 =: \tau_0 < \tau_1 < \tau_2 \cdots$, we assume that first a proportional dividend of $\beta_k = 1 - e^{-d_k}$ and then a cash dividend of α_k is paid. As a result, the stock price at a dividend date will drop by the relative amount $e^{-d_k} = 1 - \beta_k$ and the absolute amount α_k. Of course, dividends are only paid if the stock did not yet default. Hence, if we assume that the stock price process $S = (S_t)_{t \geq 0}$ only jumps due to dividends, at each dividend date $\tau_k < \tau$, we have

$$S_{\tau_k} = S_{\tau_k -} e^{-d_k} - \alpha_k \,. \tag{1.2}$$

In this setting, let us derive the value of a forward contract with delivery time T: Assume first we buy η shares today and that we short ηS_0 riskless zero bonds in order to borrow the required initial capital.[4] Since we hold the stock we will earn repo and receive the dividends it pays. To handle them, we decide to reinvest all proportional dividends and proceeds from repo contracts into the stock. Since we receive as many cash dividends as we hold units of stock, this implies that at any time τ_k before default, we receive an amount of

$$\eta \alpha_k e^{\int_0^{\tau_k} \mu_u \, du + \sum_{j \leq k} d_j} \,.$$

We will use these proceedings to buy back our initially issued debt. If the stock does not default, this implies that at time T, we hold

$$\eta e^{\int_0^T \mu_u \, du + \sum_{k : \tau_k \leq T} d_k}$$

units of stock and that we are short

$$\eta S_0 e^{\int_0^T r_u \, du} - \sum_{k : \tau_k \leq T} \eta \alpha_k e^{\int_0^{\tau_k} \mu_u \, du + \sum_{j \leq k} d_j} e^{\int_{\tau_k}^T r_u \, du}$$

$$= \eta \left(S_0 - \sum_{k : \tau_k \leq T} \alpha_k e^{\int_0^{\tau_k} (-r_u + \mu_u) \, du + \sum_{j \leq k} d_j} \right) e^{\int_0^T r_u \, du}$$

units of the zero bond. In order to be able to deliver exactly one share in time T, we chose $\eta = e^{-\int_0^T \mu_u \, du - \sum_{k : \tau_k \leq T} d_k}$ such that our terminal capital reads

$$K^{\text{no default}} = S_0 e^{\int_0^T (r_u - \mu_u) \, du - \sum_{k : \tau_k \leq T} d_k} - \sum_{k : \tau_k \leq T} \alpha_k e^{\int_{\tau_k}^T (r_u - \mu_u) \, du - \sum_{j : \tau_k < \tau_j \leq T} d_j} \,,$$

which is therefore the fair strike conditional on no default. However, if there is a default at some time $0 < \tau < T$, then we will forgo the dividends thereafter. Hence, if we receive K for the share at T, we will be short the missing dividend amounts.

---

[4]We implicitly assume that we by ourselves cannot default.

To protect ourselves against default, we need a mechanism which ensures that our terminal bank account always has the same value at time T, be there default or not. This can be achieved if we "forward-sell" the proceeds of the dividends. To this end, we sell "risky" (corporate) zero bonds with maturities $0 < \tau_1 < \cdots < \tau_N$ (where $\tau_N \leq T < \tau_{N+1}$). Each bond has a notional of

$$\alpha_k e^{-\int_{\tau_k}^{T} \mu_u \, du - \sum_{j:\tau_k < \tau_j \leq T} d_j},$$

and since we hold the appropriate amount of shares at any time before default, we will always be able to fulfill our obligations arising from shorting the bonds. However, since the bond is risky, we have to pay a risk premium of h to the buyers of these bonds, so shorting the bonds yields only

$$e^{-\int_{0}^{\tau_k} (r_u + h_u) \, du} e^{-\int_{\tau_k}^{T} \mu_u \, du - \sum_{j:\tau_k < \tau_j \leq T} d_j}.$$

Summing up, we find that the forward strike on S with maturity T is given as

$$F_t = S_0 e^{\int_{0}^{t} (r_u - \mu_u) \, du - \sum_{k:\tau_k \leq t} d_k} - \sum_{k:\tau_k \leq t} \alpha_k e^{-\int_{0}^{\tau_k} h_u \, du} e^{\int_{\tau_k}^{t} (r_u - \mu_u) \, du - \sum_{j:\tau_k < \tau_j \leq t} d_j}. \tag{1.3}$$

Hence, in the absence of cash dividends, the fair forward strike for an asset does not depend on the default risk involved. Note that F must in all cases be non-negative due to no-arbitrage constraints.

1.1.2 The Shape of Dividends to Come

Given the form of the forward (1.3), what are the implications for potential stock price processes? Between the discrete cash dividends, standard no-arbitrage arguments show that if there is "no free lunch with vanishing risk,"[5] then there exists a measure $\mathbb{P}$, equivalent to $\mathbb{Q}$, and a local $\mathbb{P}$-martingale Y such that

$$S_t = S_{\tau_{k-1}} \frac{Y_t}{Y_{\tau_{k-1}}} e^{\int_{\tau_{k-1}}^{t} (r_u + h_u - \mu_u) \, du} \quad \{\tau > t\}$$

holds for $t \in [\tau_{k-1}, \tau_k)$. In τ_k, equation (1.2) applies and we get, added up,

$$S_t = S_0 e^{\int_{0}^{t} (r_u - \mu_u) \, du - \sum_{k:\tau_k \leq t} d_k} Y_t - \sum_{k:\tau_k \leq t} \alpha_k e^{\int_{\tau_k}^{t} (r_u - \mu_u) \, du - \sum_{k:\tau_k \leq t} d_k} \frac{Y_t}{Y_{\tau_k}} \quad \text{on } \{\tau > t\}.$$

$$\tag{1.4}$$

However, Y is also subject to the constraint that the process S cannot become negative. We will now investigate the impact of this property. The following

---

[5]The notion of "no free lunch with vanishing risk" is a stronger form of "no arbitrage." Only the former is equivalent to the existence of a local martingale measure, and we will always assume we are in this setting. See Delbaen/Schachermayer [2] for a detailed analysis and examples.

discussion holds for local martingales in general, but we focus on the relevant true martingale case. For ease of exposure, let us briefly assume that $S_0 = 1$, $r \equiv 0$, $\mu \equiv 0$, $h \equiv 0$ and $d_i \equiv 0$, that is, with $\theta/\theta = \theta$,

$$S_t = Y_t - \sum_{k:\tau_k \leq t} \alpha_k \frac{Y_t}{Y_{\tau_k}} \,. \tag{1.5}$$

At any point t, the forward of the stock to a later date $T > t$ must remain non-negative. This implies that at any dividend date τ_k, the stock price must exceed the value of all forthcoming dividends,

$$S_t = S_{\tau_k} \frac{Y_t}{Y_{\tau_k}} \geq \sum_{j>k} \alpha_j \quad t \in [\tau_k, \tau_{k+1}) \,.$$

Since a martingale M with unit mean that is bounded from below by some $\ell \in [0,1]$ can be written as $M_t = M_t^+(1 - \ell) + \ell$ in terms of a non-negative martingale M^+ which has again unit mean, we can write Y in terms of some non-negative martingale X with unit mean as

$$\frac{Y_t}{Y_{\tau_k}} = \frac{X_t}{X_{\tau_k}} \frac{1 - \sum_{j>k} \alpha_j}{S_{\tau_k}} + \frac{\sum_{j>k} \alpha_j}{S_{\tau_k}} \quad t \in [\tau_k, \tau_{k+1}) \,.$$

By induction from $k = 1$ it follows that

$$S_t = \left(1 - \sum_{k=1}^{\infty} \alpha_k\right) X_t + \sum_{k:\tau_k > t} \alpha_k \,.$$

In the case of nonzero interest rates, repo rates, and default intensity, we have more general:

RESULT 1 *There exists a non-negative martingale X with unit mean such that*

$$S_t = F_t^* X_t + A_t \quad on \; \{\tau > t\} \tag{1.6}$$

with

$$F_t^* := \left(S_0 - \sum_{k=1}^{\infty} \alpha_k^*\right) R_t \tag{1.7}$$

$$A_t := \sum_{k:\tau_k > t} D_t \alpha_k^* \tag{1.8}$$

$$R_t := e^{\int_0^t (r_u + h_u - \mu_u)\,du - \sum_{k:\tau_k \leq t} d_k}$$

and

$$\alpha_k^* := \frac{\alpha_k}{R_{\tau_k}} \,.$$

We call X the "pure" stock price process.

The implication of the previous result is that we can focus on the modeling of the pure martingale part X instead of modeling S itself. This will be the subject of this part of the book. Extension to the case of stochastic interest rates or stochastic default intensities is presented in the later chapters of this book.

The previous remarks also allow us to derive the form of the total return version of the stock: Here, we reinvest the proceeds from repo rate and dividends directly back into the asset, as soon as they occur.

RESULT 2 *The* total return process $S^{(\mathrm{TR})}$ *of the stock is given as*

$$S_t^{(\mathrm{TR})} = \left(S_0 - \sum_{k:\tau_k>t} \alpha_k e^{-\int_0^{\tau_k}(r_u+h_u)\,du} \right) e^{\int_0^t (r_u+h_u)\,du} X_t 1_{\tau>t} + \sum_{k:\tau_k>t} \alpha_k e^{-\int_{\tau_k}^t(r_u+h_u)\,du} 1_{\tau>t} .$$

We can also go a step further: Since we are sure of the dividends we will receive, we may forward-sell them. To this end, assume that we buy one share and that we write risky zero bonds for $\tau_1 < \tau_2 < \cdots$ with notionals $a_k := \alpha_k e^{\int_t^{\tau_k}\mu_u\,du + \sum_{j:t<\tau_j<\tau_k} d_j}$. We will be able to honor the respective bond obligations if we reinvest the proceeds from repo rates and continuous dividends into the stock. The gain from forward-selling the dividends will be precisely A_0, as defined in (1.8). Hence, the overall price process of this asset is

$$S_t^{(\mathrm{plain})} = S_0 e^{\int_0^t r_u+h_u\,du} X_t 1_{\tau>t} = S_0 B_t^S X_t . \tag{1.9}$$

The crucial observation is that $S_t^{(\mathrm{plain})}$ is *tradable* (i.e., available for hedging purposes). This will be used in section 1.4.

Ito in the Presence of Dividends The process (1.6) exhibits jumps, in which case the standard Ito formula does not hold anymore. In our case these jumps are of finite variation, which essentially implies that if we apply Ito to some $f \in C^2$, then the second derivative of f will be integrated over the quadratic variation of the "continuous part" of S only. For convenience, let us reformulate (1.6) in terms of purely proportional but then stochastic discrete dividends. To this end we first define the deterministic functions

$$\bar{\alpha}_t := \sum_k \alpha_k 1_{\tau_k=t} \quad \text{and} \quad \bar{d}_t := \sum_k d_k 1_{\tau_k=t} , \tag{1.10}$$

which are nonzero only on the dividend dates $(\tau_k)_{k=1,\dots}$. They represent the fixed and proportional dividends paid at each time t. Accordingly,

$$S_t = S_{t-} e^{-\bar{d}_t} - \bar{\alpha}_t . \tag{1.11}$$

We can then define the *stochastic* "proportional dividend process" by accumulating the cash dividends into the exponential drift of the stock as

$$\overline{D}_t := -\log\frac{S_t}{S_{t-}} = -\log\left(e^{-\bar{d}_t} - \frac{\bar{\alpha}_t}{S_{t-}} \right) ,$$

which gives

$$S_t = X_t e^{\int_0^t (r_u - \mu_u)\,du - \sum_{u \le t} \overline{D}_u} \ . \tag{1.12}$$

Of course, if there are no fixed cash dividends α, then $\overline{D} = \overline{d}$ is deterministic. The SDE of S can now be written as

$$\frac{dS_t}{S_{t-}} = (r_t - \mu_t)\,dt - (1 - e^{-\overline{D}_t})\delta_t(dt) + \frac{dX_t}{X_t} \ , \tag{1.13}$$

where $\delta_t(\cdot)$ denotes the Dirac measure in t. If X is continuous, and if its quadratic variation is absolutely continuous with respect to the Lebesgue measure, then there exists an integrable *short-variance* process $\zeta = (\zeta_t)_{t \ge 0}$ and a Brownian motion B such that

$$X_t = \mathcal{E}_t\left(\int_0^\cdot \sqrt{\zeta_u}\,dB_u\right) \ ,$$

where we have used the *Doleans-Dade-exponential*

$$\mathcal{E}_t(Z) := e^{Z_t - \frac{1}{2}\langle Z \rangle_t} \ .$$

In this case, Ito's formula for S and $f \in C^2$ (or finite and convex) becomes

$$df(S_t) = f'(S_{t-})dS_t + \frac{1}{2}f''(S_{t-})S_{t-}^2\zeta_t - f'(S_{t-})\Delta S_t + \Delta f(S_t) \tag{1.14}$$

where $S_{t-}^2\zeta_t\,dt$ is the quadratic variation of the continuous part of S.[6] In integral form, (1.14) reads

$$f(S_T) - f(S_0) = \int_0^T f'(S_{t-})S_{t-}\left((r_t - \mu_t)dt + \sqrt{\zeta_t}\,dB_t\right) + \frac{1}{2}\int_0^T f''(S_{t-})S_{t-}^2\zeta_t\,dt$$
$$+ \sum_{t \le T}\left(f(S_{t-}e^{-\overline{D}_t}) - f(S_{t-})\right) \ .$$

Also note that the quadratic variation of S is given as

$$\langle S \rangle_T = \int_0^T S_{t-}^2\zeta_t\,dt + \sum_{t \le T}\left(e^{-\overline{D}_t} - 1\right)^2 S_{t-}^2 \ .$$

---

[6] If f is finite and convex, f'' exists as a positive measure. For example, the second derivative of $f(x) := x^+$ is the Dirac measure in zero, δ_0.

1.1.3 European Options on the Pure Stock Process

Since S is an affine transformation (1.6) of the pure stock price X, we can express the prices of European options on the former in terms of prices of European options on the latter. Indeed, let

$$\mathbb{C}(T,K) := \mathbb{E}_{\mathbb{P}}\left[B_T^{-1}\left(S_T - K\right)^+ \right].$$
(1.15)

Then,

$$\mathbb{C}(T,K) = P(0,T)F_T^* \, \mathbb{E}_{\mathbb{P}}\left[1_{T>\tau} \left(X_T - \frac{K - A_T}{F_T^*} \right)^+ \right]$$

$$= P^S(0,T)F_T^* \, \mathcal{C}\left(T, \frac{K - A_T}{F_T^*} \right),$$

where we define

$$\mathcal{C}(T,k) := \mathbb{E}_{\mathbb{P}}\left[\left(X_T - k \right)^+ \right],$$
(1.16)

which is the price of call on the pure stock price with strike k.[7]

RESULT 3 *The call price on a stock S is given in terms of a call $\mathcal{C}$ on the pure stock price X as*

$$\mathbb{C}(T,K) = P^S(0,T)F_T^* \, \mathcal{C}\left(T, \frac{K - A_T}{F_T^*} \right).$$
(1.17)

Hence, if call prices $\mathbb{C}(T,K)$ are available for all strikes and maturities, we can derive the respective prices $\mathcal{C}(T,k)$ for all "pure strikes" k from the market via

$$\mathcal{C}(T,k) := \frac{1}{P^S(0,T)F_T^*} \, \mathbb{C}\left(T, kF_T^* + A_T \right).$$
(1.18)

By put/call parity, the price of a put $\mathbb{U}$ on S with strike K and maturity T is given as

$$\mathbb{U}(K,T) := \mathbb{E}\left[B_T^{-1}\left(K - S_T\right)^+ \right] = \mathbb{C}(T,K) + P(0,T)K - P(0,T)F_T,$$

which implies the obvious lower bound

$$\mathbb{E}\left[B_T^{-1}\left(K - S_T\right)^+ \right] \geq \left(P(0,T) - P^S(0,T) \right) K = P(0,T)\mathbb{P}[\tau \leq T]K.$$

---

[7]Strictly speaking, we can call $\mathcal{C}(T,k)$ only then the price of the respective call on X, if either the market is complete (i.e., $\mathbb{P}$ is unique) or if the call on S with strike $K = kF_T^* + A_T$ and maturity T is quoted in the market, in which case its price is given under any $\mathbb{Q}$-equivalent martingale measure by (1.15).

Consequently, the "pure" put $\mathcal{U}(T, k) := \mathbb{E}_{\mathbb{P}}\left[(k - X_T)^+\right]$ on X is given in terms of the put $\mathbb{U}(T, K)$ on the original stock S as

$$\mathcal{U}(T, k) = \frac{1}{P^S(0,T)F_T^*}\left(\mathbb{U}\left(T, kF_T^* + A_T\right) - \mathbb{P}^S(0,T)\left(kF_T^* + A_T\right)\right). \qquad (1.19)$$

The above results imply that as long as we consider markets where only the stock price process S and European options are liquidly traded, we can focus entirely on the process X. The above equations, (1.17) and (1.18), respectively, allow us to convert one representation into the other. We will frequently switch between the two objects S and X, depending on the application.

1.2 IMPLIED VOLATILITY

The most famous stock price model is the *Black & Scholes model*. In our framework (1.6), it is given under the unique risk-neutral measure $\mathbb{P}$ by assuming that X is a geometric Brownian motion; that is,

$$\frac{dX_t}{X_t} = \sigma_t\,d\mathrm{W}_t \qquad (1.20)$$

for some non-negative function σ and a $\mathbb{P}$-Brownian motion W. The solution to (1.20) is

$$X_t = e^{\int_0^t \sigma_u\,d\mathrm{W}_u - \frac{1}{2}\int_0^t \sigma_u^2\,du}. \qquad (1.21)$$

In fact, this model has been introduced by Samuelson [3] and the time-dependent version above is due to Merton [4], but in practice most people refer to it as *the Black-Scholes model* (usually in the case without discrete dividends, though). The crucial contribution by Black and Scholes [5] was not so much the model itself, but the fundamental insight that any contingent claim $H(S_T)$ for a sufficiently well-behaved function H can be replicated perfectly by continuous trading in the stock. The impact of this insight cannot be underestimated: Ever since Black and Scholes published their work, a huge industry has evolved in whose core lies the idea of replication of otherwise risky payoffs. The bottom line of the idea is that since we can replicate the payoff, there is no *risk* in selling a contingent claim. Hence, the costs of replication are certain, and it is justified to call this cost the *price* of the contingent claim (we will discuss this in more detail in section 1.4).

In the Black-Scholes model, it is particularly easy to compute the prices of many standard payoffs. A standard example is the price of a European call on X with maturity T and "pure strike" k as defined in (1.16) (recall result 3, which shows that it is sufficient to consider X rather than S). Its value is given as

$$\mathcal{C}(T, k) = \mathbb{BS}\left(T, k, \sqrt{\frac{1}{T}\int_0^T \sigma_u^2\,du}\right)$$

in terms of the famous *Black-Scholes formula*

$$\mathbb{BS}(k, T; \sigma) := \mathcal{N}(d^+) - k\mathcal{N}(d^-) \quad \text{with} \quad d^\pm := \frac{-\ln k \pm \frac{1}{2}\sigma^2 T}{\sigma\sqrt{T}}.$$

To price an option on S in Black and Scholes's framework, note that the price of a call with maturity T and strike K is given as

$$\mathbb{BS}^S(T, K, \sigma^S) := P^S(0, T)F_T^* \mathbb{BS}\left(T, \frac{K - A_T}{F_T^*}, \sigma^S\right).$$

Since the Black and Scholes formula $\mathbb{BS}$ is strictly increasing in σ, it is possible to solve for the latter given a market call price $\hat{C}(T, k)$. This yields the common measure of *implied volatility* for the price of an option:

DEFINITION 1.2.1 *We call*

$$\hat{\sigma}(T, k) := \mathbb{BS}(T, k; \cdot)^{-1}\left(\hat{C}(T, k)\right) \tag{1.22}$$

the implied volatility *of X at (T, k) and*

$$\hat{\sigma}^S(T, K) := \mathbb{BS}^S(T, K, \cdot)^{-1}\left(\hat{\mathbb{C}}(T, K)\right)$$

the implied volatility of S for (T, K). Note that by construction $\hat{\sigma}(T, k) = \hat{\sigma}^S(T, kF_T^* + A_T)$.

Interpretation It should be stressed that the notion of "implied volatility" does not imply that we are actually using the Black-Scholes model. Indeed, it is evident from quoted market prices that their model is no longer sufficient to evaluate contingent claims. To see this, consider figure 1.1, where we have plotted implied volatilities of STOXX50E.[8]

The effect that implied volatility $\hat{\sigma}(T, k)$ is a decreasing function of strike is called *skew*. Most equity markets have such a shape, but some are less pronounced than STOXX50E; for example, the Japanese N225, which is shown in figure 1.2.[9] The point is that implied volatility depends strongly on the strike across all maturities. This means that the underlying stock price process cannot be explained using the Black-Scholes model, for which the implied volatility does not depend on the strike. Rather, we need to find a convenient model for X is able to produce implied volatility surfaces that such as the ones displayed in the figures. When considering alternative models, we should take into account the fact that the general shape of implied volatility is remarkably stable: Figure 1.3 on page 14 shows how the implied volatility surface of STOXX50E has changed in the last few years.

---

[8]We refer to underlyings by their Reuters code.
[9]Symmetric "smiles" are a common feature in FX markets. In other markets, such as commodities, the skew might actually be upward sloping.

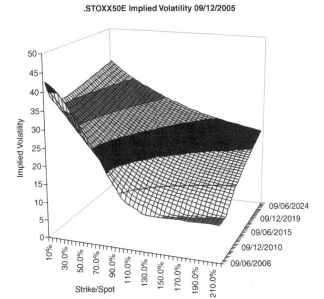

FIGURE 1.1 Implied volatilities for different strikes and maturities for STOXX50E. The graph shows a strong "skew" in strike direction for all maturities.

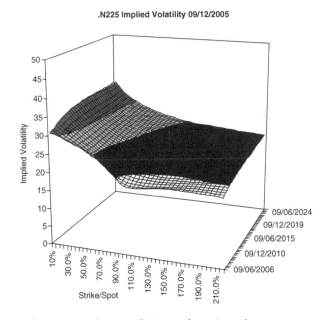

FIGURE 1.2 N225 features nearly a "smile"-type shape in strike.

1.2.1 Sticky Volatilities

Another interesting question is how implied volatility moves on an instantaneous time scale when the stock price moves. Following Balland [6], we consider *sticky strike* and *sticky delta* markets. In a sticky strike market, the implied volatility

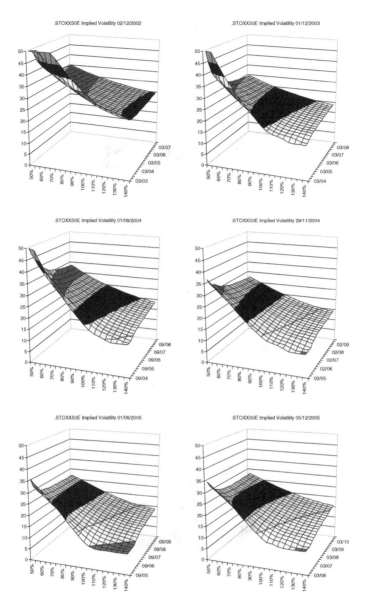

FIGURE 1.3   Historic STOXX50E implied volatility during the last few years.

$\hat{\sigma}_t^S(T,K)$ of an option on S with cash strike K is deterministic. In a sticky delta market, on the other hand, the implied volatility "relative to the forward" or, in our case, $\hat{\sigma}_t(T,k)$, is deterministic. The impact of the actual behavior of the implied volatility can best be seen in the effect on the delta of a European option (for notational simplicity, assume that $S = X$). To this end, we write the implied volatility $\hat{\sigma}^S(T,K)$ of S at time $t = 0$ as a function of S_0 as $\hat{\sigma}^S(S_0,T,K)$. The price of a call with maturity T and strike K is then

$$\hat{\mathbb{C}}(S_0,T,K) = \mathbb{BS}^S\Big(S_0,T,K,\hat{\sigma}_0^S(S_0,T,K)\Big). \qquad (1.23)$$

In a sticky strike market, the function $\hat{\sigma}_0^S$ does not depend on S_0, that is, $\hat{\sigma}_0^S(S_0, T, K) \equiv \Sigma(T, K)$, for some function Σ. In a sticky delta situation, on the other hand, we have $\hat{\sigma}_0^S(S_0, T, K) \equiv \Sigma(T, K/S_0)$. Consequently, the total derivative of (1.23) with respect to S_0 is

$$\partial_{S_0}\hat{\mathbb{C}}(S_0, T, K) = \partial_{S_0}\mathbb{BS}^S(\cdots) + \partial_{\hat{\sigma}^S}\mathbb{BS}^S(\cdots)\partial_{S_0}\hat{\sigma}_0^S(S_0, T, K)$$

$$= \Delta^{BS}(T, K) + \mathcal{V}^{BS}(T, K)\,\partial_{S_0}\hat{\sigma}_0^S(S_0, T, K)\,.$$

The symbol Δ^{BS} denotes Black and Scholes's delta (the derivative of $\mathbb{BS}^S$ is S_0) and the symbol $\mathcal{V}^{BS}$ denotes Black and Scholes's vega (the derivative in volatility). In a sticky strike situation, the derivative $\partial_{S_0}\hat{\sigma}_0^S(S_0, T, K)$ is zero (i.e., the delta of the call is given as Black and Scholes's delta). In contrast, consider a sticky delta market. In this case, we have $\partial_{S_0}\hat{\sigma}_0^S(S_0, T, K) = -K/S_0^2\,\partial\hat{\Sigma}_0(T_1K/S_0)$. Since the slope of implied volatility is typically decreasing, this means that $\partial_{S_0}\hat{\sigma}_0^S(S_0, T, K) \geq 0$, the implied volatility for a fixed cash strike K rises if stock rises (note that it is actually possible to compute the sticky delta purely from market data; cf. remark 2.3.2 on page 78). This is in contrast to market experience: At least for strikes around ATM, an increasing spot level will usually lead to a decline in volatility levels.[10] Hence, a sticky delta assumption is not compatible with market behavior.

Interestingly, both sticky strike and sticky delta behavior of the implied volatility can be characterized neatly following Balland [6]. Under the assumption that the driving stock price is a square-integrable martingale, he shows that the stock price in a sticky delta market must have independent increments, while the only stock price process that is compatible with a sticky strike market is Black and Scholes (i.e., the case without skew).

An intuitive argument for the latter result goes as follows: Assume the market is sticky strike, and that there are two calls with different strikes and the same maturity, each with a different implied volatility. However, only one of the two implied volatilities can actually be realized, which means at least in continuous time processes that only one of the two hedges can work (see also section 2.2.1). (For a thorough derivation of the result refer to Balland [6].)

REMARK 1.2.1 *This means that a volatility surface that has skew and is arbitrage free for a given spot value S_0 will no longer be arbitrage free for any other spot value.*

To see why a sticky delta model implies that the stock price process has independent increments, note that in a sticky delta model, the price of a forward started call with payoff

$$\left(\frac{S_{T_2}}{S_{T_1}} - k\right)^+$$

for $0 \leq T_1 < T_2$ is given at time T_1 as

$$\mathbb{BS}\big(T, k, \sigma_{T_1}(T, k)\big)\,.$$

---

[10]It can also lead to increase in the skew for downside strikes, hence out-of-the-money put implied volatilities may actually rise.

This is a deterministic quantity; hence, the price today of the forward started call is equal to its value at T_1 (recall that we have assumed that there are no interest rates). Since it is possible to extract the forward distribution of S_{T_2}/S_{T_1} from the forward started call prices by taking their second derivatives, it follows that the stock price has independent increments. Examples of such processes include exponential Levy processes. In contrast, stochastic volatility models such as Heston's (2.1) are *not* sticky delta because the implied volatility in such models does not move due only to the movement of the spot, but also due to the movement of the other state variables (i.e. the short volatility). Also compare remark 2.3.2 on page 78, where the delta in (very general) stochastic volatility models is computed from the market.

1.3   FITTING THE MARKET

In this section we make the idealizing assumption that European options $\hat{C}(T, k)$ on X (or S, equivalently) are traded for all strikes and maturities. In such a situation, it is very natural to ask whether the observed market prices are in some way "free of arbitrage" in that they can be reproduced with a martingale that has the required marginal distribution.

1.3.1   Arbitrage-Free Option Price Surfaces

In general, *absence of arbitrage* proves to be a tricky concept when it comes to continuous time processes. While in discrete time the former is equivalent to the existence to an equivalent martingale measure, this is not true anymore in continuous time, and examples of markets exist, which are free of arbitrage but where not even a local martingale measure exists (the standard reference on this topic is Delbaen/Schachermayer [2]). To avoid technical difficulties, we will therefore introduce a stronger notion of absence of arbitrage:

DEFINITION 1.3.1 *We say the market of European call prices* $\hat{C} = (\hat{C}(T, k))_{T \in \mathbb{R}_{\geq 0}, k \in \mathbb{R}_{\geq 0}}$ *is* strongly free of arbitrage *if there exists a non-negative true martingale X on some stochastic base* $\mathbb{W} = (\Omega, \mathcal{F}_\infty, \mathbb{F}, \mathbb{P})$ *which reprices the market, that is,*

$$\hat{C}(T, k) = \mathbb{E}_\mathbb{P}\left[\left(X_T - k\right)^+\right] \tag{1.24}$$

for all $(T, k) \in \mathbb{R}_{\geq 0}^2$.

The key contribution in this context is due to Kellerer [7]:[11]

THEOREM 1.3.1 *The market* $\hat{C} = (\hat{C}(T, k))_{T \in \mathbb{R}_{\geq 0}, k \in \mathbb{R}_{\geq 0}}$ *is strongly free of arbitrage if and only if*

(a) *For all T, the function $\hat{C}(T, \cdot)$ satisfies:*

---

[11] See Föllmer/Schied [9] for a proof.

    (i) It is continuous, strictly decreasing and convex in k.
    (ii) Its right-hand derivative in k satisfies $0 \geq \partial_k \hat{C}(T, k) \geq -1$.
    (iii) $\hat{C}(T, 0) = 1$ and $\lim_{k \uparrow \infty} \hat{C}(T, k) = 0$.[12]

(b) For all k, the function $\hat{C}(\cdot, k)$ is increasing.
(c) $\hat{C}(0, k) = (1 - k)^+$.

The martingale that reprices the market can be chosen to be Markov.

Note that the above conditions allow that $\partial_k \hat{C}(T, 0) > -1$. This is the case if the random variable X_T has a nontrivial probability mass in zero. Since X is non-negative, the state zero must be absorbing, hence, X can "default" without τ being triggered (which can be interpreted as that the company still serves its debt obligations). However, we regard this as an undesirable property and will understand, if not mentioned otherwise, that $\partial_k \hat{C}(T, k) = -1$.

EXAMPLE 1 *The "constant elasticity of variance" (CEV) model by Cox [8] is given as the unique strong solution to the SDE*

$$dX_t = \sigma X^\beta \, dW_t \tag{1.25}$$

where $\beta \in [\frac{1}{2}, 1]$.[13] *This model is occasionally used as a "local volatility" approach to incorporate skew (the resulting implied volatility exhibits an upward-sloping downside skew).*

    For all $\beta < 1$, the process X can reach zero with a nonzero probability and then "dies" there.

Theorem 1.3.1 is a convenient tool to assess whether a given market or an interpolation scheme for market prices is free of strong arbitrage. However, it does not describe how the process X can actually be computed. The best-known approach in this direction is Dupire's "implied local volatility" for continuous market price processes, which requires the knowledge of European option prices for all strikes and maturities. Madan/Yor discuss alternatives to construct pure jump processes [10]. For the discrete case where only a finite number of European options is provided, time and state discrete martingales can also be constructed, as we will show below.

1.3.2   Implied Local Volatility

The core idea of *implied local volatility* is due to Dupire [11]. His idea is intriguingly simple: Given observed market prices $\hat{C}(T, k)$ for all $k \in \mathbb{R}_{\geq 0}$ and $T \in \mathbb{R}_{\geq 0}$, we ask: is it possible to find a function $\sigma : \mathbb{R}_{\geq 0}^2 \to \mathbb{R}_{\geq 0}$ such that the solution to the SDE

$$\frac{dX_t}{X_t} = \sigma_t(X_t) \, dW_t$$

---

[12]The condition that $\hat{C}(T, 0) = 1$ ensures that any process with the correct marginals is a true martingale.
[13]For $\beta \in [0, \frac{1}{2})$, equation (1.25) has infinitely many solutions.

for a Brownian motion W exists, is unique, has the martingale property, and reprices the market? That this is indeed possible can be derived using the following theorem due to Gyöngy [12] (the original work [11] used an approach via the Fokker-Planck equation):

THEOREM 1.3.2 *If Y is an m-dimensional continuous semi-martingale of the form*

$$d\hat{Y}_t = \alpha_t \, dt + \sum_{j=1}^{n} \beta_t^j \, d\hat{W}_t^j \,,$$

with predictable bounded and integrable drift α and volatility matrix β, then the solution to

$$dY_t = a(t; Y_t) \, dt + \sum_{j=1}^{n} b^j(t; Y_t) \, d\hat{W}_t^j \,, \quad Y_0 := \hat{Y}_0$$

with

$$a(t,y) := \mathbb{E}\left[\alpha_t \mid \hat{Y}_t = y \right] \quad and \quad b^j(t,y)^2 := \mathbb{E}\left[\beta_t^{j2} \mid \hat{Y}_t = y \right]$$

exists, is unique, and has the same marginal distributions as $\hat{Y}$.

Let us assume that the "real market" price process $\hat{X} = (\hat{X}_t)_{t \geq 0}$ is a true strictly positive martingale under some measure $\hat{\mathbb{P}}$. In this case (and if the quadratic variation of the stock is absolutely continuous with respect to the Lebesgue measure),[14] there exists a $\hat{\mathbb{P}}$-Brownian motion $\hat{W}$ and a stochastic "short variance" process $\hat{\zeta} = (\hat{\zeta}_t)_{t \geq 0}$, such that $\hat{X}$ satisfies

$$\frac{d\hat{X}_t}{\hat{X}_t} = \sqrt{\hat{\zeta}_t} \, d\hat{B}_t \,.$$

The market price of a call with strike k and maturity T is then given as

$$\hat{C}(T,k) := \mathbb{E}_{\hat{\mathbb{P}}}\left[\left(\hat{X}_T - k\right)^+ \right] \,.$$

Theorem 1.3.2 implies that given some Brownian motion B on some stochastic base, the SDE

$$\frac{dX_t}{X_t} = \sigma_t(X_t) \, dB_t$$

with

$$\sigma_t(x) := \sqrt{\mathbb{E}_{\hat{\mathbb{P}}}\left[\hat{\zeta}_t \mid \hat{X}_t = x \right]}$$

---

[14]Cf. propositions 3.8 (p. 202) and 1.5 (p. 328) in Revuz/Yor [13].

has a unique strong solution which has the same marginal distribution as $\hat{X}$. Therefore, X reprices all European options; in particular, $\mathbb{E}[X_t] = \mathbb{E}_{\hat{\mathbb{P}}}[\hat{X}_t] = 1$ for all t (i.e., X is a true martingale).

To obtain an analytic form for σ, we use Ito's formula for convex payoffs:

$$(\hat{X}_T - k)^+ - (\hat{X}_0 - k)^+ = \int_0^T 1_{\hat{X}_t > k} \, d\hat{X}_t + \frac{1}{2} \int_0^T \delta_{\hat{X}_t = k} d\langle \hat{X} \rangle_t$$

$$= \int_0^T 1_{\hat{X}_t > k} \, d\hat{X}_t + \frac{1}{2} \int_0^T \delta_{\hat{X}_t = k} \zeta_t \hat{X}_t^2 \, dt \ .$$

Taking expectations and derivation in T yields

$$\partial_T \hat{\mathcal{C}}(T, k) = \frac{1}{2} \hat{\mathbb{E}} \left[\delta_{\hat{X}_T = k} \zeta_T \hat{X}_T^2 \right]$$

$$= \frac{1}{2} \hat{\mathbb{E}} \left[\hat{\mathbb{E}} \left[\delta_{\hat{X}_T = k} \zeta_T \hat{X}_T^2 \,\Big|\, \hat{X}_T \right] \right]$$

$$= \frac{1}{2} \hat{\mathbb{E}} \left[\hat{X}_T^2 \sigma(t; X_T)^2 \delta_{\hat{X}_T = k} \right]$$

$$= \frac{1}{2} k^2 \sigma(T; k)^2 \hat{\mathbb{P}}[\hat{X}_T = k] \ .$$

Since the density of $\hat{X}_T$ can be computed as $\hat{\mathbb{P}}[\hat{X}_T = k] := \partial_{kk}^2 \hat{\mathcal{C}}(T, k)$, we obtain *Dupire's formula*: given

$$\sigma_t(x)^2 := \frac{2 \, \partial_t \hat{\mathcal{C}}(t, k)}{k^2 \partial_{kk}^2 \hat{\mathcal{C}}(t, k)} \ , \tag{1.26}$$

the unique solution X to

$$\frac{dX_t}{X_t} = \sigma_t(X_t) \, dW_t \tag{1.27}$$

exists, is a martingale, and reprices the market. An example can be found in figure 1.4.

REMARK 1.3.1 *The above formula is given in terms of the calls on the pure stock price $\hat{X}$. This is much more robust than using the call prices on $\hat{S}$ via (1.18) since the effect of discontinuities in the forward (resulting from discrete dividends) are eliminated.*

It is also possible to write (1.26) in terms of implied volatility (which has the same advantage of being robust with respect to jumps in the forward, etc). To this end, one simply replaces the call prices in (1.26) by their equivalent values in terms of the Black and Scholes formula and the implied volatilities.

Conceptually, implied local volatility is a very neat approach: starting from the observable implied distribution of the underlying martingale $\hat{X}$, a diffusion X is constructed that has the same marginal distributions as the original process.

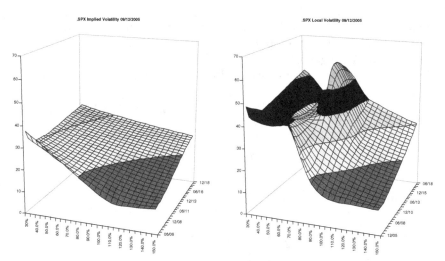

FIGURE 1.4 Implied volatility and implied local volatility of SPX. The local volatility is computed using Dupire's formula and then interpolated by a smooth spline.

This approach ensures that the resulting process X reprices all European claims correctly. In particular, skew exposure for European knock-out options and the like is taken into account properly: as an example, consider a European digital call that pays 1 if the stock is above the strike at maturity. The impact of skew on such a product is severe. The graph in figure 1.5 shows the difference between plain BS prices (computed with the strike-implied volatility) and the local volatility price. We have also provided the price given by a tight call spread, $\mathbb{E}\left[1_{X_T > K}\right] \approx \frac{1}{2\varepsilon}\left(\mathcal{C}(T, K+\varepsilon) - \mathcal{C}(T, K-\varepsilon)\right)$.

The issue with (1.26) in practice is that it is very difficult to be used directly. The main problem is that we usually have only a finite number of traded European options. In order to obtain a local volatility function using Dupire's formula (1.26), we therefore need to intra- and extrapolate option prices (or implied volatilities). The resulting European call price surface then needs to satisfy the no-arbitrage conditions of theorem 1.3.1 to ensure that (1.26) is finite and not imaginary. Moreover, the volatility function σ itself must ensure that the solution to (1.27) is unique and nonexplosive.[15] This is highly nontrivial and makes an extra- and interpolation algorithm for discretely quoted market prices difficult to implement in practice. A far more robust approach is calibration of a local volatility function via forward PDEs, as described in chapter 8.

EXAMPLE 2 *Assume that market price process is a "jump diffusion" (cf. Merton [14])*

$$\hat{X}_t = e^{\sigma W_t - \frac{1}{2}\sigma^2 t + \sum_{i=1}^{N_t} \xi_i - hmt}, \tag{1.28}$$

where N is a Poisson process with intensity h and where $\xi = (\xi_i)_i$ is an iid sequence of random variables independent of N with a nontrivial distribution; moreover, $m := \mathbb{E}_{\hat{\mathbb{P}}}\left[e^{\xi_1} - 1\right] \neq 0$. The process W is a Brownian motion and σ is a constant.

---

[15] A sufficient condition for the existence of a global unique solution to (1.27) is Lipschitz continuity; see Protter [15].

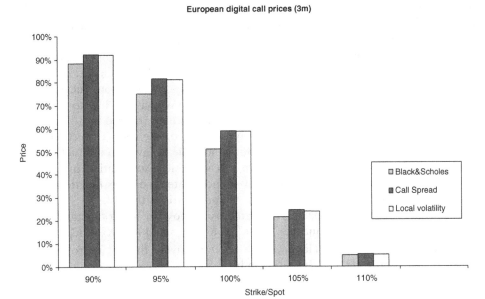

European digital call prices (3m)

Legend:
☐ Black&Scholes
■ Call Spread
☐ Local volatility

FIGURE 1.5   The prices of digital options for various strikes, computed with the Black-Scholes model, by approximation via call prices and by using implied local volatility. The example shows the importance of capturing the skew correctly when pricing nontrivial European options.

In this case, (1.26) is not well defined at $T = 0$; hence, no solution to the problem of fitting the market with a diffusion of the type (1.27) exists.

1.3.3   European Payoffs

While implied local volatility is a very valuable tool to price path-dependent options, nonvanilla European options by themselves can be priced more straightforwardly by using directly quoted vanilla options.

To this end, note that any twice differentiable function $H : \mathbb{R}_{>0} \longrightarrow \mathbb{R}$ can be written as

$$H(x) - H(x_0) = H'(x_0)(x - x_0) + \int_0^{x_0} H''(k)(x_0 - x)^+ \, dx + \int_{x_0}^{\infty} H''(k)(x - x_0)^+ \, dx \,,$$

$$(1.29)$$

that is, as long as we can trade European options $\hat{C}$ and $\hat{U}$ with all strikes at the maturity T, and under suitable integrability assumptions, we can compute

$$\mathbb{E}_{\mathbb{P}}\left[B_T^{-1} H(S_T) \right] = P(0, T)\Big(H(\hat{K}) + H'(\hat{K}) \left(F_T - K^* \right) \Big)$$

$$\int_0^{\hat{K}^*} H''(K)\hat{U}(T, K) \, dK + \int_{\hat{K}^*}^{\infty} H''(K)\hat{C}(T, K) \, dK,$$

which holds for any potential martingale measure $\mathbb{P}$ and also covers the possibility of default where the payoff at maturity is $H(0)$. The strike $\hat{K}$ is arbitrary and can be set to the forward. Note that (1.29) also holds for convex functions with their generalized derivatives. In particular, H does not need to be defined in 0: for example, the formula is also valid for the convex function $H(x) = x - 1 - \log(x)$, the price for which is infinite if the stock has a nonzero probability of default.

The advantage of using (1.29) instead of implied local volatility to price the payoff H is that (1.29) also yields a hedge for H: by construction, the formula will tell us how many European options of each strike we have to buy to perfectly replicate the payoff H. This is of great advantage, since an implied local volatility model in itself gives a hedging strategy only in terms of the spot (cf. section 1.4). Of course, in practice we will neither be willing nor able to invest in infinitely many options. Instead, we will limit ourselves to a reasonable discretization of the real line. The first step is to super-replicate H; we concentrate on convex functions since most financial payoffs are convex functions or combinations thereof.

A convex function H can be approximated from above by linear functions. That means that if we select two sequences $\hat{K} = K_0^p > K_1^p > \cdots$ and $\hat{K} = K_0^c < K_1^c < \cdots$ of strikes with $\lim_{n\uparrow\infty} K_n^p = 0$ and $\lim_{n\uparrow\infty} K_n^c = \infty$, respectively, then an approximation H_T^{sup} of H from above, $H_T^{\text{sup}} \geq H_T$, is given by

$$H_T^{\text{sup}} := H(\hat{K}) + H'(\hat{K})(S_T - \hat{K}) + \sum_{n=1}^{\infty} w_n^p \left(K_n^p - S_T\right)^+ + \sum_{n=1}^{\infty} w_n^c \left(S_T - K_n^c\right)^+ \quad (1.30)$$

with

$$w_n^c := \frac{H(K_n^c) - H(K_{n-1}^c)}{K_n^c - K_{n-1}^c} - \sum_{k=1}^{n-1} w_k^c$$

and

$$w_n^p := -\frac{H(K_n^p) - H(K_{n-1}^p)}{K_n^p - K_{n-1}^p} - \sum_{k=1}^{n-1} w_k^p \,.$$

A similar formula holds for a subreplication strategy.

If H is a function that is finite in zero and linear beyond some K^* in the sense that $H_{[K^*,\infty)}(x) = \alpha x + \beta$, we can use only a finite number of strikes: the corresponding super-replicating payoff is given by

$$\hat{H}_T^{\text{sup}} := H(\hat{K}) + H'(\hat{K})(S_T - \hat{K}) + \sum_{n=1}^{n_p} w_n^p \left(K_n^p - S_T\right)^+ + \sum_{n=1}^{n_c} w_n^c \left(S_T - K_n^c\right)^+ \quad (1.31)$$

where $0 = K_{n_p}^p < \cdots < K_0^p = \hat{K} = K_0^c < \cdots < K_{n_c}^c := K^*$. The condition that H is linear beyond some strike is necessary to be able to limit ourselves to some maximal strike. Alternatively, we could postulate that for some large strike K^*, the value of the respective call is practically zero, and will remain zero for the life of the contract we want to price. We hence assume that there is no probability mass beyond this "zero price strike" K^*. Then, (1.31) gives a super-replication price and indeed a super-hedging position for all convex payoffs.

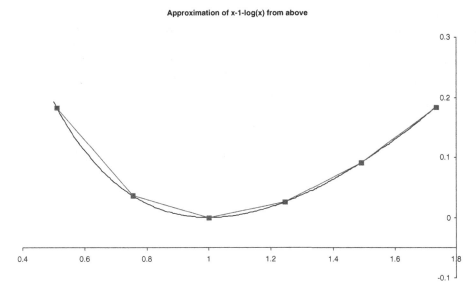

Approximation of x-1-log(x) from above

FIGURE 1.6 The super-hedge for the function $H(x) := x - 1 - \log(x)$.

Interpretation It should be noted that this approach is tantamount to assuming that the stock price will attain only discrete values in T, namely the strikes $(K_0, \ldots, K_{n_c+n_p}) := (0, K_1^p, \ldots, K_{n_p}^p, K_1^c, \ldots, K_{n_c-1}^c, K^*)$: this is because (1.30) is nothing but the price of H computed under the probability measure

$$\mathbb{P}\left[\, X_T = k_\ell \,\right] := 1 + \frac{\hat{\mathcal{C}}(T, k_{\ell+1}) - \hat{\mathcal{C}}(T, k_\ell)}{k_{\ell+1} - k_\ell} \tag{1.32}$$

where

$$k_\ell := \frac{K_\ell - A_T}{F_T^*}$$

(recall from (1.24) that $\hat{\mathcal{C}}$ are the market prices of calls on X). It is an attractive idea because it will always compute an upper bound for convex payoffs. Accordingly, we call a stock price model with (1.32) a "most expensive" model. Since the assumptions made (such as the existence of K^*) are relatively weak, it provides a good framework to assess the value of a European payoff H (of course pricing via (1.32) is not limited to convex payoffs). If we want to follow this approach for options that depend on more than one maturity, though, we also have to construct the transition probabilities between the marginal distributions (1.32). This is the subject of the next section.

1.3.4 Fitting the Market with Discrete Martingales

We will now discuss an alternative to implied local volatility which follows the construction (1.32) above. The idea here is not to assume that a smooth surface of European option prices is quoted in the market, but to give in to the fact that many of these options are traded only finitely. We saw in the previous section that such an assumption implies that we can replicate European payoffs using the liquid vanilla instruments. The same will not hold true if we construct transition densities between the marginal distributions (1.32), because these transition densities are not uniquely defined by the observable market prices. However, following Buehler [16], we will give a constructive approach identifying suitable transition matrices by imposing "secondary information." More precisely, we will choose kernels that match the prices of more exotic payoffs such as forward started options.

To be precise, assume that a discrete number of call prices $\hat{C}(T, k)_{(T,k)\in\mathcal{A}}$ can be observed in the market; we denote by $\mathcal{T}$ the set of maturities for which we have at least one call price, and we enumerate them as $0 \leq T_1 < \cdots < T_m$. For each maturity T_j, we denote by $\mathcal{K}_j := \{k : (T_j, k) \in \mathcal{A}\}$ the set of strikes for which calls are quoted. To avoid the case of local martingales we assume that $0 \in \mathcal{K}_j$ with $\hat{C}(T_j, 0) = 1$. We also assume as in the previous section that there is some (artificial and large) "zero price" strike $k^* \in \mathcal{K}_j$ such that $\hat{C}(T_j, k^*) = 0$ for all j. To ease notation, we write $0 =: k_0^j < \cdots < k_{d_j}^j = k^*$ for the strikes of calls with maturity τ_j. We will also make use of the first differences,

$$\Delta_\ell^j := \frac{\hat{C}(T_j, k_{\ell+1}^j) - \hat{C}(T_j, k_\ell^j)}{k_{\ell+1}^j - k_\ell^j}$$

for $\ell = 0, \ldots, d_j - 1$ and $\Delta_{d_j}^j := 0$. Finally, we will also need the lower convex hull of all call prices beyond some maturity, that is,

$$H_j := \sup_{f:f \text{ is convex}} \left\{ f(k) \leq \hat{C}(T_i, k) : \text{ for all } i > j \text{ and } k \in \mathcal{K}_i \right\}.$$

Note that this function is just the lower convex linear hull of all call prices with maturities T_i with $i > j$.

The following corollary is a direct consequence of theorem 1.3.1:

COROLLARY 1.3.1 *The discrete set of call prices $\hat{C}(T, k)_{(T,k)\in\mathcal{A}}$ is strongly free of arbitrage if, and only if, the following conditions hold:*

(a) **Convexity:** *For all $j = 1, \ldots, m$,*

$$-1 \leq \Delta_0^j \leq \cdots \leq \Delta_{d_j}^j = 0 .$$

(b) **Monotonicity:** *For all $j = 1, \ldots, (m-1)$ and all $k \in \mathcal{K}_j$,*

$$\hat{C}(T_j, k) \leq \hat{C}(T_{j+1}, k)$$

In particular, there exists a non-negative martingale X with states $\mathcal{K}_j$ per maturity T_j with a marginal distribution given by

$$\mathbb{P}[X_{T_j} \leq k_\ell^j] := 1 + \Delta_\ell^j \tag{1.33}$$

for $\ell = 0, \ldots, d_j$.

If, in addition, $-1 = \Delta_0^j$, then X is strictly positive.

It is quite straightforward to check these conditions for real market data. (In Buehler [16], it is also discussed how to turn data that do not satisfy the above conditions into a "close" fit which then satisfies the conditions.) The crucial point is that we can actually construct a martingale X as described in the above corollary. Before we discuss this, let us recall from the discussion in section 1.3.3 that all martingales that realized a density (1.33) are "most expensive" in the following sense: Let Y on $(\Omega^2, \mathcal{A}^2, \mathbb{P}^2, \mathbb{F}^2)$ be any other martingale (possibly with continuous state space and time) which reprices the market, that is, for all $j = 1, \ldots, m$ and $k^j \in \mathcal{K}_j$ we have

$$\mathbb{E}_2\left[(Y_{T_j} - k^j)^+\right] = \hat{\mathcal{C}}(T_j, k^j) .$$

Then X is more expensive than Y for any convex payoff $H : \mathbb{R}_{\geq 0} \to \mathbb{R}_{\geq 0}$, that is,

$$\mathbb{E}\left[H(X_{T_j})\right] \geq \mathbb{E}_2\left[H(Y_{T_j})\right]$$

for all $j = 1, \ldots, m$.

Constructing Discrete Transition Densities Let us now denote by $\mathbf{p}^j = (p_0^j, \ldots, p_{d_j}^j)$ the row vector of probabilities of X_{T_j} being exactly k_ℓ^j, that is,

$$p_\ell^j := \Delta_\ell^j - \Delta_{\ell-1}^j$$

for $\ell = 1, \ldots, d_j$ and $p_0^j := 1 + \Delta_\ell^0$. For any discrete martingale X with states $\mathcal{K}^j$ at maturity T_j, there exists a *transition kernel*

$$\mathbf{\Pi}^j = \begin{pmatrix} \Pi_{0,0}^j & \cdots & \Pi_{0,d_j}^j \\ \vdots & \ddots & \vdots \\ \Pi_{d_{j-1},0}^j & \cdots & \Pi_{d_{j-1},d_j}^j \end{pmatrix} \in \mathbb{R}^{(d_{j-1}+1)\times(d_j+1)}$$

with transition probabilities $\Pi_{u,\ell}^j$ "from k_u^{j-1} to k_ℓ^j",

$$\Pi_{u,\ell}^j := \mathbb{P}[X_{T_j} = k_\ell^j | X_{T_{j-1}} = k_u^{j-1}] .$$

Hence, the problem at hand is how to find a sequence of kernels $(\mathbf{\Pi}^j)_{j=1,\ldots,m}$ such that

$$\mathbf{p}^{j-1}\mathbf{\Pi}^j = \mathbf{p}^j$$

for all $j = 1, \ldots, m$. More precisely, we search for a sequence of matrices $(\mathbf{\Pi}^j)_j$ for which the following properties hold:

(a) Each element of $\mathbf{\Pi}^j$ is non-negative.
(b) Each row of $\mathbf{\Pi}^j$ is a probability distribution,[16]

$$\mathbf{\Pi}^j \mathit{1}^{d_j+1} = \mathit{1}^{d_{j-1}+1} .$$

---

[16] We used $\mathit{1}^n$ to denote the unit vector in $\mathbb{R}^n$.

(c) Π^j has the martingale property, that is, for $k^j = (k^j_0, \ldots, k^j_{d_j})^T$ we have

$$\Pi^j k^j = k^{j-1} .$$

(d) Π^j is compatible with the marginal distributions,

$$p^{j-1} \Pi^j = p^j .$$

The key is now that the above conditions (a)–(b) are all linear in the coefficients of Π^j. That implies that we can formulate the quest for Π^j as a linear programming problem,

$$\left. \begin{array}{r} A^j \pi^j = y^j \\ \pi^j \geq 0 \end{array} \right\} \tag{1.34}$$

where π^j is the vector of all elements of Π^j and where $A^j \in \mathbb{R}^{(d_j+2)+2(d_j+2)-2 \times (d_j+2)(d_{j-1}+2)}$ and $y^j \in \mathbb{R}^{(d_j+2)+2(d_j+2)-2}$ (two of the linear conditions are redundant). For such problems, very efficient algorithms exist, and we can solve even large systems very quickly; the existence of a solution is guaranteed by corollary 1.3.1. Note that this means that the space of solutions for (1.34) is very large—while the number of elements of Π grows quadratically, the number of conditions grows only linearly. This simply reflects the fact that many possible transition densities are compatible with the observed marginal distributions.

To put it positively, this means that we can select a transition kernel that satisfies "secondary requirements."

Repricing Forward Started Options Any of the solutions to (1.34) will perfectly reprice the observed European option prices. However, it is often desirable also to impose certain assumptions on the prices of *forward started options*: a fixed strike forward started option with "reset date" T_1 and maturity $T_2 > T_1$ has the payoff

$$\left(\frac{X_{T_2}}{X_{T_1}} - x \right)^+ .$$

While it is trivial to compute the value of such a payoff in the Black-Scholes model, it is by far not clear what the fair value of such a contract should be in the market. We will come back to this type of product at a later stage in section 2.1.6. Here, we assume that we have a good idea of the price of a few strikes for each of the options between T_{j-1} and T_j. Accordingly, we denote by $\hat{C}^j(x)$ the price of an option with payoff

$$\left(\frac{X_{T_j}}{X_{T_{j-1}}} - x \right)^+ . \tag{1.35}$$

Its price given a transition kernel $\mathbf{\Pi}^j$ is

$$C^j(x) := \sum_{u=0}^{d_{j-1}} p_u^{j-1} \sum_{\ell=0}^{d_j} \mathbf{\Pi}_{u,\ell}^j \left(\frac{k_\ell^j}{k_u^{j-1}} - x \right)^+ ,$$

which is once more just a linear expression in the elements of $\mathbf{\Pi}^j$. The idea is now to choose a transition kernel $\mathbf{\Pi}^j$, which minimizes for a range $x_1 < \cdots < x_n$ of strikes the distance between model prices and assumed market prices, that is,

$$\left\| \begin{array}{c} C^j(x_1) - \hat{C}^j(x_1) \\ \vdots \\ C^j(x_n) - \hat{C}^j(x_n) \end{array} \right\|_w$$

under an appropriate norm. This leads to an optimization problem of the form

$$\left. \begin{array}{c} \min_{\mathbf{\Pi}^j} \| \Gamma^j \pi^j - \mathbf{z}^j \|_w \\ \mathbf{A}^j \pi^j = \mathbf{y}^j \\ \mathbf{\Pi}^j \geq 0 \end{array} \right\} . \tag{1.36}$$

For $w = 1$ and $w = \infty$, this reduces again to linear programming. For $w = 2$, it is a linear least-squares problem, which can also be solved efficiently.[17]

Pricing and Hedging In a model with discrete states, it is straightforward to evaluate options whose value depends only on the dates $T_1, \ldots, T_m$. A discrete-state Monte Carlo engine, for example, just needs to invert the conditional transition probabilities, which can be accomplished very efficiently; cf. Glasserman [17]. For multi-asset applications, an ad hoc approach is to use copulas to model their interdependency (see chapter 7). The method lends itself also to backward pricing, since the necessary (expensive) inversion of the transition matrices needs to be done only once during the life of the model.

1.4 THEORY OF REPLICATION

In section 1.3.2, we introduced the concept of *implied local volatility,* where the pure stock price process X under a martingale measure $\mathbb{P}$ is given as

$$\frac{dX_t}{X_t} = \sigma_t(X_t) \, dW_t \tag{1.37}$$

for a function σ, which can in theory be implied from market quotes of European prices. One striking feature of such a model is that it is generally complete: we can *replicate* the payoff of an option by continuous trading in the stock. This is in stark contrast to the discrete model above, where such a strategy except for European payoff is not available.

---

[17]Other methods of selecting an appropriate transition kernel include the use of a "mean variance" criterion (which is also linear in the underlying probabilities). See [16] for more details.

Replicating Trading Strategies To illustrate the idea of replication, assume that we sell a European claim with payoff[18]

$$H_T \equiv H(S_T) \, .$$

To ease notation in the following, we will concentrate solely on the case of zero dividends, default probability, and interest rates (i.e., on the case where $S = X$). We comment on the general case afterward.

The question is now the following: Can we trade in X such that the result of trading plus a potential initial capital has at T the same value as H_T? This requires the concept of a *trading strategy*: a trading strategy $\Delta = (\Delta_t)_{t \in [0,T]}$ is a (random) process whose value Δ_t denotes the amount of shares we should hold at time t. This value may depend on past information, in particular the path of X up time t, but it obviously cannot include any future information of the value of X. Mathematically, we say that the process Δ must be *predictable*. We also require that the process is suitably integrable (i.e., $\int_0^T \Delta_t^2 \, d\langle X \rangle_t$ is almost surely finite) and bounded from below.[19]

To execute the trading strategy, assume we have an initial capital of H_0 and that we start at time 0 with buying Δ_0 shares. We borrow the required amount $C_0 = \Delta_0 X_0 - H_0$ from the bank,[20] so that the value of our portfolio at time 0 is $V_0 = H_0$.

Let us consider first discrete time trading, that is, that the hedging strategy Δ is constant on intervals $[(k-1)\tau, k\tau]$ for $k = 1, \dots, n$ with $\tau := T/n$, i.e. $n\tau = T$. After the end of the first interval, the value of our position in X has changed due to the movement of the stock (i.e., it is now $\Delta_0 X_\tau$), while our debt of $\Delta_0 X_0 - H_0$ did not change since we assumed that interest rates are zero. Now we rebalance our position in X according to our hedging strategy, which tells us now to hold Δ_τ units of X. Accordingly, we have to buy $(\Delta_\tau - \Delta_0)$ shares for the price of $(\Delta_\tau - \Delta_0)X_\tau$, the excess of which we need to borrow again from the bank. The overall cost to hold Δ_τ shares in τ is therefore

$$C_\tau = (\Delta_\tau - \Delta_0)X_\tau + \Delta_0 X_0 - H_0 = \Delta_\tau X_\tau - \Delta_0(X_\tau - X_0) - H_0 \, .$$

Proceeding further in time, the accumulated cost to hold $\Delta_{k\tau}$ at time $k\tau$ is

$$C_{k\tau} = \Delta_{k\tau} X_{k\tau} - H_0 - \sum_{j=1}^{k} \Delta_{(j-1)\tau} \left(X_{jt} - X_{(j-1)\tau} \right) \, .$$

The value of our portfolio including the shares is

$$V_{k\tau} := \Delta_{k\tau} X_{k\tau} - C_{k\tau} = H_0 + \sum_{j=1}^{k} \Delta_{(j-1)\tau} \left(X_{jt} - X_{(j-1)\tau} \right) \, .$$

---

[18] For technical reasons, assume that H is bounded from below.
[19] This excludes the "suicide strategy": double your bets until you *lose*.
[20] Borrowing a negative amount means to invest it in the bank.

In case of a continuous trading strategy, the same arguments hold: the right hand sum converges against the integral of Δ over X, so we have

$$V_t = H_0 + \int_0^t \Delta_u \, dX_u$$

for all $t \in [0, T]$. We now call the strategy Δ *replicating*, if the value of V_T matches the value of H_T, that is, if

$$H_T = H_0 + \int_0^T \Delta_t \, dX_t \, . \tag{1.38}$$

The point here is that the cost of replicating H_T is covered by the constant H_0, which justifies calling it the *fair price* of H_T. If such a replication strategy is possible for all payoffs of some set $\mathcal{X}$, then we say that the market $(\mathcal{X}, X)$ is *complete*.[21]

The most natural market $\mathcal{X}$ is what we call the *market of relevant payoffs*: assume we are allowed to trade in X and in some liquid instruments $C = (C^1, \ldots, C^n)$. Then the only economically relevant payoffs are those that depend functionally on X and C; this means that we will consider only payoffs that are measurable with respect to $\mathcal{F}_T^{X,C}$ for some finite T (in contrast to payoffs measurable with respect to the larger σ-algebra $\mathcal{F}_T$). As usual, we also limit ourselves to payoffs that are bounded from below. We now simply say *the market* (X, C) *is complete*, if any payoff H_T that is measurable with respect to $\mathcal{F}^{X,C}$ and bounded from below can be replicated by some trading strategy (Δ, φ) [22] in the sense that

$$H_T = \mathbb{E}_{\mathbb{P}}[H_T] + \int_0^T \Delta_u \, dX_u + \sum_{\ell=1}^n \int_0^T \varphi_u \, dC_u^\ell \, . \tag{1.39}$$

Of course, it is generally not clear that such a replication strategy exists—the reason why replication works in a local volatility model is that we have assumed that there is an equivalent measure $\mathbb{P}$ under which the process X, defined by equation (1.37), is a Markovian martingale. To this end, consider now again a payoff $H_T \equiv H(X_T)$ given in terms of a smooth, bounded function H with bounded derivatives. We can then define, somewhat ad hoc, the bounded martingale $(H_t)_{t \in [0,T]}$

$$H_t := \mathbb{E}_{\mathbb{P}}[H(X_T) \mid \mathcal{F}_t] \, .$$

Because of the Markov-property of X, this can be written as

$$H_t = \mathbb{E}_{\mathbb{P}}[H(X_T) \mid X_t] =: h_t(X_t) \, .$$

---

[21] It is an important point that the notion of a "fair price" implies the existence of a replication strategy. In incomplete markets, for example, some payoffs cannot be replicated, and therefore do not have a unique price.

[22] With $\int_0^T \Delta_u^2 \, d\langle X \rangle_u + \sum_{\ell=1}^n \int_0^T \varphi_u^2 \, d\langle C^\ell \rangle_u < \infty$.

If we assume that h is a $C^{1,2}$ function, we can apply Ito and find, using the martingale property of H_t, that

$$H(X_T) = \mathbb{E}_{\mathbb{P}}\left[\, H(X_T)\,\right] + \int_0^T \partial_X h_t(X_t)\, dX_t\, .$$

Hence, we have found a trading strategy $\Delta_t := \partial_X h_t(X_t)$, which replicates our payoff, and the price $H_0 := \mathbb{E}_{\mathbb{P}}[H(X_T)]$. Similarly, at any later time $t < T$, we can write

$$H_T = H_t + \int_t^T \partial_X h_t(X_t)\, dX_t\, ,$$

that is, the value H_t is the fair price of H_T at t.

1.4.1 Replication in Diffusion-Driven Markets

The above considerations can now also be applied to more general cases: we will now show how hedging works in a framework where a range of market instruments is driven by an underlying Markov process (we will concentrate on diffusions here). This will be put to use in section 2.3 when we discuss hedging of options on variance with variance swaps. The idea is as follows: if we want to hedge a payoff $H_T \equiv H(X_T)$, we will try to use the stock price X to hedge it, but if the market is not a local volatility model, we will need additional traded instruments to cover us against changes in the value of H_T. To this end, we assume that there are liquid instruments $C = (C^1, \ldots, C^n)$ that are traded alongside the stock. For example, think of a finite number of European options on S. We assume without loss of generalization that the price processes $C^\ell = (C^\ell_t)_{t \in [0,T]}$ for $\ell = 1, \ldots, n$ are defined until T; for an option with an earlier maturity $T^* < T$, we simply set $C^\ell_t := C^\ell_{T^*}$ for $t \in [T^*, T]$. We also assume that $C^1, \ldots, C^n$ are bounded from below.

To apply the same idea as for the case of local volatility, we now stipulate that the vector $(X, C^1, \ldots, C^n)$ of market instruments is given in terms of a finite-dimensional diffusion $\mathbf{Z} = (\mathbf{Z}_t)_{t \in [0,T]}$ with open state space $\mathcal{Z} \subset \mathbb{R}^{m+1}_{\geq 0}$ by a function $\mathbb{G}$ as

$$(X_t, C^1_t, \ldots, C^n_t) \equiv \mathbb{G}(\mathbf{Z}_t)\, .$$

The function $\mathbb{G} : \mathcal{Z} \longrightarrow \mathbb{R}^{n+1}_{\geq 0}$ is assumed to be invertible and differentiable. For all applications it will be appropriate to assume that X itself is among the state variables $\mathbf{Z}$, and we set $Z^0 := X$ accordingly. The process $\mathbf{Z}$ is thought to represent the "state factors" of the market. The inherent assumption is that the relevant information available in the entire market is incorporated in a finite set of states $\mathbf{Z}$; in the end, we could well assume that $\mathbf{Z} = (X, C^1, \ldots, C^d)$, but it is often tricky to model, say, European options along with the stock price.

We limit our attention to diffusions and assume that $\mathbf{Z}$ is the unique strong solution to an SDE

$$d\mathbf{Z}_t = \mu(\mathbf{Z}_t)\, dt + \sum_{j=1}^d \varsigma^j(\mathbf{Z}_t)\, d\mathbf{W}^j_t \quad \mathbf{Z}_0 = \mathbf{z} \in \mathcal{Z}, \qquad (1.40)$$

where $\mathbf{W} = (W^1, \ldots, W^d)$ is a d-dimensional Brownian motion. The drift vector $\mu = (\mu_0, \ldots, \mu_m) : \mathcal{Z} \to \mathbb{R}^{m+1}$ and the volatilities $\varsigma^j = (\varsigma_0^j, \ldots, \varsigma_m^j) : \mathcal{Z} \to \mathbb{R}_{\geq 0}^{m+1}$ for $j = 1, \ldots, d$ are not explicitly time dependent, but imposing, say, $z_m := 0$, $\mu_m := 1$ and $\varsigma_m^1 = \cdots \varsigma_m^d = 0$ allows to set $Z_t^m = t$.

Note, in particular, that in contrast to standard assumptions, we do not require that ς has full rank. We merely require that the SDE (1.40) has a unique strong solution. A sufficient but not necessary criterion is that μ and ς are Lipschitz continuous.

EXAMPLE 3 *Let*

$$\frac{dX_t}{X_t} = \sqrt{\zeta_t} \left(\rho W_t^1 + \sqrt{1 - \rho^2}\, W_t^2 \right)$$

$$d\zeta_t = a(\zeta_t)\, dt + b(\zeta_t)\, dW_t^1$$

such that ζ is well defined and set $\mathbf{Z}_t := (X_t, \zeta_t, t)$. Such a model satisfies the above assumptions with

$$C_t := (X_t, C_t^1),$$

where C_t^1 is the value of a European option with maturity $T^* \geq T$, for example,

$$C_t^1 \equiv \mathbb{G}^1(t; X_t, \zeta_t) := \mathbb{E}_{\mathbb{P}} \left[(X_{T^*} - K)^+ \mid X_t, \zeta_t \right].$$

EXAMPLE 4 *In the same setting as in the example before, define $Z^0 := X$, $Z^1 := \zeta$, $Z_t^3 := t$ and, additionally, $Z_t^2 := V_t(t) = \int_0^t \zeta_u\, du$; see also section 2.3. Then,*

$$C_t^1 := \mathbb{G}^1(t; X_t, \zeta_t, V_t(t)) := \mathbb{E}_{\mathbb{P}} \left[\int_0^T \zeta_u\, du \,\middle|\, X_t, \zeta_t, V_t(t) \right]$$

$$= \mathbb{E}_{\mathbb{P}} \left[\int_t^T \zeta_u\, du \,\middle|\, \zeta_t \right] + V_t(t)$$

satisfies the assumptions made before. The contract C^1 is called the variance swap *with maturity T on X. We will see in section 2.3 that these instruments are very natural hedging instruments for options on realized variance.*

Delta Hedging Works Now assume as before that we want to hedge a smooth, bounded European payoff $H_T = H(X_T)$. As before, we define the martingale $(H_t)_{t \in [0,T]}$ via

$$H_t := \mathbb{E}_{\mathbb{P}} \left[H(X_T) \mid \mathcal{F}_t \right].$$

Note that because we have assumed that H is bounded, this is a true martingale. Using the Markov property of Z, we can write again

$$H_t = h_t(Z_t) := \mathbb{E}_{\mathbb{P}} \left[H(X_T) \mid Z_t \right].$$

Since $\mathbb{G}$ is invertible, we can set $g_t(x, c^1, \ldots, c^n) := h_t\big(\mathbb{G}^{-1}(x, c^1, \ldots, c^n)\big)$, such that given X and $\mathbf{C} = (C^1, \ldots, C^n)$, we have

$$H_t = g_t\big(X_t, C_t\big) .$$

ASSUMPTION 1 *For smooth-bounded functions $H \in C_K^\infty$ with bounded derivatives and compact support, the function*

$$h_t(\mathbf{z}) := \mathbb{E}_\mathbb{P}\Big[H(X_t, C_t^1, \ldots, C_t^n) \,\Big|\, \mathbf{Z}_0 = \mathbf{z} \Big]$$

is C^1 in $\mathbf{z}$ for all t and continuous in t.

If the assumption holds, then h is differentiable in $\mathbf{z}$, and so is g (via the inverse function theorem applied to $\mathbb{G}$). An application of Ito (possibly to an approximation of g by $C^{1,2}$ functions)[23] shows that "delta hedging works,"

$$H_T = H_0 + \int_0^T \partial_X g_t(X_t, \mathbf{C}_t)\, dX_t + \sum_{\ell=1}^n \int_0^T \partial_{C^\ell} g_t(X_t, \mathbf{C}_t)\, dC_t^\ell . \qquad (1.41)$$

General Contingent Claims   To handle more general payoffs, note that we can approximate nonsmooth European payoffs by bounded smooth payoffs, and that general path-dependent payoffs of the form $H_T = H(X_{t\in[0,T]}, \mathbf{C}_{t\in[0,T]})$ can be approximated by payoffs that depend on finitely many states of X and $\mathbf{C}$. The latter payoffs, in turn, can be approximated by payoffs that are products of payoffs of the form $H_k(X_{t_k}, \mathbf{C}_{t_k})$ for a finite number of dates $t_1, \ldots, t_{n'}$; see also [18]. The crucial condition to ensure completeness of the market is that assumption 1 holds.

THEOREM 1.4.1 *Under assumption 1, the market of relevant payoffs on $(X, \mathbf{C})$ is complete.*

For example, option payoffs with prices $H_t = h_t(Z_t, \mathbf{A}_t)$, which depend not only on Z, but on some finite variation process $\mathbf{A} = (A^1, \ldots, A^q)$ can be still delta-hedged with Z,

$$H_T = H_0 + \int_0^T \partial_X g_t(X_t, \mathbf{C}_t, \mathbf{A}_t)\, dX_t + \sum_{\ell=1}^n \int_0^T \partial_{C^\ell} g_t(X_t, \mathbf{C}_t, \mathbf{A}_t)\, dC_t^\ell , \qquad (1.42)$$

where $g_t(x, \mathbf{c}, \mathbf{a}) := h_t\big(\mathbb{G}^{-1}(x, \mathbf{c}), \mathbf{a}\big)$.

---

[23]Technical details and tighter results can be found in Buehler [18].

Deterministic Dividends, Interest Rates, and Default Risk Until now, we have focused solely on the case where $S = X$, that is, we have abandoned the deterministic market data of the first section. Let us briefly comment on the impact of using

$$S_t = F_t^* X_t 1_{\tau > t} + A_t 1_{\tau > t}$$

according to (1.6). The aim is to replicate $H(S_T)$.

As a first step, we distinguish between default and no default. Since S drops to zero upon default,

$$H(S_T) = H\left(F_t^* X_t + A_t\right) 1_{\tau > T} + H(0) 1_{\tau \leq T} .$$

Hence,

$$P(0, T) \, \mathbb{E}_{\mathbb{P}} \left[H(S_T) \right] = P^S(0, T) \, \mathbb{E}_{\mathbb{P}} \left[H\left(F_T^* X_T + A_T\right) \right] + P(0, T) \left(1 - B_T^{S\,-1}\right) H(0)$$

$$= P^S(0, T) \, \mathbb{E}_{\mathbb{P}} \left[\tilde{H}\left(X_T\right) \right] + \left(P(0, T) - P^S(0, T)\right) H(0)$$

with $\tilde{H}(x) := H(F_T^* x + A_T)$. Since we can lock in $\left(P(0, T) - P^S(0, T)\right) H(0)$ by entering into a static position of risky and riskless bonds, we need to concentrate only on the replication of $\tilde{H}\left(X_T\right)$. We hence define

$$\tilde{H}_t := P(t, T) \, \mathbb{E}_{\mathbb{P}} \left[\tilde{H}(X_T) \,\middle|\, \mathcal{F}_t \right] 1_{\tau > t} . \tag{1.43}$$

As before, we assume that $\mathbf{Z} = (Z^0, \ldots, Z^m)$ with $Z^0 = X$ is uniquely given by the SDE (1.40), and that a range of traded instruments $\mathbf{C} = (C^1, \ldots, C^n)$ is given as a function of $\mathbf{Z}$. Without loss of generality we can assume with the same trick as above that each instrument C^ℓ attains zero value upon default; hence, we set

$$\mathbf{C}_t = \mathbb{G}(\mathbf{Z}_t) e^{\int_0^t (r_u + h_u)\, du} 1_{\tau > t} = B_t^S \mathbb{G}(\mathbf{Z}_t) .$$

We will also strip S of all its dividends and the repo by using the (tradable) process $S^{(plain)}$ defined in (1.9). The key is that we will use the risky bond B^S as the cash account, that is, we aim to construct a replication strategy such that

$$H(S_T) 1_{\tau > T} = \tilde{H}_0 + \int_0^T \Delta_u \, dS_u^{(plain)} + \sum_{\ell=1}^n \int_0^T \varphi_u^\ell \, dC_u^\ell + \int_0^T \beta_u \, dB_u^S .$$

As usual, the value of β is determined on the set $\{\tau > t\}$ by the self-financing requirement as

$$\beta_t := \frac{\tilde{H}_t - \Delta_t S_t^{(plain)} - \sum_{\ell=1}^n \varphi_t^\ell C_t^\ell}{B_t^S} .$$

The next step is to express, as before, the conditional expectation (1.43) in terms of $\mathbf{Z}$, rewrite it by the invertibility assumption in terms of $\mathbf{C}$, and then apply Ito. Let

$\tilde{h}_t(x, \mathbf{z}) := \mathbb{E}_{\mathbb{P}}\left[\tilde{H}(X_T) \,\middle|\, X_t = x, \mathbf{Z}_t = \mathbf{z} \right]$ and $\tilde{g}_t(x, \tilde{\mathbf{c}}) := \tilde{h}_t\left(x, \mathbb{G}^{-1}(x, \tilde{\mathbf{c}})\right)$, to which our previous results apply if g is sufficiently smooth. Defining, moreover,

$$g_t\left(S_t^{(plain)}, \mathbf{C}_t\right) := \tilde{g}_t\left(\frac{S_t^{(plain)}}{B_t^S}, \frac{\mathbf{C}_t}{B_t^S}\right),$$

yields that on $\{\tau > t\}$,

$$d\tilde{H}_t = (r_t + h_t)H_t\, dt + \partial_S g_t\left(S_t^{(plain)}, \mathbf{C}_t\right) dS_t^{(plain)} + \sum_{\ell=1}^{n} \partial_{C^\ell} g_t\left(S_t^{(plain)}, \mathbf{C}_t\right) dC_t^\ell.$$

In other words, the market is complete.

CHAPTER 2

Applications

While chapter 1 highlighted the principles of equity pricing from a rather theoretical point of view, we want to focus now on practical aspects: we will discuss a few commonly used stochastic volatility models and applications to Cliquet pricing; we will also address the pricing of payoffs that depend on the realized variance of an asset. In particular, "variance swaps" have become very liquid instruments and trading volumes are set to grow even further. The respective options on variance are an attractive new class of products on which to work.

2.1 CLASSIC EQUITY MODELS

In section 1.3.2, we discussed how we can construct martingales that fit a given initial option price surface, the most popular approach being Dupire's implied local volatility. We have already mentioned that in practice, it is rarely possible to obtain a continuum of option prices. Another problem with using an "implied" model is that it does not allow us to control the specific dynamics of the resulting actual stock price process. In this sense, we want to stress that a model that fits very well to some market does not at all guarantee that it produces acceptable prices: for example, consider a stock for which only forwards are traded, but no options. Then a "perfectly fitting" model would be given by a deterministic stock price process.[1] In this case it is obvious that this "model" cannot be correct if we want to price options on the stock. This argument can be carried over to volatility models: The mere fit of a model to European option data does not imply that it gives sensible hedges or prices for exotic payoffs. For this reason, it makes sense to take a "structural" point of view and model the stock and its volatility directly, using a particular assumption on the SDE it satisfies. We will review here a few of such classical *stochastic volatility models*.

2.1.1 Heston

By far the most popular model is probably Heston's stochastic volatility model [19]. It is given as a solution to the SDE

$$d\zeta_t = \kappa(\theta - \zeta_t)\,dt + \nu\sqrt{\zeta_t}\,dW_t^1$$

---

[1]This example is due to Peter Carr.

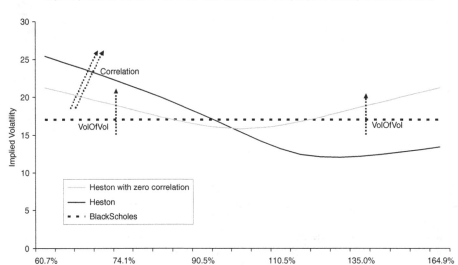

FIGURE 2.1 Stylized effects of changing vol of vol and correlation in Heston's model on the 1y implied volatility. The "Heston" parameters are $\zeta_0 = 15\%^2$, $\theta = 20\%^2$, $\kappa = 1$, $\rho = 70\%$ and $\nu = 35\%$.

$$dX_t = X_t \sqrt{\zeta_t} \, dB_t \tag{2.1}$$

$$dB_t = \rho dW_t^1 + \sqrt{1 - \rho^2} \, dW_t^2,$$

where $\mathbf{W} = (W^1, W^2)$ is a two-dimensional standard Brownian motion. We call κ the "speed of mean reversion" or "mean reversion speed," $\sqrt{\theta}$ the "long vol," ν the "vol of vol," ρ the "correlation," and the initial value $\sqrt{\zeta_0}$ the "short vol." We also refer to θ as "level of mean reversion." The two parameters vol of vol and correlation can be thought of as being responsible for the skew. This is illustrated in figure 2.1: vol of vol controls the volume of the smile and correlation its "tilt." A negative correlation produces the desired downward skew of implied volatility. The other three parameters control the term structure of the model:[2] In figure 2.2, the impact of changing short vol, long vol, and mean reversion speed on the term structure of ATM implied volatility is illustrated. It can be seen that short vol lives up to its name and controls the level of the short dated implied volatilities, while long vol controls the long end. Reversion speed controls the skewness or "decay" of the curve from the short vol level to the long vol level.

Note, however, that the distinction of the parameters by their effect on term structure and strike structure above was made for illustration purposes only: In particular, κ and ν are strongly interdependent if the model is used in the form (2.1). Indeed, κ is meant to be the "speed" of the process, but it does not feature in the volatility term of the variance. This is counterintuitive in the following sense:

---

[2]Note that the parameters ρ, ν, and ζ_0, θ, κ are not really "orthogonal"; we group them here just for illustration purposes.

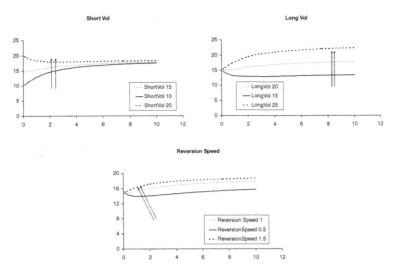

FIGURE 2.2 The effects of changing short vol, long vol, and mean-reversion speed on the ATM term structure of implied volatilities. Each graph shows the volatility term structure for 12 years. The reference Heston parameters are $\zeta_0 = 15\%^2$, $\theta = 20\%^2$, $\kappa = 1$, $\rho = 70\%$ and $\nu = 35\%$.

Consider the time change $t' := \kappa t$, such that

$$\zeta_{t/\kappa} = (\theta - \zeta_{t'/\kappa})dt' + \frac{\nu}{\sqrt{\kappa}}\sqrt{\zeta_{t'/\kappa}}\, d\tilde{W}_{t'}. \qquad (2.2)$$

The process $(\zeta_{t/\kappa})_t$ can be seen as being in "unit speed," $\kappa = 1$. From this point of view it would be more natural to parameterize the process ζ in (2.1) as

$$d\zeta_t = \kappa(\theta - \zeta_t)\, dt + \nu\sqrt{\kappa\zeta_t}\, dW_t^1.$$

Properties of Heston's Model One of the most attractive features of Heston's model is the fact that its variance is mean reverting. Such a mean-reverting feature is commonly seen in real market data; see also figure 2.3. Moreover, its calibrated correlation of around -70% is quite stable over time and produces, as we will show, a relatively good fit to the market's implied volatilities, at least for maturities beyond three months. (Figures 2.6, 2.7, and 2.10 show examples of calibrating Heston and other models to market data.)

However, Heston's popularity is probably mainly derived from the fact that it is possible to price European options on X using a semiclosed-form Fourier transformation, which in turn allows rapid calibration of the model parameters to market data.

The underlying mathematical reason for the relative tractability of Heston's model is that ζ is a squared Bessel process, which is well understood and reasonably tractable (cf. Revuz/Yor [13]). In fact, a statistical estimation on SPX by Aït-Sahalia/Kimmel [20] of $\alpha \in [1/2, 2]$ in the extended model

$$d\zeta_t = \kappa(\theta - \zeta_t)\, dt + \nu\zeta_t^\alpha\, dW_t^1$$

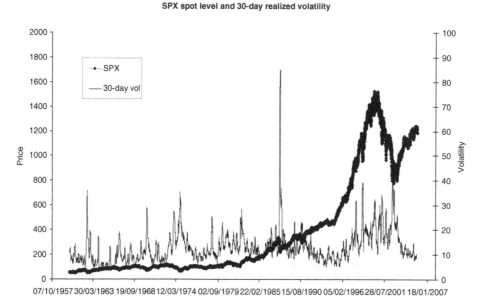

SPX spot level and 30-day realized volatility

FIGURE 2.3 Historic SPX quotes and estimated 30-day variance. Apart from occasional spikes we can identify the mean-reverting nature of the variance. It should be noted that the level of mean-reversion itself also varies over time.

has shown that, depending on the observation frequency, a value around 0.7 would probably be more adequate. What is more, the square-root volatility term means that unless

$$2\kappa\theta \geq \nu^2, \tag{2.3}$$

the process ζ can reach zero with nonzero probability. The crux is that this conditions is regularly violated if the model is calibrated freely to observed market data. While a vanishing short variance is not a problem in itself (after all, a variance of zero just implies that nobody trades), it makes numerical approximations more complicated. In a Monte Carlo simulation, for example, we have to take the event of ζ being negative into account. The same problem appears in a PDE solver: Heston's PDE becomes degenerate if the short vol hits zero (cf. section 9.4). A violation of (2.3) also implies that the distribution of short variance at some later time t is very wide (see figure 2.4).

Additionally, if (2.3) does not hold, then the stock price X may fail to have a second moment if the correlation is not negative enough in the sense detailed in proposition 3.1 in Andersen/Piterbarg [21]. Again, this is not a problem from a purely mathematical point of view, but it makes numerical schemes less efficient. In particular, Monte Carlo simulations perform much less well. Although an Euler scheme will still converge to the desired value, the speed of convergence deteriorates. Moreover, we cannot safely use control variates anymore if the payoff is not bounded.

Computing European Option Prices with Fourier Transforms To compute European option prices, we focus on the call price. Following Carr/Madan [22], we will price

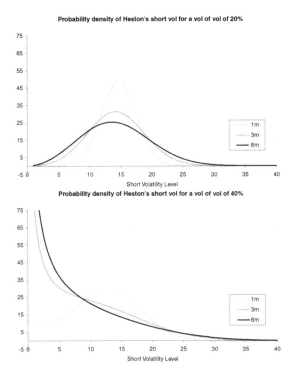

FIGURE 2.4 This graphs shows the density of ζ_t for one, three, and six months for the case where condition (2.3) is satisfied (left side) or not (right side). Apart from the vol of vol, the parameters were $\zeta_0 = 15\%^2$, $\theta = 20\%^2$, and $\kappa = 1$.

the call via Fourier inversion (see also Lewis [23] for a detailed overview of the subject). Let, as before,

$$\mathcal{C}(T, e^k) := \mathbb{E}\left[\left(X_T - e^k\right)^+\right].$$

Since the call price itself is not an L^2 function in k, we define a *dampened call*

$$c(T, k) := e^{\alpha k}\mathcal{C}(T, e^k)$$

for an $\alpha > 0$ (see Carr/Madan [22] for a discussion on the choice of α). We also denote by ϕ_t the density and by φ_t the characteristic function of $\log X_t$. Then,

$$\begin{aligned}
\psi_t(z) &:= \int_{\mathbb{R}} e^{ikz} c(t, k)\, dk \\
&= \int_{\mathbb{R}} e^{ikz + \alpha k} \int_{\mathbb{R}} 1_{x > k} \left(e^x - e^k\right) \phi_t(x)\, dx\, dk \\
&= \int_{\mathbb{R}} \int_{-\infty}^{x} \left(e^{(iz+\alpha)k + x} - e^{(iz+\alpha+1)k}\right) dk\, \phi_t(x)\, dx \\
&= \int_{\mathbb{R}} \frac{e^{(iz+\alpha+1)x}}{(iz+\alpha)(iz+\alpha+1)} \phi_t(x)\, dx = \frac{\varphi_t\left(z - i(\alpha+1)\right)}{(iz+\alpha)(iz+\alpha+1)}.
\end{aligned}$$

We can then price a call on X using

$$C(T, e^k) = \frac{e^{-\alpha k}}{\pi} \int_0^\infty e^{-izk} \psi_t(z) \, dz.$$

The method also lends itself to Fast-Fourier transformation if a range of option prices for a single maturity is required.

Heston's Characteristic Function Let us now show how we can compute Heston's characteristic function,

$$\psi_T(z) := \mathbb{E}\left[e^{iz \log X_T} \right].$$

We present here an approach that is mathematically not rigorous, but very intuitive. See Heston's original work for a more precise derivation of the characteristic function. We have

$$\psi_T(z) = \mathbb{E}\left[e^{iz \log X_T} \right]$$

$$= \mathbb{E}\left[e^{iz \int_0^T \sqrt{\zeta_u} \, dB_u - \frac{iz}{2} \int_0^T \zeta_u \, du} \right]$$

$$= \mathbb{E}^z\left[e^{-\frac{iz + z^2}{2} \int_0^T \zeta_u \, du} \right],$$

where $\mathbb{P}^z$ is the complex measure associated with the density $e^{iz \int_0^T \sqrt{\zeta_u} \, dB_u + \frac{z^2}{2} \int_0^T \zeta_u \, du}$. We have $B_t = B_t^z + \int_0^t iz\sqrt{\zeta_u} \, du$ for a $\mathbb{P}^z$-Brownian motion B^z. This implies that under $\mathbb{P}^z$, the process ζ satisfies

$$d\zeta_t = \tilde{\kappa}(\tilde{\theta} - \zeta_t) \, dt + \nu\sqrt{\zeta_t} \, dW_t^z \quad \text{with } \tilde{\kappa} := \kappa - \rho i z \nu \text{ and } \tilde{\theta} := \frac{\kappa}{\tilde{\kappa}}\theta.$$

Here, W^z is a $\mathbb{P}^z$-Brownian motion with a correlation of ρ with respect to B^z. We can therefore compute ψ using the more general function

$$\eta_T(\mu, h; x_0) := \mathbb{E}\left[e^{-\mu x_T - h \int_0^T x_u \, du} \right]$$

for a process

$$dx_t = (m - kx_t) \, dt + \xi\sqrt{x_t} \, dW_t.$$

To this end, note that because of the Markov property of x, the process $e^{-h \int_0^t x_u \, du} \eta_{T-t}(\mu, h; x_t)$ is a martingale on $[0, T]$. Hence, by using Ito and division by $e^{-h \int_0^t x_u \, du}$, we obtain the PDE

$$0 = -h\eta_{T-t}(\mu, h; x) + -\partial_T \eta_{T-t}(\mu, h; x)$$

$$+ (m - kx)\partial_x \eta_{T-t}(\mu, h; x) + \frac{1}{2}\xi^2 x \partial_{xx}^2 \eta_{T-t}(\mu, h; x)$$

$$= -h\eta_{T-t}(\mu, h; x) + -\partial_T \eta_{T-t}(\mu, h; x) + m\partial_x \eta_{T-t}(\mu, h; x)$$

$$+ x\left(-k\partial_x \eta_{T-t}(\mu, h; x) + \frac{1}{2}\xi^2 \partial_{xx}^2 \eta_{T-t}(\mu, h; x) \right)$$

with boundary condition $\eta_0(\mu, h; x) = e^{-\mu x}$. Since x is affine, we guess that η is an exponential of an affine function,

$$\eta_T(\mu, h; x) = e^{-xA_T(\mu, h) - mB_T(\mu, h)}. \tag{2.4}$$

By solving the above PDE for this function, we obtain

$$A_T(\mu, h) = \frac{\alpha + ae^{\gamma t}}{\beta + be^{\gamma t}} \tag{2.5}$$

and

$$B_t(\mu, h) = \int_0^T A_t(\mu, h)\, dt = \frac{\alpha b \gamma t + (a\beta - \alpha b)\log \frac{\beta + be^{\gamma t}}{\beta + b}}{\beta b \gamma}. \tag{2.6}$$

with the constants

$$\alpha := h(\gamma + b) - 2\mu$$
$$a := h(\gamma - b) + 2\mu$$
$$\beta := -\xi^2 h + \gamma - k$$
$$b := \xi^2 h + \gamma + k$$
$$\gamma := -\sqrt{k^2 + 2\xi^2 \mu}.$$

For the case where m is time-dependent, see section 2.1.5 below.

Simulating Heston Once we have calibrated the model using the aforementioned semiclosed form solution for the European options, the question is how to evaluate complex products. At our disposal are PDEs and Monte Carlo schemes. We briefly comment on the Monte Carlo approach: we want to simulate the Heston process (2.1) in an interval $[0, T]$. Since the conditional transition density of the entire process is not known, we have to refrain from solving a discretization of the SDE (2.1). To this end, assume that we are given fixing dates $0 = t_0 < \cdots < t_N = T$ and let $\Delta t_i := t_{i+1} - t_i$ for $i = 0, \ldots, N - 1$. Moreover, we denote by ΔW_i for $i = 0, \ldots, N - 1$ a sequence of independent normal variables with variance Δ_i, and by ΔB_i a corresponding sequence where ΔB_i and ΔW_i have correlation ρ.

When using a straightforward Euler scheme, we will face the problem that ζ can become negative. It works well simply to reduce the volatility term of the variance to the positive part of the variance, that is, to simulate

$$\zeta_{t_{i+1}} = \zeta_i + \kappa(\theta - \zeta_i)\Delta_i + v\sqrt{\zeta_i^+}\,\Delta W_i.$$

A flaw of this scheme is that it is biased. This is overcome by using the moment-matching scheme

$$\zeta_{t_{i+1}} = \theta \Delta t_i + \left(\zeta_{t_i} - \theta\right) e^{-\kappa \Delta t_i} + \left(v\zeta_{t_i}^+ \sqrt{\frac{1 - e^{-2\kappa \Delta t_i}}{2\kappa}}\right) \Delta W_i, \tag{2.7}$$

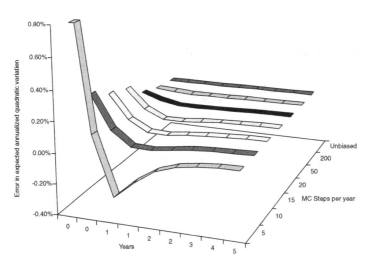

FIGURE 2.5 Plain Euler with various steps per year vs. the unbiased scheme. The model parameters were $\zeta_0 = 30\%^2$, $\theta = 20\%^2$, $\kappa = 2$, $\rho = -70\%$, $\nu = 35\%$. The graph shows the error between the true and the simulated value of $\mathbb{E}[\int_0^T \zeta_t \, dt]/T$.

which works well in practice, see figure 2.5. Higher-order schemes such as Milstein cannot be used with this process since the square root is not differentiable at 0 (this is not such a big problem if we ensure that (2.3) is satisfied). A similar approach is used to compute the stock price: Here, we note that the integral over ζ_t in the interval $[t_i, t_{i+1}]$ conditional on ζ_{t_i} is given as

$$\Delta_i V := \theta \Delta t_i + \left(\zeta_{t_i} - \theta\right) \frac{1 - e^{-\kappa \Delta t_i}}{\kappa} \; ;$$

hence, we set

$$X_{t_{i+1}} := X_{t_i} \exp\left\{\sqrt{\Delta_i V} \Delta B_i - \frac{1}{2}\Delta_i V\right\}.$$

A powerful tool to improve the convergence of the estimation of an expectation are control variates (for the case where (2.3) holds). The idea is as follows: Assume we want to compute the expectation of a random variable X (the payoff) and denote by $\mathbb{E}^n[X]$ the estimated value of X using n Monte Carlo paths. The standard deviation of the error in this estimate is given by $\sqrt{\text{Var}[X]/n}$ (i.e., it is worthwhile to try to reduce the variance of the variable we estimate). Now assume that there is a second random variable Y (the control variate) whose expectation $\mathbb{E}[Y]$ we know analytically.

The idea is that we estimate the value of $X - hY$ and add back the value of hY. It is clear that this scheme is unbiased if our original Monte Carlo scheme was unbiased. To compute the ideal ρ, note $X - hY$ has the variance $\text{Var}[X] - 2h\text{Var}[X, Y] + h^2\text{Var}[Y]$, which is minimized if we set

$$h := \frac{\text{Var}[X, Y]}{\text{Var}[Y]}.$$

Since we usually do not know $\text{Var}[X, Y]$ and $\text{Var}[Y]$, we can replace the above quantities by the estimates on the nth path. Extension of this idea to a number of control variates is straightforward (a good reference on Monte Carlo in practice is Glasserman [17]).

An efficient control variate depends by construction on the actual payoff, but if no other variance reduction techniques are used, using the integrated variance and the stock price is usually a good choice. To this end, we track in addition to ζ and X also $V_{i+1} := V_i + \Delta_i V$, which is an unbiased estimator of the integrated variance

$$\mathbb{E}\left[\int_0^{t_i} \zeta_u \, du\right] = \theta t_i + (\theta - \zeta_0)\frac{1 - e^{-\kappa t_i}}{\kappa}.$$

2.1.2   SABR

The *SABR model* introduced by Hagan et al. [24] is given as

$$\begin{aligned}
d\alpha_t &= v\alpha_t \, dW_t^1 \\
dX_t &= X_t^\beta \alpha_t \, dB_t \\
dB_t &= \rho \, dW_t^1 + \sqrt{1 - \rho^2} \, dW_t^2,
\end{aligned} \tag{2.8}$$

for $\beta \in [\frac{1}{2}, 1]$ and $X_0 = x$ and $\alpha_0 > 0$. It is a blend between the *CEV* model (cf. example 1) and a log-normal volatility model: the former is obtained from (2.8) by using $v = 0$, while the latter corresponds to $\beta = 1$. This model is very popular in interest rate modeling due to the fact that it is possible to derive approximations for the implied volatility directly from the model parameters. These approximations can then be used to interpolate the implied volatility surface in an arbitrage-free way without the need to compute European option prices numerically with subsequent computation of implied volatilities. The implied volatility for a strike k at maturity T is approximated in [24] as

$$\hat{\sigma}(k, T) \approx \frac{z\alpha_0}{\chi \, (xk)^{(1-\beta)/2}} \frac{1 + \left[\frac{(1-\beta)^2\alpha^2}{24}(xk)^{\beta-1} + \frac{\alpha\beta v\rho}{4}(xk)^{(\beta-1)/2} + \frac{2-3\rho^2}{24}v^2\right]T}{1 + \frac{(1-\beta)^2}{24}\log^2\frac{x}{k} + \frac{(1-\beta)^4}{1920}\log^4\frac{x}{k}} \tag{2.9}$$

with

$$z := \frac{v}{\alpha}(xk)^{(1-\beta)/2}\log\frac{x}{k} \quad \text{and} \quad \chi := \log\frac{\sqrt{1 - 2\rho z + z^2} + z - \rho}{1 - \rho}.$$

While this model is convenient for marking implied volatilities, it has a few drawbacks when used for pricing equity options. The first issue is that for the case $\beta < 1$, the stock price itself becomes zero with a nonzero probability just as the CEV process in example 1. While this might be acceptable for single stocks,

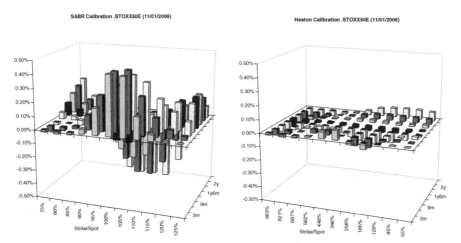

FIGURE 2.6 Calibration of SABR and unconstrained Heston to STOXX50E data for maturities from 3m to 2y. Heston appears to fit better to most indices at the time of writing. The calibrated values were $\alpha_0 = 15.9\%$, $\rho = -46.9\%$, $\nu = 78.0\%$, $\beta = 0.58$ and $X_0 = 0.75$ for SABR and $v_0 = 15.7\%^2$, $\theta = 40.2\%^2$, $\kappa = 0.30$, $\rho = -68.5\%$ and $\nu = 38.3\%$ for Heston. The SABR fit is only marginally worse for fixed $\beta = 1$ and $X_0 = 1$, in which case the remaining parameters become $\alpha_0 = 15.9\%$, $\rho = -46.9\%$ and $\nu = 78.0\%$.

this is rarely a desirable feature for index price processes. Another issue is that in the case $\beta = 1$ and $\rho > 0$, the stock price in this model is not a martingale, as Jourdain shows in [25]. He also shows that the model has moments up to order $1/(1 - \rho^2)$; hence, the second moment does not exist for $\rho > -1/\sqrt{2}$. These problems stem from the fact that the model has a log-normal volatility, which implies that volatility can grow exponentially. However, most historic data indicate that an unbounded volatility process is rather unlikely, and that volatility should be mean-reverting in some sense (to this end, see figure 2.3 on page 38). Nonetheless, the model offers an alternative to the Heston model because it can be calibrated very quickly to observed European market prices using (2.9). At the moment, however, it does not seem to beat Heston in terms of fitting the market, as figure 2.6 shows.

The SABR model has been extended in several ways. In [26] Hagan et al. discuss the model with a more general local volatility function F,

$$
\begin{aligned}
d\alpha_t &= \nu \alpha_t \, dW_t^1 \\
dX_t &= F(X_t) \alpha_t \, dB_t \\
dB_t &= \rho \, dW_t^1 + \sqrt{1 - \rho^2} \, dW_t^2,
\end{aligned}
$$

for which they also present analytical approximations. Moreover, Henry-Labordère [27] discusses approximation formulas for much more general models than (2.8). In particular, he introduces a mean-reverting drift into the SDE for α and, additionally, shows how the local volatility function F in the above equations must be chosen to perfectly match the short-end skew. In a recent paper, Bourgade and Croissant [28] also work in this extended framework.

2.1.3 Scott's Exponential Ornstein-Uhlenbeck Model

Scott [29] has proposed a short-variance process, which is modeled as an exponential Ornstein-Uhlenbeck (OU) process,

$$
\begin{aligned}
dv_t &= \kappa(\theta_t - v_t)\,dt + v\,dW_t^1 \\
dX_t &= X_t\sqrt{e^{v_t}}\,dB_t \\
dB_t &= \rho\,dW_t^1 + \sqrt{1-\rho^2}\,dW_t^2.
\end{aligned}
\tag{2.10}
$$

This process has been investigated in depth by Fouque et al. in [30]. This model shares with the preceding SABR model the loss of the martingale property for $\rho > 0$ and the limitations if the second moment is to be retained (in fact, Jourdain discusses in [25] both models). From a practical point of view the problem with (2.10) is that no straightforward method is available that allows the efficient computation of European option prices or implied volatilities. It should be noted, however, that the process v itself is very easy to simulate. The complication is to simulate the stock price X, for which we have to revert to solving the SDE (2.10) via discretization. The use of control variates as discussed above improves the convergence of a Monte Carlo scheme, but again this limits us to the case where X has a second moment. However, if we want to price European options, we can make use of the following observation: let $\zeta_t := e^{v_t}$, then

$$
\mathbb{E}\left[\left(X_T - k\right)^+\right] = \mathbb{E}\left[\,\mathbb{E}\left[\left(e^{\rho\int_0^T \sqrt{\zeta_t}\,dW_t^1 + \sqrt{1-\rho^2}\int_0^T \sqrt{\zeta_t}\,dW_t^2 - \frac{1}{2}\int_0^T \zeta_t\,dt} - k\right)^+ \,\middle|\, W_{t:t\le T}^1\right]\right]
$$

$$
= \mathbb{E}\left[Y_T \mathbb{BS}\left(T, kY_T^{-1}, \sqrt{\frac{1-\rho^2}{T}\int_0^T \zeta_t\,dt}\right)\right]
$$

with

$$
Y_T := e^{\rho\int_0^T \sqrt{\zeta_t}\,dW_t^1 - \frac{1}{2}\rho^2 2\int_0^T \zeta_t\,dt}.
$$

Hence, we have reduced the computation of a European option to a one-factor problem. This obviously works for all "pure" stochastic volatility models where the volatility does not depend functionally on the stock price level.

2.1.4 Other Stochastic Volatility Models

The list of stochastic volatility models that have been proposed for option pricing is long. However, apart from Heston-type and SABR-type models, most stochastic volatility models do not admit an easy access to the pricing of European options or their implied volatilities.[3] In contrast, for many Levy models proposed in the literature (see, for example, Overhaus et al. [31] and Shoutens [32]), the characteristic function is available, such that the approach discussed on page 38 can be used

---

[3]Schoebel/Zhou [34] have shown that it is possible to obtain the characteristic function of logarithm of the stock price if the short volatility itself is given as an OU process. This model, however, is somehow unnatural since the short volatility can become negative.

to price Europeans. Numerical methods for such models tend to be more involved than for diffusion-based models; see Cont/Tankov [33] for a good account on using Levy models in finance.

2.1.5 Extensions of Heston's Model

Using Heston's model (2.1) as a basis, we can develop a range of related models that still admit a characteristic function that can be computed more or less quickly. The first extension is a model in which the level of mean reversion is time dependent: assume that $\theta = (\theta_t)_{t \geq 0}$ is a non-negative function and set

$$
\begin{aligned}
d\zeta_t &= \kappa(\theta_t - \zeta_t)\,dt + v\sqrt{\zeta_t}\,d\mathrm{W}_t^1 \\
dX_t &= X_t\sqrt{\zeta_t}\,dB_t \\
dB_t &= \rho d\mathrm{W}_t^1 + \sqrt{1 - \rho^2}\,d\mathrm{W}_t^2 .
\end{aligned}
\tag{2.11}
$$

A good example, which we will pick up again in section 2.3.3, is $\theta_t := m + (\theta_0 - m)e^{-ct}$. Following the computations for Heston's model, we find that we can still write the characteristic function of $\log X$ as an exponential of an affine function as in (2.4). Indeed, the only change is that now, instead of (2.6),

$$
B_T(h, \mu) := \int_0^T \theta(T - t)A_t(h, \mu)\,dt .
$$

If time dependency of the other parameters of Heston's model is required, we can revert to the case of piecewise constant parameters. Indeed, let us set

$$
\begin{aligned}
d\zeta_t &= \kappa_t(\theta_t - \zeta_t)\,dt + v_t\sqrt{\zeta_t}\,d\mathrm{W}_t^1 \\
dX_t &= X_t\sqrt{\zeta_t}\,dB_t \\
dB_t &= \rho_t d\mathrm{W}_t^1 + \sqrt{1 - \rho_t^2}\,d\mathrm{W}_t^2 .
\end{aligned}
\tag{2.12}
$$

with functions κ, θ, v and ρ, which are piecewise constant on $0 = t_0 < \cdots < t_n$. Assume that $t_k < T \leq t_{k+1}$. The characteristic function of $\log X_T$ is then given as

$$
\mathbb{E}\left[e^{iz \log X_T} \right] = \mathbb{E}\left[\mathbb{E}\left[e^{iz \log X_T} \mid \mathcal{F}_{t_k} \right] \right] = \mathbb{E}\left[e^{iz \log X_{t_k}} e^{-v_{t_k}\tilde{A}_k(z) - \kappa_{t'_k}^{m_{t_k}}\tilde{B}_k(z)} \right]
$$

for some constants $\tilde{A}_k(z)$ and $\tilde{B}_k(z)$. By iteration, we obtain once again an exponential affine characteristic function of $\log X_T$.

In a different direction, Heston's model can be extended by adding jumps to the return process. A popular example is Bates's "Heston Jump Diffusion" [35], which is a combination of Heston's model and the jump diffusion model with normal jumps in the return as in example 2 on page 20. Since the characteristic function of the jump diffusion part can be computed easily and since the jumps and the Brownian motions are independent, the characteristic function of Bates's model is just the product of the characteristic functions of Heston's model and the Jump Diffusion model with zero short volatility (i.e., $\sigma = 0$ in (1.28)). The parameters of this model can also be made time dependent with piecewise constant values.

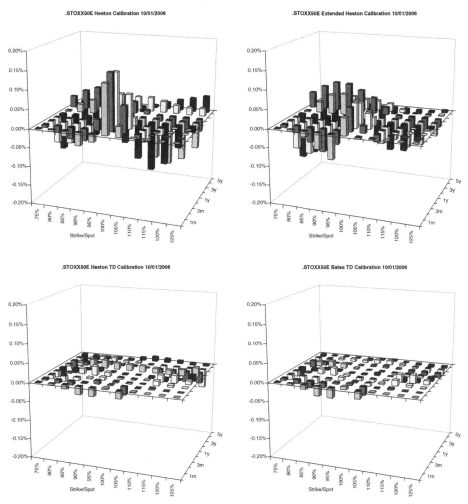

FIGURE 2.7 Various models fitted to STOXX50E for maturities from 1m to 5y. The introduction of time dependency clearly improves the fit. Figure 2.8 on page 48 shows a summary of the calibration for STOXX50 while figure 2.9 on page 48 and figure 2.10 on page 49 show the summaries for SPX and FTSE, respectively.

When the number of parameters in a model increases, it will usually also fit better to the implied volatility. In particular, the extension (2.11) is a good way of improving the short-end fit of Heston's model to the implied volatility market. If a much better fit is required, the piecewise constant time-dependent Heston model with or without jumps can be used, as is illustrated in figures 2.7 through 2.10.

However, it should be noted that by introducing piecewise constant time-dependent data, we lose much of a model's structure. It is turned from a time-homogeneous model that "takes a view" on the actual evolution of the volatility via its SDE into a kind of an arbitrage-free interpolation of market data: If calibrated without additional constraints to ensure smoothness of the parameters over time, this is reflected in large discrepancies of the parameter values for distinct periods.

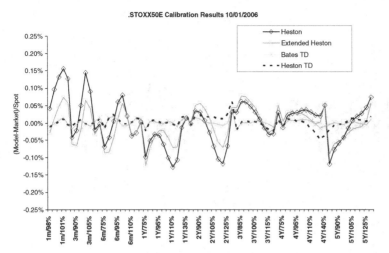

FIGURE 2.8 A summary view of the calibration for STOXX50E. The extension of Heston via (2.11) in particular improves the fit of Heston's model to the short end, which is a common problem of the original model.

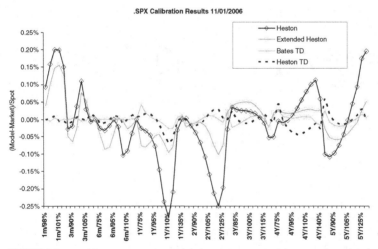

FIGURE 2.9 Calibration results for SPX. The naïve calibration for Heston gives a very bad fit that exceeds the desired 0.10% error threshold frequently.

For example, the excellent fit of the time-dependent Heston model in figure 2.8 is achieved with the following parameter values (short volatility $\sqrt{\zeta_0}$ was 15.0%):

	6m	1y	3y	∞
Long vol $\sqrt{\theta}$	20.7%	23.6%	36.1%	46.5%
Reversion speed κ	5.0	3.2	0.4	0.3
Correlation ρ	−55.2%	−70.9%	−80.1%	−69.4%
VolOfVol ν	78.7%	81.5%	35.3%	60.0

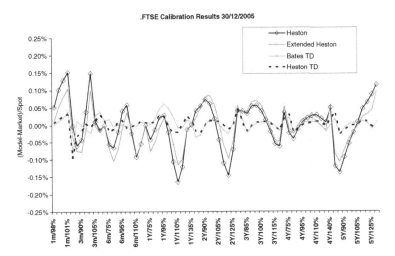

FIGURE 2.10 Calibration results for FTSE.

Moreover, the increased number of parameters makes it more difficult to hedge in such a model in practice. Even though both Heston and the time-dependent Heston models create complete markets, as discussed in section 1.4.1, we will always need to additionally protect our position against moves in the parameters values of our model. Just as for vega in Black and Scholes, this is typically done by computing "parameter greeks" and neutralizing the respective sensitivities. Clearly, the more parameters are involved, and the less stable these are, this "parameter hedge" becomes less and less reliable.

2.1.6 Cliquets

A classic group of "volatility products" in equity markets is called *Cliquets*. The term generally refers to contracts whose payoff depends one way or the other on the performance of an asset over a future period of time. For example, a globally floored Cliquet with a local floor of 2.5% and a cap of 5% over the reset dates $0 = t_0 < \cdots < t_n = T$ pays

$$\left(\sum_{i=1}^{n} -2.5\% \vee \left(\frac{S_{t_i}}{S_{t_{i-1}}} - 1 \right) \wedge 5\% \right)^{+} \tag{2.13}$$

where we used the notation $a \vee b := \max\{a, b\}$ and $a \wedge b := \min\{a, b\}$. Other, more exotic payoffs include:

- Napoleons:

$$\left\{ \prod_{i=1}^{n} \left(90\% \vee \frac{S_{t_i}}{S_{t_{i-1}}} \wedge 110\% \right)^{+} - 100\% \right\}^{+},$$

- Multiplicative Cliquets:

$$\left\{\left(\prod_{i=1}^{n}\max\left(\frac{S_{t_i}}{S_{t_{i-1}}},1\right)\right)-1\right\}^{+},$$

- Reverse Cliquets:

$$\left\{C-\sum_{i=1}^{n}\left(k-\frac{S_{t_i}}{S_{t_{i-1}}}\right)^{+}\right\}^{+}$$

for $C > 0$ and $k > 0$.

The evaluation of such products is by far not trivial and the market has not yet settled for an agreed reference model. In fact, at least for single underlying products, a big step forward would be if it were possible to price and, more importantly, actually hedge plain *forward-started options* consistently. For example, a forward-started call has the payoff

$$\left(\frac{S_{t_2}}{S_{t_1}}-k\right)^{+}\quad(t_1 < t_2).\tag{2.14}$$

Puts are defined accordingly.[4]

If we want to price a forward-started option of the type above, it is clear that at the reset date t_1, the contract turns into a plain European option. Since such options are liquidly traded, this price must be very accurate. In other words, any model we may propose should internally be able to produce future implied volatility shapes (i.e., European option prices) that are consistent with historic behavior: we have already discussed in section 1.2.1 that the general shape of the implied volatility surface is similar over time. However, we do not necessarily need to fit the entire implied volatility surface perfectly. Intuitively, the main importance is to fit and explain well those implied volatilities at time-to-maturity of the length of the period $\tau := t_i - t_{i-1}$, so typically one month, three months, six months, or one year.

Stochastic Implied Volatility Under these circumstances, the most natural modeling approach is to model directly the implied volatility surface (or, equivalently, the implied forward distribution or the European option prices). The first such *stochastic implied volatility* model (to our knowledge) was proposed by Brace et al. in [36].[5] It has also been discussed by Cont et al. [38] and Haffner [39]. The idea is relatively

---

[4]The form (2.14) is called a *fixed notional* forward started call; the *variable notional* form has the payoff

$$\left(S_{t_2}-S_{t_1}k\right)^{+}\quad(t_1 < t_2).$$

[5]In an earlier work, Schoenbucher [37] discusses an implied volatility model for a single strike K.

straightforward: Let us denote by $\sigma_t(T, k)$ the implied volatility in our model at time t for a strike k and a maturity T. We now want to model this quantity directly as a stochastic process. While it is possible to formulate this idea in terms of stochastic functions in the spirit of Brace et al. [36], we consider here the more direct approach of writing σ in terms of a sufficiently well-behaved function G and an m-dimensional parameter process $\mathbf{Z} = (\mathbf{Z}_t)_{t \geq 0}$ as

$$\sigma_t(T, k) := G\left(\mathbf{Z}_t;\, T - t, \frac{k}{X_t}\right).$$

For example, we use a d-dimensional Brownian motion $\mathbf{W} = (W^1, \ldots, W^d)$ and assume that the m-dimensional process Z is the unique strong solution to an SDE

$$d\mathbf{Z}_t = \mu(\mathbf{Z}_t)\, dt + \sum_{j=1}^{d} \varsigma^j(\mathbf{Z}_t)\, dW_t^j$$

for vectors $\mu(z), \sigma^1(z), \ldots, \sigma^d(z) \in \mathbb{R}^m$.

The function G is chosen such that it gives a reasonable shape of the implied volatility for all possible parameter values $\mathbf{z} \in \mathcal{Z}$. This is why we have written $G(\mathbf{z}; x, c)$ as a function of the natural coordinates' time-to-maturity $x = T - t$ and relative strike $c = k/X_t$ instead of fixed maturities and cash strikes. Ideally, the parameters of the process $\mathbf{Z}$ would have a direct interpretation such as level, skew, kurtosis, and term structure of the implied volatility surface. However, it should be clear that the specification of such a function and the dynamics of $\mathbf{Z}$ are constrained by no-arbitrage conditions: In particular, the price process of each European option should be a local martingale.[6]

The price of a call with cash strike k and maturity T at time t is given by

$$\mathcal{C}_t(T, k) = X_t\, \mathbb{BS}\left(T - t, \frac{k}{X_t}, \sigma_t\left(T - t, \frac{k}{X_t}\right)\right) =: \mathbb{G}(X_t, \mathbf{Z}_t;\, T - t, k).$$

If the implied volatility surface is well defined, then it follows from the continuity of the stock price process that X is given in the form $X_t = \mathcal{E}_t(\int_0^\cdot \sqrt{\zeta_s}\, dB_s)$ for some Brownian motion B and with a short variance process ζ, which is the square of the instantaneously maturing implied volatility, $\zeta_t = \sigma_t(0; X_t)^2$.[7] In other words, the call price is a function of X and $\mathbf{Z}$, and as such we can apply Ito. As a result, we obtain

---

[6]The existence of a local martingale measure is equivalent to "no free lunch with vanishing risk"; see Delbaen/Schachermayer [2].

[7]To see this, note that ζ is the derivative of the instantaneously maturing variance swap. Moreover, the instantaneous squared implied volatility is equal to the instantaneous variance.

a regularity condition on the interplay between $\mathbb{G}$, μ, ς and ζ.

$$0 = -\partial_x \mathbb{G} + \frac{1}{2}\partial_{X_t^2}^2 \zeta_t \mathbb{G}$$

$$+ \sum_{i=1}^{m} \partial_{Z_t^i} \mu_i(\mathbf{Z}_t)\,\mathbb{G} + \frac{1}{2}\sum_{j=1}^{d}\sum_{i,k=1}^{n} \sigma_i^j(\mathbf{Z}_t)\sigma_k^j(\mathbf{Z}_t)\partial_{Z_t^i,Z_t^k}^2 \mathbb{G}(\mathbf{Z}_t)$$

$$+ \sum_{j=1}^{d}\sum_{i=1}^{m} \sigma_i^j(\mathbf{Z}_t)\sqrt{\zeta_t}\rho^j \frac{1}{2}\partial_{Z_t^i,X_t}^2 \mathbb{G}(\mathbf{Z}_t)$$

This expression can be expanded using the standard derivatives for the Black & Scholes formula, which results in a complex PDE for ς and μ (see Brace et al. [36] for details). While this approach is very appealing, it has the unfortunate drawback simply that no "stochastic implied volatility" model has yet been published that is not from the start a stochastic volatility model. The main problem of the entire approach is that it is very difficult to find a function G that actually ensures that the European option prices at any time t are strongly arbitrage free in the sense of definition 1.3.1 on page 16; if a model produces arbitrage situations in itself, then the "price" of a derivative computed with this model is meaningless. Indeed, it seems that the only functional forms for G so far known are those that stem from starting with price process X in the first place: this is one of the motivations of using the SABR model discussed above, for which we have approximative formulas for the implied volatilities. However, even if we use the implied volatility surface function given by, say, a Heston model (2.1) and simply see it as a function

$$G : z := (\zeta_0, \theta, \kappa, \nu, \rho) \longmapsto G(z; \cdot, \cdot)$$

which maps the parameters of the model to an implied volatility surface, the restrictions imposed by the no-arbitrage equation derived above are severe (also see the comments in example 5 on page 75).

REMARK 2.1.1 *Instead of modeling implied volatility, we could also consider alternatives such as the call prices on the stock, its implied distribution, or the implied local volatility. The latter has been discussed by Derman/Kani in the related context of their implied trees [40].*

2.1.7 Forward-Skew Propagation

To price Cliquets, we have to revert to less ambitious approaches. Note that it is, of course, possible to price a forward-started option using the Black-Scholes formula. For a given flat volatility σ, the price of such a call (2.14) on X is given as

$$\mathcal{C}^{\mathrm{BS}}(t_1, t_2, k) := \mathbb{BS}\left(t_2 - t_1, k;\, \sigma\right).$$

Just as before, this allows us to define what is called the *forward implied volatility* of a given market price $\hat{\mathcal{C}}(t_1, t_2, k)$ for the call as

$$\hat{\sigma}(t_1, t_2, k) := \mathbb{BS}\left(t_2 - t_1, k;\, \cdot\right)^{-1}\left(\hat{\mathcal{C}}(t_1, t_2, k)\right).$$

This quantity is often used as a way to quote the price of a forward-started option. For example, we call $k \mapsto \hat{\sigma}(t_1, t_1 + \tau, k)$ the *forward skew* at t_1 for the period $\tau := t_2 - t_1$. Given a particular model, this forward skew can be used to compare the prices of forward-started options with the same reset period τ but with different starting dates: see, for example, the fourth graph in figure 2.12 on page 82, which shows how the forward skew for τ is equal to three-month changes with the start date in a Heston model. We can clearly see that the skew becomes more and more U-shaped.

Sometimes it is required that a model "propagates the skew," that is, that the forward skew matches the current skew for the same time-to-maturity as closely as possible. One way to achieve this works as follows: As before, denote by τ the period between two reset dates, and we assume that we can extract the distribution of S_{t_1} from the market using the second derivative in strike of standard spot-started European options. The idea is now to assume that

$$Y_i := \frac{S_{t_i}}{S_{t_{i-1}}}$$

is independent of Y_j, $j = i - 1, \ldots, 1$ and that it has exactly the same distribution as Y_1. This implies that the discrete stock price is given as a product of independent variables,

$$S_{t_i} = \prod_{j=1}^{i} Y_j.$$

Such a model is called an *independent increment model* and by construction it will perfectly "preserve the skew."[8] Apart from the unrealistic assumption that the increment of a stock price does not depend on its past behavior in any way, this model also has the drawback that the prices of spot-started European options with maturities $t_2, \ldots, t_n$ are completely determined by the initial distribution of Y_1. Consequently, the ATM spot-started options will usually not fit to the market prices. To alleviate this obvious drawback, it has been proposed to maintain the ATM implied volatility for the forward-started options in Black and Scholes and to apply a certain skew to them. These forward starts are then used to back out the assumed distribution of Y_i, which is possible because of the assumption of independent increments: If all forward-started call prices are known, the forward distribution is as usual given by the second derivative of these prices in strike. Hence, a simple model of this type can be realized by jumping independently between the reset dates t_i according to the forward distributions implied by the forward-started call prices.[9]

---

[8]There are many ways to obtain such a model. The easiest approach is to use a Levy process (CGMY or Merton's model) and calibrate it only to options with maturity τ. The resulting fit for the spot-started options is usually good enough to obtain an idea of the approximate price level of a Cliquet. An alternative approach is to use directly the distribution inferred by the European options with maturity τ.

[9]To obtain an idea of the impact of such a model, calibrate a Merton-model with time-dependent volatility parameters: first, the jump parameters are calibrated to the τ-maturity

Blending the Skew Instead of using purely independent increments, it is often desirable to introduce some interdependency between the increments while retaining the possibility of controlling closely the shape of the forward distribution. In fact, what is needed is a model where each Y_i is distributed according to some distribution μ, which is parameterized by a parameter-vector χ. If these parameters are the same for all $i = 1, \ldots, n$, then the model is an independent increment model.

We want to discuss such a model now: It allows us to blend between a pure independent increment model and a real stochastic volatility model. The idea is to use the distribution in Heston's model for the forward distribution. Using previous results, we can combine the various forward distributions such that it is possible to blend between a pure Heston model and an independent increment model. Let us therefore define for the first interval $t \in [0, t_1]$ the initial process

$$
\begin{aligned}
d\zeta_t^1 &= \kappa^1(\theta^1 - \zeta_t^1)\, dt + \nu^1 \sqrt{\zeta_t^1}\, dW_t \\
dX_t / X_t &= \sqrt{\zeta_t^1}\, d\left(\rho W_t + \sqrt{1 - \rho^2} W_t^{\perp} \right).
\end{aligned}
$$

The distribution of X_{t_1} is then controlled by the parameters $\chi^1 = (\zeta_0^1, \theta^1, \kappa^1, \rho^1, \nu^1)$. To model the next increment, we again want to use Heston's model. Hence, set for $t \in (t_1, t_2]$

$$
\begin{aligned}
d\zeta_t^2 &= \kappa^2(\theta^2 - \zeta_t^2)\, dt + \nu^2 \sqrt{\zeta_t^2}\, dW_t \\
dX_t / X_t &= \sqrt{\zeta_t^2}\, d\left(\rho W_t + \sqrt{1 - \rho^2} W_t^{\perp} \right).
\end{aligned}
$$

The key is that we can introduce a dependency on the values of the previous process by letting

$$
\zeta_{t_1}^2 := \alpha^2 \zeta_0^2 + (1 - \alpha^2)\zeta_{t_1}^1,
$$

where we usually set $\zeta_0^2 := \mathbb{E}\left[\zeta_t^1 \right] = \theta^1 + (\zeta_0^1 - \theta^1)e^{-\kappa^1 \tau}$ to avoid jumps in the forward variance curve of the model. The blending parameter α^2 allows us to blend from the independent increment case ($\alpha^2 = 1$) to the pure (piecewise time-dependent) Heston case ($\alpha^2 = 0$). The parameters for the second maturity are $\chi^2 = (\theta^2, \kappa^2, \rho^2, \nu^2; \alpha^2)$. This process can then be iterated to yield a sequence of semidependent short volatilities for each interval. Additionally, the sequence $\theta^1, \ldots, \theta^n$ can be used to fit the model to the ATM spot options.

While the other parameters could be chosen freely, it is in the spirit of the approach—propagating the skew—to keep κ, ρ and ν constant, because this implies that the forward distribution of X_{t_i} for $i = 2, \ldots, n$ has the general properties of the initial distribution for X_{t_1}. The parameter α can be varied to assess the impact of co-correlation between the increments. Indeed, if $\alpha = 0$ and if θ and the start values for each interval, $(\zeta_0^i)_{i=1,\ldots,n}$, are kept constant, then the model simply is an independent increment model with identically distributed increments.

---

options. Then, a time-dependent volatility coefficient for the Black and Scholes diffusion part of the model is calibrated to the strip of ATM options.

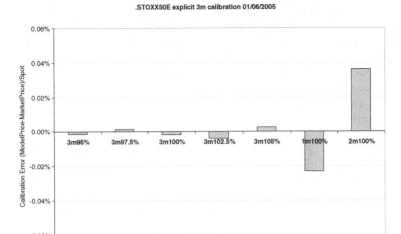

FIGURE 2.11 The fit of the Heston model to the 3m skew. The calibrated parameters are $\zeta_0 = 11.25\%^2$, $\theta = 17.39\%^2$, $\kappa = 2.75$, $\rho = -65\%$, and $\nu = -51.69\%$ (note that condition (2.3) is violated).

Of course, the general idea of randomizing the parameters of the distribution can be applied to any stock price model, but the "blended Heston skew" model described here has the advantage that the characteristic function of the logarithm of the stock price can be computed easily: in each interval, a formula of the type (2.4) holds. For $i = 1, \ldots, n$ we can find constants A^i and B^i such that

$$\mathbb{E}\left[e^{-\mu \zeta_{t_i}^i - b \int_{t_{i-1}}^{t_i} \zeta_s^i \, ds} \,\middle|\, \zeta_{t_{i-1}} \right] = e^{\zeta_{t_{i-1}} A^i + \theta^i B^i \kappa^i}.$$

Iteration yields a closed form for the characteristic function. To match the very short-term options better it is possible to add a jump diffusion component along the lines of Bates [35].[10]

Example As an example, assume we want to price a Cliquet structure with three monthly reset periods. We have calibrated a Heston model to the following options: 3m calls on 100%, 102.5%, and 105%; 3m puts on 95% and 97.5%; and 1m and 2m calls on 100%. Since the reset period of the Cliquet we want to price is three months, we have given the 3m options twice as much weight as the other two options.

The resulting Heston model fits very well to the calibration instruments, as shown in figure 2.11.

As a next step, we have set up the above model with $\theta^i := \theta$, $\nu^i = \nu$, $\rho^i = \rho$ and $\zeta_0^i := \mathbb{E}\left[\zeta_{t_i}^{i-1} \right]$ for $i = 1, \ldots, n$. As a result, the model is just the calibrated Heston

---

[10]An additional stochastic interdependency can be modeled by setting $\theta^i := y_{t_i}$ for an independent square root diffusion y with SDE $dy_t = c(m_t - y_t) \, dt + \mu \sqrt{y_t} \, dW_t^y$, which has a piecewise constant mean-reversion level m in order to match the ATM-Europeans or the variance swap term structure.

model as long as $\alpha^i = 0$, while it is an independent increment model if we set $\alpha^i = 1$; note that the increments are not exactly identically distributed because the short vol parameters ζ_0^i vary. The interesting point is now the impact on the forward skew of changing α between these extreme values: Figure 2.12 shows how α blends between a skew-preserving model and a true homogeneous Markovian model.

Finally, we can assess the impact of the blending of the skew when pricing a Cliquet structure. As an example, we show in figure 2.13 what happens when we price the globally floored Cliquet (2.13).

REMARK 2.1.2 *The last graph of figure 2.12 shows the usual effect that in stochastic volatility models the forward skew for start dates that are farther away tends to become more "U-shaped." The reason for this behavior can be explained as follows: For a time-homogeneous stochastic volatility model such as Heston, the price of a forward-started call on X with reset date t_1, maturity t_2, and strike k is given as*

$$\mathbb{E}\left[\left(\frac{X_{t_2}}{X_{t_1}} - k\right)^+\right] = \mathbb{E}\left[\mathbb{E}\left[\left(\frac{X_{t_2}}{X_{t_1}} - k\right)^+ \bigg| \zeta_{t_1}\right]\right] = \mathbb{E}\left[c(\zeta_{t_1}; t_2 - t_1, k)\right]$$

with

$$c(\zeta; \tau, k) := \mathbb{E}\left[\left(\frac{X_\tau}{X_0} - k\right)^+ \bigg| \zeta_0 = \zeta\right].$$

At time t_1, the implied volatility for the relative strike k and time-to-maturity $\tau := t_2 - t_1$ is according to (1.22) given as

$$\hat{\sigma}_{t_1}(\tau, k) := \mathbb{BS}(\tau, k; \cdot)^{-1}\left(\hat{c}(\zeta_{t_1}; \tau, k)\right),$$

that is, it is a function of the random short variance ζ_{t_1}. Due to the homogeneity of the model, the skew $k \mapsto \hat{\sigma}_{t_1}(\tau, k)$ will be very similar in shape to $k \mapsto \hat{\sigma}_0(\tau, k)$ for all reasonable values of ζ_{t_1}. In particular, the "expected future skew" $k \mapsto \mathbb{E}\left[\hat{\sigma}_{t_1}(\tau, k)\right]$ is nearly the same as $k \mapsto \hat{\sigma}_0(\tau, k)$ (see figure 2.14). The quantity "forward skew," on the other hand, is given as

$$\sigma(t_1, t_2, k) := \mathbb{BS}(\tau, k; \cdot)^{-1}\left(\mathbb{E}\left[\hat{c}(\zeta_{t_1}; \tau, k)\right]\right).$$

Since $\mathbb{BS}(\tau, k; \cdot)^{-1}$ is concave for out-of-the-money options, it follows from Jensen that we obtain the observed U-shape. It seems theoretically more natural to preserve the expected future skew instead of the forward skew. The former is a genuine property of all homogeneous stochastic volatility models.

2.2   VARIANCE SWAPS, ENTROPY SWAPS, GAMMA SWAPS

We have seen that under the assumption that sufficiently many European options on the underlying S, or X, are traded, we can price European payoffs uniquely using (1.29) or its discrete version (1.30). A particularly popular application of (1.29) is the pricing of *variance swaps*, suggested first by Neuberger. We also present two relatively new products, *entropy swaps* and *gamma swaps*.

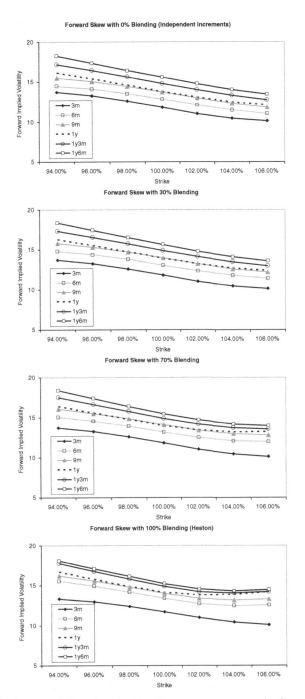

FIGURE 2.12 The impact of changing the blending parameter α on the forward skew. We can clearly see the usual increasingly upward-sloping forward skew in the classic Heston model.

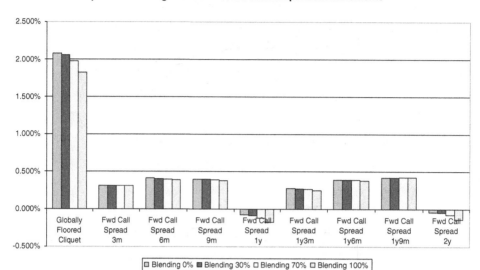

FIGURE 2.13 The price of the globally floored Cliquet (2.13) with maturity in two years along with the values of the prices of the involved forward-started call spreads. The price differences stem mostly from the difference in the prices of the forward-started options, rather than the global floor.

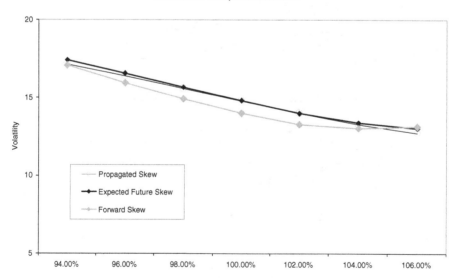

FIGURE 2.14 Forward skew and expected future skew in the Heston model.

2.2.1 Variance Swaps

A *variance swap* with maturity T is a contract that pays the *realized variance* of the return of the stock over the period $[0, T]$ in exchange for a previously agreed strike, K^2 (the strike is usually quoted in "volatility," K). In the absence of any proportional or fixed dividends, and no risk of default, the realized variance is commonly defined as

$$V^n(T) := \frac{252}{n-1} \sum_{k=1}^{n} \left(\log \frac{S_{t_k}}{S_{t_{k-1}}} \right)^2 \qquad (2.15)$$

where $0 = t_0 < \cdots < t_n := T$ are the business days in the period $[0, T]$. The *scaling factor*

$$\frac{1}{[T]} := \frac{252}{n-1}$$

"annualizes" the returned variance: the number 252 is the standardized number of business days per year; we can think of $[T]$ as being approximately T. If the stock price pays dividends and is subject to default risk, then we use here

$$V^n(T) := \frac{1}{[T]} \sum_{k=1}^{n} \left(\log \frac{\left(S_{t_k} + \overline{\alpha}_{t_k} \right) e^{\overline{d}_{t_k}}}{S_{t_{k-1}}} 1_{\tau > t_k} \right)^2, \qquad (2.16)$$

where $\overline{\alpha}_{t_k}$ denotes the discrete cash dividend paid at t_k and where $1 - e^{-\overline{d}_{t_k}}$ is the proportional dividend for this date, cf. (1.10). The idea of this convention is that we do not want to count movements of the stock price that are due to (previously known) dividend payments. Indeed, if no further dividends are paid in (t_{k-1}, t_k), we obtain (cf. equation (1.6) on page 7):

$$\frac{\left(S_{t_k} + \overline{\alpha}_{t_k} \right) e^{\overline{d}_{t_k}}}{S_{t_{k-1}}} 1_{\tau > t_k} = \frac{S_{t_k-}}{S_{t_{k-1}}} 1_{\tau > t_k} = \frac{F^*_{t_{k-1}} X_{t_k} + A_{t_{k-1}}}{F^*_{t_{k-1}} X_{t_{k-1}} + A_{t_{k-1}}} \frac{R_{\tau_k}}{R_{\tau_{k-1}}} 1_{\tau > \tau_k}$$

In practice, default risk is not excluded as in (2.16), but by imposing a cap on the overall realized variance (discussed on page 64 ff). Moreover, dividends are in practice taken out only for single stocks; for indices, (2.15) is used. See remark 2.2.1 for the impact of dividends. Let us first consider the case where dividends are taken out (i.e., (2.16)).

Given dividend dates $0 = \tau_0 < \cdots < \tau_m = T$, we have

$$V^n(T) \approx \frac{1}{[T]} \sum_{j=1}^{m} \left(\langle \log S^\tau \rangle_{\tau_j-} - \langle \log S^\tau \rangle_{\tau_{j-1}} \right) . \qquad (2.17)$$

We will assume that the right-hand side is in fact the definition of *realized variance* (cf. remark 2.2.1 below). A *variance swap* pays the actual realized variance up to its maturity T in exchange for a previously agreed strike K^2. Its payoff is therefore

$$V^n(T) - K^2 .$$

We will denote by $\mathbb{V}_t(T,K)$ the value at time t of a variance swap with strike K and maturity T. Since both $\frac{1}{[T]}$ and K are constants, it is sufficient to compute the expectation (2.17) for the purpose of evaluating a variance swap, which is given by

$$V_t(T) := \frac{\mathbb{V}_t(T,K) + K^2}{P(t,T)} [T] .$$

If $\mathbb{P}$ is a pricing measure, and if there are no cash dividends, this means that

$$V_t(T) = \mathbb{E}_{\mathbb{P}} \left[\langle \log X \rangle_T \mid \mathcal{F}_t \right] .$$

The *fair strike* $K^*(T)$ for this maturity, which renders the initial value of the trade zero, is therefore

$$K^*(T) := \sqrt{\frac{1}{[T]} V_0(T)} .$$

REMARK 2.2.1 *Note that approximation (2.17) works well if we want to price variance swaps. However, the pathwise approximation of realized variance by quadratic variation is not perfect, as is illustrated in figure 2.15. This is particularly important if we price nonaffine payoffs of realized variance; see Barnorff-Nielsen et al. [41] for a discussion on the properties of the error.*

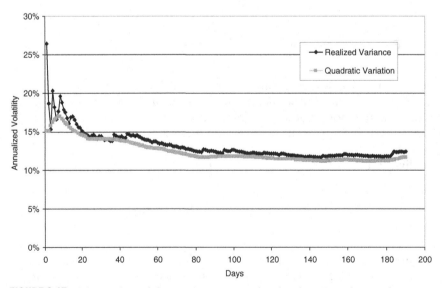

FIGURE 2.15 The quality of the approximation of realized variance by quadratic variation. The graph shows an example path of each of the two quantities for Heston's model with the calibrated parameters from figure 2.6.

Pricing and Hedging Following Demeterfi et al. [42], we henceforth assume that the pure stock price X is continuous, and that $\langle X \rangle_t$ is absolutely continuous with respect to the Lebesgue measure. We have mentioned already in section 1.1.2 that this implies that there exists a stochastic short variance process $\zeta = (\zeta_t)_{t \geq 0}$ and a Brownian motion B such that

$$X_t = \mathcal{E}_t(Z) \quad Z_t := \int_0^t \sqrt{\zeta_u}\, dB_u,$$

where $\mathcal{E}_t(Y) := e^{Y_t - \frac{1}{2}\langle Y \rangle_t}$ denotes again the Doleans-Dade-exponential. Accordingly, the quadratic variation of the returns of X is given as

$$\langle \log X \rangle_T = \int_0^T \zeta_u\, du.$$

On $[\tau_{j-1}, \tau_j)$ with $\tau > \tau_j$, we have $_t = (F^*_{\tau_{j-1}} X_t + B_{\tau_{j-1}}) R_t / R_{\tau_{j-1}}$. Hence,[11]

$$d\langle \log S \rangle_t = \left(\frac{F^*_{\tau_{j-1}} R_{\tau_{j-1}}}{F^*_{\tau_{j-1}} X_t R_t + B_{\tau_{j-1}} R_t} \right)^2 d\langle XR \rangle_t$$

$$= -2 \frac{F^*_{\tau_{j-1}} R_{\tau_{j-1}}}{F^*_{\tau_{j-1}} X_t R_t + B_{\tau_{j-1}} R_t} d(XR)_t + -2d\log(F^*_{\tau_{j-1}} X_t R_t + B_{\tau_{j-1}} R_t)\,.$$

Hence,

$$\langle \log S \rangle_{\tau_{j-}} - \langle \log S \rangle_{\tau_{j-1}} = - \int_{\tau_{j-1}}^{\tau_{j-}} \frac{2}{S_{t-}} d\left(S_t - R_t \frac{B_{\tau_{j-1}}}{R_{\tau_{j-1}}} \right) - 2\log\left(1 + \frac{\overline{\alpha}_{\tau_j}}{S_{\tau_j}} \right) + d_{\tau_j}\,. \tag{2.18}$$

Let us focus for a moment on the case when there are no discrete cash dividends. We obtain

$$\mathcal{V}^n(T) = \frac{1}{[T]} \langle \log X \rangle_T$$

and, using $X_t = S_t / F^*_t$,

$$\langle \log X \rangle_T = -2\log \frac{S_T}{F^*_T} + 2 \int_0^T \frac{dX_t}{X_{t-}} = -2\log \frac{S_T}{S_0} + 2 \int_0^T \frac{dS_t}{S_{t-}}\,. \tag{2.19}$$

This means that we can replicate realized variance by holding a static position in a log-contract with payoff $-2\log S_T$ and by dynamic delta-hedging with a delta of $\Delta_t := 2/S_{t-}$ (for clarity of exposure we ignore discounting here). One particular point is that the *cash-delta* $\Delta^\$_t := S_t \Delta_t = 2$ (2.19) is constant: we hold at all times the value 2 in the stock. Similarly, the gamma $\Gamma_t := 1/S_t^2$ implies that our *cash gamma* of $\Gamma^\$_t := S_t^2 \Gamma_t$ is constant, too. (In the light of the discussion below this makes a variance swap particularly suited to "trade volatility.") For (2.18), the expression

---

[11]
$$\langle X_t + Y_t \rangle = \langle X \rangle_t + \langle Y \rangle_t + 2\langle X, Y \rangle_t$$

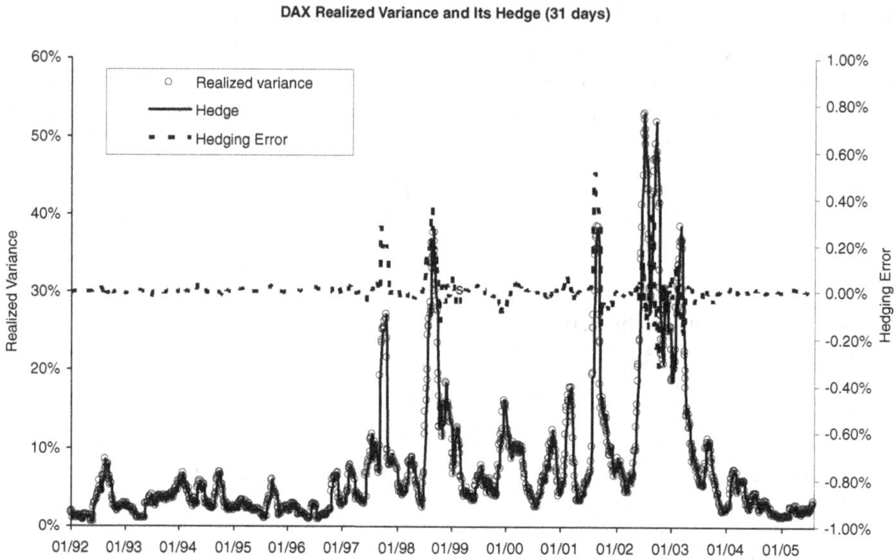

FIGURE 2.16   The quality of hedging variance swaps with (2.19). The graph shows daily the realized variance over 31 business days, the return from the hedging strategy (2.19), and the hedging error.

is slightly more complicated, but it is still of the same basic structure. (Note that additional terms are European-type payoffs on S, whose value can be computed using formula (1.29).)

To assess the quality of the hedging strategy implied by this equation, we have used historic DAX returns and priced a variance swap against two log-contracts plus their daily delta-hedge. Figure 2.16 shows the impressive performance of this hedge.

To calculate the cost of exercising this strategy, note that under any equivalent matringale $\mathbb{P}$, the expectation of the right hand side of (2.19) is given as

$$V_0(T) := -2\mathbb{E}\left[\log X_T\right]. \tag{2.20}$$

To compute $\mathbb{E}\left[\log X_T\right]$, note that this value is equal to $\mathbb{E}\left[H(X_T)\right]$ with $H(x) = x - 1 - \log x$, the function shown in figure 1.6 on page 23.

This function can also be used to center the strip of options around some "reference strike" $\hat{K}$. To this end, note that $H(x/\hat{K})$ has a minimum of zero in $\hat{K}$. We have

$$H\left(\frac{S_T}{K}\right) - H\left(\frac{S_0}{K}\right) = -\log S_T + \log S_0 - \frac{\hat{K} - S_T}{\hat{K}} + \frac{\hat{K} - S_0}{\hat{K}},$$

that is,

$$\mathcal{V}^n(T) = \frac{2}{[T]}\left\{H(S_T) - H(S_0) + \frac{S_0 - S_T}{K}\right\} + \frac{2}{[T]}\int_0^T \frac{dS_t}{S_{t-}}. \tag{2.21}$$

Following this strategy, that is, taking a static position in $H(S_T/\hat{K})$ instead of $-\log S_T$, requires an additional position in a future. See Demeterfi et al. [42] for an extensive discussion of this subject. Also, Carr/Madan discuss various extensions of the idea of pricing volatility-sensitive options via hedging arguments similar to (2.21) in [43]. For example, it can be shown that pricing H via (1.31) means that in actual fact, a *corridor variance swap* is priced, that is, the returns in the sum (2.16) will be counted only if the stock price is between the lowest and highest strike of (2.21). Therefore, a sufficiently wide strike range should be used. Corridor variance swaps and their hedging are discussed in Carr/Lewis [44].

REMARK 2.2.2 *In some contracts, in particular for indices, realized variance is defined using equation (2.15), even if dividends are present. In that case, we have to evaluate*

$$\langle \log S \rangle_T = \int_0^T \zeta_t \, dt + \sum_{t \leq T} \overline{D}_t^2.$$

The additional terms $\overline{D}_t^2$ (of which there are only finitely many) can be hedged and priced with European options using formula (1.29).

Trading Volatility Apart from the fact that variance swaps can be hedged and priced using European options and a clearly defined delta-hedging strategy, what are the reasons to trade this product?

One motivation to trade in volatility is that apart from the stock, the price of an equity derivative is massively dependent on the volatility of the stock price. Practitioners therefore seek to protect themselves against moves in volatility. A very common method works as follows (assume that $X = S$): To price an option with payoff $H(X_T)$, we use the Black-Scholes model with a constant volatility σ,

$$\frac{dX_t^\sigma}{X_t^\sigma} = \sigma \, dB_t, \tag{2.22}$$

where we estimate a reasonable σ from European options traded at maturity T. For example, we might decide that the payoff H is sufficiently close to a call with maturity T and strike k with a market price of $\hat{C}_0(T,k)$ at time zero. Its implied volatility (cf. definition 1.2.1) is denoted by $\hat{\sigma}_0(T,k)$, and we choose to use this implied volatility for our Black-Scholes model (2.22) by setting $\sigma := \hat{\sigma}_0(T,k)$. Let us use $\hat{X} = (\hat{X}_t)_{t\geq 0}$ to denote the real market price process.

Then, our price for H is given as

$$h_t(\hat{X}_0, \sigma) := \mathbb{E}^{\mathrm{BS}}\left[H(X_T^\sigma) \mid X_0^\sigma = \hat{X}_0 \right].$$

At some later time t, the value of H given the observed spot $\hat{X}_t$ is then computed as

$$h_t(\hat{X}_t, \sigma) := \mathbb{E}^{\mathrm{BS}}\left[H(X_T^\sigma) \mid X_t^\sigma := \hat{X}_t \right]. \tag{2.23}$$

That works well if the real price process $\hat{X}$ is a Black-Scholes diffusion with volatility σ. In reality, though, that is unlikely. Assume, for example, that in fact

$$\frac{d\hat{X}_t}{\hat{X}_t} = \sqrt{\zeta_t} \, d\hat{B}_t \tag{2.24}$$

for some stochastic short variance $\zeta = (\zeta_t)_{t \geq 0}$. Then, our price (2.23) evolves as

$$dh_t(\hat{X}_t, \sigma) = \partial_t h_t(\hat{X}_t, \sigma)\, dt + \frac{1}{2}\partial^2_{XX} h_t(\hat{X}_t, \sigma)\, \hat{X}_t^2 \zeta_t\, dt$$
$$+ \partial_X h_t(\hat{X}_t, \sigma)\, d\hat{X}_t.$$

Using the fact that h is a Black-Scholes price for H and that it therefore satisfies the Black-Scholes PDE

$$0 = \partial_t h(t, x, \sigma) + \frac{1}{2}\partial^2_{XX} h(t, x, \sigma) x^2 \sigma^2,$$

we have

$$H(\hat{X}_T) - h_0(\hat{X}_0, \sigma) = \frac{1}{2}\int_0^T \partial^2_{XX} h_t(\hat{X}_t, \sigma)\, \hat{X}_t^2 \left(\zeta_t - \sigma^2\right) dt$$
$$+ \int_0^T \partial_X h_t(\hat{X}_t, \sigma)\, d\hat{X}_t.$$

(See also the results from El Karoui, Jeanblanc-Picquè and Shreve [45].) The cost of our strategy to replicate $H(X_T)$ via its Black-Scholes hedge is therefore not covered by the initial price $h_0(\hat{X}_0, \sigma)$. The term

$$\frac{1}{2}\int_0^T \partial^2_{XX} h_t(\hat{X}_t, \sigma)\, \hat{X}_t^2 \left(\zeta_t - \sigma^2\right) dt \tag{2.25}$$

shows that we will have an additional contribution from the mismatch in volatility weighted by *cash gamma* $\Gamma^\$:= \partial^2_{XX} h_t(\hat{X}_t, \sigma)\, \hat{X}_t^2$.[12] For convex payoffs, cash gamma will be positive, so we see that we lose money if the real variance ζ stays above σ, and we will gain if our initial guess was larger than the real variance. Equation (2.25) also reveals that it is not sufficient for a perfect hedge that the realized variance, $\int_0^T \zeta_u\, du$, equals $\sigma^2 T$.

Vega Hedging To protect ourselves against the profit and loss swings arising from a wrong volatility assumption in (2.25), it is natural to readjust the Black-Scholes volatility during the life of the product. After all, if we price the call (T, k) itself, we will not match the market as soon as its implied volatility changes.

Assume therefore that at some later time t, the call trades at some $\hat{C}_t \equiv \hat{C}_t(T, k)$. We can then infer its implied volatility $\hat{\sigma}_t \equiv \hat{\sigma}_t(T, k)$ by inverting the Black-Scholes price for the call,[13]

$$C_t^{\text{BS}}\left(X_t, \hat{\sigma}_t\right) := X_t \mathbb{BS}\left(T, \frac{k}{X_t}, \hat{\sigma}_t^2(T - t)\right).$$

---

[12]The second derivative of the price with respect to the stock is called *gamma*, and we call its product with the square of the stock price *cash gamma*.

[13]Note that in contrast to the discussion in section 1.2, the current stock price level is not based on unity here, hence the additional scaling by X_t.

Hence, the our price process for H is now given as

$$h\left(t; \hat{X}_t, \hat{\sigma}_t\right).$$

A common practice is to protect the position against the change in volatility by *vega hedging*. The idea is to buy as many calls $\hat{C}_t$ such that the overall sensitivity of the position to changes in both $\hat{X}_t$ and $\hat{\sigma}_t$ is zero (recall that the derivative of a price with respect to volatility is called vega; hence the name *vega hedging*). In our case, this means first to define the Black-Scholes delta-neutral portfolio

$$\mathcal{C}_t^{\Delta-\text{neutral}} := \mathcal{C}_t - \partial_X \mathcal{C}_t^{\text{BS}}(\hat{X}_t, \hat{\sigma}_t)\hat{X}_t ,$$

and then build a hedging position

$$\partial_X h_t(\hat{X}_t, \hat{\sigma}_t)\,\hat{X}_t + \partial_\sigma h_t(\hat{X}_t, \hat{\sigma}_t)\,\frac{1}{\partial_\sigma \mathcal{C}_t^{\text{BS}}(\hat{X}_t, \hat{\sigma}_t)}\,\mathcal{C}_t^{\Delta-\text{neutral}}.$$

The first observation is that this strategy applied to the payoff $H(X_T) := (X_T - k)^+$ will yield a perfect hedge: we simply hold $\hat{C}$. This is an advantage over the pure delta-hedging strategy discussed initially.

However, it is clear that we still do not cover the cost of this hedge with our initial price, $h_0(\hat{X}_0, \hat{\sigma}_0)$. Heuristically, we expect that the hedge above works better, but it is not clear that this is actually true in practice. Another problem with this approach is that it requires us, at least in this pure form, to select a reference option that can be used for vega hedging. In light of today's strong volatility skews, the choice of a strike is a tricky problem and requires a good knowledge of the product that we want to risk manage.[14]

Here is where the variance swaps come in: Their price does not depend on a strike. Moreover, their payoff is directly the realized variance; hence, variance swaps are a more natural instrument to hedge against changes in volatility. Indeed, variance swap trades are in practice quoted in units of vega.

The idea behind trading vega is as follows: In terms of the variance swap volatility $\sigma := K^*(T)$, a variance swap with maturity T pays out the quantity σ^2. This payoff has a vega of

$$\partial_\sigma \left(\frac{1}{[T]} V_0(T)\right) \equiv 2\sigma.$$

If we now assume that we have an overall vega exposure $\mathcal{V}$ in our trading book, we can neutralize this exposure by buying

$$N := \frac{\mathcal{V}}{2\sigma} \qquad (2.26)$$

units of variance swaps (the quantity N is the "notional" of a trade of $\mathcal{V}$). This approach is consistent with the idea of hedging volatility exposure with variance swaps. (For a thorough account on this approach, see section 2.3). However, it

---

[14]Since we can always revert to a time-dependent volatility in the Black-Scholes model, the maturity of the option is not such an issue.

requires that the vega of the portfolio is the sensitivity of the portfolio with respect to changes in the fair strike of the variance swap. In particular, it requires us to compute all option payoffs with a model that at least reprices the Europeans in (1.30) and therefore the variance swap itself.

More commonly, though, the vega of a book is an accumulated sum of Black-Scholes vegas across strikes (and possibly maturities), as discussed above. In this case, it seems sensible to assign the Black-Scholes vegas per strike weights according to (1.30). Of course, such an approach does not generally produce a perfect hedge, and it also disrespects changes in skew and kurtosis of the implied volatility surface.

Volatility as an Asset Class   Apart from the potential use of variance swaps for vega hedging, they also offer the investor a way to invest in volatility. This can be attractive for many reasons. One of the most interesting properties is that volatility tends to be anticorrelated to movements of the market. Volatility increases if the market is falling and often decreases if the market rallies. (Note, though, that during the dotcom boom both price levels and volatility rose; cf. figure 2.3.) Now, most market participants would probably prefer to trade implied volatility in some way.

The drawback of using plain implied volatility as an underlying, however, is that once a strike of the respective option, to which the implied volatility refers, is fixed (for example at-the-money), this strike can entirely change its characteristics depending on the movements of the stock price. For example, if we start off with a strike at-the-money and the market starts to fall, we end up with an out-of-the money strike above current spot level. Implied volatility in this region often appears to be "cheap." (For most indices, upside implied volatility is lower than at-the-money implied volatility.) Moreover, the farther out the strike, the less liquid the corresponding option becomes, with the effect of increasing transaction costs.

Here, variance swaps are a good and relatively inexpensive alternative (in terms of transaction costs). They offer exposure to volatility in a way that does not depend on the level of the market in the sense above. Indeed, *cash gamma* of a variance swap is simply constant 2, if we use the static replication strategy (2.21). In fact, we could also define the variance as the contract that has a constant cash gamma, that is, as the contract that always has the same sensitivity to changes in realized variance, regardless of the level of the stock. See Demeterfi et al. [42] for this approach. A linear cash gamma can be realized using gamma swaps, which are discussed below.

REMARK 2.2.3 *The market's interest in trading volatility has led to the introduction of "variance indices," notably VIX for SPX and VDAX for the GDAXI. These indices can be seen as rolling the square-root of variance swaps with a fixed maturity, a property that makes them very costly to replicate.*

It is also noteworthy that trading in options on VIX futures started on CBOE in February 2006.

As soon as trading in variance swaps began, it became clear that variance swaps on single names are very sensitive to large price moves in the underlying asset, as can be seen easily from equation (2.15). In particular, the payout will be infinite if the asset defaults (recall that in practice, the case of default is not excluded by using definition (2.16)). For this reason, investors who *sold* variance swaps have requested to impose a cap on the potential payout of a variance swap. Typically, this cap is around 250% of K^2; that is, the payoff of such a capped variance swap is, in the absence of dividends,

$$\min \left\{ V^n(T), 2.5K^2 \right\} - K^2 .$$

This is equivalent to

$$\left\{ \left(V^n(T) - K^2 \right) - \left(V^n(T) - 2.5K^2 \right)^+ \right\} 1_{\tau > T} + 2.5\, K^2 1_{\tau \leq T}$$

The latter payoff is also valid in the presence of dividends if (2.16) is used plus the additional payoff of $250\% K^2$ in the event of default.

By requesting protection against extreme stock price movements, investors who sold the capped variance swaps essentially bought out-of-the-money calls on variance. The availability of such products then spurred the development of more standard options: common *options on variance* that are available today are simple calls

$$\left(V^n(T) - K^2 \right)^+ , \tag{2.27}$$

and puts

$$\left(K^2 - V^n(T) \right)^+ \tag{2.28}$$

but also *volatility swaps* with payoff

$$\sqrt{V^n(T)} - K .$$

(Note that value of a zero-strike volatility swap is always less than the value of a zero-strike variance swap.) More recently, options on forward variance swaps have emerged. For example, a call on forward variance between T_1 and T_2 has at time T_1 the payoff

$$\left(\frac{V_{T_1}(T_1, T_2)}{[T_2 - T_1]} - K^2 \right)^+$$

where $V_t(T_1, T_2)$ is the price at time t of the variance between T_1 and T_2, that is,

$$V_t(T_1, T_2) = V_t(T_2) - V_t(T_1).$$

It should be noted that this contract has a different nature than a forward starting call on variance swap, which pays at T_2 the quantity

$$\left(\frac{V^n(T_2) \cdot [T_2] - V^n(T_1) \cdot [T_1]}{[T_2 - T_1]} - k \frac{V_{T_1}(T_1, T_2)}{[T_2 - T_1]} \right)^+ ,$$

where k is now a relative strike.

REMARK 2.2.4 (Quoting Conventions) *European options on variance such as (2.27) and (2.28) are usually quoted in terms of "vol points,"*

$$\frac{Price}{2\,K^*(T)}$$

As before, $K^*(T)$ denotes the variance swap volatility.

2.2.2 Entropy Swaps

Since variance swaps offer exposure to the realized volatility of the returns of the stock X, they are relatively insensitive to the level of the stock price.[15] As an alternative measure of variance, it is possible to define the payoff of what we will call an *entropy swap* as

$$\int_0^T X_t\, d\langle \log X\rangle_t = \int_0^T X_t \zeta_t\, dt. \tag{2.29}$$

Intuitively, this "entropy variance" has the convenient property that if stock price and short variance are negatively correlated, then rises in one quantity are offset by falls of the other. Moreover, if the market drifts sideways (i.e., the level of X does not change much), then the payoff behaves roughly like a variance swap: If the instantaneous correlation between X and ζ is zero, then the value of weighted variance and standard variance are equal. Price and hedging strategy of such a swap can be computed using the same ideas as above. To this end, note that

$$\int_0^T X_t\, d\langle \log X\rangle_t = \int_0^T \frac{1}{X_t}\, d\langle X\rangle_t$$

$$= -2\int_0^T \log X_t\, dX_t + 2\left(X_T \log X_T - X_T\right) - 2\left(X_0 \log X_0 - X_0\right),$$

Hence, pricing an entropy swap boils down to approximate the convex and bounded function $H(x) := x\log x - x + 1$ via (1.29); while the weights for evaluating a variance swap via (1.29) are given as $1/k^2$, they are $1/k$ in the case of an entropy swap. Since X is a martingale with $X_0 = 1$, we can compute the value of an entropy swap with maturity T at time 0 as

$$E_0(T) = 2\mathbb{E}_{\mathbb{P}}\left[X_T \log X_T\right].$$

Let us define the *stock price measure* $\mathbb{P}^X$ by setting $\mathbb{P}^X[A] := \mathbb{P}[1_A X_T]$ for all $A \in \mathcal{F}_T$ and all $T < \infty$. This measure is given by using X itself as a numeraire, and the above expression shows that $\frac{1}{2}E_0(T)$ is simply the *relative entropy* of $\mathbb{P}^X$ with respect to $\mathbb{P}$, hence the name *entropy swap*.

---

[15] Indeed, in classical stochastic volatility model such as Heston's (cf. (2.24)), where the short variance ζ is not functionally dependent on X, the delta of a variance swap is zero. This is not true for local volatility models or other models where the volatility is functionally dependent on the spot level.

Shadow Options The connection between an entropy swap and the measure $\mathbb{P}^X$ goes further: we have

$$E_t(T) = \mathbb{E}\left[\int_0^T X_t \zeta_t \, dt\right] = \int_0^T \mathbb{E}[X_t \zeta_t] \, dt = \int_0^T \mathbb{E}^X[\zeta_t] \, dt = \mathbb{E}^X\left[\int_0^T \zeta_t \, dt\right].$$

In other words, the price of an entropy swap is the value of a variance swap under $\mathbb{P}^X$. With regard to this measure, recall that we used $\mathcal{U}(T, k)$ to denote a put on X with strike k and maturity T. Hence,

$$\mathcal{U}(T, k) = \mathbb{E}\left[(k - X_T)^+\right] = k \mathbb{E}\left[X_T\left(\frac{1}{X_T} - \frac{1}{k}\right)^+\right]$$

$$= k \mathbb{E}^X\left[\left(\frac{1}{X_T} - \frac{1}{k}\right)^+\right] := k \mathcal{C}^X\left(T, \frac{1}{k}\right),$$

where we call $\mathcal{C}^X$ following Lewis [23] the "shadow call" on X. It is the call on X_T^{-1} under the numeraire X. The shadow put $\mathcal{U}^X$ is defined similarly; together we have

$$\mathcal{C}^X(T, k) := k \mathcal{U}(T, 1/k)$$
$$\mathcal{U}^X(T, k) := k \mathcal{C}(T, 1/k).$$

Hence, the shadow option prices can be read from the market. So, in principle, we could compute the value of an entropy swap, $E_0(T) = \mathbb{E}^X[\log X_T]$, using (1.29) in terms of shadow options.

2.2.3 Gamma Swaps

While entropy swaps are an interesting alternative to variance swaps, they are not particularly well suited for real-life investments, because they require us to strip dividends, repo, and interest rates from the traded stock price, S, in order to obtain X. This is very unnatural from an economic point of view and inconveniences the investor. This drawback can be overcome by using what are called *gamma swaps* or *weighted variance swaps*: A gamma swap pays at maturity the *weighted variance* of the stock price,

$$\frac{252}{n-1} \sum_{k=1}^n \frac{S_{t_k}}{S_0} \left(\log \frac{S_{t_{k-}}}{S_{t_{k-1}}} 1_{\tau > t_k}\right)^2. \tag{2.30}$$

Assuming that there are no cash dividends, we approximate (2.30) as

$$\int_0^T \frac{S_t}{S_0} \, d\langle \log X \rangle_t.$$

A gamma swap has the same attractive property as the entropy swap of being exposed to correlation between stock price and volatility. See figure 2.17 for past

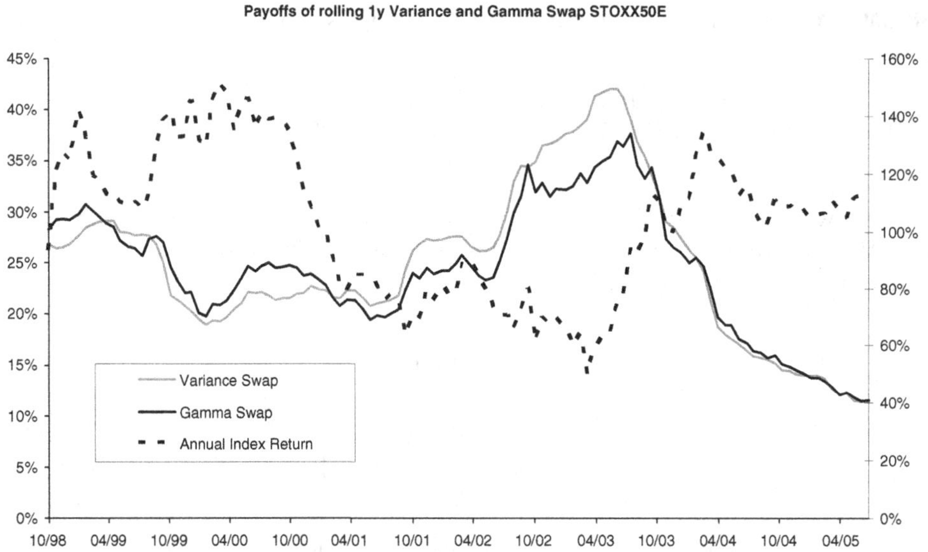

Payoffs of rolling 1y Variance and Gamma Swap STOXX50E

FIGURE 2.17 Past performance of 1y variance and gamma swaps on STOXX50E. We have also plotted the return performance of the index.

performance of gamma swaps. Under the assumption of continuity of X, the price of a gamma swap is

$$\Gamma_0(T) := \mathbb{E}\left[\int_0^T \frac{S_t}{S_0} d\langle \log X \rangle_t\right] = \int_0^T \mathbb{E}\left[\frac{S_t}{S_0} \zeta_t\right] dt$$

$$= \int_0^T \frac{F_t^*}{S_0} \mathbb{E}[X_t \zeta_t], dt$$

$$= \int_0^T \frac{F_t^*}{S_0} (\partial_T E_0)(t) dt$$

(recall the symbols F_t^* and A_t from page 7). In other words, a gamma swap is a sequence of forward variance swaps and forward entropy swaps. We can approximate its price as

$$\Gamma_0(T) \approx \sum_{i=1}^n \left\{ \frac{F_{t_i}^*}{S_0} (E_0(t_i) - E_0(t_{i-1})) \right\}.$$

When it comes to hedging a gamma swap, let $h \equiv 0$ and define $H(x) := x \log x - x + 1$ as above. Let us also recall equation (1.12) and Ito's formula (1.13). They give us again a hedging program,

$$\int_0^T \frac{S_t}{S_0} \zeta_t \, dt = \frac{2}{S_0} \left\{ H(S_T) - H(S_0) - \int_0^T \log S_{t-} \, dS_t \right\}, \qquad (2.31)$$

similar to (2.19). Here, we can see why the product is called *gamma swap*: The *cash gamma* $\Gamma_t^\$:= S_t^2 \Gamma_t$ for this product is $\Gamma_t^\$ = S_t/S_0$ (i.e., linear in spot). The

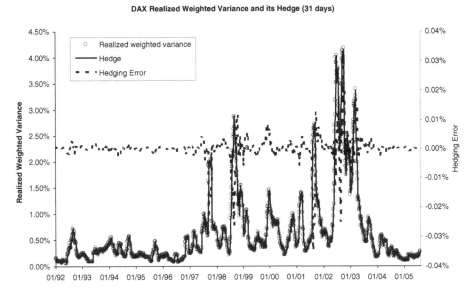

DAX Realized Weighted Variance and its Hedge (31 days)

FIGURE 2.18 The quality of hedging weighted variance swaps with (2.31). The graph shows the daily realized weighted variance over 31 business days, the return from the hedging strategy (2.19), and the hedging error.

performance of this hedge for real-life gamma swaps is as good as it is for variance swaps, as figure 2.18 shows.

2.3 VARIANCE SWAP MARKET MODELS

While the evaluation of variance swaps, entropy swaps and gamma swaps is relatively model independent, such formulas are not known for *options on realized variance*, as introduced in section 2.2.1.[16] To price and hedge a call (2.27) on realized variance on a stock where only European options are traded, we have to use a particular stock price model. In this section we will discuss a general modeling approach that is based on the idea to hedge options on variance with variance swaps. As an illustration, figure 2.19 shows the term structure of variance swap fair strikes K^* for a few major indices. The aim is to model the entire curve of variance swaps as a random variable and then derive in a *second* step the dynamics of a stock price process that realizes the modeled variance. (We do not attempt to develop a model that prices variance swaps; rather, their prices are input parameters for the model.) Of course, a model that describes well the evolution of variance swap price curves cannot only be used to hedge options on realized variance. Since we will also provide an "associated stock price process" in the model (and an intuitive meaning of correlation), we can use such a model to price and hedge any exotic derivative. For example, it is natural to hedge Cliquet-type products as discussed in section 2.1.6 using forward

---

[16]In the particular situation where the skew is symmetric in the logarithm of the strike (i.e., if the instantaneous correlation is zero), it is possible to infer the distribution of integrated variance. See Carr/Lee [46].

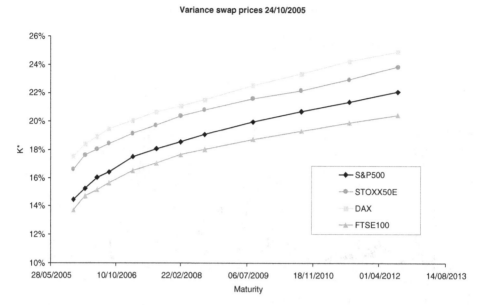

Variance swap prices 24/10/2005

FIGURE 2.19 Variance swap fair strikes for major stock price markets.

started variance swaps.[17] This approach is particularly appealing in the light of recent trading volumes in variance swaps.

The entire approach is very similar to the Heath-Jarrow-Merton (HJM) approach [47] in interest rates. There, the dynamics of the forward interest rates are modeled as stochastic variables; we will consider *forward variance*. The basic assumption is that alongside the "pure" stock X, at any time t, (zero-strike) variance swaps for all finite maturities with prices

$$\frac{1}{[T]}V_t(T)$$

are liquidly traded. Under the assumption of "no free lunch with vanishing risk," there exists an equivalent measure $\mathbb{P}$ under which both X and all variance swap price processes and therefore $V = (V(T))_{T \geq 0}$ are local martingales (for ease of exposure we will frequently refer to $V(T)$ as the price process of a variance swap even though, strictly speaking, the price process is $V(T)/[T]$). While variance swap prices V are readily available in the market, they are slightly difficult to model directly: Since the prices $V_t = (V_t(T))_{T \geq t}$ of variance swaps have to be increasing in T at any time t, it is more natural to work instead with the *forward variances*

$$v_t(T) := \partial_T V_t(T). \tag{2.32}$$

Forward variance is "the market's expectation" at time t of the variance at time T, just as the forward rate in interest rates is the expectation of the short interest rate under the forward measure. (Note that in contrast to a forward rate, a forward

---

[17]This has also been proposed by Bergomi [48].

variance of zero is a natural state, for example, on weekends.) The main point is that due to its definition (2.32), forward variance itself is tradable and must therefore be a local martingale under a pricing measure, if such a measure exists.

As with interest rates, it is much more natural to look at the evolution of the forward variance curve over time in "fixed time-to-maturity," rather than a fixed maturity. We expect the properties of forward variance $v_t(T)$ to change markedly during the remaining time to maturity $T - t$: for example, very long-term forward variance should not be as volatile as short-term forward variance. It is therefore more convenient to use the *Musiela parametrization*[18] of forward variance,

$$u_t(x) := v_t(x + t). \tag{2.33}$$

Accordingly, the price of a variance swap (modulo scaling by the inverse of time-to-maturity) in Musiela-parametrization is

$$U_t(x) := \int_0^x u_t(y)\, dy.$$

HJM Theory for Variance Swaps The idea of "variance curve models" as introduced by Buehler [49] is now to *start* by specifying the dynamics of the family $u = (u(x))_{x\geq 0}$ itself, just as HJM-type interest rate models are specified by starting with the forward rate dynamics. The additional complication in the case of forward variance is that we do not only want to model the variance swap prices in this way, but we also need to model a consistent stock price process whose expected realized variance is the price of the respective variance swap. We ignore the effects of dividends in this section.

To formalize our setup, assume that we have a d-dimensional Brownian motion $\mathbf{W} = (W^1, \dots, W^d)$ under a measure $\mathbb{P}$, which creates the filtration $\mathbb{F} = (\mathcal{F}_t)_{t\geq 0}t$. We will model the variance curves directly under their martingale measure; the ideas from section 1.4 will then be used to derive conditions on market completeness. Assume that $u = (u(x))_{x\geq 0}$ is a family of non-negative processes $u(x) = (u_t(x))_{t\geq 0}$ given by

$$du_t(x) = \alpha_t(x)\, dt + \sum_{j=1}^d \beta_t^j(x)\, dW_t^j \tag{2.34}$$

for some integrable predictable processes α and $\beta = (\beta^1, \dots, \beta^d)$. Reversing the construction above, we can then define the forward variance processes $v = (v(T))_{T\geq 0}$ by setting

$$v_t(T) := \begin{cases} u_t(T - t) & T \geq t \\ v_T(T) & T < t \end{cases} \tag{2.35}$$

(note that $v_t(T)$ is well-defined for $t > T$). Equivalently, the variance swap price processes for finite maturities T are defined as

$$V_t(T) := \int_0^T v_t(r)\, dr.$$

---

[18]Musiela introduced this concept for interest rates in [50].

DEFINITION 2.3.1 *We call u given by (2.34) a variance curve model if v(T) given by (2.35) is a local martingale for all T < ∞ and if there exists a local martingale X for the stock price such that*

$$\mathbb{E}_{\mathbb{P}}\left[\left.\langle \log X \rangle_T \right| \mathcal{F}_t\right] = V_t(T).$$

for all t and all T < ∞.

Let us assess when a curve u is indeed a variance curve model.[19] First of all, it is natural to assume that all initial variance swap prices are finite, that is,

$$\int_0^x u_0(y)\,dy < \infty$$

for all $x < \infty$. Indeed, if this does not hold, the expected value of the logarithm of X cannot exist. Second, we have to ensure that for each $T < \infty$, the process $v(T)$ is a local martingale. To this end, we require that β is in C^1 and its derivative $\partial_x \beta(x)$ is integrable with respect to Brownian motion. Then,

$$dv_t(T) = \left(\alpha_t(T-t) - \partial_x v_t(T-t)\right)dt + \sum_{j=1}^d \beta_t^j(T-t)\,dW_t^j,$$

which implies that the following *HJM drift condition for forward variance* must hold:

$$\alpha_t(x) = \partial_x u_t(x).$$

As a next step, note that the process

$$\zeta_t := u_t(0) \tag{2.36}$$

is an adapted non-negative process. Since $\mathbb{E}_{\mathbb{P}}[\int_0^T \zeta_t\,dt] = V_0(T) < \infty$, its square root $\sqrt{\zeta}$ is integrable with respect to any Brownian motion B. Each such Brownian motion B can be written in terms of W as

$$B_t = \sum_{j=1}^d \int_0^t \rho_s^j\,dW_s^j, \tag{2.37}$$

where $\rho = (\rho^1, \ldots, \rho^d)$ is some potentially stochastic "correlation vector" with values in $[-1, +1]^d$, which always has unit norm, $\|\rho_t\|_2 = 1$. This means that

$$X_t := \mathcal{E}_t\left(\int_0^{\cdot} \sqrt{\zeta_s}\,dB_s\right)$$

---

[19]For a more technically detailed exposure, refer to Buehler [49] and [18].

is a well-defined local martingale with the property that

$$\mathbb{E}_{\mathbb{P}}\left[\left.\langle \log X\rangle_T \,\right|\, \mathcal{F}_t\right] = \mathbb{E}_{\mathbb{P}}\left[\left. \int_0^T \zeta_s\,ds \,\right|\, \mathcal{F}_t\right] = V_t(T),$$

just as required. We call X an *associated stock price process* to u.

The Brownian motion B or, alternatively, the correlation vector ρ was arbitrary in the construction of X. Indeed, B plays the role of a "correlation" or "skew" parameter: If the dynamics of u in the form of β are given, then the specification of ρ links the movement of the variance curve with the stock price movement. In particular, this implies that volatility structure of the variance curve and its correlation with the stock price movement can be estimated one after the other.

However, the general formulation of a variance curve above in terms of equation (2.34) plus the requirement of non-negativity is more subtle than it may appear in the first place. Indeed, it is very difficult to assess whether a general stochastic integral (2.34) will remain non-negative. In particular it means that we cannot—as in the HJM-framework for interest rates—specify the volatility structure β independently of the initially observed forward variance curve u_0.

A natural approach to this problem is to model u as an exponential,

$$u_t(x) = u_0(x)e^{w_t(x)},$$

where w satisfies the integral equation

$$dw_t(x) = a_t(x)\,dt + \sum_{j=1}^{d} b_t^j(x)\,d\mathrm{W}_t^j.$$

Applying our previous results implies the HJM-type drift condition

$$a_t(x) = \partial_x w_t(x) - \frac{1}{2}\sum_{j=1}^{d} b^j(x)^2.$$

This approach is well suited for statistical estimation of a volatility structure independent of the initial state u_0 of the variance curve, for example, via a PCA-type estimation of the factors driving the curve. However, it should be noted that this approach also excludes all those classical stochastic volatility models that allow the volatility to reach zero, such as Heston's. Moreover, it is usually more complicated to ensure a true martingale property for the process X if u is given in the form above: recall in particular Jourdain's results [25] for the SABR model and for Scott's model, which we discussed in sections 2.1.2 and 2.1.3, respectively. Nonetheless, given a "volatility structure" w that ensures the martingale property for all initial values u, the above formulation can be used to "fit the market." This will be discussed in section 2.3.3.

2.3.1 Finite Dimensional Parametrizations

One drawback of our approach so far is that we formulated the dynamics for u in a very general way. But in practice, the formulation of u in terms of a predictable integral equation (2.34) is inconvenient for numerical purposes. Moreover, this formulation implies that the entire curve u is the state of the process, an object difficult to handle on a computer. What we are really interested in is a *finite-dimensional* representation of the curve u. Indeed, in real life, a finite number of variance swap market quotes is usually interpolated or approximated by some non-negative increasing functional $\mathbb{G}$, which itself depends on only a finite number of parameters $z \in \mathcal{Z} \subset \mathbb{R}^m$. If $\mathbf{Z}_t$ is the parameter vector at time t, this means that the price at time t of a variance swap starting in t with time-to-maturity x is given as

$$U_t(x) = \mathbb{G}(\mathbf{Z}_t; x).$$

Since the function $\mathbb{G}$ must be increasing in x, we can set $G(\mathbf{z}; x) := \partial_x \mathbb{G}(\mathbf{z}; x) \geq 0$ such that the forward variance process is given as

$$u_t(x) = G(\mathbf{Z}_t; x). \tag{2.38}$$

The process $\mathbf{Z} = (\mathbf{Z}_t)_{t \geq 0}$ is called the *parameter process* of the functional G. The idea is to restrict the dynamics of $\mathbf{Z}$ to ensure that the forward variances $v_t(T) = G(\mathbf{Z}_t; T - t)$ are local martingales.

To this end, recall the definition of the *driving diffusion* in section 1.4, equation (1.40). There, we have assumed that the entire market of tradable instruments has been given as a functional of a finite-dimensional diffusion $(Z^0, \ldots, Z^m)$ where Z^0 represented the stock price X itself. We have shown that such a framework is naturally complete in the sense that "delta hedging works" if assumption 1 on page 32 holds. Consequently, we will use the last m parameters $\mathbf{Z} = (Z^1, \ldots, Z^m)$ to drive the parameters of the function G, and incorporate the associated stock price $X = Z^0$ afterwards. To this end, assume that on the open set $\mathcal{Z} \subset \mathbb{R}^m_{\geq 0}$, the SDE

$$dZ_t = \mu(Z_t)\,dt + \sum_{j=1}^{d} \varsigma^j(Z_t)\,dW_t^j \quad Z_0 \in \mathcal{Z}$$

for a drift vector $\mu : \mathcal{Z} \to \mathbb{R}^m$ and volatility vectors $\varsigma = (\varsigma^1, \ldots, \varsigma^d)$ with $\varsigma^j : \mathcal{Z} \to \mathbb{R}^m_{\geq 0}$ has a unique, strong solution. Moreover, assume that the *variance curve functional* $G : \mathcal{Z} \times \mathbb{R}_{\geq 0} \longrightarrow \mathbb{R}_{\geq 0}$ is a $C^{2,2}$ function with finite variance swap prices for all states $\mathbf{z} \in \mathcal{Z}$, i.e. $\int_0^T G(\mathbf{z}; x)\,dx < \infty$ for all $T < \infty$. A direct application of Ito shows that the family u defined by (2.38) is a variance curve model if, and only if, the "consistency condition"

$$\partial_x G(\mathbf{z}, x) = \mu(\mathbf{z})\,\partial_z G(\mathbf{z}, x) + \frac{1}{2}\varsigma^2(\mathbf{z})\,\partial_{xx}^2 G(\mathbf{z}; x) \tag{2.39}$$

holds for all $(\mathbf{z}, x) \in \mathcal{Z} \times \mathbb{R}_{\geq 0}$ and if $v(T)$ is a true martingale for all finite T.[20]

---

[20] For technical details cf. [49].

REMARK 2.3.1 *It should be noted that we look at the heat equation (2.39) here in a nonclassical way: obviously, if the process Z is given, then (2.39) is satisfied for all functions G defined as $G(z; x) := \mathbb{E}[g(\mathbf{Z}_x) \mid \mathbf{Z}_0 = z]$ in terms of a suitably well-behaved function g.*

In contrast, here we start with the function G and ask when a process Z exists to satisfy (2.39): The idea is that we observe the variance swap market data and then choose a suitable function G, which interpolates these data well. Afterwards we use (2.39) to derive constraints on the dynamics on the parameters that drive the curve to ensure that the resulting variance swap price processes are local martingales. The entire approach is very closely related to the idea of a "finite dimensional parametrization" of a variance curve, cf. [49]. This concept has been developed in the context of interest rate theory by Björk/Svensson [51], Filipovic [52] and Filipovic/Teichmann [53].

The Associated Stock Price Once we have obtained what we call a *consistent pair* (G, Z), the next step is again to construct an associated stock price process X. From the considerations of the previous section, we know that the short variance of X is given by $u_t(0) = G(\mathbf{Z}_t; 0)$. It remains to model an appropriate correlation structure; to this end, assume that $\rho = (\rho^1, \ldots, \rho^d)$ is a "local" correlation vector; that is, ρ^j for $j = 1, \ldots, d$ is a measurable function $\rho^j : \mathcal{Z} \times \mathbb{R}_{\geq 0} \to [-1, +1]$ such that $\|\rho(z, s)\|_2 = 1$ for all (z, s). Then, the stock price X is the strong unique solution to

$$dX_t = \sum_{j=1}^{d} \rho^j(\mathbf{Z}_t; X_t) X_t \sqrt{G(\mathbf{Z}_t; 0)} \, dW_t^j, \quad X_0 = 1.$$

The solution exists and is unique because $\rho^j(\mathbf{Z}_t; x)x$ is process Lipschitz for all $j = 1, \ldots, d$, hence is a well-defined non-negative local martingale, and we call the triplet (G, Z, ρ) a *variance curve market model*. It models all relevant market instruments jointly in an arbitrage-free way. This setting also includes local volatility models (in which case X itself is part of the vector Z) and, naturally, stochastic volatility models. Moreover, the current framework fits into the settings of section 1.4: The vector $\hat{Z} = (X, Z^1, \ldots, Z^m)$ is Markov by construction; the market instruments are the stock X itself and the variance swaps with price processes

$$V_t(T) = \int_0^{T-t} G(\mathbf{Z}_t; x) \, dx + V_t(t).$$

The process $V_t(t) = \int_0^t \zeta_s \, ds$ with $dV_t(t) = G(\mathbf{Z}_t; 0) \, dt$ represents the running variance of $\log X$. Without loss of generality we can assume that $Z_t^m = V_t(t)$. Let us then define variance swap price functional

$$\mathbb{G}^*(z, x) := z_t^m + \mathbb{G}(z; x) = z_t^m + \int_0^x G(z; y) \, dy,$$

which gives the price of a variance swap with maturity $T > t$ in terms of Z as $V_t(T) = \mathbb{G}^*(\mathbf{Z}_t; T - t)$. If this functional can be inverted locally in the sense that there is some $\varepsilon > 0$ and some time-to-maturities $x_M > \cdots x_1 > \varepsilon$ such that the function

$$\mathbf{z} \longmapsto \left(\mathbb{G}^*(\mathbf{z}, x_1 - t), \ldots, \mathbb{G}^*(\mathbf{z}, x_M - t) \right)$$

is invertible for $0 < t < \varepsilon$, then it is possible to extract locally the vector Z_t from the observation of only $V_t(t)$ and a finite number of variance swaps with maturities $T_i = x_i + t$. If this function and therefore also its inverse is C^1, then the results of section 1.4 can be applied, which means that under assumption 1 the market given by $(G, \mathbf{Z}, \rho)$ is complete. Moreover, all the payoffs depending on the value processes of X and the variance swaps can be replicated by trading in stock and variance swaps (see Buehler [54] for technical details).

REMARK 2.3.2 (Delta in Stochastic Volatility Models) *In the particular case where the correlation vector ρ does not depend on X, the stock price at some later time T depends on the current level X_t only through its initial value. This allows us to compute the delta of a European option directly from market data without the need to calibrate a model: We can write the price of a call with maturity T and strike k as*

$$C_t(T, k) = \mathbb{E}\left[\left. (X_T - k)^+ \,\right|\, X_t, \zeta_t \right] = \mathbb{E}\left[\left. \left(X_t e^{\int_t^T \sqrt{\zeta_u}\, dB_u - \frac{1}{2}\int_t^T \zeta_u\, du} - k \right)^+ \,\right|\, X_t, \zeta_t \right]$$

$$= X_t \,\mathbb{E}\left[\left. \left(e^{\int_t^T \sqrt{\zeta_u}\, dB_u - \frac{1}{2}\int_t^T \zeta_u\, du} - \frac{k}{X_t} \right)^+ \,\right|\, \zeta_t \right].$$

Hence, the "stochastic volatility delta" for any model that is well fitted to the market is given as

$$\partial_{X_t} C_t(T, k) = \frac{1}{X_t} C_t\left(T, \frac{k}{X_t} \right) - \frac{1}{X_t^2} (\partial_k C_t)\left(T, \frac{k}{X_t} \right).$$

That implies, in particular, that two different stochastic volatility models of this type that fit the market prices perfectly will have the same delta. Hence, the only way "pure" two-factor models can be distinguished is via their "vega hedge." [21]

It is sometimes assumed that stochastic volatility models have a sticky strike delta due to the computation above. However, this is not the case since the implied volatility given in such a model for a relative strike remains the same only in the (zero-probability) case that all other state parameters remain constant.

---

[21] Also note that jump models in which the jump parameters do not depend on the stock price level have the same delta.

2.3.2 Examples

Let us now assess a few examples of variance curve functionals. Obviously, a rich source of such functionals is to start with a stochastic volatility model and use the variance swap curve functional given by this model as a starting point. The natural question is then which other processes can drive the same variance curve.

EXAMPLE 5 *A consistent parameter process* $\mathbf{Z}$ *for the "linearly mean-reverting" variance curve functional*

$$G(\mathbf{z}, x) := z_2 + (z_1 - z_2)e^{-z_3 x}$$

must follow an SDE of the form

$$
\begin{aligned}
dZ_t^1 &= Z_t^3(Z_t^2 - Z_t^1)\, dt &&+ \varsigma^1(Z_t)\, dW_t \\
dZ_t^2 &= &&+ \varsigma^2(Z_t)\, dW_t \\
dZ_t^3 &= 0.
\end{aligned}
$$

One popular example is Heston's model (2.1).

The interpretation of this observation is that if variance swaps are priced using Heston's model, which in turn is calibrated every day to market data, then the speed of mean reversion, Z^3, must theoretically be kept constant. Using entropy swaps, it can also be shown [54], that the product of "vol of vol" and "correlation" in Heston's model must in theory be kept constant.

Also note that this example covers by a simple coordinate transformation the Nelson-Siegel interpolation function for interest rates, $G(\mathbf{z}; x) = z_1 + (z_2 + z_3)e^{-z_4 x}$. More generally, assume that G is a polynomial exponential, that is, that G is of the form

$$G(\mathbf{z}; x) := \sum_{i=1}^{n} p_k(\mathbf{z}; x)e^{-z_i x} \tag{2.40}$$

for polynomials $p_i(\mathbf{z}; x) = \sum_{k=1}^{n_i} \gamma_{ik}(z)x^k$ and $n \le m$. Using (2.39), it is straightforward to show that the "speeds of mean reversion" $Z^1, \ldots, Z^n$ for any consistent parameter process must be constant. A similar result holds for functions of the form $G(\mathbf{z}; x) := \exp\left\{\sum_{i=1}^{n} p_k(\mathbf{z}; x)e^{-z_i x}\right\}$, in which case the parameters $z_1, \ldots, z_n$ must not only be constant, but also need to come in pairs in which one is twice the value of the other parameter. The observation that speeds of mean reversion must generally be constant for interest rate models was first shown by Björk/Christensen [55] and further investigated by Filipovic [52].

Another example of functionals of the class (2.40) is given by, $G(\mathbf{z}; x) = z_1 + (z_2 + z_3)e^{-z_4 x} + z_4 e^{-z_5 x}$. Following Buehler [49], we use the following reparametrization, which makes it easier to ensure that the function remains positive:

EXAMPLE 6 *The "double linearly mean-reverting" variance curve functional is defined for positive constants κ and c as*

$$G(\mathbf{z}, x) := z_3 + (z_1 - z_3)e^{-\kappa x} + (z_2 - z_3)\frac{\kappa}{\kappa - c}\left(e^{-cx} - e^{-\kappa x}\right) \qquad (2.41)$$

with a well-defined limit for $\kappa = c$. A consistent parameter process follows an SDE of the form

$$\begin{aligned}
dZ_t^1 &= \kappa(Z_t^2 - Z_t^1)\,dt &+ \varsigma^1(Z_t)\,dW_t\\
dZ_t^2 &= c(Z_t^2 - Z_t^3)\,dt &+ \varsigma^2(Z_t)\,dW_t\\
dZ_t^3 &= &+ \varsigma^3(Z_t)\,dW_t.
\end{aligned}$$

For the case in which $Z^1, \ldots, Z^3$ are square roots of affine functions, such a process fits in the affine framework of Duffie et al. [56]. The curve (2.41) has proven to be a good interpolation for actual market data; an example is given in figure 2.20. Also recall that we have shown in section 2.1.5 that in the case $\varsigma^1(\mathbf{z}) = v\sqrt{z_1}$ and $\varsigma^2 = \varsigma^3 = 0$, a semi-closed form for European option prices can be derived. We will discuss a model based on (2.41) below.

While the linearly mean-reverting models admit a range of possible parameter processes, this is not generally true. Here is an example of a curve that admits only one parameter process:

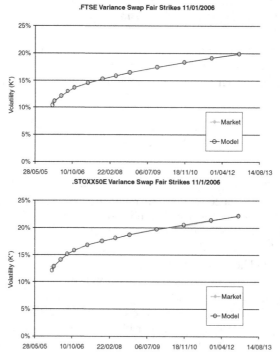

FIGURE 2.20   Fit of the double mean-reverting functional (2.41) to FTSE and STOXX50E market data.

EXAMPLE 7 *For the "exponential linearly mean-reverting" variance curve functional*

$$G(\mathbf{z}, x) := \exp \left\{ z_2 + (z_1 - z_2)e^{-z_4 x} + \frac{z_3}{4}(1 - e^{-2z_4}) \right\},$$

any parameter process $\mathbf{Z}$ is constant in Z^2, Z^3 and Z^4. The parameter Z^1 follows an Ornstein-Uhlenbeck process

$$dZ_t^1 = Z_t^4 (Z_t^2 - Z_t^1) \, dt + \sqrt{Z_3} \, dW_t \; ;$$

that is, G is driven only by Scott's exponential OU model.

It is also interesting to see whether a functional admits a parameter process at all. To this end, note that sometimes functions like $g(\mathbf{z}; x) = z_1 + z_2 \sqrt{x + \varepsilon}$, $g(\mathbf{z}; x) = z_1 + z_2 / \sqrt{x + \varepsilon}$ (for $\varepsilon > 0$) or $g(\mathbf{z}; x) = z_1 + z_2 \log(1 + x)$ are used to interpolate the term structure of implied volatility. Applied to variance swap curves, though, it can be seen easily that such an interpolation of the variance swap volatility, that is, using $G(\mathbf{z}, x) := x g^2(\mathbf{z}; x)$, does not admit a consistent parameter process. This observation means that at least in the case of flat skew, implied volatility cannot consistently be interpolated with such functions.

REMARK 2.3.3 *The results here are of a theoretical nature. In practice, the speed of mean reversion of a Heston model must be calibrated to market data, and we cannot enforce a constant value over a long period of time without considerably weakening the fit of the model to the market. Moreover, it should be clear that a real trading desk faces many more inconsistencies arising from trading in the real world.*

From this point of view, the results here regarding a constant mean reversion should be merely taken as advice to avoid strong movements of the parameter as a result of the daily recalibration of the model. Indeed, in our experience, imposing a penalty on movements of the speed of mean reversion during calibration leads to a much more stable daily recalibration of, for example, Heston's model.

A Double Mean-Reverting Model   Following example 6, a convenient parametrization to drive the double linearly mean-reverting curve functional (2.41) is given by

$$\begin{aligned}
d\zeta_t &= \kappa(\theta_t - \zeta_t)\, dt &&+ \nu \zeta_t^\alpha \, dW_t^\zeta \\
d\theta_t &= c(m_t - \theta_t)\, dt &&+ \mu \theta_t^\beta \, dW_t^\theta \\
dm_t &= &&+ \eta m_t \, dW_t^m
\end{aligned} \qquad (2.42)$$

and

$$\frac{dX_t}{X_t} = \sqrt{\zeta_t} \, dB_t.$$

The correlation structure of the involved Brownian motions is given in terms of the parameters ρ_ζ, ρ_θ, $r_{\theta,\zeta}$ and ρ_m as

$$\begin{aligned}
B_t &= W_t^1 \\
W_t^\zeta &= \rho_\zeta B_t + \hat{\rho}_\zeta \, W_t^2 \\
W_t^\theta &= \rho_\theta B_t + \hat{\rho}_\theta \left(r_{\zeta,\theta} W_t^2 + \hat{r}_{\zeta,\theta} W_t^3 \right) \\
W_t^m &= \rho_m B_t + \hat{\rho}_m \, W_t^4
\end{aligned}$$

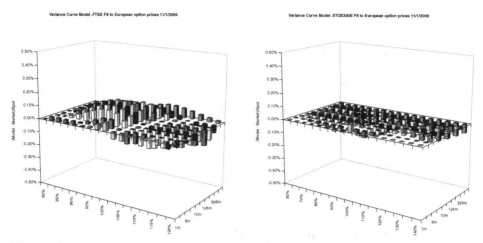

FIGURE 2.21 Calibration of the double mean-reverting model (2.42) to FTSE and STOXX50E market data. The variance swap fits are shown in figure 2.20.

(we used the notation $\hat{\rho} := \sqrt{1 - \rho^2}$). The exponentials α and β are assumed to be from $(0.5, 1)$ to ensure that (2.42) has a unique strong solution. To ensure that X is a true martingale, we assume that ρ_ζ, ρ_θ and ρ_m are negative.

The dynamics of this model are very intuitive: The short variance ζ is a mean-reverting process whose mean-reversion itself is stochastic. Such a behavior is often observed in real markets. The stochasticity of m has been introduced to fit the market slightly better, but in general and in the interest of parsimony, we usually set $\eta = 0$.

The calibration of the initial states ζ_0, θ_0, and m_0, along with the reversion speeds κ and c, can be done by fitting (2.41) to the observed variance swap market data. The remaining parameters v, μ, α, β, ρ_ζ, and ρ_θ ($r_{\zeta,\theta}$ is usually set to zero), on the other hand, require quite an expensive calibration via Monte Carlo. This is numerically far less robust than the calibration of, say, a Heston model. Indeed, to reduce the time spent during the calibration, we typically calibrate to only five maturities with three options per maturity. (While being theoretically attractive, such a model is necessary only if we want to price spread-type products such as forward-started options on variance). Figure 2.21 shows the calibration results for this model to STOXX50E and FTSE market data.

To assess the impact of the model choice, we also calibrated the model (2.11) with $\theta_t := m + (\theta_0 - m)e^{-ct}$ and piecewise constant vol of vol and correlation to the same market data. It can be written as

$$\begin{aligned} d\zeta_t &= \kappa(\theta_t - \zeta_t)\,dt + v_t\sqrt{\zeta_t}\,dW_t \\ d\theta_t &= c(m_0 - \theta_t)\,dt, \end{aligned} \qquad (2.43)$$

and it also has the variance curve (2.41). The calibration results are shown in figure 2.22. Given the calibrated model, we can now price arbitrary options on variance. Figures 2.23 and 2.24 display the prices of calls on variance computed with the two calibrated models (all prices here are computed using Monte Carlo simulation with control variates on the variance swaps).

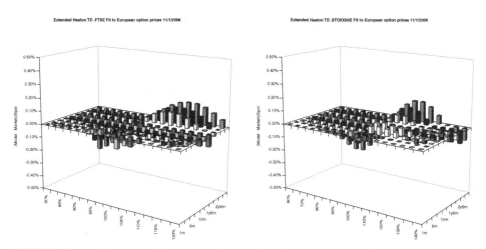

FIGURE 2.22 Calibration of the extended time-dependent Heston model (2.43) to FTSE and STOXX50E market data. The variance swap fits are shown in figure 2.20.

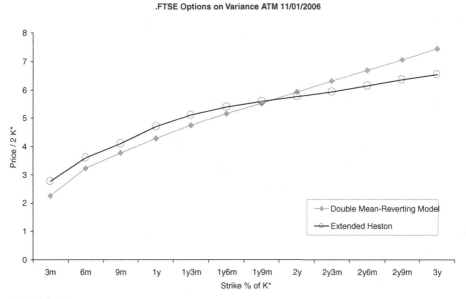

FIGURE 2.23 Prices of ATM calls on realized variances with the calibrated double mean-reverting and the calibrated extended Heston model (2.43).

2.3.3 Fitting to the Market

The previous sections discussed how we can model consistently the idea of "interpolating the variance swaps": We assumed that if we find a suitable function $\mathbb{G}$ that interpolates well the variance swaps at any time t, then we can derive no-arbitrage conditions on the dynamics of the parameters of this function. This approach is in spirit the idea of Björk/Christensen [55], who first introduced this concept of "consistency" for interest rates. However, by far more popular interest rate models are those that serve only two purposes: a perfect fit to the interpolated discount

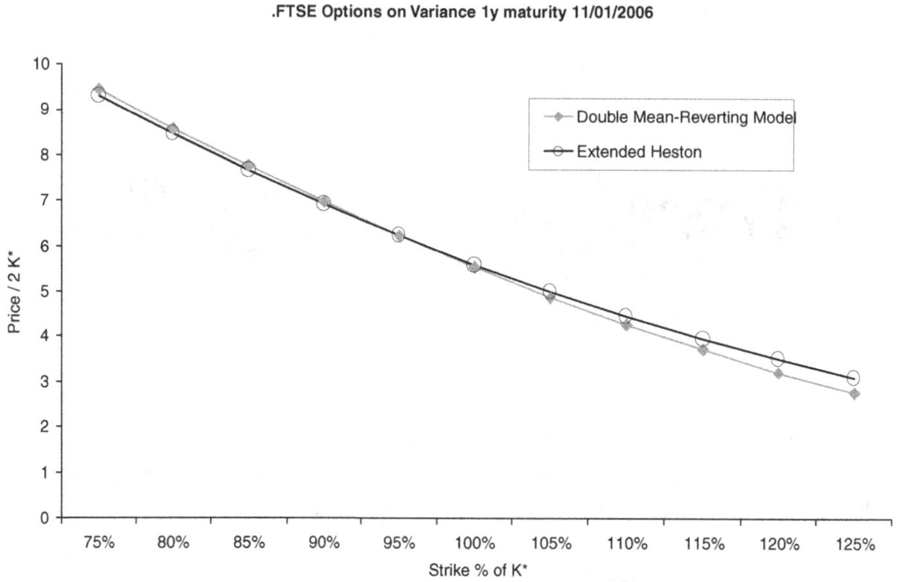

FIGURE 2.24   Prices of 1y calls on realized variances with the calibrated double mean-reverting and the calibrated extended Heston model (2.43).

bonds, regardless of the interpolation method used, and a parsimonious specification of the volatility structure of the model. The best known models of this class are the one- and two-factor extended Vasicek or Hull-White models; see chapter 3.

We will now discuss similar approaches for variance curves and thereby forgo the consistency approach. The aim is now to fit the market and to be able to describe the volatility structure of variance in a parsimonious way. We assume that we observe a sufficiently smooth variance swap market curve $U_0 = (U_0(x))_{x \geq 0}$ with forward non-negative forward variance curve $u_0(x) := \partial_x U_0(x)$. Recall the fixed time-to-maturity quantities $v_t(T) := u_t(T - t)$ and $V_t(T) := U_t(T - t)$.

EXAMPLE 8 *Dupire [57] proposed a "fitting stochastic volatility" model based on an exponential representation of the forward variance curve, that is,*

$$v_t(T) := u_0(T)\mathcal{E}_t\left(\int_0^{\cdot} v_s \, dW_s^1\right)$$

where v is a deterministic volatility function.

Indeed, this approach can easily be generalized. To this end, assume that we are given a variance swap curve model $(G, \mathbf{Z})$. Then,

$$u_t(x) := \frac{u_0(x + t)}{G(\mathbf{Z}_0; x + t)} \, G(\mathbf{Z}_t; x) \tag{2.44}$$

can be seen to be a variance curve model that reprices the variance swap market (i.e., $u_0 \equiv u_0$). A model very similar to Dupire's is therefore given by using Scott's exponential OU model,

$$u_t(x) := u_0(x+t)\frac{e^{w_t}}{\mathbb{E}[e^{w_t}]}, \tag{2.45}$$

where $dw_t = -\kappa w_t\, dt + v\, dW_t$ is an Ornstein-Uhlenbeck process. We call this model "fitted log-normal." It can be extended to a sum of correlated Ornstein-Uhlenbeck processes, as proposed by Bergomi [48]. However, following Jourdain [25], care should be taken with (2.44) to ensure that the associated stock price process is a true martingale (the *local* martingale property is ensured if the original model yields a local martingale for the stock price).

REMARK 2.3.4 *Sin [58] makes the following observation: a local martingale*

$$\frac{dX_t}{X_t} = \sqrt{\zeta_t}\, dB_t \quad (X_0 = 1)$$

with nonexplosive short variance ζ is a true martingale if, and only if, the process ζ does not explode under the measure $\mathbb{P}^X$ associated to the numeraire X.[22]

Using this result we can show that (2.44) applied to Heston's model will retain the martingale property of the associated stock price as long the correlation ρ is not positive.

The drawback of the "fitted log-normal" model is that it is to our knowledge not possible to efficiently compute European option prices. That implies that we have to revert to expensive numerical methods if the model is to be calibrated to European prices. A model that does not have this drawback can be constructed from example (2.43) given earlier: we have discussed that European prices for

$$\begin{aligned}
d\zeta_t &= \kappa(\theta_t - \zeta_t)\, dt + v\sqrt{\zeta_t}\, dW_t \\
d\theta_t &= c(m_0 - \theta_t)\, dt
\end{aligned} \tag{2.46}$$

can be computed relatively efficiently using Fourier transforms provided θ is non-negative. Since

$$\mathbb{E}[\zeta_t] = \int_0^t e^{-\kappa s}\theta_s\, ds$$

it is easy to see that if we set $\theta_t := \kappa u_0(t) + \partial_x u_0(x)$, then we fit the market: $\mathbb{E}[\zeta_t] = u_0(t)$. The non-negativity condition on θ essentially implies that u_0 must have the form $u_0(x) = e^{-\kappa x} f(x)$ for some increasing function f. As long as this condition is satisfied, we obtain a "fitted Heston model" that reprices the initial

---

[22] To see this, let $\tau_n := \inf\{t : \zeta_t \ge n\}$ such that $(X^n)_{n\in\mathbb{N}}$ with $X_t^n := X_{t\wedge\tau_n}$ is a true (discrete time) martingale on the filtration $(\mathcal{F}_{\tau_n\wedge T})_{n\in\mathbb{N}}$. Fix $T > 0$ and define $\mathbb{P}^n$ on $\mathcal{F}_{\tau_n\wedge T}$ by $\mathbb{P}^n[A] := \mathbb{E}[X_T^n 1_A]$. Assuming that $(\Omega, \mathcal{F}_T)$ is Polish, there exists by Kolmogorov extension a probability measure $\mathbb{P}^X$ on $\mathcal{F}_T$ such that $\mathbb{P}^X[A] = \mathbb{P}^n[A]$ for all $A \in \mathcal{F}_{\tau_n\wedge T}$, and for all $B \in \mathcal{F}_T$, we have then via Lebesgue decomposition that $\mathbb{P}^X[B] = \mathbb{E}[X_T 1_B] + \mathbb{P}^X[B \cap \{\tau \le T\}]$. Using $B = \Omega$ yields the desired result.

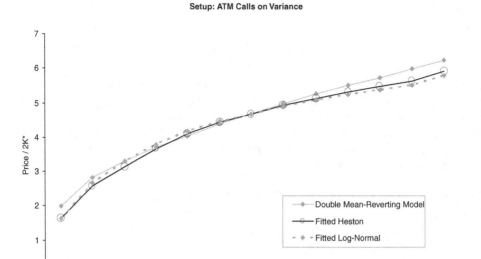

FIGURE 2.25 We have adjusted the parameters for the fitted Heston and fitted log-normal model by hand to roughly match ATM calls on variance between 1y and 2y of the double mean-reverting model. The graph shows the quality of the match and the impact on the short and long end of the ATM curve.

variance curve, which has a parsimonious parameter structure and which allows the calibration of these "volatility parameters" κ, ν and ρ via European options. Additionally, the volatility parameters can be made piecewise time dependent; cf. (2.12) and the discussion thereafter.[23]

Model Dependency If we use a specific model to price and hedge an exotic payoff, we are subject to model risk. Hence, it is important to assess the impact of the choice of a model. To this end, we present here a few results on the comparison between the fitted Heston model, the fitted log-normal model and the double mean-reverting model (2.42). To be able to compare the models, we interpolate the variance swaps using the variance swap curve function (2.41). Next, we price a 100% ATM call on variance using the double mean-reverting model using the parameters calibrated in the examples before. Then, we adjust the parameters ν and κ in the fitted Heston and fitted log-normal model such that they both have very similar option prices for the 1y to 2y 100% ATM calls (the correlation parameters do not have a big impact on pricing of options on variance).

   Having matched the models in this way, we can now compare the impact of the choice of a model first by comparing ATM calls with different maturities and second by comparing the prices of out-of-the-money calls. This is shown in figures 2.25 and 2.26. It is remarkable how similar prices the two fitted models produce: once

---

[23]In this section, we construct models that mainly serve the purpose of fitting the market. As in other fitting models, this can easily lead to economically counterintuitive calibration results.

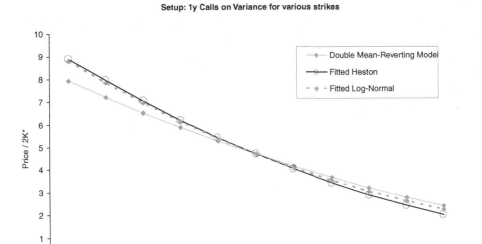

FIGURE 2.26   This graph shows the prices of 1y calls for the three models shown in figure 2.25.

the fitted log-normal and the fitted Heston agree for the ATM option, they produce very similar OTM option prices. Because of this very similar fit, the two models also produce very similar "VarSwapVegas"; hence, both price and hedge of a European option on realized variance are relatively robust with respect to model choice once the ATM calls are matched.

Equity Interest Rate Hybrids

CHAPTER 3

Short-Rate Models

3.1   INTRODUCTION

When pricing equity derivatives, we generally need to model only a single market instrument: the stock price.[1] The interest rate world, on the other hand, consists of many instruments: futures, swaps, and the like, all of which can move independently. These are generally combined to form the yield curve, commonly expressed in terms of zero coupon bond prices $P(t, T)$ (i.e., the value seen at time t of 1 unit of currency paid at time T) or the zero coupon rate $R(t, T)$, defined by

$$P(t, T) = \exp\left(-R(t, T)(T - t)\right).$$

Another useful representation is in terms of the forward rate, $f(t, T)$. This is defined as the rate, fixed at time t, for instantaneous borrowing at time T. If we agree at time t that we will invest 1 at time T for an infinitesimal period δ, the amount we will get back at time $T + \delta$ is $1 + f(t, T)\delta$. We can hedge this by shorting the zero coupon bond with maturity T and buying $1 + f(t, T)\delta$ units of the zero coupon bond with maturity $T + \delta$, making

$$f(t, T) = \lim_{\delta \to 0} \frac{1}{\delta}\left(\frac{P(t, T)}{P(t, T + \delta)} - 1\right)$$

$$= -\frac{\partial}{\partial T} \ln P(t, T).$$

The EUR yield curve is shown in terms of $R(0, T)$ and $f(0, T)$ in figure 3.1.

Two different approaches to interest rate modeling are

- *Market models,* where we model the market instruments such as LIBOR[2] or CMS[3] rates directly. Examples of market models include the well-known BGM model [59].

---

[1]Treating volatility as an asset class in its own right.

[2]The LIBOR (London Inter-Bank Offer Rate) is the uncompounded rate fixed at t for a loan or investment at t, paid back at T. The value of one unit of currency at time t is worth the promise of $1 + LIBOR(t, T)(T - t)$ units at time T, so

$$LIBOR(t, T) = \frac{1}{T - t}\left(\frac{1}{P(t, T)} - 1\right).$$

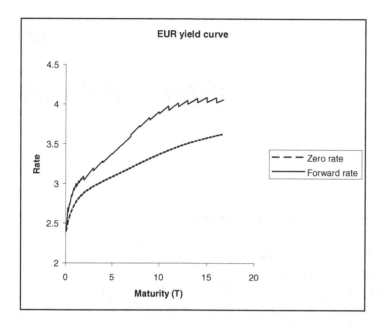

FIGURE 3.1   EUR yield curve in terms of the zero rate, $R(0, T)$, and the forward rate, $f(0, T)$.

- *HJM models* [60], where we model the evolution of the entire forward curve $f(t, T)$.

When pricing equity-interest rate hybrids we will automatically have at least two stochastic factors (the equity and the interest rate), so to keep the problems tractable it is often convenient to use a simple one-factor model for the interest-rate component. One such family of models is the short-rate family (a subset of the HJM models). These are particularly tractable and allow us to use PDE methods for pricing derivatives, unlike some market models.

The short rate, r_t, is the instantaneous borrowing rate. It is not observed directly in the market, but can be expressed in term of zero-coupon bonds as

$$r_t = - \left. \frac{\partial (\ln P(t, T))}{\partial T} \right|_{T=t}$$
$$= f(t, t).$$

We will ignore the small differences between the LIBOR fixing date and the accrual start date, and the LIBOR payment date and accrual end date. For convenience, we will refer to LIBOR rates whatever the actual currency (instead of using terms like EURIBOR, etc.).

[3]The n-year CMS (Constant Maturity Swap) rate at time t is the rate that gives an n-year swap, starting at t, zero value. If the payment dates in the swap are T_1 to $T_m = t + n$ (in an annual swap, for example, we have $T_i = t + i$), we have

$$\text{CMS} = \frac{1 - P(t, T_m)}{\sum_{i=1}^{m} \delta_i P(t, T_i)},$$

where δ_i is the day-count fraction $T_i - T_{i-1}$ (with $T_0 = t$).

In a short-rate model, the short rate is modeled as some specified stochastic process. For a general single-factor model we will have

$$dr_t = \mu(t, r_t)dt + \sigma(t, r_t)dW_t,$$

where W_t is a Brownian motion in the risk-neutral measure, $\mathbb{Q}$, where the money market account,

$$B_t = \exp\left(\int_0^t r_s ds\right),$$

is the numeraire.

Three examples of popular short-rate models are the Hull-White or Vasicek model ([61], [62]):

$$dr_t = (\theta_t - \kappa_t r_t)dt + \sigma_t dW_t, \qquad (3.1)$$

the Black-Karasinski model ([63]):

$$d \ln r_t = (\theta_t - \kappa_t \ln r_t)dt + \sigma_t dW_t,$$

and the Cox-Ingersoll-Ross model ([64]):

$$dr_t = (\theta_t - \kappa_t r_t)dt + \sigma_t \sqrt{r_t} dW_t.$$

Each of these models is capable of fitting the entire term structure of interest rates if the yield curve obeys certain constraints. For example, the Black-Karasinski model requires that the forward rate,

$$f(0, t) = -\frac{\partial \ln P(0, t)}{\partial t},$$

is positive for all t. The function θ_t can be calibrated so that the models fit the initial yield curve, that is,

$$P(0, t) = \mathbb{E}\left[\exp\left(-\int_0^t r_s ds\right)\right].$$

The volatility parameters, σ_t and κ_t, can also be calibrated. While these parameters do affect the fit to the yield curve, they will generally be calibrated to swaption and/or cap prices. For any set of volatility parameters, we must adjust the drift term θ_t to fit the yield curve.

Since we only have a one-factor model, the ways in which the yield curve can evolve are limited, with changes to all forward rates being perfectly correlated. Figure 3.2 shows some possible changes to the forward curve in a simple Hull-White model, whereas figure 3.3 shows actual changes to the forward curve. While one-factor models may capture the dynamics of individual rates, they cannot capture the relationship between different rates. As a consequence, one-factor models are not suitable for pricing derivatives that depend on differences between two market rates, such as CMS spread options.

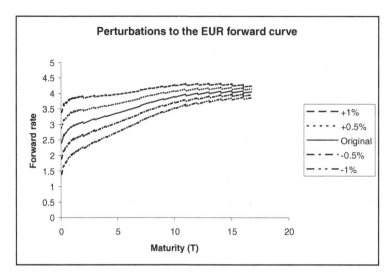

FIGURE 3.2 Possible changes to the forward curve from a single-factor Hull-White model using a mean reversion of 10%. A change to the short rate (the front end of the curve) decays away exponentially with maturity.

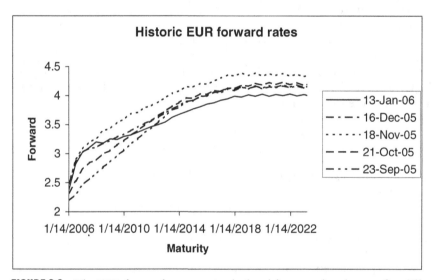

FIGURE 3.3 The EUR forward rate curve calculated from market data on five different dates, shown as a function of maturity.

3.2   ORNSTEIN-UHLENBECK MODELS

We will consider a useful family of short-rate models that can be constructed by expressing the short rate as some function of a variable, x_t, following an Ornstein-Uhlenbeck process:

$$\mathrm{d}x_t = -\kappa_t x_t \mathrm{d}t + \sigma_t \mathrm{d}W_t \tag{3.2}$$

as

$$r_t = r_t(x_t, \bar{x}_t, t). \tag{3.3}$$

If we let $r_t = x_t + \bar{x}_t$, we recover the Hull-White or Vasicek model. If we let $r_t = \exp(x_t + \bar{x}_t)$, we get the Black-Karasinski model (and the Black-Derman-Toy model ([65]) if we set $\kappa = 0$). To have more control over the relationship between the short rate and its volatility, we can find some parameterization that interpolates between a normal and a log-normal model, such as

$$r_t = \frac{1}{\beta} \left(\exp(\beta(x_t + \bar{x}_t)) - 1 \right) + \beta.$$

In this model, the limit $\beta = 0$ corresponds to the Hull-White or Vasicek model and the limit $\beta = 1$ corresponds to the Black-Karasinski model.

3.3 CALIBRATING TO THE YIELD CURVE

3.3.1 Hull-White Model

The Hull-White or Vasicek model is particularly popular as it is the most analytically tractable nontrivial interest rate model. Closed form solutions exist for several options since we have closed forms for both the short-rate distribution and the money market account (our numeraire). In this model we can express the drift θ_t in terms of the initial yield curve $P(0, t)$. However, the expression involves the second derivative of $P(0, t)$, which means we must use some smooth function like a cubic spline for the yield curve. This may not always be ideal as these functions tend to have unwanted nonlocal behavior. However, with a simple change of variables we can remove the need to calculate θ_t and the need to use smooth functions for $P(0, t)$.

As mentioned above, we can rewrite the Hull-White model in terms of some variable x_t whose simple SDE (given by equation (3.2)) does not involve θ_t. We do this by letting

$$r_t = x_t + \bar{x}_t$$

where $\bar{x}_t$ obeys

$$d\bar{x}_t = (\theta_t - \kappa_t \bar{x}_t)dt.$$

Adding this to equation (3.2) recovers the usual Hull-White SDE in equation (3.1). If we choose $\bar{x}_0 = f(0, 0)$, we have $x_0 = 0$ and $E[x_t | F_0] = 0$, so $\bar{x}_t$ is just the expected future short rate in the risk-neutral measure.

Integrating equation (3.2) we have

$$x_s = x_t \exp(-\Lambda_{ts}) + \int_t^s \exp(-\Lambda_{us}) \sigma_u dW_u,$$

where

$$\Lambda_{ts} = \int_t^s \kappa_u du.$$

To show how $\bar{x}_t$ relates to the yield curve, we need to price a zero-coupon bond:

$$
\begin{aligned}
P(t,T) &= \mathbb{E}\left[\exp\left(-\int_t^T r_s ds\right) | F_t\right] \\
&= \exp\left(-\int_t^T \bar{x}_s ds\right) \mathbb{E}\left[\exp\left(-\int_t^T x_s ds\right) | F_t\right] \\
&= \exp\left(-\int_t^T \bar{x}_s ds - x_t \hat{B}(t,T)\right) \mathbb{E}\left[\exp\left(-\int_t^T \sigma_s \hat{B}(s,T) dW_s\right) | F_t\right] \\
&= \exp\left(-\int_t^T \bar{x}_s ds - x_t \hat{B}(t,T) + \frac{1}{2}\int_t^T \sigma_s^2 \hat{B}(s,T)^2 ds\right), \qquad (3.4)
\end{aligned}
$$

where

$$\hat{B}(t,T) = \int_t^T \exp(-\Lambda_{ts}) ds. \qquad (3.5)$$

If we let $t = 0$ and differentiate the log of equation (3.4), we get

$$
\begin{aligned}
f(0,T) &= \bar{x}_T - \frac{1}{2}\frac{d}{dT}\int_0^T \sigma_s^2 \hat{B}(s,T)^2 ds \\
&= \bar{x}_T - \int_0^T \sigma_s^2 \hat{B}(s,T)\exp(-\Lambda_{sT}) ds.
\end{aligned}
$$

We can use this equation to calculate $\bar{x}_t$ from the initial yield curve, should we need to. We can also use it to eliminate $\bar{x}_t$ from the expression for the $P(t,T)$ given in equation (3.4), giving

$$P(t,T) = \frac{P(0,T)}{P(0,t)} \exp\left(-x_t \hat{B}(t,T) + \frac{1}{2}\int_0^t \sigma_s^2 [\hat{B}(s,t)^2 - \hat{B}(s,T)^2] ds\right).$$

Since the short rate is not observable in the market, there is no reason why we should explicitly need r_t. Instead, we can use x_t when simulating Monte Carlo paths or writing PDEs for derivatives prices. However, for finding closed-form solutions it is often simpler to work with a slightly different variable,

$$
\begin{aligned}
x_t' &= r_t - f(0,t) \\
&= x_t + \int_0^t \sigma_s^2 \hat{B}(s,t)\exp(-\Lambda_{st}) ds. \qquad (3.6)
\end{aligned}
$$

This has zero expectation in the t−forward measure, $\mathbb{Q}_t$. We can price derivatives as

$$V = P(0, t)\mathbb{E}^{\mathbb{Q}_t}[\text{Payoff}(x'_t, t)],$$

for which we need the probability density of x'_t in $\mathbb{Q}_t$.

To calculate the distribution of x'_t, we could use the dynamics of x_t in $\mathbb{Q}$ (i.e., equation (3.2)), then change measure to $\mathbb{Q}_t$. The Radom-Nikodym derivative is just the ratio of the numeraires, so we need an expression for the money market account:

$$
\begin{aligned}
B_t &= \exp\left(\int_0^t r_s \mathrm{d}s\right) \\
&= \exp\left(\int_0^t (x_s + \bar{x}_s)\mathrm{d}s\right) \\
&= \frac{1}{P(0, t)} \exp\left(\int_0^t x_s \mathrm{d}s + \frac{1}{2}\int_0^t \sigma_s^2 \hat{B}(s, t)^2 \mathrm{d}s\right) \\
&= \frac{1}{P(0, t)} \exp\left(\int_0^t \int_0^s \sigma_u \exp(-\Lambda_{us})\mathrm{d}W_u \mathrm{d}s + \frac{1}{2}\int_0^t \sigma_s^2 \hat{B}(s, t)^2 \mathrm{d}s\right) \\
&= \frac{1}{P(0, t)} \exp\left(\int_0^t \sigma_s \hat{B}(s, t)\mathrm{d}W_s + \frac{1}{2}\int_0^t \sigma_s^2 \hat{B}(s, t)^2 \mathrm{d}s\right).
\end{aligned}
$$

The Radom-Nikodym derivative is therefore

$$\frac{\mathrm{d}\mathbb{Q}_t}{\mathrm{d}\mathbb{Q}} = \frac{1}{B_t P(0, t)} = \exp\left(-\int_0^t \sigma_s \hat{B}(s, t)\mathrm{d}W_s - \frac{1}{2}\int_0^t \sigma_s^2 \hat{B}(s, t)^2 \mathrm{d}s\right).$$

The SDE followed by x under $\mathbb{Q}_t$ is therefore

$$\mathrm{d}x_s = -\kappa_s x_s \mathrm{d}s + \sigma_s \mathrm{d}W_s^{\mathbb{Q}_t} - \sigma_s^2 \hat{B}(s, t)\mathrm{d}s,$$

with solution

$$x_t = -\int_0^t \sigma_s^2 \hat{B}(s, t)\exp(-\Lambda_{st})\mathrm{d}s + \int_0^t \sigma_s \exp(-\Lambda_{st})\mathrm{d}W_s^{\mathbb{Q}_t}.$$

Comparing this to equation (3.6), we see that

$$x'_t = \int_0^t \sigma_s \exp(-\Lambda_{st})\mathrm{d}W_s^{\mathbb{Q}_t}.$$

To price derivatives in $\mathbb{Q}_t$ we also need zero-coupon bond prices. Using equation (3.6) to substitute for x_t in equation (3.4) gives

$$P(t, T) = \frac{P(0, T)}{P(0, t)} \exp\left(-x'_t \hat{B}(t, T) - \frac{1}{2}\hat{B}(t, T)^2 \int_0^t \sigma_s^2 \exp(-2\Lambda_{st})\mathrm{d}s\right). \tag{3.7}$$

3.3.2 Generic Ornstein-Uhlenbeck Models

In this section we look at fitting the generic short-rate model given in equation (3.3) to the yield curve. Traditionally, this has been done by using forwards induction on trees (see Jamshidian [66] and Hull and White [67]). We present a conceptually very similar approach, using PDEs instead of trees.

Let $V(x,t)$ be the price of a derivative depending on the stochastic interest rates, seen at time t when the parameter governing the short rate is x. Since we are working in the risk-neutral measure, $V(x,t)/B_t$ is a martingale and so

$$\mathrm{d}\left(\frac{V(x,t)}{B_t}\right) = \frac{1}{B_t}\left(\frac{\partial V}{\partial t} - r(x,t)V - \kappa_t x \frac{\partial V}{\partial x} + \frac{1}{2}\sigma^2 \frac{\partial^2 V}{\partial x^2}\right)\mathrm{d}t$$

$$+\text{ a martingale.}$$

It follows that the price $V(x,t)$ must obey the PDE

$$\frac{\partial V}{\partial t} - r(x,t)V - \kappa_t x \frac{\partial V}{\partial x} + \frac{1}{2}\sigma^2 \frac{\partial^2 V}{\partial x^2} = 0. \tag{3.8}$$

Now define the t–forward measure probability density of x as $\phi(x,t)$. This must obey

$$V(x_0,0) = P(0,t)\mathbb{E}^{\mathbb{Q}_t}[V(x,t)]$$

$$= P(0,t)\int_{-\infty}^{\infty} V(x,t)\phi(x,t)\mathrm{d}x. \tag{3.9}$$

Note that the left-hand side of this equation does not depend on t. This can hold only if ϕ obeys certain conditions. Differentiating the above equation with respect to t gives

$$0 = P(0,t)\int_{-\infty}^{\infty}\left(\phi\frac{\partial V}{\partial t} + V\frac{\partial \phi}{\partial t} - f(0,t)\phi V\right)\mathrm{d}x.$$

Substituting for $\frac{\partial V}{\partial t}$ using equation (3.8) and integrating by parts gives

$$0 = \int_{-\infty}^{\infty} V\left(\frac{\partial \phi}{\partial t} + (r(x,t) - f(0,t))\phi - \kappa_t\frac{\partial(x\phi)}{\partial x} - \frac{1}{2}\frac{\partial^2(\sigma^2\phi)}{\partial x^2}\right)\mathrm{d}x$$

$$+\text{ boundary terms.}$$

The boundary terms vanish if we assume that ϕ goes to zero sufficiently quickly as $x \to \pm\infty$. Since the above equation must hold for any derivative payoff $V(x,t)$, the term in brackets must be zero.[4] We have the following PDE for ϕ:

$$\frac{\partial \phi}{\partial t} + (r(x,t) - f(0,t))\phi - \kappa_t\frac{\partial(x\phi)}{\partial x} - \frac{1}{2}\frac{\partial^2(\sigma^2\phi)}{\partial x^2} = 0. \tag{3.10}$$

---

[4]This follows by setting V equal to the term in brackets making it the integral of $(\ldots)^2$, so $(\ldots)$ must be zero.

Assuming all of the coefficients of the above equation are well behaved, we can always find some solution ϕ. However, in order for the model to match the yield curve, we must be able to price zero-coupon bonds correctly. Going back to equation (3.9) and letting $V(x,t) = 1$ (and so $V(x_0, 0) = P(0,t)$) we have

$$1 = \int_{-\infty}^{\infty} \phi(x,t) \mathrm{d}x.$$

Obviously, if this is not satisfied, then ϕ cannot be the t−forward measure probability density. Differentiating the above equation with respect to t, using equation (3.10) and integrating by parts we get

$$\int_{-\infty}^{\infty} (r(x,t) - f(0,t)) \phi(x,t) \mathrm{d}x = 0. \tag{3.11}$$

Again, we have used the properties of ϕ as $x \to \pm\infty$ to set the boundary terms to zero. Equations (3.10) and (3.11) together let us fit the model to the yield curve.

Recall that the parameter for fitting the yield curve is embedded in the expression for $r(x,t)$. Going back to our earlier notation, we wrote

$$r = r(x, \overline{x}_t, t),$$

so assuming we know $\phi(x,t)$ up to some time t, the problem of fitting the model to the yield curve is simply the problem of finding $\overline{x}_t$ so that equation (3.11) is satisfied.

As an example, in the Hull-White model we wrote

$$r(x,t) = x + \overline{x}_t$$
$$= x' + f(0,t)$$

and so we have

$$\int_{-\infty}^{\infty} x' \phi(x,t) \mathrm{d}x = 0,$$

which we know to be true since x' has zero expectation in $\mathbb{Q}_t$.

We can bootstrap this calibration along since knowledge of $\phi(x,t)$ allows us to find $\overline{x}_t$, which in turn allows us to find $\phi(x, t + \delta t)$ using some numerical PDE solver.

This simple bootstrapping will give us errors in the propagation from t to $t + \delta t$ of order $(\delta t)^2$ since we only work out $\overline{x}_t$ using information at the start of the time-step, and so our approximation for the average $\overline{x}$ in t to $t + \delta t$ has an error of order δt and we are using it to propagate the PDE a distance δt. However, having done this first step, we then have a solution $\phi(x, t + \delta t)$ that is accurate to $\mathrm{O}((\delta t)^2)$ and so we can calculate $\overline{x}_{t+\delta t}$ to order $(\delta t)^2$ and from this get an $\mathrm{O}((\delta t)^2)$ solution for the average $\overline{x}$ in the period. We therefore can find $\phi(x, t + \delta t)$ with errors of $\mathrm{O}(\delta t^3)$, so after $\frac{T}{\delta t}$ steps, we have an error in ϕ and $\overline{x}$ of $\mathrm{O}(\delta t^2)$.

In figures 3.4 and 3.5, we show the results of fitting a BK model to the EUR yield curve. We used a constant volatility of 10% and a mean reversion of 1%. Note that $\overline{x}$ has discontinuities corresponding to the discontinuities in the forward rate in figure 3.1.

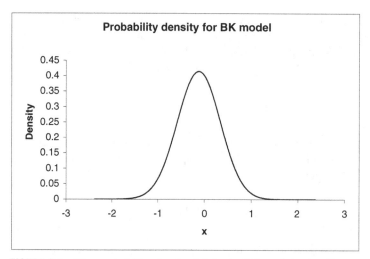

FIGURE 3.4 The probability density (ϕ) in the BK model using the EUR yield curve, a volatility of 10% and a mean reversion of 1%.

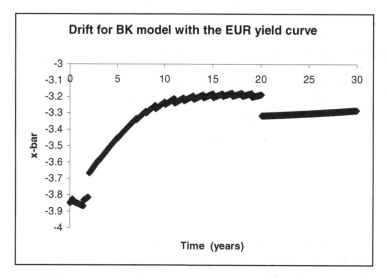

FIGURE 3.5 The integrated drift ($\bar{x}$) for a BK model using the EUR yield curve, a volatility of 10% and a mean reversion of 1%.

3.4 CALIBRATING THE VOLATILITY

In this section we discuss how to calibrate the parameters that govern the volatility structure of short-rate models. In this case, that means the volatility of x and the mean reversion. Mean reversion has the effect of reducing the overall volatility so it must be calibrated alongside the volatility parameters. We will generally want to calibrate the volatility parameters to fit some liquid volatility-dependent instruments such as caps and swaptions.

3.4.1 Hull-White/Vasicek

As before, we will treat the case of the Hull-White/Vasicek model separately as it allows for several closed-form or near-closed-form solutions. In particular, we have closed forms for the zero-coupon bond and the distribution of r_t (see section 3.3.1).

A cap is a string of caplets, which are options to receive LIBOR. We will assume we have dates $T_i, 0 \le i \le n$, describing n caplet periods. The i'th caplet runs from T_{i-1} to T_i, with the LIBOR being fixed (and the exercise decision being made) on date T_{i-1} and the payment being received on date T_i. The i'th LIBOR is

$$L_i = \frac{1}{\delta_i} \left(\frac{1}{P(T_{i-1}, T_i)} - 1 \right),$$

where $\delta_i = T_i - T_{i-1}$ is the day-count fraction for the i'th period. The value of the i'th caplet seen on its exercise date is therefore

$$c_i(T_{i-1}) = P(T_{i-1}, T_i)\delta_i (L_i - K)^+$$
$$= (1 - (1 + K\delta_i)P(T_{i-1}, T_i))^+$$

We can now use the results of section 3.3.1 to get a closed-form solution for the price of a caplet. Substituting equation (3.7) into the above equation gives

$$c_i(T_{i-1}) = \left(1 - \frac{(1 + K\delta_i)P(0, T_i)}{P(0, T_{i-1})} \exp \left(-B(T_{i-1}, T_i)x'_{T_{i-1}} \right. \right.$$
$$\left. \left. - \frac{1}{2}B(T_{i-1}, T_i)^2 \int_0^{T_{i-1}} \sigma_s^2 \exp(-2\Lambda_s T_{i-1} \, \mathrm{d}s) \right) \right)^+ .$$

To evaluate this, let $Z_i = B(T_{i-1}, T_i)x'_{T_{i-1}}$ so that Z_i is normally distributed with variance $u_i = B(T_{i-1}, T_i)^2 \int_0^{T_{i-1}} \sigma_s^2 \exp(-2\Lambda_s T_{i-1})\mathrm{d}s$. Since the exponential is monotonic in Z_i, the caplet will be exercised if

$$Z_i > A = \ln \left(\frac{(1 + K\delta_i)P(0, T_i)}{P(0, T_{i-1})} \right) - \frac{1}{2}u_i,$$

giving a price of

$$c_i(0) = P(0, T_{i-1})N(d_{1i}) - (1 + K\delta_i)P(0, T_i)N(d_{2i}),$$

where

$$d_{1i} = -\frac{\ln \left(\frac{(1+K\delta_i)P(0,T_i)}{P(0,T_{i-1})} \right)}{\sqrt{u_i}} + \frac{\sqrt{u_i}}{2}$$
$$d_{2i} = d_1 - \sqrt{u_i}.$$

The price of the cap is therefore

$$\text{Cap} = \sum_{i=1}^{n} P(0, T_{i-1})N(d_{1i}) - (1 + K\delta_i)P(0, T_i)N(d_{2i}),$$

For pricing swaptions, we can either use a closed-form approximation, or a near-closed-form exact solution. We'll deal with the exact solution first.

A swaption is an option on a swap. We will assume we have an option to pay coupons of K and receive LIBOR. If we also assume the LIBOR fixing, accrual, and payment dates are all aligned, then the i'th LIBOR payment is worth

$$P(t, T_{i-1})\mathbb{E}^{QT_{i-1}}[L_{i-1}\delta_i P(T_{i-1}, T_i)] = P(t, T_{i-1})\mathbb{E}^{QT_{i-1}}[(1 - P(T_{i-1}, T_i)]$$

$$= P(t, T_{i-1}) - P(t, T_i),$$

and so the floating side of the swap is worth $P(t, T_0) - P(t, T_n)$. The whole swap is worth

$$\text{Swap}(t) = P(t, T_0) - P(t, T_n) - K\sum_{i=1}^{n} \delta_i P(t, T_i).$$

On the exercise date, which we will assume is T_0, the swaption is worth

$$\text{Swaption}(T_0) = \left(1 - P(T_0, T_n) - K\sum_{i=1}^{n} \delta_i P(T_0, T_i)\right)^+.$$

Substituting for $P(T_0, T_i)$ using equation (3.7) gives

$$\text{Swaption}(T_0) = \left(1 - \sum_{i=1}^{n} a_i \exp\left(-\hat{B}(T_0, T_i)x'_{T_0}\right)\right)^+, \qquad (3.12)$$

where

$$a_i = \frac{(\Delta_{in} + K\delta_i)P(0, T_i)}{P(0, T_0)} \exp\left(-\frac{1}{2}\hat{B}(T_0, T_i)^2 \int_0^{T_0} \sigma_s^2 \exp(-2\Lambda_{sT_0})ds\right)$$

and Δ_{in} is the Kronecker delta. The swaption is therefore the sum of a series of options on zero-coupon bonds, the strikes being determined by the solution of the equation

$$\sum_{i=1}^{n} a_i \exp\left(-\hat{B}(T_0, T_i)x^*\right) = 1.$$

As the left-hand side of this equation is clearly monotonically decreasing in x^*, we can solve this very efficiently using a Newton-Raphson method. Once we have found x^*, we can price the swaption as

$$F(x^*, T_0, T_0) - F(x^*, T_0, T_n) - K \sum_{i=1}^n \delta_i F(x^*, T_i),$$

where $F(x^*, t, T)$ is the price of an option to receive a zero coupon bond $P(t, T)$ at t if $x_t' > x^*$, that is,

$$F(x^*, t, T) = \frac{P(0, T)}{\sqrt{2\pi V_t}} \int_{x^*}^{\infty} \exp\left(-\hat{B}(t, T)x' - \frac{1}{2}\hat{B}(t, T)^2 V_t\right) \exp\left(-\frac{x'^2}{2V_t}\right) dx'$$

$$= P(0, T) N\left(-\frac{x^*}{\sqrt{V_t}} - \hat{B}(t, T)\sqrt{V_t}\right),$$

where V_t is the variance of the short-rate distribution at time t,

$$V_t = \int_0^t \sigma_s^2 \exp(-2\Lambda_{st}) ds.$$

Alternatively, we can find a closed-form approximation for the swaption price as was first done by Jamshidian [68]. We approximate the sum in equation (3.12) by a single exponential as

$$\sum_{i=1}^n a_i \exp\left(-\hat{B}(t, T_i)x'\right) \approx G \exp\left(-Hx' - \frac{1}{2}H^2 V_t\right). \tag{3.13}$$

If we want to match the expectation of this under the t–forward measure (and thus the price of the swap), we have

$$G = \frac{P(0, T_n) + K \sum_{i=1}^n \delta_i P(T_0, T_i)}{P(0, T_0)}.$$

We can choose H to match the expectation of the slope of the function. Differentiating both sides of equation (3.13) with respect to x and taking the expectation gives

$$H = \frac{P(0, T_n)\hat{B}(T_0, T_n) + K \sum_{i=1}^n \delta_i P(T_0, T_i)\hat{B}(T_0, T_i)}{P(0, T_n) + K \sum_{i=1}^n \delta_i P(T_0, T_i)}.$$

In figure 3.6, we show an example for a 1y20y swaption with $\kappa = 0.1$, $\sigma = 0.1$, and zero initial interest rates.

Given this approximation, we can express the swaption price as

$$P(0, T_0)\left(N\left(-\frac{\ln G}{H\sqrt{V_{T_0}}} + \frac{H\sqrt{V_{T_0}}}{2}\right) - GN\left(-\frac{\ln G}{H\sqrt{V_{T_0}}} - \frac{H\sqrt{V_{T_0}}}{2}\right)\right).$$

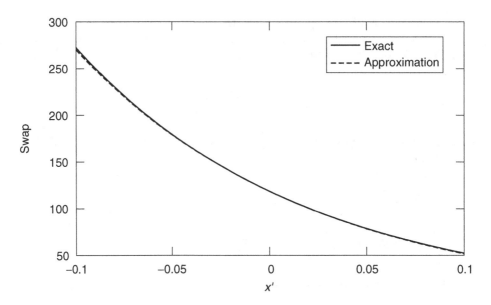

FIGURE 3.6   Log-normal swap approximation for a 1y20y swap.

Note that the swaption price depends on σ only up to the exercise date of the swaption. This means that if we fix the mean reversion, we can bootstrap the volatility term-structure. Alternatively, since we can find analytic expressions for the derivatives of the swaption prices with respect to the volatility and mean reversions we could use some Newton-Raphson-based minimization strategy.

3.4.2   Generic Ornstein-Uhlenbeck Models

In this section we discuss calibrating the volatility structure for models that do not have closed-form solutions for swaptions/caps. The important thing is to be able to price caps and swaptions as efficiently as possible. We can use PDE methods to get accurate prices given a set of parameters (kappas, sigmas, and other parameters that the model might have) and then embed the pricing in some minimization algorithm.

Traditionally, we would price a swaption with finite differences by propagating the values of the payments in the swap back to the exercise date, calculating the value of the swaption there, then propagating that price back to the evaluation date. To price an *nymy* swaption (i.e., a swaption that is exercised after n years into an m year swap) we would have to propagate for $n + m$ years on the PDE grid. However, for each new set of parameters, we must recalibrate $\overline{x}_t$, and in doing so we calculate $\phi(x, t)$, the probability density of x in the t−forward measure. We therefore do not have to propagate all the way back to the evaluation date, but can propagate the swap price to the exercise date, then use ϕ to calculate the swaption price with

$$\text{Swaption} = P(0, T_0) \int_{-\infty}^{-\infty} \phi(x, T_0) \text{Swap}(x, T_0)^+ dx.$$

This reduces the computational cost of pricing the swaption to just propagating m years on the grid.

In the general problem, the price of the *nymy* swaption depends on the volatility up to the end of the swap (through the drift term $\bar{x}_t$), so it is not possible to bootstrap the volatility. Instead, we have to calibrate the entire volatility term structure simultaneously with some appropriate nonlinear minimization algorithm (see section 3.6).

3.5 PRICING HYBRIDS

In this section we assume we have a stochastic stock process as well as stochastic interest rates. We will model the stock price as

$$\frac{dS_t}{S_t} = (r_t - v_t)dt + \sigma^S(S, t)dW_t^S, \tag{3.14}$$

where v_t incorporates the dividends (assumed to be proportional to the stock price) and the repo rate. We assume the interest rates follow an Ornstein-Uhlenbeck model given by equation (3.3). To distinguish between the stock price process and the interest rate process we will write

$$dx_t = -\kappa_t x_t dt + \sigma_t^r dW_t^r.$$

We assume we have some correlation structure

$$\langle dW_t^r, dW_t^S \rangle = \rho dt.$$

Recall that we defined

$$r_t = r_t(x_t, \bar{x}_t, t).$$

The volatility of the stock may depend on S_t (i.e., local volatility) or be just a function of time. Calibrating the volatility is the subject of chapter 8, but for now we just mention that the equity process volatility is affected by the interest rate volatility assuming we are calibrating to a market of European options.

We can remove the dividends and repo from the problem by changing variables as follows. Let

$$S_t = S_0 \exp(y_t) \frac{\exp\left(-\int_0^t v_s ds\right)}{P(0, t)}.$$

We will work in terms of y_t instead of S_t as it is continuous. The analogous SDE to equation (3.14) is

$$dy_t = \left[r_t - f(0, t) - \frac{1}{2}(\sigma_t^S)^2\right]dt + \sigma_t^S dW_t. \tag{3.15}$$

3.5.1   Finite Differences

To find the PDE followed by the prices of the hybrid products we assume we have some derivative whose price depends only on the short-rate driving variable (x_t) and the stock price (or equivalently y_t): $V(x, y, t)$. The value of the derivative discounted by the money market account B_t must be a martingale, so we have

$$
\mathrm{d}(V/B) = \left[\frac{\partial V}{\partial t} - r_t V + \frac{\partial V}{\partial x}(-\kappa_t x) + \frac{\partial V}{\partial y}\left(r_t - f(0, t) - \frac{1}{2}(\sigma_t^S)^2 \right) \right.
$$
$$
\left. + \frac{(\sigma_t^r)^2}{2}\frac{\partial^2 V}{\partial x^2} + \rho \sigma_t^S \sigma_t^r \frac{\partial^2 V}{\partial x \partial y} + \frac{(\sigma_t^S)^2}{2}\frac{\partial^2 V}{\partial y^2} \right] \mathrm{d}t
$$
$$
+ \text{a martingale part.}
$$

This gives the following PDE for V:

$$
\frac{\partial V}{\partial t} - r_t V + \frac{\partial V}{\partial x}(-\kappa_t x) + \frac{\partial V}{\partial y}\left(r_t - f(0, t) - \frac{1}{2}(\sigma_t^S)^2 \right)
$$
$$
+ \frac{(\sigma_t^r)^2}{2}\frac{\partial^2 V}{\partial x^2} + \rho \sigma_t^S \sigma_t^r \frac{\partial^2 V}{\partial x \partial y} + \frac{(\sigma_t^S)^2}{2}\frac{\partial^2 V}{\partial y^2} = 0.
$$

To improve the accuracy slightly, we can work with the deterministically discounted value of the derivative by defining $U(x, y, t) = V(x, y, t)P(0, t)$. This gives the PDE

$$
\frac{\partial U}{\partial t} - (r_t - f(0, t))U + \frac{\partial U}{\partial x}(-\kappa_t x) + \frac{\partial U}{\partial y}\left(r_t - f(0, t) - \frac{1}{2}(\sigma_t^S)^2 \right)
$$
$$
+ \frac{(\sigma_t^r)^2}{2}\frac{\partial^2 U}{\partial x^2} + \rho \sigma_t^S \sigma_t^r \frac{\partial^2 U}{\partial x \partial y} + \frac{(\sigma_t^S)^2}{2}\frac{\partial^2 U}{\partial y^2} = 0.
$$

Unless we represent the yield curve by at least a cubic spline, the forward curve $f(0, t)$ will be discontinuous and so will the short rate r_t. The difference between the two will generally have smaller discontinuities than the short rate itself and is continuous in the Hull-White/Vasicek model and in the limit of zero interest rate volatility. For this reason, U is generally better to work with than V. Note that the PDE for the Vasicek case in terms of r_t involves the drift term θ_t. By writing the PDE in terms of x instead, we have removed the need to calculate this term (which depends on the second derivatives of the zero-coupon bonds). By using U instead of V, we have also removed the need to calculate the forward rate $f(0, t)$ (which depends on the first derivative of the zero-coupon bonds) since $r_t - f(0, t)$ can be expressed in terms of x using equation (3.6) as

$$
r_t - f(0, t) = x_t + \int_0^t \sigma_s^2 \hat{B}(s, t)\exp(-\Lambda_{st})\mathrm{d}s.
$$

We therefore not only do not need twice-differentiable yield curves, or even once-differentiable ones—we can get away with discontinuous forward rates.

3.5.2 Monte Carlo

An alternative method for pricing derivatives is to use Monte Carlo simulation. For that we need to be able to simulate paths of the SDEs followed by x and y. We will treat two cases here—the full problem with local volatility and non-Gaussian interest rates and the special case of the Hull-White/Vasicek model with a term structure of equity volatility; in this case we have a closed form for the Greens function and can therefore take large steps in the simulation.

Vasicek + Term Structure of Log-Normal Equity Volatilities We need to simulate paths of x_t and y_t given by equations (3.2) and (3.15), and the money market account, which follows the process

$$dB_t = r_t B_t dt. \tag{3.16}$$

We will consider the changes from t to T. The solution of equation (3.2) is

$$x_T = x_t \exp(-\Lambda_{tT}) + \int_t^T \sigma_s^r \exp(-\Lambda_{sT}) dW_s^r. \tag{3.17}$$

We can rewrite equation (3.15) as

$$dy_t = \left(x_t + \frac{1}{2} \frac{d}{dt} \int_0^t \sigma_s^{r2} \hat{B}(s,t)^2 ds - \frac{1}{2} \sigma_t^{S2} \right) dt + \sigma_t^S dW_t^S,$$

where $\hat{B}$ is defined in equation 3.5. Using equation (3.17) to substitute for x_T we get

$$y_T = y_t + x_t \hat{B}(t,T) + \frac{1}{2} \left(\int_0^T \sigma_s^{r2} \hat{B}(s,T)^2 ds - \int_0^t \sigma_s^{r2} \hat{B}(s,t)^2 ds \right)$$

$$- \frac{1}{2} \int_t^T \sigma_s^{S2} ds + \int_t^T \sigma_u^r \hat{B}(u,T) dW_u^r + \int_t^T \sigma_s^S dW_s^S.$$

To simulate the money market, we rewrite equation (3.16) as

$$d\ln(B_t P(0,t)) = x_t + \frac{1}{2} \frac{d}{dt} \int_0^t \sigma_s^{r2} \hat{B}(s,t)^2 ds.$$

Once again, we use equation (3.17) to substitute for x_t, giving

$$\ln B_T = \ln B_t + \ln P(0,t) - \ln P(0,T) + x_t \hat{B}(t,T) + \int_t^T \sigma_u^r \hat{B}(u,T) dW_u^r.$$

In order to simulate the steps from t to T, we must sample from the integrals

$$I_1 = \int_t^T \sigma_s^r \exp(-\Lambda_{sT}) dW_s^r,$$

$$I_2 = \int_t^T \sigma_s^r \hat{B}(s,T) dW_s^r,$$

$$I_3 = \int_t^T \sigma_s^S dW_s^S.$$

We can sample from these if we know the covariance matrix C_{ij}, where

$$C_{11} = \int_t^T \sigma_s^{r2} \exp(-2\Lambda_{sT}) ds$$

$$C_{22} = \int_t^T \sigma_s^{r2} \hat{B}(s,T)^2 ds$$

$$C_{33} = \int_t^T \sigma_s^{S2} ds$$

$$C_{12} = \int_t^T \sigma_s^{r2} \hat{B}(s,T) \exp(-\Lambda_{sT}) ds$$

$$C_{13} = \rho \int_t^T \sigma_s^r \sigma_s^S \exp(-\Lambda_{sT}) ds$$

$$C_{23} = \rho \int_t^T \sigma_s^r \sigma_s^S \hat{B}(s,T) ds.$$

Let D_{ij} be the Cholesky decomposition of C, so

$$C = D^T D.$$

If we sample three independent normal variables, Z_1, Z_2, Z_3, we can write

$$I_i = \sum_j D_{ij} Z_j.$$

We can therefore simulate paths of the short rate, stock price, and money market account.

Generic Ornstein-Uhlenbeck Models   For the more general model given by equations (3.2) and (3.3), we can still simulate x_t exactly, but not the money market account or the stock price. We will therefore have to take small steps in the Monte Carlo simulation where we can find the distribution approximately. Letting $T - t = \delta t$, we have the change in the money market account as

$$\ln B_T = \ln B_t + \int_t^T r(x_s, s) ds$$

$$\approx \ln B_t + r(x_t, t) \delta t,$$

The change in the stock variable is given by

$$y_T = y_t + \int_t^T \left(r_s - f(0,s) - \frac{1}{2}\sigma_s^{S2} \right) ds + \int_t^T \sigma^S(s, y_s) dW_s^S$$

$$\approx y_t + \left(r(x_t, t) - f(0, t) - \frac{1}{2}\sigma_s^{S2} \right) \delta t$$

$$+ \sigma^S(t, y_t) \int_t^T dW_s^S + \frac{\partial \sigma^S}{\partial y} \sigma^S(t, y_y) \int_t^T \int_t^s dW_u^S dW_s^S$$

$$\approx y_t + \left(r(x_t, t) - f(0, t) - \frac{1}{2}\sigma_s^{S2} \right) \delta t$$

$$+ \sigma^S(t, y_t) \int_t^T dW_s^S + \frac{\partial \sigma^S}{\partial y}\sigma^S(t, y_y) \left[\left(\int_t^T dW_u^S \right)^2 - \delta t \right].$$

We therefore need to sample from the following stochastic integrals:

$$I_1 = \int_t^T \sigma_s^r \exp(-\Lambda_{sT}) dW_s^r,$$

$$I_4 = \int_t^T dW_s^S,$$

with covariances

$$C_{11} = \int_t^T \sigma_s^{r2} \exp(-2\Lambda_{sT}) ds$$

$$C_{44} = \delta t$$

$$C_{14} = \rho \int_t^T \sigma_s^{r2} \exp(-\Lambda_{sT}) ds.$$

Overall, this simulation has strong order 1. The interest rate process is simulated exactly and the Milstein scheme we use for the equity process has strong order 1, as does the simulation of the money market account. See Kloeden and Platen [69] for details of Milstein schemes.

3.6 APPENDIX: LEAST-SQUARES MINIMIZATION

When calibrating the parameters of an interest rate model to swaption/cap data, the problem generally reduces to trying to fit m prices by adjusting n parameters. If we have $m > n$, we cannot necessarily fit all of the prices simultaneously, so we must try to minimize the error in the price in some norm. A commonly chosen norm is the L^2 norm, where we find the least-square error. If we let the parameters be $\mathbf{x} = (x_1, x_2, \ldots x_n)$ and the differences between the market prices and the model prices be $\mathbf{y}(\mathbf{x}) = (y_1, y_2, \ldots y_m)(\mathbf{x})$, then the problem is to find the vector $\mathbf{x}$ that minimizes

$$\sum_j y_j(\mathbf{x})^2.$$

While we could use some general algorithm for minimizing a single function of many variables, by reducing the vector $\mathbf{y}$ to a single number we throw away useful information about the individual components of $\mathbf{y}$. Many techniques exist for this style of minimization, but here we will just describe two, Newton-Raphson and Broyden's methods, as these are particularly easy to implement. More details can be found in Press et al. [70].

3.6.1 Newton-Raphson Method

When the Jacobian $J_{ij} = \frac{\partial y_i}{\partial x_j}$ can be calculated simply, such as when calibrating the Hull-White model to swaptions/caps, we can use the Newton-Raphson method to minimize the L^2 norm. If we have a good trial solution $\mathbf{x}^k$, with residual errors $\mathbf{y}^k = \mathbf{y}(\mathbf{x}^k)$, we can get a better solution by linearizing the problem about this point, giving

$$\mathbf{y}(\mathbf{x}^k + \delta\mathbf{x}^k) \approx \hat{\mathbf{y}}(\mathbf{x}^k + \delta\mathbf{x}^k) \equiv \mathbf{y}^k + \sum_i \frac{\partial \mathbf{y}}{\partial x_i}\delta x_i^k.$$

We want to minimize

$$\sum_j \hat{y}_j^2 = \sum_j (y_j^k)^2 + 2\sum_{ij} y_j^k \frac{\partial y_j}{\partial x_i}\delta x_i^k + \sum_{ijl} \frac{\partial y_j}{\partial x_i}\frac{\partial y_j}{\partial x_l}\delta x_i^k \delta x_l^k$$

$$= A + 2\mathbf{v}^T\delta\mathbf{x}^k + \delta\mathbf{x}^{kT}\mathbf{M}\delta\mathbf{x}^k.$$

Differentiating with respect to $\delta\mathbf{x}$ and setting the result to zero, we have

$$\delta\mathbf{x} = -\mathbf{M}^{-1}\mathbf{v}.$$

The new trial solution is

$$\mathbf{x}^{k+1} = \mathbf{x}^k - \mathbf{M}^{-1}\mathbf{v}.$$

If we have a linear problem, this technique will solve it in one iteration; for nonlinear problems, the number of iterations will depend on how far away from the linear regime our starting solution is. To handle constraints on the parameters, we can use the sequential quadratic programming method (see [71]) or re-express the original problem in terms of unconstrained parameters. For instance, if we have one original parameter, x, which we know must be strictly positive, we can re-express the problem in terms of $x' = \log(x)$ instead. The new parameter, x', is free to assume any real value, and ensures that $x = \exp(x') > 0$.

3.6.2 Broyden's Method

To handle the case where we do not know the derivatives, we can use Broyden's method to estimate them. Here at each step we only have an approximate estimate of the Jacobian

$$J_{ij} = \frac{\partial y_i}{\partial x_j} \approx B_{ij}.$$

At each step, k, of our iterative procedure, we use the approximate Jacobian to calculate the matrix $\mathbf{M}$ and vector $\mathbf{v}$ and get the new trial solution $\mathbf{x}^{k+1}$, then update the estimated Jacobian to be consistent with the previous step. Given that the k'th step is $\delta\mathbf{x}^k = \mathbf{x}^{k+1} - \mathbf{x}^k$ and $\mathbf{y}$ changes by $\delta\mathbf{y}^k = \mathbf{y}^{k+1} - \mathbf{y}^k$, with an estimated Jacobian of $\mathbf{B}^k$, we can compute an updated Jacobian, $\mathbf{B}^{k+1}$, that satisfies

$$\delta\mathbf{y}^k = \mathbf{B}^{k+1}\delta\mathbf{x}^k.$$

There is no unique solution to this, but a good thing to use in practice is Broyden's method, where we let

$$\mathbf{B}^{k+1} = \mathbf{B}^k + \frac{(\delta \mathbf{y}^k - \mathbf{B}^k \delta \mathbf{x}^k) \times \delta \mathbf{x}^k}{\delta \mathbf{x}^k \cdot \delta \mathbf{x}^k},$$

since

$$\delta \mathbf{y}^k = \left(\mathbf{B}^k + \frac{(\delta \mathbf{y}^k - \mathbf{B}^k \delta \mathbf{x}^k) \times \delta \mathbf{x}^k}{\delta \mathbf{x}^k \cdot \delta \mathbf{x}^k} \right) \delta \mathbf{x}^k.$$

For more details, see Press et al. [70].

CHAPTER 4

Hybrid Products

In this chapter we discuss when it is necessary to use stochastic rates to price a derivative and what effects they have on the prices, giving the conditional trigger swap TARN, convertible bond and exchangeable bond as examples.

All options depend on interest rates through the discounting of future payments. If we treat interest rates as stochastic, then the money market account (often used as our numeraire) becomes stochastic. So apart from the explicit hybrid products, where we receive payments based on both interest rate market observables (LIBOR and CMS rates) and equities, we may also need to consider stochastic interest rates when pricing options where the value of some equity/index affects the time when we receive some payments. A good example of this is the target redemption note (see section 4.3).

4.1   THE EFFECTS OF ASSUMING STOCHASTIC RATES

Whether or not we choose to price a particular option with stochastic rates will depend on what risks we think are significant and against which we need to hedge ourselves. Interest rates tend to be less volatile than equities, with typical short-rate volatilities being around a few percent, whereas equity volatilities may be of the order 10% to 100%. Often, the effect of stochastic rates will be swamped by the effects of the more volatile equities, and it will not be necessary to use a more CPU-intensive two-factor model.

Stochastic LIBOR and CMS rates   The most obvious effect of stochastic interest rates is to make quantities such as LIBOR and CMS[1] rates stochastic. If we have an option with a payoff dependent on a combination of these and an equity performance, there is a good chance we will need to model the interest rates as stochastic. However, as mentioned, the interest rate volatilities may be so low as to make this unnecessary. Examples of derivatives that depend on stochastic interest rates in this way are conditional trigger swaps (see section 4.2) and hybrid best-of products, which pay coupons of the form

$$\max(LIBOR, a.(S_t/S_0 - 1)).$$

---

[1] See footnote on page 91.

These derivatives tend to depend strongly on the assumed correlation between the interest rate and equity processes.

Note that derivatives containing a stream of LIBOR payments that cannot be terminated early do not necessarily need to be modeled using stochastic interest rates as we can hedge the payments in a way that does not depend on what happens to the LIBOR rates.[2]

Stochastic numeraires The second effect of assuming stochastic rates is to make the money market account and zero-coupon bond prices stochastic. These are often used as numeraires, so the time value of money is affected. Any option where the time of a given payment is uncertain will be affected by stochastic interest rates. Examples of such options are

- Bermudan/American callable options. Here the timing of the strike payment depends on when the holder decides to exercise; that decision will depend on what has happened to the interest rates.
- Target redemption notes (TARNs; see section 4.3) where the overall level of return is guaranteed, but how the return is distributed throughout the life of the option depends on an equity performance.
- Any option in which you receive a payment the first time an event happens (e.g., a barrier is breached).
- Any option with a stream of LIBOR payments that can be called/knocked out, such as the floating side of a conditional trigger swap.

The longer the maturity of an option, the greater will be the effect of stochastic rates. A 1% change in interest rates will have only a 1% effect on the price of a one-year zero-coupon bond, but the effect on the price of a 30-year bond will be compounded up to more like 30%. For this reason, many options will be considered to be hybrid options once their maturity becomes large enough, say five or ten years.

---

[2]If we have to make a payment of LIBOR, fixed at T_1 and paid at T_2, we can hedge this by buying the zero-coupon bond with maturity T_1 and shorting the zero-coupon bond with maturity T_2. At T_1, the T_1 bond is worth 1; we use this to buy more of the T_2 zero-coupon bond, giving us

$$\frac{1}{P(T_1, T_2)} - 1 = (T_2 - T_1)LIBOR(T_1, T_2)$$

units of the T_2 bond. At T_2, we use this to make the LIBOR payment.

If we have a stream of back-to-back LIBOR payments (as in the floating side of a swap) with fixing dates $T_0 \rightarrow T_{n-1}$ and payment dates $T_1 \rightarrow T_n$, we can hedge this by buying the T_0 zero-coupon bond and shorting the T_n zero-coupon bond. At T_0, we invest 1 in the T_1 ZCB; at T_1 we sell this, invest 1 in the T_2 ZCB and use the remainder to pay back the LIBOR. We repeat this until we reach T_n, where we have to pay back the LIBOR and buy back the T_n ZCB for 1. In this way, paying a stream of LIBOR payments is equivalent to borrowing 1 at T_0 and paying it back at T_n.

Adjusted local volatilities The final effect of stochastic rates that we will mention here is more subtle. It is not so much a direct effect of stochastic rates on the payoff of a product as a breakdown of our usual modeling assumptions for long-dated options. Interest rates affect the stock price process through the drift term; in the risk-neutral measure the drift of the stock price is just the short rate r_t. Ignoring dividends, we can write the stock price at time t as

$$S_t = S_0 \exp\left(\int_0^t r_s ds\right) \mathcal{E}_t\left(\int_0^t \sigma_s^S dW_s^S\right), \tag{4.1}$$

where σ_s^S is the equity process volatility (which may be stochastic), W^S is the Brownian motion driving the stock price process in the risk-neutral measure and $\mathcal{E}$ is the Doleans-Dade exponential.[3]

When we assume interest rates are deterministic, all of the volatility of the terminal stock price, S_t, comes from the final exponential in the above equation and so we calibrate σ_s^S to implied volatilities. In reality, since interest rates are stochastic, the first exponential in the above equation is also a source of randomness and so the equity process (local) volatility must be adjusted to match the implied volatility surface (for more details of this, see chapter 8). Note that this effect exists even when the interest rates are uncorrelated with the equity process. If we are always calibrating to market implied volatilities, the terminal stock price distribution in the t−forward measure (and thus the prices of European-style equity options) is unaffected by our assumptions about stochastic rates.[4] However, options that are more directly sensitive to the local volatility than the implied volatility will be affected.

In particular, options with a knock-out feature will be affected. Consider an option that pays a fixed coupon c semiannually up to the first time the stock rises above some barrier B on one of the coupon dates, T_i. The probability of being above the barrier at time t (in the t−forward measure) is unaffected by our rate assumptions.[5] However, the more positive the correlation between stochastic rates and the equity process, the less the equity local volatility will be and so the more correlated the stock prices on adjacent barrier dates will be.

We can write the present value of the coupon payment on date T_n as

$$PV_n = cP(0, T_n)\text{Prob}_{Q_n}(S_1 < B \cap S_2 < B \ldots \cap S_n < B).$$

---

[3]

$$\mathcal{E}_t(Z) = \exp\left(Z_t - \frac{1}{2}\langle Z\rangle_t\right)$$

[4] The discussion in European payoffs in section 1.3.3 applies here as well.
[5] We can write a call price in terms of the T−forward measure as $C(K, T) = P(0, T)\mathbb{E}_{Q_T}[(S_T - K)^+]$. Differentiating with respect to K gives $-\frac{1}{P(0,T)}\frac{\partial C}{\partial K} = \mathbb{E}_{Q_T}[1_{S_T > K}]$, i.e., the probability of the stock being above the barrier.

This probability can be rewritten as

$$\text{Prob}(S_1 < B) \times \text{Prob}(S_2 < B | S_1 < B) \times \ldots \times \text{Prob}(S_n < B | \max(S_1 \ldots S_{n-1}) < B).$$

If the local volatility is reduced by introducing stochastic interest rates, the terms in the above expression will also be reduced as there is less volatility to allow the stock to move over the barrier at date T_i, given that it wasn't over the barrier at date T_{i-1}.

Note that the first exponential in equation (4.1) will be correlated with the short rate at time t, r_t. Even if there is no instantaneous correlation between the equity process and the interest rate process (i.e., dS and dr are uncorrelated), the terminal values (S_t and r_t) will be correlated, so derivatives with a payoff sensitive to this correlation will be affected by modeling rates as stochastic even if we assume no instantaneous correlation.

4.2   CONDITIONAL TRIGGER SWAPS

A conditional trigger swap is like a standard swap in that the holder (or issuer) receives coupons in exchange for paying LIBOR. However, what would normally be fixed coupons depend on the performance of an equity. Additionally, the whole trade knocks out if the equity ever goes above some barrier.

In each of the example trades here, the underlying is the Nikkei (N225) index and the payments are made in Japanese yen. The holder pays JPY LIBOR semiannually on dates T_i and receives c_1 at date T_1, then subsequently receives

$$
\begin{array}{lll}
c_1 & \text{if} & S(T_i) < B_c \\
c_2 & \text{if} & S(T_i) \geq B_c,
\end{array}
$$

at date T_i where B_c is a barrier set below the current spot level. If the index performs well, the holder will receive a string of large coupons, whereas if the index plunges below the barrier, he will receive only the small coupons.

On top of this, the whole structure knocks out if the index goes above B_k on date T_i, where B_k is a knock-out barrier level set above the current spot. On the date when the structure knocks out, the LIBOR and coupon payments are still made, but subsequent ones are not.

The payoff is shown graphically in figure 4.1.

Without the knock-out barrier, this deal would not require stochastic rates at all. We can value the floating side payments as we normally would, as $1 - P(T_0, T_N)$. We can decompose the fixed side payments into the guaranteed amounts δc_1, where δ is the appropriate day-count fraction, and a series of digital options paying $\delta(c_2 - c_1)$ if $S_{T_i} > B_c$, which can be completely hedged with European options.

We can think of the floating side of the option as being equivalent to paying 1 at T_0 and receiving 1 at maturity or when the option knocks out. This is shown

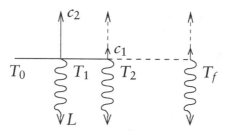

FIGURE 4.1 Cash flows for a conditional trigger swap. T_f is the first observation date T_i at which $S(T_i) > B_k$ or maturity.

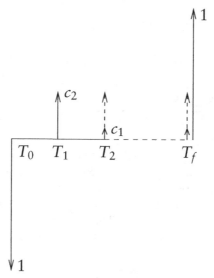

FIGURE 4.2 Alternative cash flows for a conditional trigger swap. T_f is the first observation date T_i at which $S(T_i) > B_k$ or maturity.

in figure 4.2. The floating side payments in the option are therefore sensitive to stochastic rates because the time when the holder effectively pays back the notional is stochastic. The value of the stream of LIBOR payments can be written as

$$\text{float side} = 1 - P(T_0, T_1) + P(T_0, T_1)\mathbb{E}^{Q_{T_1}}[1_{S_1 < B_c}(1 - P(T_1, T_2))]$$
$$+ P(T_0, T_2)\mathbb{E}^{Q_{T_2}}[1_{S_1}S_2 < B_c(1 - P(T_2, P_3))] + \dots$$

For now we will ignore the effect of the stochastic rates on the distribution of the time T_f and just note that each of the terms

$$1 - P(T_i, T_{i+1})$$

is positively correlated with interest rates. The more positively correlated the terms

$$1_{S_1, \dots, S_i < B_c}$$

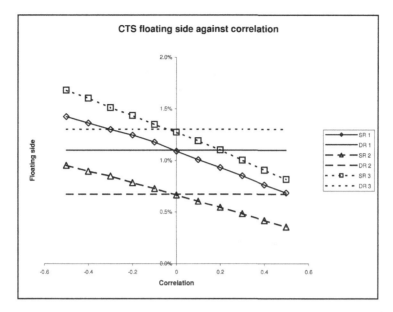

FIGURE 4.3 Effect of correlation on the floating side of a sample of conditional trigger swaps. SR and DR refer to stochastic rates and deterministic rates, respectively.

are with interest rates, the greater each of the expectations will be. The greater the index/interest rate correlation, the less positively correlated the above terms will be with interest rates, and the smaller the PV of the LIBOR payments will become. As the correlation increases, the value of the floating side decreases.

The other effect to consider is the change in the local volatility. As correlation increases, the local volatility decreases and so the probability of the option's knocking out by a particular date decreases. Consequently, as correlation increases, the expected lifetime of the option (the expectation of T_f) increases. This is a smaller effect than the one discussed above, so is not noticeable in the floating side, but we can see that the PV of the fixed side payments do indeed increase slightly with correlation.

Figures 4.3 and 4.4 show the effect of correlation on the PV of the float and fixed side payments for some representative trades. Note that although the maturities of these deals are 15y or 30y, the expected lifetimes are actually much smaller, so the stochastic interest rates have only a small impact on the prices.

The details of the trades are as follows:

Trade	Maturity	Small coupon (c_1)	Large coupon (c_2)	Coupon barrier (B_c)	Knock-out barrier (B_k)
1	30y	0.1%	2.0%	10,064	12,764
2	15y	0.0%	0.0%	10,220	12,716
3	30y	0.8%	2.9%	10,220	13,163

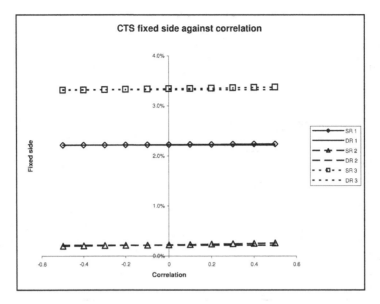

FIGURE 4.4 Effect of correlation on the fixed side of a sample of conditional trigger swaps. SR and DR refer to stochastic rates and deterministic rates, respectively.

4.3   TARGET REDEMPTION NOTES

4.3.1   Structure

The target redemption note (TARN) is a coupon-bearing, capital-guaranteed structure that pays an attractive coupon for the first year or two, and that furthermore pays a guaranteed[6] *total* coupon amount, distributed among the remaining coupon dates of the structure. The structure's maturity might be eight years or more.

The defining features of the TARN structures we consider here are:

- The sum of coupons paid (*TARN level*) is guaranteed and the capital protected.
- For an initial period, coupon payments are fixed.
- The timing of the residual coupon and of the redemption payment are not guaranteed, but are dependent on the performance of an underlying.

So the market risk is in the *timing* of the payments, not in their aggregate size.

A wide variety of instruments can be used as the underlying for a TARN. The structure originated as an interest rate derivative: Equity-linked TARNs are a more recent development (since around 2003). Equity-linked underlyings can be indices

---

[6]The term *guaranteed* should invariably be interpreted as carrying an implicit "assuming no default of the issuer" *caveat*. There is nothing absolute about these guarantees in the absence of additional arrangements such as escrow accounts, which take the funds out of the control of the issuer.

(e.g., Dow Jones Euro Stoxx50), baskets (of as many as 20 stocks) or worst-of baskets (having just a few constituents in the basket, perhaps just three). A CPPI strategy (chapter 5) can also serve as the underlying for a TARN.

We will adopt a typical example TARN to study, with terms as follows:

- 10-year maturity.
- Underlying is the Dow Jones Euro Stoxx 50 index.
- TARN level of 13.5%.
- Annual coupons $C_{i,1 \leq i \leq 10}$ at anniversary dates $t_{i,1 \leq i \leq 10}$.
- The first two coupon amounts are fixed: $C_1 = C_2 = 4.5\%$.

The remaining coupons are equity linked and given in terms of the performance of the underlying since the inception of the structure, $P_i = S(t_i)/S(0) - 1$, thus:

$$C_i = \text{Min} \left\{ \left(P_i - \sum_{j=1}^{i-1} C_j \right)^+, \text{TARN level} - \sum_{j=1}^{i-1} C_j \right\}, \, 3 \leq i \leq 9$$

$$C_{10} = \text{TARN level} - \sum_{j=1}^{9} C_j.$$

In words: The equity-linked coupons, before the last one, pay the excess of the stock's performance, up to the coupon date, over the accumulated coupons prior to that time; the total aggregated coupon being however capped at the TARN level. The final coupon "tops up" the total aggregated coupon to equal the TARN level irrespective of the underlying stock's performance.

When the total aggregated coupon reaches the TARN level, the capital is returned and the structure terminates. Neither the total income from the structure nor the repayment of capital is therefore in doubt: just the timing of the income and redemption payments, and hence the yield (to maturity or to early redemption). The structure attracts the investor who believes that it will be called early; say, after three or four years. In that case, he will have received attractive coupons from a medium-term note. He must believe that it is not unreasonable to suppose that the index will have risen by 13.5% in three or four years.

To illustrate the risk taken on this market view, we may look at the *internal rate of return* (IRR) arising from various possible redemption scenarios. Table 4.1 lists the most favorable scenario (which is that the instrument is called after just three years), the two extreme scenarios at four-year termination (the ones generating the minimum and maximum coupon at three years), the most favorable five-year termination case and the ten-year case. We note that even the most favorable four-year termination reduces the IRR by more than 1% and the most favorable five-year termination by nearly $1\frac{3}{4}$%. The investor's yield drops abruptly if his favorable early-termination scenarios are not realized. Worse still, if the market falls and does not recover, he is trapped in a structure that provides a yield far below risk free. A further conclusion from the table is that the dominant factor in the realized IRR is the timing of the *redemption* payment, not the details of how the coupon is distributed amongst the anniversary dates.

TABLE 4.1 Internal rates of return for TARN redemption scenarios

Payments	Year of Termination				
	3	4	4	5	10
Initial	−100.00%	−100.00%	−100.00%	−100.00%	−100.00%
Year 1	4.50%	4.50%	4.50%	4.50%	4.50%
Year 2	4.50%	4.50%	4.50%	4.50%	4.50%
Year 3	104.50%	0.00%	4.49%	4.49%	0.0%
Year 4		104.50%	100.01%	0.00%	0.0%
Year 5				100.01%	0.0%
Year 10					104.5%
IRR	4.50%	3.39%	3.43%	2.77%	1.37%

Compare also figures 4.10 and 4.11 showing how the TARN's value derives from the distribution of early- and late-termination cases.

While this is not an atypical structure, there are variants on the theme. One such caps each coupon payment, potentially preventing the TARN level being reached at some coupon date and thereby lengthening the structure when the basic TARN would have redeemed early. In the above expression for the coupon amounts,

$$\left(P_i - \sum_{j=1}^{i-1} C_j \right)^+$$

is in this case replaced by

$$\text{Min} \left(\left(P_i - \sum_{j=1}^{i-1} C_j \right)^+, \text{Cap} \right).$$

4.3.2 Back-Testing

For the purposes of marketing a structured derivative, it is common to perform back-testing. This procedure evaluates how the structure *would have* performed had it been purchased at some time in the past. In particular, it is common to evaluate the results of having, hypothetically, made the investment in the structure on each business day during an appropriate time interval, using historical daily time series for all relevant underlyings.[7]

Although back-testing is no part of derivative valuation, we apply it to our example TARN to illustrate some of its features. The Stoxx50 index is available from January 1987, so derivatives of ten-year maturity can be back-tested meaningfully, assuming one "clone" of the structure to be initiated per business day during the ten

---

[7]It is also common to speak loosely of the results as giving probabilities of particular outcomes: this is not correct.

years between January 1, 1987, and December 31, 1996. It transpires that even the latest starting of the simulated structures would have terminated by December 31, 1999. Accordingly, we can calculate their realized IRRs and plot them: Figure 4.5 shows the realized IRR for each trial, and figure 4.6 shows their distribution into the maximum possible IRR and percent-wide bands below it.

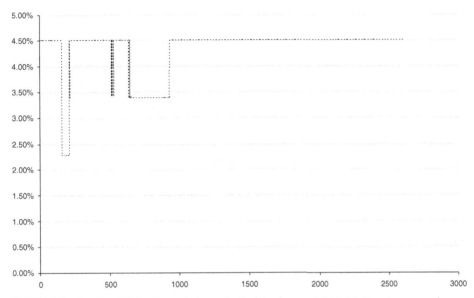

FIGURE 4.5 Realized IRRs for each hypothetical back-tested TARN. One is assumed to have been started each business day for ten years from January 1, 1987.

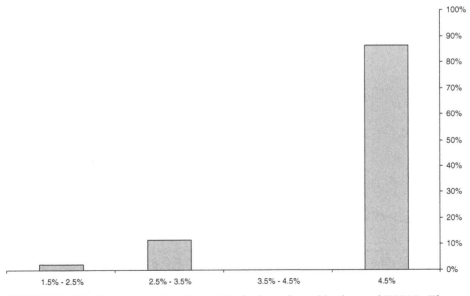

FIGURE 4.6 The distribution of realized IRRs for hypothetical back-tested TARNs. The gap in the histogram corresponds to the gap between the three-year termination case and the most favorable four-year case in the last row of Table 4.2.

We have the surprising result that 86% of the simulated TARN issues terminate after three years (the market rose at least 13.5%).

This is in fact a nice illustration of the power of back-testing: If the investor believes that this behavior is representative of the outcome for an investment he is considering, he will see the investment as extremely attractive. The risk-neutral probability of markets rising 13.5% in three years is, of course, nowhere near this high.

We may gain some intuition for this high percentage by observing the time series for the index over the relevant interval (see figure 4.7). The vertical lines in the graph mark the start date of the last simulated TARN, and its redemption date. (It is clear by inspection that it terminates after three years, and in fact no simulated TARN survives later than this.) We can see that the back-testing interval is dominated by rising markets and excludes (because even the latest-starting TARNs have terminated) the decline from the markets' peak in 2000, hence the excellent back-testing performance of this structure.

Now we are in a position to understand how the TARN offers such an attractive early coupon and what the pitfall is. The early coupons are paid for by the probability that the capital will be tied up for a long time, earning no great return, in the event that the early redemption scenarios are not realized. The larger the initial coupon, the lower the probability of early redemption and the longer it will be necessary to lock up the capital in order to make the structure value work. In structuring a TARN, there is a balance to be struck between initial coupons sufficient to attract investors, the probability that early redemption will not happen, and the length of time for which the investor's capital will be locked up in the structure if it is not redeemed early.

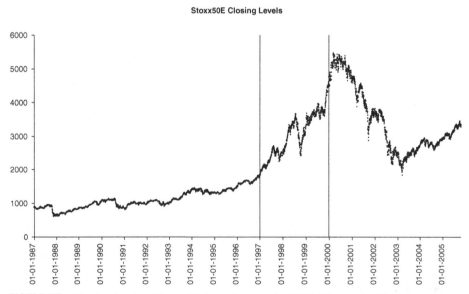

FIGURE 4.7 Closing levels of Stoxx50 from January 1, 1987. The vertical lines mark the inception date of the latest simulated TARN and its redemption date.

In the following sections, we extract the risks embedded in the structure, and indicate how the various models in which the structure can be valued quantify these risks.

4.3.3 Valuation Approach

Apart from the initial fixed-coupon payments, the TARN embeds a strip of call spreads, where the lower strike depends on the past performance, and a payment of the redemption amount on the first anniversary on which the performance reaches the barrier (i.e., TARN level), 113.5% of initial spot in our example. Hence, we may investigate the interest rate risk, the embedded lookback call spreads, and the barrier risk.

Barrier Risk We first concentrate on the barrier risk at $K = 113.5\%S_0$. The barrier in question pays the redemption amount as soon as the stock reaches K, or at maturity if the stock never reaches this level. A barrier can generally be seen as a limit of call spreads. As such, the impact of using a Black-Scholes-type model is severe: It neglects the presence of the skew around the barrier.

In formulae, this rests on the fact that

$$
\begin{aligned}
\text{Digital}(K) &= -\partial_K \text{Call}(K) \\
&= -\partial_K \text{Call}^{\text{BS}}(K, \hat{\sigma}(K)) \\
&= \text{Digital}^{\text{BS}}(K, \hat{\sigma}(K)) - \text{Vega}^{\text{BS}}(K, \hat{\sigma}(K))\, \partial_K \hat{\sigma}(K) \\
&\neq \text{Digital}^{\text{BS}}(K, \hat{\sigma}(K))
\end{aligned}
$$

(Here $\hat{\sigma}(K)$ denotes the implied Black-Scholes volatility of a call with strike K and the BS superscript indicates Black-Scholes-type formulae.) To illustrate the impact of the vega term, we may evaluate the digital in the Black-Scholes Model and compare it with approximations to the derivative of the call price using call spreads of $\pm \epsilon$ around the barrier K.[8]

$$
\text{Digital}(K) \approx \frac{\text{Call}(K - \epsilon K) - \text{Call}(K + \epsilon K)}{2\epsilon K}
$$

The results of this test for the digital at 18-month maturity are given in table 4.2. (Compare also figure 1.5, in which similar comparisons are illustrated.)

The wide discrepancy here forces us to use a model that takes into account the skew, such as local volatility. In principle, such models reprice all European vanillas correctly. Consequently, as we can see in table 4.3, they give consistent prices for the barriers. (Again, compare figure 1.5.)

---

[8]The actual size of the spread is determined by trading considerations, because the call spread also allows one to constrain the possible delta positions occurring during the life of the trade.

TABLE 4.2   The Black-Scholes digital compared to call spread approximations

ϵ	BS Digital	Call Spread
0.5%	16.12%	20.60%
0.25%		20.60%
0.05%		20.59%
0.01%		20.59%
0.001%		20.59%

TABLE 4.3   The Black-Scholes digital compared to call spread approximations and local volatility prices at various maturities. Data for Stoxx50, June 2005

Maturity	BS Digital	Call Spread	Local Volatility
1y6m	16.1%	20.6%	20.6%
2y	18.8%	24.4%	24.4%
2y6m	21.8%	28.5%	28.6%
3y	22.4%	29.7%	29.7%

Lookback Elements   The next elements for consideration in the TARN are the embedded call spreads. The coupons have the form:

$$C_1 = 4.5\%$$

$$C_2 = 4.5\%$$

$$C_3 = \mathrm{Min}\left(13.5\%, \left(\frac{S_3}{S_0} - 109\%\right)^+\right)$$

$$C_4 = \mathrm{Min}\left(13.5\%, \left(\frac{S_4}{S_0} - \left\{\left(\frac{S_3}{S_0} - 109\%\right)^+ + 109\%\right\}\right)\right)$$

$$= \mathrm{Min}\left(13.5\%, \left(\frac{S_4}{S_0} - \mathrm{Max}\left(\frac{S_3}{S_0}, 109\%\right)\right)^+\right)$$

$$C_5 = \mathrm{Min}\left(13.5\%, \left(\frac{S_5}{S_0} - \mathrm{Max}\left(\frac{S_4}{S_0}, \frac{S_3}{S_0}, 109\%\right)\right)^+\right),$$

which shows that later coupons are lookback-type call spreads.[9] In general, such structures might depend strongly on future skew and interdependency between the increments S_i/S_0 and S_{i-1}/S_0. Such effects are not always well captured by local volatility models.

---

[9]A lookback on the maximum is a payoff of the form: $F(S_n, \mathrm{Max}_{i<n}S_i)$ for $t_0 < \ldots < t_n$.

To assess the impact of using a "structural" model (as opposed to a "fitting" model like local volatility) that still fits the European prices along the barrier K well, but that also has self-consistent implied volatility dynamics, we calibrate a Heston-type extended stochastic volatility model to the market. Carrying out the comparison between these two models and plain Black-Scholes and the call spread yields the comparison in figure 4.8 for the 113.5% barrier of our example. The same comparison for the TARN using a BS model (i.e., term structure of implied volatility along K), a local volatility model and a stochastic volatility model is shown in figure 4.9.

The TARN can be thought of as two guaranteed coupons of 4.5%, plus an option to receive the notional when a barrier of 13.5% is reached, plus an extra 4.5% paid somewhere between year 3 and year 10. Well-calibrated stochastic or local volatility models should agree on the prices of the fixed coupons and the barrier option, as well as the value of the first variable coupon. It is only the remainder of the deal that behaves like the sum of lookback options (and then only if the index falls within the narrow range of 109% to 113.5%). It is perhaps not too surprising that the choice of the stochastic versus local volatility model does not have a large effect on the price.

Impact of Stochastic Rates   Although there is no explicit dependence on interest rates in this product, the choice of deterministic versus stochastic rate models and of the correlation between the index and the rates can still have a significant effect on the price.

This behavior can be understood from looking at figures 4.10 and 4.11, where we show the probabilities of the TARN expiring at a particular date and the corresponding contributions to the overall price.

As the correlation between the index and the rates is increased, two effects occur:

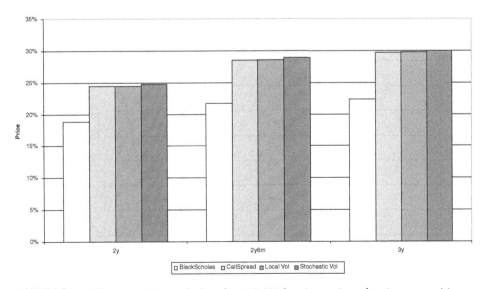

FIGURE 4.8   Different models applied to the 113.5% barrier option of various maturities.

- The local volatility of the index process has to decrease (as the effect of the stochastic rates on the implied volatilities becomes stronger).
- The cash bond becomes more positively correlated with the index level.

The first effect increases the correlation between the index prices on consecutive fixing dates, which increases the probability that if the index is above the barrier on date i, then it was also above the barrier on date $i-1$. The probability of the TARN expiring in each of periods 4 to 9 is therefore reduced (figure 4.10). The

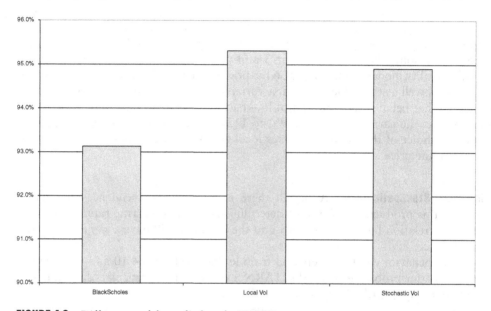

FIGURE 4.9   Different models applied to the TARN structure.

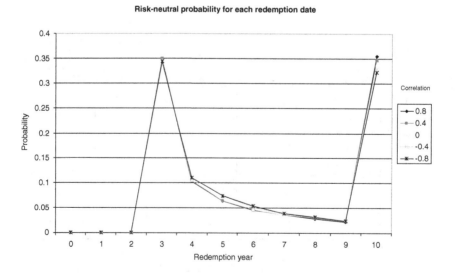

FIGURE 4.10   Risk-neutral probabilities of redemption on the possible expiry dates.

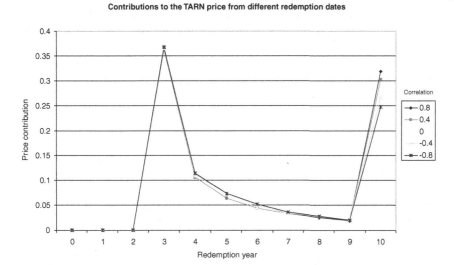

FIGURE 4.11 Contributions to the TARN value from the possible expiry dates.

second effect means that paths where the index performed badly (and so the TARN expired after ten years) have a smaller cash bond and so the final payment in less strongly discounted and so worth more, seen from today. This can be seen from figure 4.11, where the correlation has a very large effect on the contribution to the TARN price of the paths expiring after ten years. Note that the second effect becomes more pronounced for later maturities thanks to compounding up of the cash bond. The net effect is that the TARN value increases with increasing index versus rate correlation, as shown in figure 4.12.

4.3.4 Hedging

Once the deal is priced, a hedging strategy to manage the risk must be employed. The considerations necessary to hedge the product are similar to the pricing considerations: We are faced with some fixed coupons (for which we do not need any hedging), a barrier, and a stream of lookback call spreads.

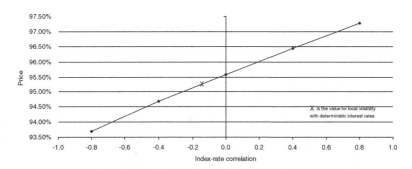

FIGURE 4.12 The effect on the calculated TARN value of correlation between the index and the EUR short rate, in a local volatility model with stochastic short rates.

Barrier Hedging   The risk in hedging a barrier is that the delta becomes very large when we approach the barrier, and suddenly collapses when the barrier is reached. We then face the problem of not being able to unwind our delta position fast enough and face a gap risk. To alleviate the situation, call spreads can be used to approximate the barrier. However, the size of the call spread is crucial: set too large, the product becomes too expensive; too low, and the gap risk becomes too strong. In general, the size of the spread lies in the experience of the trader and depends on the liquidity of the stock, the size of the position, any other positions in the book, and so forth.

Lookback Call Spreads   The specific nature of the lookback call-spreads embedded in the TARN is that the payment of one spread determines the lower strike of the preceding call.

One possible strategy is therefore to set up call spreads for all times $t_i : i \geq 3$ with upper strike K (the barrier) and lower strike initially at $109\% S_0$. The later strikes might also be adjusted by the probabilities of the process reaching the barrier up to t_i. Clearly, this initial portfolio of calls must be adjusted during the life of the trade to account for the actual movement of the stock, taking into account the transaction costs for each repositioning.

4.4   CONVERTIBLE BONDS

4.4.1   Introduction

In this chapter we consider an intensity-based framework for pricing convertible bonds (CBs; see, for example, Overhaus et al. [31]) in a "two-and-a half-factor" setting. The two factors are the stock price and the interest rate. The hazard rate (the *half factor*) is modeled as a deterministic function of the stock, the interest rate, and time. We account explicitly for the stock price behavior and holder's rights in the event of default as well as the recovery value of the bond. Most comparable existing models are special cases of this general setting.

There are three main issues on the modeling side:

- Whether the stock value or the firm value is the main underlying factor
- Whether there are additional stochastic factors, such as an interest rate or hazard rate
- How default is modeled and what happens upon default to the state variables, the CB holders' rights, and the convertible value.

In general, credit risk models fall into two main categories: structural and reduced form (see Chapter 6). In *structural models* (see [72]–[82]) the state variable is usually the value of the firm or firm asset value, which moves randomly. All claims on the firm's value are modeled as derivative securities with the firm value as the underlying. Default occurs when the value of the firm hits or crosses a boundary. It is necessary to specify the process for the firm value, the location of the barrier, and the form and amount of recovery upon default. These models provide a link between the equity and debt instruments issued by a firm, which may be necessary, for example, in the valuation of CBs and callable bonds; they can be used, at least in theory, to optimize the capital structure, and default risk is endogenized and measured based on the share price and fundamental data only. However, the firm value is unobservable and often difficult to model. The volatility of the firm value is particularly hard to estimate. Also, models become too complex for reasonable capital structures. Finally, they are not well suited for pricing and hedging of credit instruments. In *reduced form models* (see [77], [83]–[88]) default is exogenous, occurring at the first jump time τ of a counting process, N_t, with jump intensity λ_t. The main issues in reduced form models are the specification of processes for the riskless short rate r_t, the hazard rate λ_t, and the recovery value.

The early models of convertible bonds (Ingersoll [89] and Brennan and Schwartz [90]) follow Merton [73] in using the value of the firm with geometric Brownian motion as the sole state variable. Brennan and Schwartz [91] and more recently Nyborg [92] and Carayannopoulos [93] included in addition a stochastic interest rate. Brennan and Schwartz and Nyborg assumed the short rate follows a mean-reverting log-normal process; Carayannopoulos assumed the short rate follows the Cox, Ingersoll, and Ross [94] model. Default risk is usually incorporated structurally by capping payouts to the bond by the value of the firm.

Recent literature, on the other hand, mainly uses the stock price as a state variable and either ignores credit risk (Zhu and Sun [95]; Epstein, Wilmott, and Haber [96]; Barone-Adesi, Bermúdez, and Hatgioannides [97]; Bermúdez, and Nogueiras [107]), incorporates it via a credit spread (McConnell and Schwartz [99], Cheung and Nelken [100], Ho and Pfeffer [101]), or models it in a reduced form setting as an exogenously specified default process (see Duffie and Singleton [87]). However, some authors have pointed out (see Schonbucher [102]) that given the hybrid nature of convertibles, asset-based models are the right class to consider in order to account for credit risk. Arvanitis and Gregory [103] implemented and compared both type of models for CB valuation. Bermúdez and Webber [104] proposed an asset-based model that incorporates both endogenous and exogenous default, as well as endogenized recovery.

In the equity-based approach most authors use a single-factor model, although some allow interest rates to be stochastic in addition. The Vasicek [105] or else the extended Vasicek (Hull and White [106]) model is used by Epstein, Haber, and Wilmott [96]; Barone-Adesi, Bermúdez, and Hatgioannides [97], Bermúdez and Nogueiras [107]; and Davis and Lischka [108]. Ho and Pfeffer [101] used the Black, Derman, and Toy [109] model; and Zvan, Forsyth, and Vetzal [110] and Yigitbasioglu [111] used the Cox, Ingersoll, and Ross [94] model. Cheung and Nelken [112] adopted the model developed by Kalotay, Williams, and Fabozzi [113].

Very few authors model the hazard rate stochastically (Davis and Lischka [108], Arvanitis and Gregory [103]). Most recent papers model the hazard rate as a deterministic function of the state variables (also called a quasi-factor or half factor) instead. To model the credit spread as a function of the state variables is very intuitive and appears to provide realistic valuations, sensitivities, and implied parameters, but it does constrain the credit spread to have an explicit relationship with the stock price. This suggests developing a model in which both stock prices and credit spreads follow separate but correlated random processes, as proposed by Davis and Lischka [108]. As these authors point out, although there are three sources of uncertainty—stock price, interest rate and credit spread—more than two factors tend to be avoided for computational tractability. From the implementation point of view, stochastic hazard rates offer the same complexity as stochastic interest rates, given that the dynamics for both processes are often very similar and their role in the valuation PDE is analogous (Duffie and Singleton [87]).

The first authors to have modeled default exogenously, in the spirit of reduced form models, were Davis and Lischka [108] (DL) and later Takahashi, Kobayahashi, and Nakagawa [114] (TKN). They assumed that default occurs at the first jump of a Poisson process, and they modeled the intensity of the jump as a deterministic function of the stock price. They assumed that upon default the stock price jumps to zero. DL modeled the recovery as a constant fraction R of the par value of the bond, whereas TKN modeled recovery as a fraction of the market value of the bond prior to default. However, it can be argued that these approaches penalize the equity upside of the CB. The value of a convertible bond has components of different default risk; the value contributed to the bond by its conversion rights can be argued not to be subject to the same risk treatment as the fixed payments. Therefore, it may be convenient, or even essential, to split the CB value into a bond part and an equity part. In general, the value of the debt and equity components will be linked, and the valuation problem reduces to solving a coupled system of equations. *Splitting models* allow one to apply a different credit regime to the debt and equity components. Moreover, they may be of interest to investors in order to identify different sources of risk and be able to hedge them. How to split the convertible value, though, is an open and controversial matter.

The first authors presenting splitting and writing the model as a coupled system of equations were Tsiveriotis and Fernandes [115] (TF). The value of the equity component and the value of the bond component were discounted differently to reflect their supposed different credit risk. Ayache, Forsyth, and Vetzal [116], [117] (AFV) extended previous literature by proposing a general specification of default in which the stock price jumps by a given percentage η upon default and the issuer has the right either to convert or to recover a given fraction R of the bond part of the convertible. The way they define the bond part is different from the original definition of Tsiveriotis and Fernandes.

We consider a unified framework for pricing convertible bonds incorporating interest rate and credit risk. We assume a jump-diffusion process for the stock price and a mean-reverting process for the interest rate. We model the intensity as a deterministic function of the stock and the interest rate, leading to an extra so-called quasi-factor or half factor. Upon default, the model has an arbitrary loss rate η on the stock price, and an arbitrary default value V^* for the convertible that may be a function of the state variables. The model contains many other models as special cases. We identify most of the previous models, and we show that the main difference between them is the specification of the recovery value.

DL and TKN implement their model in a lattice. TF use explicit finite differences and an explicit algorithm to solve the coupled system of equations. AFV use a modified Crank-Nicolson method combined with a penalty method for the free boundaries and an implicit algorithm to solve the coupled system of equations. In chapter 9 we discretize using a Lagrange-Galerkin method, and use an iterative method to deal with the free boundaries.

In the next section we present the general valuation framework. Section 4.4.3 provides a detailed specification of the model, namely the interest rate model, the hazard rate, the recovery value, and the conversion rights upon default. Also in this section, previous models that are special cases of the general framework are identified. Section 4.4.4 provides the analytical solution for a special bond convertible just at expiry.

4.4.2 The Governing Equation

We follow a standard procedure given, for instance, by Protter [118]. Suppose that the value S_t of the underlying asset follows a jump-augmented geometric Brownian motion under the objective measure, P^*,

$$dS_t = \left(\mu_S - d_t - q_t\right) S_{t_-}\, dt + \sigma_S S_{t_-}\, dZ_t^{S^*} - \eta_t S_{t_-}\, dN_t, \tag{4.2}$$

where $Z_t^{S^*}$ is a standard Brownian motion under P^*, d_t is the continuous dividend yield, and q_t is the repo rate. N_t is a counting process with intensity λ_t^*. η_t is a deterministic loss rate. N_t models exogenous default events. At a jump time τ for N_t the equity value falls by a proportion η_τ,

$$S_\tau = S_{\tau_-}\left(1 - \eta_\tau\right). \tag{4.3}$$

It is well known that the process $v_t^* = \lambda_t^* t$ is the P^*−compensator of N_t, that is, the unique finite-variation previsible process such that $N_t - \lambda_t^* t$ is a martingale under P^*.

Under the equivalent martingale measure (EMM), P, associated with the money market account, $B_t = \exp\left(\int_0^t r_s ds\right)$, the relative price $\frac{S_t}{B_t}$ is a martingale, so

$$dS_t = \left(r_t - d_t - q_t\right) S_{t_-}\, dt + \sigma_S S_{t_-}\, dZ_t^S - \eta_t S_{t_-}\left(dN_t - \lambda_t dt\right), \tag{4.4}$$

where Z_t^S is a standard Brownian motion under P and $v\left(dt\right) = \lambda_t dt$ is the P−compensator of the jump component.

Notice that the setup defined by equation (4.4) is an incomplete market, meaning that there is at least one contingent claim that cannot be hedged. Equivalently, under the assumption of no arbitrage, there is no unique equivalent martingale measure with which to price a contingent claim. However, given that the loss rate, η_t, is deterministic, the market can be completed by adding a defaultable bond issued by the firm whose equity is modeled by S_t.

Let us also assume that the short rate follows the stochastic process

$$dr_t = \mu_r dt + \sigma_r dZ_t^r, \tag{4.5}$$

where μ_r and σ_r are the expected rate of return and volatility of the spot interest rate, which may be functions of the short-rate level as well as time. Z_t^S and Z_t^r are both Brownian motions that may be correlated

$$< dZ_t^r dZ_t^S > = \rho_t dt, \qquad \text{with} \quad -1 \leq \rho_t \leq +1. \tag{4.6}$$

We suppose that the firm has issued a convertible bond with market value V_t. The bond matures at time T with face value F. At any time up to and including time T the bond may be converted to equity. Its value upon conversion at time t is $n_t S_t$, where n_t is the conversion ratio (which may be zero). The bond may be called by the issuer for a call price M_{C_t} and also it may be redeemed by the holder for a put price M_{P_t}. We assume that call and put prices include already accrued interest, which must be paid by the issuer upon call and upon put.

By Ito's lemma (see Jacod and Shiryaev [119]), the process followed by V_t is

$$dV_t = \left(\frac{\partial V_t}{\partial t} + \frac{1}{2}\sigma_S^2 S_t^2 \frac{\partial^2 V_t}{\partial S_t^2} + \rho S_t \sigma_S \sigma_r \frac{\partial^2 V_t}{\partial S_t \partial r_t} + \frac{1}{2}\sigma_r^2 \frac{\partial^2 V_t}{\partial r_t^2} \right.$$

$$\left. + (r_t - d_t - q_t + \lambda_t \eta_t) S_t \frac{\partial V_t}{\partial S_t} + \mu_r \frac{\partial V_t}{\partial r_t} \right) dt$$

$$+ \sigma_S S_t \frac{\partial V_t}{\partial S_t} dZ_t^S + \sigma_r \frac{\partial V_t}{\partial r_t} dZ_t^r + \Delta V(S_{t-})$$

where $\Delta V(S_{t-}) = V_t^*(S_t, t) - V_t(S_{t-}, t)$ and $V_t^*(S_t, t) = V_t^*(S_{t-}(1 - \eta_t), t)$ is the value of the convertible bond if a jump occurs at time t.

Under the EMM the relative price $\frac{V_t}{B_t}$ is a martingale. Imposing this condition, we have

$$r_t V_t = \frac{\partial V_t}{\partial t} + \frac{1}{2}\sigma_S^2 S_t^2 \frac{\partial^2 V_t}{\partial S_t^2} + \rho S_t \sigma_S \sigma_r \frac{\partial^2 V_t}{\partial S_t \partial r_t} + \frac{1}{2}\sigma_r^2 \frac{\partial^2 V_t}{\partial r_t^2}$$

$$+ (r_t - d_t - q_t + \lambda_t \eta_t) S_t \frac{\partial V_t}{\partial S_t} + \mu_r \frac{\partial V_t}{\partial r_t} \qquad (4.7)$$

$$+ \lambda_t \mathbb{E}_{t-} \left[V_t^*(S_t, t) - V_t(S_{t-}, t) \right].$$

Notice that $\lambda_t \mathbb{E}_{t-} \left[V_t^*(S_t, t) - V_t(S_{t-}, t) \right] dt$ is the compensator of the jump $\Delta V(S_{t-})$. When V_t^* is a deterministic function of $S_t = S_{t-}(1 - \eta_t)$, equation (4.7) reduces to

$$(r_t + \lambda_t) V_t = \frac{\partial V_t}{\partial t} + \frac{1}{2}\sigma_S^2 S_t^2 \frac{\partial^2 V_t}{\partial S_t^2} + \rho S_t \sigma_S \sigma_r \frac{\partial^2 V_t}{\partial S_t \partial r_t} + \frac{1}{2}\sigma_r^2 \frac{\partial^2 V_t}{\partial r_t^2}$$

$$+ (r_t - d_t - q_t + \lambda_t \eta_t) S_t \frac{\partial V_t}{\partial S_t} + \mu_r \frac{\partial V_t}{\partial r_t} + \lambda_t V_t^*(S_t, t). \qquad (4.8)$$

Inequality constraints that follow from the optimal conversion, redemption, and call strategies, as defined by Brennan and Schwartz [90], make the convertible bond valuation problem a free-boundary problem that can be formulated as a variational inequality. This is modeled below via a Lagrange multiplier p, which adds or subtracts value to ensure that the constraints are being met.

We will use the notation:

$$\mathcal{L} = \frac{\partial}{\partial t} + \frac{1}{2}\sigma_S^2 S_t^2 \frac{\partial^2}{\partial S_t^2} + \rho S_t \sigma_S \sigma_r \frac{\partial^2}{\partial S_t \partial r_t} + \frac{1}{2}\sigma_r^2 \frac{\partial^2}{\partial r_t^2} \qquad (4.9)$$

$$+ (r_t - d_t - q_t + \lambda_t \eta_t) S_t \frac{\partial}{\partial S_t} + \mu_r \frac{\partial}{\partial r_t}$$

to write the valuation equation in short as

$$p_t = \mathcal{L}V_t - (r_t + \lambda_t) V_t + \lambda_t V_t^*(S_t, t), \qquad (4.10)$$

together with conditions

$$\max \{n_t S_t, M_{P_t}\} \le V_t \le \max \{M_{C_t}, n_t S_t\}, \tag{4.11}$$

$$\max \{n_t S_t, M_{P_t}\} < V_t < \max \{M_{C_t}, n_t S_t\} \implies p_t = 0, \tag{4.12}$$

$$V_t = \max \{n_t S_t, M_{P_t}\} \implies p_t \le 0, \tag{4.13}$$

$$V_t = \max \{M_{C_t}, n_t S_t\} \implies p_t \ge 0. \tag{4.14}$$

If the bond pays coupons discretely, typically every year or half year, let $K(r_t, t_c)$ [10] be the amount of discrete coupon paid on date t_c. Then the following condition must be imposed in order to avoid arbitrage opportunities:

$$V_t\left(r_t, S_t, t_c^-\right) = V_t\left(r_t, S_t, t_c^+\right) + K(r_t, t_c). \tag{4.15}$$

Such discrete cash flows may be incorporated in the governing valuation equation by adding a Dirac delta function term $-K\delta(t - t_c)$ to the RHS of (4.10).

The final condition for the convertible bond is the exercise condition at the maturity time T,

$$V_T(r_T, S_T, T) = \max(n_T S_T, F + K(r_T, T)) = \max\left(n_T S_T, \widetilde{F}\right), \tag{4.16}$$

where we have introduced the adjusted face value $\widetilde{F} = F + K(r_t, T)$.

Solving (4.10) − (4.14) subject to boundary, final, and jump conditions gives the theoretical value of the convertible bond.

Splitting Procedures Given the hybrid nature of convertibles, it is possible and often desirable to split the value V of the convertible into a bond part W and an equity part U. Early models valued CBs by replication as a portfolio of a bond and a warrant. Unfortunately, this approach is limited to the case when the bond is convertible only at expiry and there are no other embedded options, such as call and put features. In general, the two parts are linked and the valuation problem is a coupled system of equations. Splitting models allows a different credit treatment to be applied to the debt and equity parts. This may be of interest to investors in order to identify their risks and be able to hedge them.

Let us assume the value of the bond is split into an equity part U and a bond part W. U is the part related to payments in equity, and therefore includes the conversion and call option. W is related to payments in cash, and includes the coupons and the put option. In general, both are derivatives on the underlying stock price and the instantaneous interest rate, and will follow partial differential equations similar to (4.10) with default values given by W^* and U^*, respectively. The two parts have embedded early exercise features and therefore follow inequalities with Lagrange multipliers p^W and p^U,

$$\mathcal{L}W_t - (r_t + p_t) W_t + \lambda_t W_t^*(S_t, t) = p_t^W, \tag{4.17}$$

$$\mathcal{L}U_t - (r_t + p_t) U_t + \lambda_t U_t^*(S_t, t) = p_t^U. \tag{4.18}$$

---

[10] Most CBs pay fixed coupons. Some pay float, hence $K(r_t, t_c)$.

To be fully specified we need to supply inequality constraints and final conditions to (4.17) and (4.18). At the final time the payoff to the convertible is given by (4.16).

$$V_T(r_T, S_T, T) = \max\left(n_T S_T, \widetilde{F}\right). \qquad (4.19)$$

The splitting determines how V_T is allocated between W_T and U_T. How to decompose the convertible value, or equivalently how to define the bond and equity parts, is an open and controversial matter. Three possible splittings are (see figure 4.13):

- Splitting 1. U_T: asset or nothing call, W_T: cash or nothing put
- Splitting 2. U_T: equity, W_T: equity premium (put)
- Splitting 3. U_T: risk premium (warrant), W_T: bond floor

The motivation of the splitting is to apply a different credit treatment to equity and debt. Originally, in the TF model, the main objective was to use a different discount factor for the debt part and the equity part, such that the bond part is discounted with the risky rate and the equity part with the risk-free rate. The same effect may be achieved without the splitting by modeling the hazard rate as a function of the stock price. However, if we want to use a different recovery in bond and equity, a splitting is necessary in order to define the recovery value of the convertible. It will be mandatory to solve a coupled system of equations only when the default value of the convertible V^* depends explicitly on one or both of the values of the equity part U and the bond part W.

4.4.3   Detailed Specification of the Model

In this section we discuss in detail the remaining components of the model, namely the hazard-rate specification, the recovery value, and the conversion rights upon default.

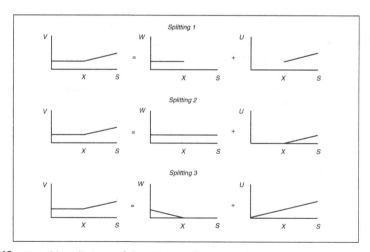

FIGURE 4.13   Possible splittings of the CB payoff at maturity.

TABLE 4.4 Models for the hazard rate

Davis and Lischka [108]	λ_t
Olsen [120] Takahasi, Kobayahashi, and Nakagawa [114] Ayache, Forsyth, and Vetzal [117]	$c + k/S^a$
Arvanitis and Gregory [103]	$k \exp\left[-aS_t + d\right]$
Das and Sundaram [121]	$k \exp\left[br_t + c(T - t) + d\right]/S^a$

The Hazard-Rate Process As an alternative to stochastic hazard rate (chapter 3, Davis and Lischka [108]), herein we may use a deterministic function of the state variables and time. Many parameterizations could be applied; table 4.4 shows some specifications that have been used in the literature. Several authors model the hazard rate as a function of the stock price only, and impose negative correlation via a power or an exponential function. In both specifications the spread is a monotonic decreasing function of the stock price; but only the power function guarantees an infinite hazard rate for zero stock price, which may be a desirable property (see Olsen [120]). Recently Das and Sundaram [121] have combined an exponential dependency on the interest rate with a power dependency on the stock price, and have added the time to maturity. They calibrated the hazard rate using market prices of CDSs and historical data, and they tested this approach empirically by pricing some real convertible bonds. Their results seem very satisfactory. Andersen and Buffum [122] are concerned with the simultaneous calibration of the hazard rates and the volatility smiles; they point out the need to make the hazard rate time dependent to avoid mispricing.

The Recovery Value Regarding the *recovery* of defaultable claims, many models (as reviewed by Schonbucher [102] and Bielecki and Rutowski [124]) have been proposed in the literature: recovery of treasury (RT), recovery of par (RP), multiple defaults (MD), recovery of market value (RMV), zero recovery (ZR) and stochastic recovery.

The RT is very convenient from the computational point of view. The reason is that the price of a defaultable issue under RT is a weighted average of the default-free instrument and the price under zero recovery, which is usually easy to compute. However, the RT can lead to unrealistic shapes of spread curves and lead to recoveries above 100%. The RP and RMV models are similar for issues close to par. The RMV is more consistent for the pricing of credit risk derivatives, but it does less well in pricing downgraded and distressed debt. The RMV is very elegant, in the sense that pricing of financial instruments can be done by discounting with the adjusted defaultable rate $r + \lambda(1 - R)$, where λ is the hazard rate and R is the recovery rate. In RP the pricing is more complicated. Both models are suited for the calibration of the implied credit spreads, although in RMV it is not possible to separate the calibration of the hazard rate, λ, and the loss rate, $(1 - R)$. RMV cannot be used with firm-value models, whereas the RP can be used in intensity-based and firm-value models. Finally, the intuition behind both models is different: the RMV is motivated by the idea of reorganization and renegotiation of debts; the RP is motivated by the idea of bankruptcy proceedings under an authority ensuring strict relative priority.

Suppose default occurs at time τ. We define the recovery value on the CB, V^*, as the sum of the recovery values on the bond and equity parts, W^* and U^*, respectively,

$$V^* = W^* + U^*. \tag{4.20}$$

Conversion Rights upon Default Another issue regarding the default value is whether or not the model should allow for conversion upon default. Realdon [129] showed that it can be rational for CB holders to convert when the debtor approaches distress. In the pricing literature, only AFV allow for conversion upon default. This is consistent with the assumption that the stock price falls on default by a given fraction η and does not necessarily vanish. We adopt their assumption and redefine the bond value upon default as the maximum between the conversion price and the recovery value. In this case the pricing equations can be written as

$$p_t = \mathcal{L}V_t - (r_t + \lambda_t)\,V_t + \lambda_t \max\left\{n_t S_t\,(1-\eta),\,V_t^*\right\}. \tag{4.21}$$

No other models explicitly consider holder rights on default. However, given that DL and TKN assume the stock price jumps to zero upon default, the conversion option is worthless.

Previous Models as Special Cases of General Framework Most of the previous models fit into the general framework presented above. The particular specification of the hazard rate, the loss rate, and the recovery value will determine the difference. We have summarized why in table 4.5.

- Davis and Lischka

    Their equation is a special case of (4.10) for deterministic interest rate, loss rate η equal to 1, and recovery of par.

- Takahasi, Kobayahashi, and Nakagawa

    Their equation is a special case of (4.10) for deterministic interest rate, loss rate η equal to 1, and recovery of market value.

- Tsiveriotis and Fernandes

TABLE 4.5 Comparison of previous models

Model	Loss rate η	Default value $V_\tau^* = U_\tau^* + W_\tau^*$	
		U_τ^*	W_τ^*
TF	0	U_τ	RW_τ
TKN	1	RU_τ	RW_τ
DL	1	0	RF
AFV	η	$(nS_\tau\,(1-\eta) - RW_\tau) \wedge 0$	RW_τ
AFV total default	1	0	0
AFV partial default	0	nS_τ	0

Although TF do not discuss default, and they model credit risk via a credit spread, a posteriori we could identify their model in the more general setting of the previous section. The equation they propose for the total value of the convertible is the one-factor counterpart of (4.10) for zero loss rate, η, constant hazard rate, λ, equal to the credit spread, r_c, and value upon default, V^*, equal to the equity part of the bond, U,

$$\eta_t = 0, \tag{4.22}$$

$$\lambda_t = r_c, \tag{4.23}$$

$$V_t^* = U_t. \tag{4.24}$$

This means that in the event of default the stock price does not jump. Also the bond part vanishes, and therefore the holder is not entitled to any cash flows, but conversion is allowed at any time after default. This was pointed out by AFV.

We would rather give the following interpretation. If we write the credit spread, r_c, as the product of a hazard rate, λ, and a loss rate $1 - R$, where R is the recovery rate on the bond part, it can be easily shown that the default value of the convertible turns out to be $V_t^* (S_t, t) = U_t (S_t, t) + R W_t (S_t, t)$. This means that on default the total equity part is recovered, which is consistent with the fact that the stock price does not jump on default, or equivalently the recovery on equity is one. On the other hand, the recovery on the bond part is not zero. Therefore, TF can be seen as a special case of (4.10) with zero loss rate η and recovery a fraction of bond and equity part.

4.4.4 Analytical Solutions for a Special CB

We consider a special case for which an analytical solution is available: a zero coupon bond, which is convertible only at expiry. It is well known that the value of such a convertible may be written as the sum of the value of the straight bond plus n call options on the underlying stock with strike price $X = F/n$. Indeed

$$\begin{aligned} V (r, S, T) &= \max (nS, F) \\ &= \max(nS - F, 0) + F \\ &= n \max(S - \tfrac{F}{n}, 0) + F. \end{aligned} \tag{4.25}$$

For simplicity, we assume the default value on the bond, V^*, is independent of the state variables, although it may depend on time. This includes, for example, the RP and RT models. Closed-form solution under other recovery models can easily be found. The value of the convertible may be written as

$$\begin{aligned} V (r, S, t) &= F Z (r, t, T) \\ &\quad + n \left(S_t e^{- \int_t^T (d_s - q_s - \lambda_s \eta_s) ds} N (d_1) - X Z (r, t; s) N (d_2) \right) \\ &\quad + \int_t^T \lambda_s V^* (s) Z (r, t; s) SV (t, s) \, ds, \end{aligned} \tag{4.26}$$

where

- $Z(r, t; s)$ is the Vasicek discount factor from time t to time s
- $SV(t, s)$ is the survival probability of the issuer from time t to time s
- And

$$d_1 = \frac{1}{\sqrt{Var}} \ln \left(\frac{S_t e^{-\int_t^T (d_s - q_s - \lambda_s \eta_s) ds}}{X Z (\lambda_t, t; T)} \right) + \frac{1}{2} \sqrt{Var},$$

$$d_2 = d_1 - \sqrt{Var},$$

with

$$Var = \int_0^T \sigma_S^2 (s)\, ds + \int_0^T \sigma_r^2 (s)\, ds + 2 \int_0^T \rho(s)\, \sigma_S(s)\, \sigma_r(s)\, ds.$$

4.5   EXCHANGEABLE BONDS

The valuation of convertible bonds (CBs) under stochastic short-rate models and deterministic hazard rates is well established. In this section we introduce a minor extension that nevertheless introduces an interesting new feature.

We consider the case of a bond that is convertible into stock at the option of the holder, exactly as for a standard CB, but which is issued by an issuer other than the company into whose stock the bond is convertible. Such instruments are known as *exchangeable* bonds.[11] A typical use of this latter structure is for a company to issue bonds convertible into shares of another company in which it already has a stake, thereby reducing its exposure to that stock, and effectively selling its stake in the event that the bond is converted.

The principal new feature for modeling that arises here is the exposure to two credits. The company whose stock underlies the bond can default, or the issuer can default, and the consequences for the bondholder of these two possible defaults are quite different. We do not consider here any correlation between the defaults.

4.5.1   The Valuation PDE

We use the following diffusion processes for the equity and short rate processes:

$$\frac{dS_t}{S_t} = \left(r_t + \lambda_t^S \right) dt + \sigma_t^S dZ_t^S - dN_t$$

$$dr_t = (\theta_t - \kappa_t r_t) dt + \sigma_t^r dZ_t^r$$

$$E\left(dZ_t^S dZ_t^r \right) = \rho(S_t, r_t, t)\, dt,$$

where

---

[11]Or occasionally as *synthetic* convertible bonds.

- r_t is the instantaneous short rate, modeled as a Vasicek process (section 3.3.1).
- σ_t^S is the volatility of the share, which requires calibration as in chapter 8.
- N_t is a Poisson process with a deterministic intensity λ_t^S (hazard-rate function).
- θ_t and κ_t are the long-term mean and mean reversion speed, respectively.
- σ_t^r is the volatility of the short rate.
- Z_t^S and Z_t^r are correlated Wiener processes.
- N_t models exogenous default events of the company that issued the stock. At a jump time for N_t, the share price is assumed to fall to zero.

Let $V(S_t, r_t, t)$ be the price of an exchangeable bond. Since V is subject to two sources of default risk, the issuer and the underlying risk, we introduce λ_t^B for the deterministic hazard rate function of the issuer. $V(S_t, r_t, t)$ then satisfies the following PDE:

$$\frac{\partial V}{\partial t} + \frac{1}{2}\sigma_t^S S_t^2 \frac{\partial^2 V}{\partial S_t^2} + \rho S_t \sigma_t^S \sigma_t^r \frac{\partial^2 V}{\partial S_t \partial r_t} + \frac{1}{2}\left(\sigma_t^r\right)^2 \frac{\partial^2 V}{\partial r_t^2} + \left(r_t + \lambda_t^S\right) S_t \frac{\partial V}{\partial S_t}$$

$$+ (\theta_t - \kappa_t r_t)\frac{\partial V}{\partial r_t} - \left(r_t + \lambda_t^B + \lambda_t^S\right) V + \lambda_t^S R_S(t, r_t) + \lambda_t^B R_B(t) = 0 \qquad (4.27)$$

In (4.27) we introduce the following quantities:

- $R_B(t)$ is the value recovered by the holder in case of default of the issuer: The "recovery value" of the exchangeable bond. We may decompose this value a little, thus

$$R_B(t) = P(t, t + TLP) \times LP$$

in which

— LP is the *liquidation proceeds*: the amount eventually received by the holder, delayed perhaps some while after the default event, by an interval known as the *time to liquidation proceeds*.
— TLP is the *time to liquidation proceeds*: the interval that elapses, or is assumed to elapse for modeling purposes, between the default and the eventual payment of the liquidation proceeds.
— $P(t, t + TLP)$ is the discount factor from the default time t to $t + TLP$.

The liquidation proceeds may in turn be broken down thus:

$$LP = RR \times \left(PP(t) + \text{accrued}\right)$$

in which

— PP is the *principal payable*: the amount due to bondholders in the event of default. It could in principle be a function of time (Original Issue Discount bonds, zero coupon bonds issued at a large discount to par, might have this feature) but will typically be the full notional.

— RR is the *recovery rate*: the fraction of the amount due to a bondholder which the issuer actually pays (or, again, is assumed to pay for the purposes of modelling).

— The accrued is of course the amount accrued, at the time of default, on the coupon accruing at that time.

■ $R_S(t, r_t)$ is the value of the exchangeable bond if the underlying defaults. After the underlying defaults, the exchangeable loses all its equity value (the value due to the holder's conversion right), but the issuer is still obliged to make the coupon and redemption payments. Accordingly, the residue is simply an ordinary bond, although it retains its issuer call feature.

However, the call feature will not have any value once the stock price has dropped to zero: if it is a soft call, then the trigger level will manifestly not be satisfied, and if not, then the call price would, in practice, be set sufficiently high as not to terminate the pure bond without equity content. Hence, $R_S(t, r_t)$ can be approximated by the price of a standard coupon-bearing bond under Vasicek interest rates. Note that this is a risky bond, subject to default of the issuer, with recovery value equal to R_B. The closed-form solution for such a bond is given by

$$R_S(t, r_t) = \sum_i K_i SV^B(t, t_i) P(r, t, t_i)$$
$$+ N \times R \times SV^B(t, T) P(r, t, T)$$
$$+ RV(r, t),$$

where

— $i = 1, ..., N$ runs over the remaining coupons.
— K_i is the coupon amount payable at t_i.
— $SV^B(t, t_i)$ is the survival probability of the issuer from t to t_i.
— $P(r, t, t_i)$ is the zero-coupon bond price seen at time t and maturing at t_i, given r.
— N is the notional.
— R is the redemption factor (generally equal to 1, but greater than 1 for premium redemption bonds).
— $RV(r, t)$ is the expected value of recovery in case of default of the issuer as of time t.

This function depends on time t and the state variable r, so it needs to be evaluated at every node in the FD grid. The recovery contribution to the value of the bond, $RV(r, t)$, is given by

$$RV(r, t) = \int_t^T R_B(s) SV^B(t, s) P(r, t, s) \lambda_s^B ds.$$

4.5.2 Coordinate Transformations for Numerical Solution

In order to use (4.27) directly, the drift term θ_t is needed. The expression for this function involves second derivatives of $P(0, t)$, so a piecewise linear function for $P(0, t)$ (or the yield $R(0, t)$) is not sufficiently smooth. We can transform the problem such that θ_t, or first derivatives of $P(0,t)$, are not required. In this we follow section 3.3.1.

The variable

$$y_t = r_t - f(0,t)$$

is introduced. This follows the process

$$dy_t = (\Sigma(t) - \kappa_t y_t)dt + \sigma_t^r dW_t^r,$$

where $\Sigma(t)$ is the variance of r_t

$$\Sigma(t) = \int_0^t (\sigma_s^r)^2 \exp(2(\Lambda_s - \Lambda_t))ds$$

and

$$\Lambda_{0t} = \int_0^t \kappa_s ds.$$

Since $f(0,t)$ is the expected future short rate in the t–forward measure, PDE grids that remain centered on $y_t = 0$ will always capture the relevant region.

The process for the equity becomes

$$\frac{dS_t}{S_t} = (y_t + f(0,t) + \lambda_t^S)dt + \sigma_t^S dW_t^S - dN_t,$$

which contains the possibly nonsmooth functions $f(0,t)$ and h_t^S. To remove this, we use the variable

$$x_t = \log(SV^S(0,t)P(0,t)S_t/S_0)$$

where $SV^S(0,t)$ is the survival probability of the underlying stock, given by

$$SV^S(0,t) = \exp\left(-\int_0^t \lambda_s ds\right).$$

We have the processes

$$dx_t = (y_t - \tfrac{1}{2}(\sigma_t^S)^2)dt + \sigma_t^S dW_t^S,$$
$$dy_t = (\Sigma(t) - \kappa_t y_t)dt + \sigma_t^r dW_t^r.$$

If $V(S_t, r_t, t) = X(x,y,t)$ the pricing PDE in terms of the x-y variables becomes

$$\frac{\partial X_t}{\partial t} + \frac{1}{2}\sigma_t^S \frac{\partial^2 X_t}{\partial x_t^2} + \rho \sigma_t^S \sigma_t^r \frac{\partial^2 X_t}{\partial x_t \partial y_t} + \frac{1}{2}\left(\sigma_t^r\right)^2 \frac{\partial^2 X_t}{\partial y_t^2} + (y_t - \tfrac{1}{2}(\sigma_t^S)^2)\frac{\partial X_t}{\partial x_t}$$

$$+ (V(t) - \kappa_t y_t)\frac{\partial X_t}{\partial y_t} - \left(y_t + f(0,t) + \lambda_t^B + \lambda_t^S\right)X_t + \lambda_t^S R_S(t,r_t) + \lambda_t^B R_B = 0.$$

This has removed second derivatives of the yield curve (θ_t), and $f(0,t)$ and λ_t^S from the convection (drift) term. However, the PDE still contains $f(0,t)$, λ_t^S and λ_t^B in the reaction (discounting) term. To remove those (and improve convergence in the event of discontinuous forward or hazard rates), we can solve for a deterministically risky discounted form of X, that is,

$$Y(x,y,t) = X(x,y,t)P(0,t)SV^B(0,t)SV^S(0,t) = X(x,y,t)\Psi(0,t)$$

where

$$\Psi(0,t) = P(0,t)SV^B(0,t)SV^S(0,t)$$

This follows the PDE

$$\frac{\partial Y_t}{\partial t} + \frac{1}{2}\sigma_t^S \frac{\partial^2 Y_t}{\partial x_t^2} + \rho\sigma_t^S\sigma_t^r \frac{\partial^2 Y_t}{\partial x_t \partial y_t} + \frac{1}{2}\left(\sigma_t^r\right)^2 \frac{\partial^2 Y_t}{\partial y_t^2} + (y_t - \tfrac{1}{2}(\sigma_t^S)^2)\frac{\partial Y_t}{\partial x_t}$$
$$+ (V(t) - \kappa_t y_t)\frac{\partial Y_t}{\partial y_t} - y_t Y_t + \left(\lambda_t^S R_S(t,r_t) + \lambda_t^B R_B\right)\Psi(0,t) = 0. \tag{4.28}$$

In practice, at every time step from time t_1 to time t_2, with $t_2 < t_1$, we solve for the function

$$\widetilde{Y}(x,y,t) = \frac{Y(x,y,t)}{\Psi(0,t_1)}.$$

Notice that, at a known time step, t_1, we have

$$\widetilde{Y}(x,y,t_{1.}) = X(x,y,t_1).$$

In particular, at maturity

$$\widetilde{Y}(x,y,T) = X(x,y,T);$$

therefore, solving for $\widetilde{Y}$, we do not need to rescale the payoff. The PDE for $\widetilde{Y}(x,y,t)$ becomes

$$\frac{\partial \widetilde{Y}}{\partial t} + \frac{1}{2}\sigma_t^S \frac{\partial^2 \widetilde{Y}}{\partial x_t^2} + \rho\sigma_t^S\sigma_t^r \frac{\partial^2 \widetilde{Y}}{\partial x_t \partial y_t} + \frac{1}{2}\left(\sigma_t^r\right)^2 \frac{\partial^2 \widetilde{Y}}{\partial y_t^2} + (y_t - \tfrac{1}{2}(\sigma_t^S)^2)\frac{\partial \widetilde{Y}}{\partial x_t}$$
$$+ (V(t) - \kappa_t y_t)\frac{\partial \widetilde{Y}}{\partial y_t} - y_t\widetilde{Y} + \left(\lambda_t^S R_S(t,r_t) + \lambda_t^B R_B\right)\frac{\Psi(0,t)}{\Psi(0,t_1)} = 0 \tag{4.29}$$

where

$$\frac{\Psi(0,t)}{\Psi(0,t_1)} = \frac{1}{\Psi(t,t_1)} = \frac{1}{P(t,t_1)SV^B(t,t_1)SV^S(t,t_1)}.$$

After solving this equation between two times t_1 and t_2, we can multiply by the risky discount factor between these two times

$$\Psi(t_2, t_1) = \frac{P(0,t_1)SV^B(0,t_1)SV^S(0,t_1)}{P(0,t_2)SV^B(0,t_2)SV^S(0,t_2)}.$$

This is equivalent to solving for $X(x, y, t)$.

Local Volatility The implied volatility of a European option is affected by both equity volatility and interest rate volatility, and the calibration of the equity local volatility needs to take this into account as described in chapter 8, alongside the possible jump to zero of the stock. This done, the algorithm will correctly reprice European options in the presence of deterministic default.

Implementation The recovery of the exchangeable $R_B(t)$ in the event of issuer default is a function only of time if the *time to liquidation proceeds* is assumed to be zero. Otherwise, it is an approximation to drop the r-dependence. (The same calculation appears in the evaluation of a CB in a deterministic interest rate model, and in the valuation of a straight defaultable bond with recovery in a similar model.)

The value of the exchangeable bond at the time the underlying defaults $R_S(t, r_t)$ enters the PDE (4.29) alongside $R_B(t)$ in the source term

$$\left(\lambda_t^S R_S(t, r_t) + \lambda_t^B R_B \right) \frac{\Psi(0, t)}{\Psi(0, t_1)}.$$

This quantity is evaluated at every point on the r-grid, at every time step.

An Example To make the discussion less abstract, we can consider a real example. In 2004, Banca Monte Dei Paschi Di Siena S.p.a. (Banca MPS) issued a bond convertible into the stock of Banca Nazionale Del Lavoro S.p.a. (BNL). Both are Italian banks listed on the Milan exchange[12]; the former is the world's oldest bank and the latter one of Italy's largest banking groups. Both are, unsurprisingly, good credits: as of late 2005, 5-year Banca MPS credit default swaps traded below 20 bps (basis points), rising to around 25 at ten years; five-year BNL credit default swaps traded around 35 bps, rising to 45 at ten years.

The exchangeable bond in question matures in July 2009; carries a 1% coupon, payable annually; and is convertible at any time after January 15, 2006, and callable by Banca MPS after July 2007, subject to the stock trading above €3.09 for 20 out of the preceding 30 business days. We can compare the valuations obtained for this bond with a hypothetical bond issued by BNL (a marginally worse credit) on its own stock; i.e., a standard convertible. Thus we keep the equity details unchanged in the comparison. Moreover, as the hazard rate appearing in the $\partial/\partial S$ term in (4.27) is that of BNL, the stock drift term is itself unaltered in the comparison.

We also make a recovery assumption: for illustration, we will assume recovery ratios of zero and 30% on default of the issuer. (In the exchangeable case, the separate default of the stock does not need a recovery assumption.) The comparison

---

[12]Reuters codes BMPS.MI and BANI.MI, respectively.

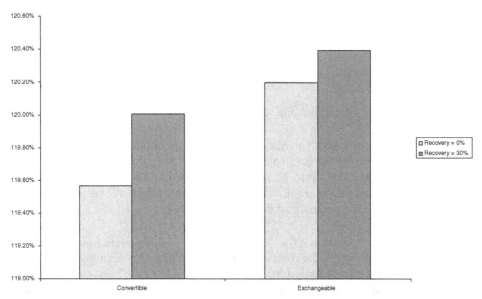

FIGURE 4.14   Prices of exchangeable and hypothetical plain convertible bonds in percent of notional, for zero and 30% recovery assumptions.

is shown in figure 4.14. The better credit of Banca MPS naturally tends to raise the fair price for the exchangeable. We should also bear in mind that the issuer being Banca MPS rather than BNL itself softens the effect of a potential default of BNL, as in the exchangeable case such a default would yield the full value of the coupon-bearing bond to the holder rather than, say, 30% of notional, which would be the case if the issuer were BNL.

CHAPTER 5

Constant Proportion Portfolio Insurance

5.1   INTRODUCTION TO PORTFOLIO INSURANCE

Portfolio insurance is a family of investment strategies designed to give the investor the possibility to limit downside risk while benefiting from rallying markets. These strategies protect the investor from falling markets and allow him to recover his initial capital or less commonly a percentage of it. One well-known portfolio insurance strategy is constant proportion portfolio insurance (CPPI). This was introduced by Perold in 1986 for fixed income instruments and by Black and Jones in 1987 for equity instruments.

In this chapter, we will introduce CPPI and discuss options on CPPI portfolios. CPPI is a trading strategy intended to keep a constant proportional exposure to a certain risky asset while guaranteeing a minimum value of the portfolio throughout its life. Let us define a strategy as a pair of evolving weights $(a(t), b(t))$. The portfolio consists of a risky fund denoted $RF(t)$ and a floor denoted $Floor(t)$. The value of the strategy denoted $CPPI(t)$[1] is then given by

$$CPPI(t) = a(t)RF(t) + b(t)Floor(t).$$

The risky asset could be an equity, commodity, or any other risky underlying. The floor is almost always a bond, either a coupon-bearing bond or a zero bond.

Let us first introduce some standard key words that are commonly used when dealing with CPPIs. Note that this section is essential to the understanding of the rest of the chapter.

CPPI Key Words:

- Floor: The reference level to which the CPPI value is compared; it could be seen as the present value of the protected amount at maturity
- Cushion: CPPI − Floor
- Cushion%: Cushion/CPPI
- Multiplier: A fixed number symbolizing how much leverage we put into the structure; also called the gearing

---

[1]This also referred to as net asset value (NAV).

- InvestmentLevel: The percentage invested in the risky asset portfolio; this is also known as the exposure.

$$= \text{Multiplier} \times \text{Cushion}\%$$

$$e = m \times c$$

Allocation Mechanism The rebalancing of the money between the risky asset and the riskless bond is done in the following way:

The investment level is computed first as follows:

$$IL_t = m \frac{CPPI_t - Floor_t}{CPPI_t}$$

And the CPPI index value is then computed as follows:

$$CPPI_t = CPPI_{t-1} \left[1 + IL_{t-1} \left(\frac{RF_t}{RF_{t-1}} - 1 \right) + (1 - IL_{t-1}) \left(\frac{Floor_t}{Floor_{t-1}} - 1 \right) \right]$$

This algorithm corresponds to the most basic CPPI in which we do not have any special features. This will be discussed in detail in the following sections.

The CPPI itself is a hybrid underlying and needs a hybrid modeling framework in order to account for the various risks embedded in it. The risky asset portfolio could itself be a hybrid, as is the case in most of the strategies on hedge funds and mutual funds. Indeed, hedge funds and especially fund of funds do execute investment strategies that involve different types of underlyings.

Moreover, as we will see in section 5.5, flexi-portfolio CPPIs in general and momentum and rainbow CPPIs in particular can be defined on a basket of hybrid underlyings involving various asset classes ranging from equity to interest rates to credit to commodities.

The remainder of this chapter will be organized as follows. First, we discuss the most basic form of the CPPI, the classical CPPI. We then introduce various restrictions and discuss their impact on the CPPI strategy. Pricing and hedging options on the CPPI index is next. Finally, we introduce some nonstandard CPPIs, namely off-balance-sheet, momentum, and perpetual CPPIs.

5.2 CLASSICAL CPPI

The classical CPPI is a self-financing strategy that rebalances the money between the risky asset and the riskless one, depending on the performance of the former, throughout its life. It has the following characteristics:

- The floor is a zero bond whose redemption is the guaranteed capital.
- No restriction is imposed on the investment level.
- No fees are taken out of the CPPI index (see section 5.3.2).
- No ratcheting (lock-in) is applied to the floor (see section 5.3.2).

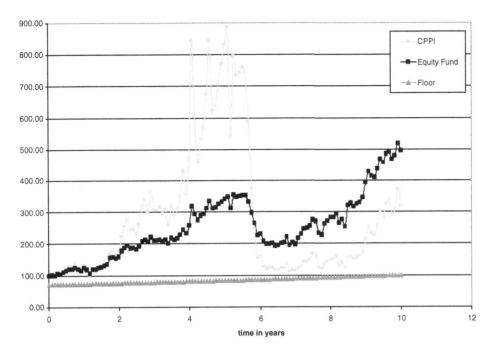

FIGURE 5.1 Example of a simulated CPPI strategy that does not deleverage.

There are other structures that relax the above restrictions and will be discussed later.

When pricing an ATM option on a classical CPPI, the only risk we are dealing with is the gap risk (assuming, of course, that we don't have any liquidity issues).

The Gap Risk In extreme market conditions, the CPPI index could rapidly fall below the floor before the insurance manager has the chance to rebalance his portfolio. The CPPI index will not have a chance to recover, as the investment level will have reached zero and the manager will be unable to repay the guaranteed investment.

It is easily seen that the risky asset has to fall by more than $1/m$ (m being the multiplier) between two rebalancing dates for the CPPI index to drop below the floor. Moreover, the greater the leverage, the greater is the risk on the fund value to drop at a rate proportional to the leverage as the risky asset falls, allowing correspondingly less opportunity to the fund manager to execute the rebalancing. This means that we have a crash put option with a strike of $1-1/m$ embedded in the strategy and the strategy is no longer a delta one[2] strategy.

The graphs in figures 5.1 and 5.2 give examples of simulated outcomes of a classical CPPI strategy: It can be seen from figure 5.2 that any upside gains made by the strategy at the beginning fade away as soon as the risky asset drops, the investment level can become zero, and the strategy will not recover. A series of restrictions may be added to the classical CPPI strategy in order to allow the investor

---

[2]A delta one product is a product whose payoff is linear in the underlying risky asset, a product whose risk could be hedged entirely by the risky asset.

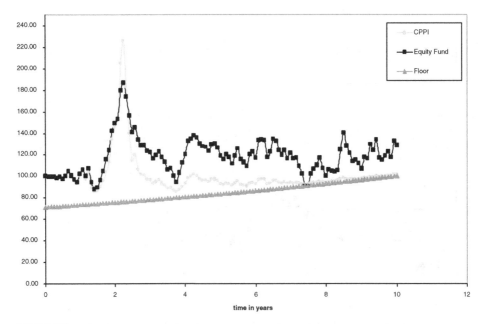

FIGURE 5.2   Example of a simulated CPPI strategy that deleverages completely.

to benefit from any upsides whenever they happen, even in cases where the classical CPPI would have completely deleveraged.

The Continuous Time Classical CPPI   If we consider a continuous time strategy with no constraints on the floor or investment level, the pricing of options on a CPPI resembles the one of power options. To illustrate this, let's call V_t and F_t the values of the CPPI index and the floor at time t, respectively. We can therefore write

$$dV_t = (V_t - E_t)\frac{dF_t}{F_t} + E_t\frac{dS_t}{S_t}$$

where we have $V_0 = 1$, $F_{maturity} = 1$, $V_t = C_t + F_t$, $E_t = mC_t$ and $dF_t = rF_t dt$, where C_t is the cushion at time t. The variation of the latter is given by:

$$dC_t = dV_t - dF_t$$

$$= (V_t - E_t)\frac{dF_t}{F_t} + E_t\frac{dS_t}{S_t} - dF_t$$

Assuming that the risky asset S_t is log-normal, $dS_t = S_t\left(\mu dt + \sigma dW_t\right)$, we have the following result[3]

$$C_t = \alpha_t S_t^m$$

$$\alpha_t = \frac{C_0}{S_0^m}\exp\left(\beta t\right), \text{ where } \beta = r - m\left(r - \frac{\sigma^2}{2}\right) - \frac{m^2\sigma^2}{2}$$

---

[3] See appendix B for details of the computation.

Finally, the value of the portfolio is given by

$$V_t = \alpha_t S_t^m + F_t$$

This result means that in the limit of continuous trading an option on the CPPI strategy is nothing other than a power option on the risky asset. However, the rebalancing in most CPPI strategies is not continuous, and moreover most of them contain one or more restricting features. In the next section we present the most common restrictions imposed on the classical CPPI strategy.

5.3   RESTRICTED CPPI

The traditional CPPI strategy can be restricted or modified depending on the appetite and whim of the investor. In this section, we examine some of the modifications that may be made. Typically, these are motivated by risk aversion, legal constraints, or performance.

5.3.1   Constraints on the Investment Level

In this section, we depart from the classical CPPI by introducing restrictions on the fraction of the fund that may be invested in the risky asset, and we look briefly at the implications on the CPPI and ATM options on the CPPI.

Minimum Investment Level As mentioned previously, if the risky asset falls substantially and the investment level becomes zero, there is no chance for the strategy to recover. To allow the strategy to pick up from a downturn, a minimum level of investment in the risky asset may be imposed (also called minimum delta).

From the graph in figure 5.3 we can see that the CPPI index is not guaranteed to end above par due to the minimum investment level restriction. This risk of not recovering the initial investment implies that the value of an ATM option on the CPPI index will increase. Indeed, the increase in the probability of not guaranteeing the initial capital will increase the option value.

Maximum Investment Level A maximum investment level is sometimes imposed on the CPPI strategy in order to reduce the gap risk and avoid an unbounded leverage. In a classical CPPI, as the risky asset rises, the investment level becomes greater and greater (the gearing effect) and the CPPI index becomes more like the pure risky asset. As an example, in the case of the underlying risky asset being a mutual fund or a basket of mutual funds, the investment level is capped at 100% due to legal restrictions.

5.3.2   Constraints on the Floor

In the previous section, the implications of restrictions on the investment level were considered. Restrictions or modifications may also be placed on the other component of the CPPI fund, the floor. We examine those in the current section.

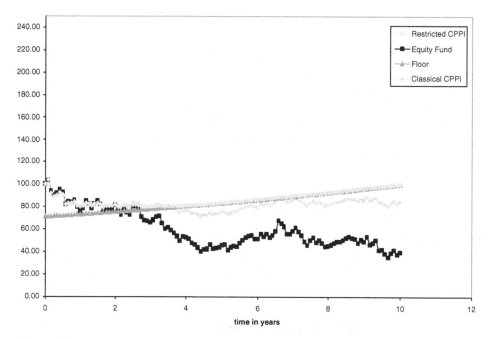

FIGURE 5.3   Example of a CPPI strategy with a minimum investment level of 30%.

Ratcheting   When the market rallies, any gains made by the CPPI strategy could be lost if a downturn occurs. Therefore, the investor is not guaranteed to benefit from those gains. Ratcheting is introduced to allow the investor to lock in gains made from upside movements of the market.

Ratcheting operates as follows: Whenever the CPPI strategy performs well and reaches a new maximum, a percentage RP of that maximum is guaranteed to the client (we say that we ratchet at $RP\%$). This raising of the floor of the strategy reduces the exposure to the risky asset, introduces a lookback effect to the strategy, and adds, in some cases, more vega to the option by increasing the gap risk.

If we compare figures 5.2 and 5.4, we can see the benefit of ratcheting to the investor. In these graphs, we have looked at the same simulated paths of the risky asset and the guaranteed amount with ratcheting is far bigger than without. In the former case, the floor remains at a low level while on the latter it is raised, taking advantage of the sharp rise in the risky asset early in the life of the strategy.

Protected Fees   When an investment manager manages a portfolio such as a CPPI strategy for a client, he will be paid some fees in one way or another depending on the performance of the portfolio. Distributors to retail market also get paid fees for the service.

In the case of a CPPI strategy, fees are usually taken from the CPPI index, but there are cases in which they are taken from the risky asset portfolio. They, then, are equivalent to a proportional dividend on the CPPI index paid at each rebalancing date. These fees are cash amounts paid to the fund manager or to the investor. From the perspective of the investor they are effectively coupons.

Usually, the fees continue to be paid out from the CPPI index even if the latter drops close to or below the floor. This penalizes the CPPI portfolio, as it is likely to

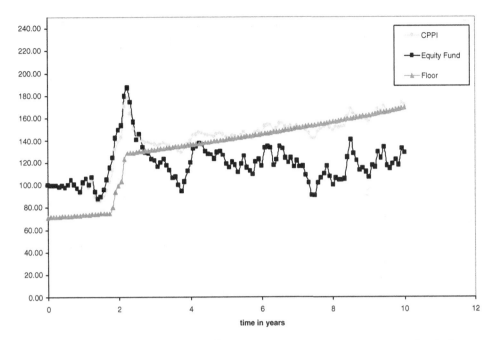

FIGURE 5.4   Effect of ratcheting on a CPPI strategy with minimum investment level of 30%.

end up below par in the case of a classical CPPI, for example. The remedy for this is to protect the fees.

When the fees of the strategy are protected, they are often added back to the floor and the latter then becomes a coupon-bearing bond instead of a zero bond. This lowers the investment level, lowers the leverage, and reduces the value of an ATM CPPI option (it is like raising the strike level), which means less gap risk.

Straight-Line Floor   Investors wanting to benefit from a drop in interest rates might prefer a straight-line floor, one that varies linearly with time and so does not correspond to a bond as in the classical case. Indeed, as interest rates fall, a bond floor rises and the investment level reduces, which limits the benefit from the risky asset performance (negative correlation between equity and bond prices, when the equity market is doing badly the interest rates are in general cut to boost the economy, inducing a rise in bond prices). Accordingly, stochasticity of interest rates plays a role in the pricing of options on the CPPI index.

In cases in which the investor is relying on an early exit from the strategy, a straight-line floor proves to be effective, as he or she knows with certainty what the level of the floor will be at any time because the floor is insensitive to interest rates.

5.3.3   An Example Structure

We consider the structure outlined in figure 5.5 and whose term sheet is presented in section 5.8, appendix C. The risky underlying is Eurostoxx50E and the riskless asset is a coupon bond (protected fees). The ratcheting is applied during the first five years at 100% (to invite more subscriptions) and at 85% thereafter (see section 5.3.2 for more details on ratcheting).

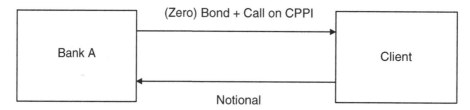

FIGURE 5.5 Example of CPPI structure.

5.4 OPTIONS ON CPPI

5.4.1 The Pricing

The pricing is done within the framework presented in chapter 3, concerning interest rate hybrids. We can add jumps to this framework to account for the gap risk. A Monte Carlo simulation of the strategy is performed. The complexity of the structure imposes the use of different models depending on the risks embedded in the structure.

Indeed, depending on the nature of the underlying risky asset (e.g., a hedge fund vs. a well-known index), the bond floor (emerging markets currency vs. USD or EUR, for example), and the various features contained in the contract, the structure could, for example, be very sensitive to the volatility of interest rates, to jumps in the risky asset, or to both.

Therefore, the model used to price an option on a CPPI index could vary from one structure to another depending on the risks embedded in each structure, as explained above.

5.4.2 Delta, Gamma, and Vega Exposures

An option on a classical CPPI strategy is not a delta one product, as the gap risk introduces optionality. As soon as we introduce restrictions (and fees) on the strategy, we introduce even more optionality. A similar conclusion could be drawn about the vega exposure. Indeed, the vega of an option on a classical CPPI is not zero, precisely because of gap risk, and as soon as we introduce restrictions, we usually increase the vega exposure.

Dividends affect the strategy in a similar way to fees, with the difference being that the dividends are taken only from the risky asset rather than from the CPPI index. This lowers the forward of the strategy, because the risky asset drops, and introduces more vega.

The frequency of rebalancing in a CPPI strategy could be different from the hedging frequency (e.g., monthly rebalancing versus daily hedging), and this creates a large gamma exposure when approaching rebalancing dates.

5.4.3 Hedging

Classical CPPI, if managed correctly and continuously, will always end up at or above the guaranteed level, except if downward jump occurs. An ATM European put on a classical CPPI will not have any value and therefore any greeks. A model incorporating jumps in the risky asset, such as Merton's jump-diffusion model [4] is the only way to price this option (i.e., price the gap risk).

Risk management becomes more qualitative than quantitative. In many cases it is difficult to hedge the greeks given by the model (when the risky asset is hedge funds, mutual funds, etc.). In the case where the CPPI is managed by a third party, the risk manager must ensure that the manager of the CPPI stays within the limits so that the CPPI does not carry additional risk beyond the unavoidable gap risk.

Gap risk can be hedged by selling *stability notes*. These are basically a series of knock-out OTM Cliquet puts (see section 2.1.6 for more details about Cliquet structures) with a resetting frequency matching that of the CPPI (i.e., daily, weekly, monthly). So the implied gap risk is redefined as a Cliquet put.

In the following section, we depart further from the classical CPPI and present some nonstandard CPPI strategies that use techniques borrowed from the asset management world.

5.5 NONSTANDARD CPPIs

The CPPI strategy is an innovation that comes from the asset management perspective. People often refuse to think of it as a derivative product, and this is why several features, characteristics, and ways of thinking are inspired from there. The fee structure we present here is just an another example of emulating what is done within the fund industry.

5.5.1 Complex Fee Structures

High-Water-Mark Fee Structure The initial motivation behind the development of this strategy is the fact that clients are used to dealing with fund managers who are paid on the relative performance of the fund over a certain period, a year in general, which is well known in the hedge fund industry as *high-water mark*.[4] In this strategy, at every rebalancing date we lock in the highest performance of the CPPI index, and the incentive fees are paid only if the new index level is higher than the previous locked in value. Extra fees are taken on a regular basis, accounting for administrative and running expenses.

The CPPI algorithm looks like

$$CPPI_t = CPPI_{t-1} \left(\frac{RA_t}{RA_{t-1}} \times IL_{t-1} + \frac{B_t}{B_{t-1}} (1 - IL_{t-1}) - f^r \Delta t \right)$$
$$- f^i \left(\text{lockin}_t - \text{lockin}_{t-1} \right)^+$$
$$\text{lockin}_t = \max \left(\text{lockin}_{t-1}, CPPI_t \right), \ \text{lockin}_0 = CPPI_0$$

where f^r and f^i denote the running and incentive fees, respectively, and RA_t, B_t, and IL_t denote the values of the risky asset, bond floor, and the investment level, respectively, at a given time t.

---

[4] See section 5.8, appendix A for the definition of *high-water mark*.

Similar to the high-water mark fee structure, structures exist in which the fees are tied to the investment level rather than the CPPI index. The philosophy behind this choice is basically to make the asset manager's earnings linked only to the risks he manages and not to the riskless part of the fund; it is a risk-reward approach.

5.5.2 Dynamic Gearing

The multiplier serves as a leveraging and deleveraging tool and is fixed, in general, for the life of the strategy. Its value is usually between 2.5 and 6, depending on the risky asset. Ideally, one would like to leverage more when the risky asset portfolio is performing well and less for the opposite scenario. This is achieved by exploiting the anticorrelation between the volatility and the performance of the asset, and considering the multiplier as a decreasing function of the realized volatility over a certain period of time (one month in general).

As an example, we can define the multiplier as follows:

$$m_t = \min \left(cap, \frac{1}{Vol_t} \right)$$

where Vol_t is the monthly realized volatility for the period $[t - 1month, t]$.

This would decrease the multiplier for a falling market and would prevent it from reaching very high levels in case of a rallying market thanks to the introduction of a cap.

5.5.3 Perpetual CPPI

A perpetual CPPI is, as its name suggests, a strategy in which there is no maturity. This means that the asset manager will be paid a minimum fee even if the strategy does not perform. If the strategy deleverages, no fees are paid until the index bounces back. In case of a massive drop (gap risk), the manager bears the risk and has to ensure that the index is back to the floor level. Then, the index grows, say, at the money market rate and the income generated by the protection asset is put into the risky asset, and the index starts to leverage again, but slowly.

Any early gains made by the strategy are locked in and could be cashed in at any time; hence, this strategy is also known as a *fixed threshold strategy*. This is advantageous compared to the standard ratcheting strategy in which the client has to wait until maturity to benefit from the performance of the CPPI index. This does, of course, come at a cost as the investor puts some capital at risk as the floor stays at the same level in the case of continuous underperformance of the index.

The CPPI (fund) is an open-end[5] structure (fund) that terminates only if the client unsubscribes from the fund or there is not enough money under management. In practice, the fixed threshold strategy is likely to terminate the first time it drops to or below the floor level as the speed of bouncing back is hindered by the fact that it relies on the money market growth for it to leverage again.

The investor avoids interest rate risk by being sure of the amount that he or she is going to cash in at a given time (after any lock-in, the floor is a horizontal line, that is, constant in time), and the only interest rate risk could come from the fact that the underlying risky asset is itself sensitive to the volatility of interest rates.

---

[5]See appendix A for a definition of open-end fund.

5.5.4 Flexi-Portfolio CPPI

Actively Managed CPPIs An actively managed fund is a fund in which the risky asset and floor portfolios can change during its life. This is the case for most hedge funds and mutual funds. This means that the asset manager has some freedom in the choice of the underlyings in which to invest. He remains, however, subject to regulatory constraints, especially for mutual funds, as they are typically required to limit their exposure to high-risk assets in order to avoid spectacular losses, as sometimes occurs for hedge funds. However, the asset manager does not have any constraints when it comes to picking his risky portfolio as long as the latter remains within the horizon defined by the regulator or investment guidelines. (See the example of investment guidelines in section 5.8, appendix C.)

An example of actively managed CPPI is the *flexi-basket CPPI*, which is a strategy where the underlying risky asset is a basket whose underlyings are chosen from a horizon of names. The idea is similar to the cheapest-to-deliver concept, where you do not specify the name of the bond you deliver. The selection of the basket is left to the fund manager, who does the rebalancing of the CPPI portfolio. This enables the asset manager to select the stocks or funds that he or she believes will perform better, taking advantage of the information available during the life of the strategy.

As opposed to actively managed funds or CPPIs where the risky underlying is not known beforehand or can change throughout the life of the strategy, passively managed funds are tied to a predefined set of underlyings that constitute the risky asset portfolio.

Passively Managed CPPIs Passively managed funds follow a predefined investment strategy. The fund manager is literally executing an algorithm, which is designed to take advantage of the performances of the assets in a predefined basket. In what follows, we present the momentum and rainbow CPPI strategies, where the allocation mechanism within the risky portfolio is done following the concept of the classical equity structures, momentum, and rainbow.

Momentum CPPI An example of a momentum structure is an option written on an exotic basket of underlyings, whose payoff at maturity is equal to the initial capital invested plus a geared performance of the underlying basket above some reference level.

Note that we mean by performance the value of the asset at some time in the future compared to its value at the last rebalancing date before this time.

The momentum CPPI is based on the momentum structure philosophy and is intended to imitate the asset manager's behavior and way of payment. Indeed, at each rebalancing date, say monthly, the risky asset of the CPPI is calculated as a weighted sum of the performances, above some reference level, of the various underlyings in the basket. A large weight is assigned to the best performer, the following largest weight to the next-best performer, and the smallest weight to the worst performer. The reference level is in general a one-month interest rate future.

Considering a basket of n underlyings $(S_i)_{1 \leq i \leq n}$ and a vector of n ordered weights (w_i) such that $w_n \leq w_{n-1} \leq \cdots \leq w_1$, the risky asset value at a given time t

is given by

$$RF_t = RF_{\varphi(t)} \sum_{i=1}^{n} w_i \frac{S_t^{(i)}}{S_{\varphi(t)}^{(i)}}$$

where $\varphi(t)$ is the last rebalancing date before t and $S^{(i)}$ is the the underlying asset with the *ith* performance at time $\varphi(t)$.

Note that if the performance of the underlyings in the basket are below the reference level, they are replaced by the reference level (Libor, Euribor, etc.).

The rebalancing of the momentum CPPI is then done similarly to the classical case in which we have one underlying.

Another strategy similar to the momentum CPPI is the *rainbow CPPI*. The idea of the rainbow CPPI strategy is likewise based on the classical rainbow structure. The difference between the two strategies, momentum and rainbow, is the fact that in the latter the weights are set and used on the same rebalancing date, whereas in the momentum CPPI, they are set on the previous rebalancing date.

These two structures are very sensitive to the correlation and are appealing for clients who believe in trends. We can incorporate all the features mentioned before, namely ratcheting and minimum investment level, to make the investor benefit from the potential gains made by the strategy at different times throughout its life.

The underlying basket for these structures could range from an all-equity basket to a very diversified one containing, for example, a fixed income index, an equity index, a foreign exchange index, a commodity underlying, a mutual fund, and a hedge fund. Note, however, that in case of small or medium-sized mutual funds or hedge funds, being constituents of the momentum basket, these strategies can disrupt the fund management if the amounts traded are large compared to the size of the funds. For example, if a good performance of the underlying fund in one period is followed by a sharp drop in its value in the next, then the algorithm requires the CPPI manager to buy and then sell a substantial fraction of the fund. This will create serious disruptions within the fund if the amounts traded are substantial compared to the fund's size.

The above strategy ideas could be extended to accommodate some other popular exotic structures containing "worst-off" and/or "best-off" features. The innovation in this field is very rapid in an attempt to respond to the variety of investors and their risk appetites.

5.5.5 Off-Balance-Sheet CPPI

An off-balance-sheet CPPI is a CPPI strategy managed entirely by a third party. The client is guaranteed a payoff that depends on a fund managed by somebody else, where the latter executes a CPPI algorithm (see Figure 5.6). The liability is there but the assets are not on the books, hence the term *off balance sheet*.

Regulatory requirements have in part been behind the introduction of this family of CPPIs. Indeed, asset managers and pension fund managers are not allowed to call a fund, portfolio, or product *capital guaranteed* unless it is really true for all cases. Those institutions are not allowed or unwilling to take the gap risk so they buy the guarantee from outside.

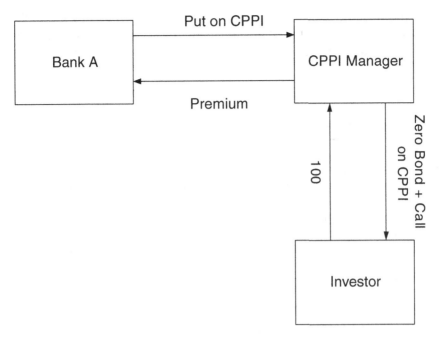

FIGURE 5.6 Example of off-balance-sheet CPPI structure.

On the other hand, after the collapse of Enron and WorldCom, the U.S. accounting standards for derivatives were changed. Profits cannot be taken up front unless they are 100% locked in. A party who sold a CPPI can take the management fees only on an ongoing basis rather than up front, as the structure still bears the gap risk. A purchase of the protection enables the manager of the CPPI to show the profits up front, as all potential risks have been hedged out.

Hedging such exposure is quite tricky, as it is not always easy to trade the underlying fund. Risk management becomes more qualitative than quantitative. In many cases, the manager is not able to hedge the greeks given by the model (e.g., when the risky asset is a hedge fund, mutual fund, etc.). The risk manager must furthermore ensure that the manager of the CPPI stays within the limits so that CPPI does not carry more risk than the gap risk.

A clear reporting line with the CPPI manager needs to be established. The guarantor provides the CPPI manager with the theoretical exposure coming out of the CPPI algorithm, and the CPPI manager must report its portfolio allocation to the guarantor.

In case of early redemption, *break clauses* need to be negotiated between the guarantor and the CPPI manager. Should the manager not follow the instructions of the guarantor, the guarantee is canceled.

Off-balance-sheet CPPIs can be offered in different forms:

- European or American put on the CPPI
- Bank guarantee on the fund following a CPPI algorithm
- An option embedded in the fund

Usually, the value of the CPPI at time 0 is protected, except when the CPPI strategy contains a ratcheting feature implying a profit lock-in in case the strategy performs well. Then the guarantor guarantees at maturity the amount: LockIn(maturity) − CPPI(maturity).

5.6   CPPI AS AN UNDERLYING

The popularity of the CPPI strategies in the marketplace, the growth of the hedge fund community, and the familiarity of investors with the strategy have resulted in the birth of complex structures treating the CPPI strategy as an underlying itself.

TARNs (target redemption notes, section 4.3) on CPPI are a popular structure. Momentum- and rainbow- type structures can have CPPI indices as their underlyings, to mention a few. Basically, any exotic structure written on classical underlyings, be it equity, interest rates, credit, funds, or commodities could be extended to incorporate CPPI strategies.

5.7   OTHER ISSUES RELATED TO THE CPPI

5.7.1   Liquidity Issues (Hedge Funds)

When a hedge fund is considered as the risky underlying for the CPPI strategy, liquidity issues have to be taken into account, as there is sometimes a large asymmetry in the settlement dates between a buyer and a seller. A buyer settles at $T + 5$ (meaning that settlement occurs 5 days after the agreement) whereas a seller would settle at $T + 30$ or $T + 60$. This makes life difficult for the CPPI manager, as he has to rebalance his portfolio, say, quarterly. This is not an issue when we deal with standard underlyings, as there is no asymmetry and all parties settle at $T + 2$.

Note that the settlement periods mentioned here are just examples for illustration.

5.7.2   Assets Suitable for CPPIs

The classical CPPI is by nature a self-financing strategy that performs a rebalancing of the underlying portfolio throughout its life, which makes the investor exposed to the realized volatility rather than implied volatility. Therefore, assets with high implied volatility compared to realized volatility are good underlyings for the CPPI strategy. In general, upward trending assets with low volatility (e.g., funds) and no cyclicality are prime candidates as underlyings for a CPPI strategy.

In the case of emerging markets where no mature option market exists, a CPPI strategy is a good instrument that gives access to the upside with very small vega exposure (mainly gap risk). It needs, however, to be engineered, taking into account liquidity constraints and country-specific risk. Diversification is always desirable in order to lower the volatility and the risk of quick deleveraging.

5.8 APPENDIXES

5.8.1 Appendix A

In this section, we give some background on the various types of hedge funds, which are classified based on their investment strategies. Thereafter, we give definitions of some keywords widely employed within the fund community.

Types of Hedge Funds **Merger arbitrage:** Funds involved in event-driven investments such as mergers and acquisitions and leveraged buy-outs, taking advantage of the fact that the stock of a target company rises and the stock of a buying company depreciates.

High yield: Funds specializing in securities whose underlying companies are in difficulty, which could range from corporate restructuring to inability to honor payments to complete bankruptcy. These funds enter into investment strategies that involve taking opportunistic positions in debt, stock, and credit derivatives on the company.

Convertible arbitrage: This involves managing a portfolio of convertible bonds and hedging the interest rate exposure and equity risk by buying or selling the securities in question (e.g., bonds, stocks).

Fixed income relative value: Funds in which managers try to take advantage of price inefficiencies and mispricings between a related set of fixed income securities and neutralize any interest rate exposure.

Equity arbitrage: Similar to fixed income relative value funds, equity arbitrage fund managers seek to profit from price ineffencies between a related set of equity instruments while neutralizing the risk to directional market movements.

Macro arbitrage: Managers of these funds make forecasts about the shift in world economies and anticipate movements in stock markets, fixed income securities, interest rates, inflation, and foreign exchange due to political changes and global shifts in supply and demand of commodities.

Fund Keywords **Open-end fund:** Holding a share in an open-end fund is like holding a stock. This is the most common structure, and deals are done on a stock exchange and in a secondary market.

Closed-end fund: A hedge or mutual fund that has stopped accepting subscriptions from investors, at least temporarily, and are traded on a secondary market only by professionals.

Fund of funds: An investment vehicle consisting of shares in various hedge or mutual funds. The vehicle could have a strategy focus, the underlying funds following a given investment strategy, or a diversified one in which the fund managers have different strategies. An investment in a fund of funds offers many structural benefits compared to one in a classic hedge or mutual fund. Indeed, funds of funds offer more transparency and provide frequent portfolio updates. The barrier to entry is another advantage, with levels of minimum investment many times less than single funds being very common. The fee structure is in general complex, as the investor has to pay the incentive and running fees for both the fund of funds and the underlying funds.

Prime brokerage: Large financial institutions often have a prime brokerage group that is dedicated to providing hedge funds with administrative, back-office, and financing services. Other services like providing offices, infrastructure, and initial capital are sometimes offered to help fund managers start their business.

Master feeder fund: A common structure in the United States through which a fund can run two funds, one onshore for U.S.-based investors and another one offshore for non-U.S.-based investors. The underlying funds are called feeder funds, and the father entity is called the master fund. This is created to allow U.S. and non-U.S. investors to have participation in a single fund.

Drawdown: The percentage difference between the maximum and minimum asset values of a fund over a certain period. It is often used as a measure of the risk of a fund.

High-water mark: This is a provision that ensures that the asset manager receives incentive fees only for real profits. He is, in fact, paid only on the basis of the performance attained above the highest net asset value realized previously.

Hurdle rate: The minimum return required from the asset manager. The latter receives incentive fees only for the extra return above it.

Sharpe ratio: Introduced by William R. Sharpe, this is the extra return, above the risk-free one, realized by a fund in units of the risk taken. It is calculated as the difference between the average annualized return and the risk-free rate divided by the annualized volatility of the fund.

Venture capital: Also called capital risk, this is money given to starting funds (start-ups in general) that seek high-return investments.

5.8.2 Appendix B

In this section, we give more details about the computations for the continuous time strategy. Recall that: $V_0 = 1$, $F_{maturity} = 1$, $V_t = C_t + F_t$, $E_t = mC_t$ and $dF_t = rF_t dt$.

The change in V_t and C_t is given by the following equations:

$$dV_t = (V_t - E_t)\frac{dF_t}{F_t} + E_t\frac{dS_t}{S_t}$$

$$dC_t = (V_t - E_t)\frac{dF_t}{F_t} + E_t\frac{dS_t}{S_t} - dF_t$$

The log-normality of the risky asset implies

$$dC_t = (C_t + F_t - mC_t)\frac{dF_t}{F_t} + mC_t\left(\mu dt + \sigma dW_t\right) - dF_t$$

$$= (C_t - mC_t)\,rdt + mC_t\left(\mu dt + \sigma dW_t\right)$$

$$= C_t\left[(1 - m)\,r + \mu m\right]dt + m\sigma\,dW_t.$$

Therefore,

$$C_t = C_0 \exp\left(\left[(1-m)\,r + \mu m - \frac{m^2\sigma^2}{2}\right]t + m\sigma\,W_t\right).$$

On the other hand, we know that

$$S_t^m = S_0^m \exp\left(\left[\mu m - \frac{m\sigma^2}{2}\right]t + m\sigma\,W_t\right).$$

From these two results we can conclude that

$$C_t = \alpha_t S_t^m$$

$$\alpha_t = \frac{C_0}{S_0^m}\exp(\beta t)\,,\text{where }\beta = r - m\left(r - \frac{\sigma^2}{2}\right) - \frac{m^2\sigma^2}{2}.$$

Finally,

$$V_t = \alpha_t S_t^m + F_t.$$

5.8.3 Appendix C

Example of Matrix of Investment Guidelines

Local Limitations

Name	Bloomberg	Maximum Allocation	Minimum Allocation
EMI Index France	GPEMIFR FP Equity	50%	0%
Groupama France Stock	GPINFRA FP Equity	50%	0%
Groupama Croissance	GRPCRSS FP Equity	50%	0%
EMI Index Euro	GPEMIEU FP Equity	50%	0%
Groupama Euro Stock	GPACFRA FP Equity	50%	0%
Euro Gan	EURGNSV FP Equity	50%	0%
Groupama Avenir Euro	FIGRAVE FP Equity	25%	0%
Actions Nouvelle Europe	GRPAMOR FP Equity	20%	0%
Groupama Actions Internationales	GPACINT FP Equity	80%	0%
Groupama Actions Mid Cap US	GPACMUS FP Equity	25%	0%
Groupama US Stock	FIFINUS FP Equity	50%	0%
Groupama ASIE	GRPASIE FP Equity	20%	0%
Actions Croissance Japan	FIACROJ FP Equity	50%	0%
Groupama Japan Stock	NPPNGAC FP Equity	50%	0%
Groupama Euro Crédit MT	FIOBECR FP Equity	25%	0%
Groupama Euro Crédit LT	GPOBLIF FP Equity	25%	0%
Groupama Institutions LT	GRINSLT FP Equity	100%	20%
Groupama Index Inflation LT	GRINILT FP Equity	100%	0%

Name	Bloomberg	Maximum Allocation	Minimum Allocation
Groupama US Etat LT	GRGETLT FP Equity	100%	20%
Groupama Etat Monde LT	GRPCAPT FP Index	100%	20%
Groupama Alternatif Equilibre	GRALTEQ FP Equity	15%	0%
Global Limitations			
Emerging Markets Equity		20%	0%
North America Equity		50%	0%
Developed Europe Equity		50%	0%
Japan/Developed Asia Equity		50%	0%
High Yield (emerging markets, credit, etc.)		25%	0%
Equity in Total		80%	0%
Equity (mid-cap, small cap)		25%	0%
Fixed Income (investment grade)		100%	20%

Example Term Sheet   An example term sheet is given on the following two pages.

Principal Protected Note on CPPI on Stoxx50E

Indicative Terms and Conditions   CPPI invests in the reference asset (the underlying fund(s)) and a reserve asset (zero-coupon bond). The allocation between the two is done on a monthly basis following the allocation mechanism. If the CPPI increases in value, it will invest more in the reference asset to increase leverage. If the CPPI decreases in value, it will invest less in the reference asset to protect the capital.

Summary of Terms and Conditions

Issuer	Deutsche Bank AG, London
Currency	EUR
Maturity	10 years
Notional	10,000,000 EUR
Business Days	London, modified following
Calculation Agent	Deutsche Bank AG, London
Payoff at maturity	$Notional + Notional$

$$* Max\left(0, \frac{MAX(CPPI_{final}, LockIn_{final})}{CPPI_0} - 100\%\right)$$

CPPI on the Stoxx50E

Description of CPPI   The CPPI consists of two components: (a) the reference asset and (b) the reserve asset, in different proportions, as determined and computed by the calculation agent. The allocation between (a) and (b) will be performed daily and determined by the allocation mechanism. The allocation will be adjusted to protect the CPPI on the downside and to provide return on the upside.

Sponsor	Deutsche Bank AG, London
Business Days	London, modified following
Composition	The index will consist of: The reference asset and the reserve asset
Reference Asset	Stoxx50E index
Reserve Asset	EUR-denominated zero-coupon bond
Allocation	Means, in relation to an index business day, the proportion of the index invested in the reference asset
Mechanism	("investment level"). The investment level is a function of the distance between the current index level and the protected amount. The index sponsor will adjust the investment level according to the following formula:

$$IL_t = Min\left(MaxIL, Max\left(MinIL, m \times \left(\frac{CPPI_t - Floor_t}{CPPI_t}\right)\right)\right)$$

with $CPPI(t)$ = CPPI valuation on such index business days

$Floor(t)$ = value of the floor at time t

m = multiplier = 5

$MaxIL$ = Maximum investment level = 100%

$MinIL$ = Minimum investment level = 0%

$IL(0)$ = initial investment level = 71.80%

CPPI Valuation

$$CPPI_t = CPPI_{t-1} \times \left(1 + \left(\frac{Index_t}{Index_{t-1}} - 1\right) \times IL_{t-1}\right.$$
$$\left. + \left(\frac{ZB_t}{ZB_{t-1}} - 1\right) \times MAX(0, 1 - IL_{t-1}) - \frac{Fee_t \times (d_t - d_{t-1})}{365}\right)$$

where $Index(t)$ = level of the reference asset at time t

$IL(t)$ = investment level in fund at time t

d_t = calendar day at time t

$Fee(t)$ = 1.90% if $CPPI(t) > floor(t)$ otherwise $fee(t)$ = 0.90%

Lock In

$$LockIn_t = MAX(LockIn_{t-1}, p^*CPPI_t)$$

where p = 1.0 for the first 5 years and 0.85 thereafter.

$LockIn(0)$ = 100%

Floor

$$Floor_t = Bond_t^* LockIn_t$$

where $Bond(t)$ = clean price of a EUR-denominated bond with a coupon of 0.90% p.a.

Equity Credit Hybrids

CHAPTER 6

Credit Modeling

6.1 INTRODUCTION

The growth witnessed in the credit derivatives market in recent years has led to the introduction of equity hybrid structures that depend on the creditworthiness and the performance of an equity underlying. Convertible bonds constituted the first generation of these structures and are still the most liquid of them, while the equity default swap remains the main innovation in this field.

This chapter presents a methodology to value derivative securities written on equity underlyings subject to credit risk. Arbitrage-free valuation techniques are employed, and the methodology is applied to derivative securities written on assets subject to default risk as well as to pure credit derivative instruments.

6.2 BACKGROUND ON CREDIT MODELING

The risk of default is the financial loss that a counterparty would bear if a reference entity does not honor its commitments. This is in general called a credit event and could range from downgrades by a rating agency to failure to pay debt to complete liquidation. In theory, every financial transaction embeds this kind of risk regardless of the counterparties involved. Estimating the likelihood of occurrence of a credit event is the center of any methodology aiming at modeling credit risk or default risk. However, this is not sufficient for the pricing of contingent claims sensitive to default risk. Indeed, we need to model the loss given default (or recovery), risk-free interest rates, and in the case of multiname securities, the dependency between the credit events.

There are two main routes to modeling default risk, the structural approach and the reduced-form or intensity, based approach. In the first approach, we make explicit assumptions about the capital structure of the company, its debt, and the dynamics of its assets. In the reduced-form approach, the dynamics of the default are exogenously given by a default rate (intensity). Intensity-based models focus directly on describing the conditional probability of default without the definition of the exact default event. The use of a Poisson process framework to describe default captures the idea that the timing of a default takes the investor by surprise. Technically speaking, either the default time τ is a stopping time in the asset filtration (structural models) or it is a stopping time in a larger filtration (intensity models).

6.2.1 Structural Approach

The firm value model was introduced by Black and Scholes in 1973 and Merton in 1974. It consists of defining the default time as the time τ that the underlying process, the assets of the firm, hits a certain barrier.

Standard Approach Consider a company with market value V_t at time t, which represents the expected discounted value of its future cash flows. The company has a debt modeled as a zero-coupon bond with face value D and maturity T. If the company cannot honor its commitments at maturity, the debtors take control of the company.

The firm value V_t (also called asset price) is modeled as geometric Brownian motion and its dynamics are given as follows:

$$\frac{dV_t}{V_t} = \mu dt + \sigma_V dW_t \qquad (6.1)$$

$$V_0 > 0$$

The default event is defined as the inability of the company to pay its debt at maturity; that is, $V_T < D$. The default probability is therefore given by

$$P(0,T) = \mathbb{Q}(V_T < D)$$

$$= \mathbb{Q}\left(\left(\mu - \frac{\sigma_V^2}{2}\right)T + \sigma_V W_T < \log\left(\frac{D}{V_0}\right)\right)$$

$$= \mathcal{N}\left(\frac{\log\left(\frac{D}{V_0}\right) - \left(\mu - \frac{\sigma_V^2}{2}\right)T}{\sigma_V\sqrt{T}}\right),$$

where $L = \frac{D}{V_0}$ is the leverage ratio.

The bondholder receives at maturity $D(T,T) = \min(V_T, D)$, which could be written as

$$D(T,T) = D - (D - V_T)^+.$$

Therefore, the bondholder is long a default-free bond with a face value D and short a put option on the assets of the company.

On the other hand, the equity value $E_T = \max(V_T - D, 0)$ is a call option on the assets of the company. The values today of the debt and equity of the company are given by

$$D(0,T) = B(0,T)e^{\mu T}V_0\mathcal{N}(-d_1) + B(0,T)D\mathcal{N}(d_2)$$

$$E_0 = B(0,T)e^{\mu T}V_0\mathcal{N}(d_1) - B(0,T)D\mathcal{N}(d_2)$$

$$d_1 = \frac{\log\left(\frac{V_0}{D}\right) + \left(\mu + \frac{\sigma_V^2}{2}\right)T}{\sigma_V\sqrt{T}}, \text{ and } d_2 = d_1 - \sigma_V\sqrt{T},$$

where $B(0,T)$ is the default-free zero-coupon bond.

The credit spread is defined as the excess return, above the risk-free rate, demanded by investors for bearing the default risk of the underlying entity. Its expression, using the formulas above, is given by

$$sp\,(0,T) = -\frac{1}{T}\log\left(\frac{D\,(0,T)}{B\,(0,T)\,D}\right)$$

$$= -\frac{1}{T}\log\left(\frac{e^{\mu T}V_0\mathcal{N}(-d_1)}{D} + \mathcal{N}(d_2)\right).$$

First-Passage Approach In the standard approach, the value of the company can reach any value between today and the maturity without triggering the default event (value of the company at any point in time before maturity can be below the face value of the debt). The test for default or no default is done only at maturity. The first-passage approach, on the other hand, defines the default event as the first time the value of the company drops below a predefined barrier H.

Given the dynamics (6.1), the probability of default is given as follows:

$$P\,(0,T) = 1 - \mathbb{Q}\left(\min_{t\leq T} V_t > H, V_T > D\right)$$

$$= \mathcal{N}\left(\frac{\log\,(L) - \left(\mu - \frac{\sigma_V^2}{2}\right)T}{\sigma_V\sqrt{T}}\right) + \left(\frac{H}{V_0}\right)^{\left(\frac{2\mu}{\sigma_V^2}-1\right)}\mathcal{N}\left(\frac{\log\left(\frac{H^2}{DV_0}\right) + \left(\mu - \frac{\sigma_V^2}{2}\right)T}{\sigma_V\sqrt{T}}\right)$$

Within this approach the bondholder receives at maturity

$$D\,(T,T) = V_T - (V_T - D)^+\,\mathbf{1}_{\min_{t\leq T} V_t > H}$$

$$= V_T - (V_T - D)^+ + (V_T - D)^+\,\mathbf{1}_{\min_{t\leq T} V_t < H}$$

$$= D + V_T - D - (V_T - D)^+ + (V_T - D)^+\,\mathbf{1}_{\min_{t\leq T} V_t < H}$$

$$= \underbrace{D - (D - V_T)^+}_{\text{standard approach}} + (V_T - D)^+\,\mathbf{1}_{\min_{t\leq T} V_t < H}.$$

The bondholder is therefore long a default free zero coupon bond with face value D, a down-and-in call on the assets of the company, and short a put on the assets of the company.

On the other hand, the equity value at maturity is given as follows:

$$E_T = (V_T - D)^+\,\mathbf{1}_{\min_{t\leq T} V_t > H};$$

that is, the equityholder is long a down and out call on the assets of the company. The values $D(0, T)$ and E_0 of the debt and equity today are given by

$$D(0, T) = D(0, T)^{\text{standard}} + B(0, T) e^{\mu T} V_0 \left(\frac{H}{V_0} \right)^{\left(\frac{2\mu}{\sigma_V^2} + 1 \right)}$$

$$\times \mathcal{N}(\delta_1) - B(0, T) D \left(\frac{H}{V_0} \right)^{\left(\frac{2\mu}{\sigma_V^2} - 1 \right)} \mathcal{N}(\delta_2)$$

$$E_0 = E_0^{\text{standard}} - B(0, T) e^{\mu T} V_0 L^{\left(\frac{2\mu}{\sigma_V^2} + 1 \right)} \mathcal{N}(\delta_1) + B(0, T) DL^{\left(\frac{2\mu}{\sigma_V^2} - 1 \right)} \mathcal{N}(\delta_2)$$

$$\delta_1 = \frac{\log \left(\frac{H^2}{DV_0} \right) + \left(\mu + \frac{\sigma_V^2}{2} \right) T}{\sigma_V \sqrt{T}}, \text{ and } \delta_2 = \delta_1 - \sigma_V \sqrt{T}$$

where E_0^{standard} and $D(0, T)^{\text{standard}}$ are the values of the equity and debt at time 0 given in the standard approach described above.

The derivation of these formulas could be found in [130].

The credit spread is therefore expressed as follows:

$$sp(0, T) = \frac{-1}{T} \log \left(\frac{L}{B(0, T)} \left(e^{\mu T} \left(\frac{H}{V_0} \right)^{\left(\frac{2\mu}{\sigma_V^2} + 1 \right)} \mathcal{N}(\delta_1) + \mathcal{N}(-d_1) \right) + \mathcal{N}(d_2) \right.$$

$$\left. + \left(\frac{H}{V_0} \right)^{\left(\frac{2\mu}{\sigma_V^2} - 1 \right)} \mathcal{N}(\delta_2) \right)$$

Discussion The calibration of structural models is problematic, as the value of the firm is not directly observable in the market. The face value and the maturity of the debt is not easy to estimate from the balance sheet given the complexity of the capital structure of the company. Indeed, we often have a mixture of short-, medium-, and long-term debts as well as different seniorities. The barrier level, in the case of a first-passage approach, is another parameter that is not easy to estimate, and its definition is generally ad hoc and conditions the occurrence of default event.

Another drawback of the two approaches described above is the fact that the default cannot happen immediately. This has been addressed by random barrier models such as credit grades. However, this adds even more complexity in terms of the calibration as we need to calibrate the volatility of the barrier level in addition to all other parameters.

Nevertheless, this approach could be useful to provide predictive tools related to upcoming default events. Indeed, a pre-default event could be defined as the first time the asset value is below a certain level higher than, but close to, the default barrier, and users of structural models observe the evolution of the so-called "distance-to-default" or the marginal default probabilities. From a mathematical point of view, this means that the default time τ is predictable, a stopping time with respect to the asset filtration. Unfortunately, market reality is different, as we do witness spread movements as well as jumps to default that happen in a surprising way.

The inability of structural models to properly describe the default event is a drawback well described by Madan in "Pricing the Risks of Default" (2000):

> ...*default is often a complicated event and specifying the precise conditions under which it must occur are easily misspecified. The conditions one writes down may be too stringent so that it often occurs before these conditions are met, or the conditions are too weak and default fails to occur when all the requisite conditions have been met.*

6.2.2 Reduced-Form Approach

In reduced-form or intensity-based models, the dynamics of the default are described exogenously and directly under the pricing measure. We model the instantaneous likelihood of default through the hazard-rate process.

Definition of the Hazard Rate of a Default Time

Hazard rate: Deterministic case Let us consider a security with default time τ. τ is a continuous random variable measuring the length of time from today to the default time.

Let $F(t)$ denote the distribution function of τ:

$$F(t) = \mathbb{Q}\left(\tau \leq t\right), t \geq 0 \qquad (6.2)$$

$$F(0) = 0$$

We also define the survival function $S(t)$ by

$$S(t) = 1 - F(t) = \mathbb{Q}\left(\tau > t\right), t \geq 0 \qquad (6.3)$$

$$S(0) = 1.$$

As to the probability density function, it is given by

$$f(t) = F'(t) = -S'(t) = \lim_{\Delta \to 0^+} \frac{\mathbb{Q}\left(t \leq \tau < t + \Delta\right)}{\Delta}.$$

The distribution of the random variable default time can be specified with the hazard-rate function, which gives the instantaneous default probability for a security that has attained time x, given survival to this time:

$$\mathbb{Q}\left(x \leq \tau < x + \Delta x | \tau \geq x\right) = \frac{F\left(x + \Delta x\right) - F\left(x\right)}{1 - F\left(x\right)} \qquad (6.4)$$

$$\approx \frac{f(x)}{1 - F\left(x\right)}\Delta x$$

The function

$$h(x) = \frac{f(x)}{1 - F(x)},$$

used in statistics under the name of hazard-rate function, is the conditional probability density function of τ at time x, given survival to that time.

The hazard-rate function can easily be linked to the survival function as follows

$$\begin{cases} h(x) &= -\frac{S'(x)}{S(x)} \\ S(0) &= 1 \end{cases}.$$

We get

$$S(t) = \exp\left(-\int_0^t h(s)ds\right). \tag{6.5}$$

In the same way,

$$\mathbb{Q}(\tau > t + x | \tau \geq x) = \frac{S(t + x)}{S(x)}$$

$$= \exp\left(-\int_x^{t+x} h(s)ds\right). \tag{6.6}$$

Lastly, distribution and density functions of the default time τ can be expressed as a function of the hazard rate function as follows:

$$F(t) = 1 - S(t) = 1 - \exp\left(-\int_0^t h(s)ds\right) \tag{6.7}$$

$$f(t) = S(t) \times h(t) \tag{6.8}$$

These relationships show that modeling a default process is equivalent to modeling a hazard-rate function.

Hazard rate: General case Let us define the default process by $N_t = 1_{\tau \leq t}$, where τ is the default time. It is assumed that the increasing one-jump process N_t admits an absolutely continuous compensator Δ_t, where Δ_t is a predictable and increasing process such that $N_t - \Delta_t$ is a martingale [131]:

$$\Delta_t = \int_0^{t \wedge \tau} h_s ds$$

where the non-negative predictable process h stands for the intensity process or hazard rate. With a constant intensity h, for example, default is a Poisson process with intensity h. More generally, for $t < \tau$, h_t can be viewed as the conditional rate of arrival of default at time t, given all information available up to that time. Roughly speaking, for a small time interval of length Δt, the conditional probability that default occurs between t and $t + \Delta t$, given survival to t, is given by $h_t \Delta t$.

We consider two increasing and complete information filtrations $\mathcal{F}_t \subset \mathcal{G}_t$ such that

$$\begin{cases} \tau & \in \mathcal{G}_t \\ h_t & \in \mathcal{F}_t \end{cases},$$

the default time τ being outside the span of $\mathcal{F} = \mathcal{F}_T$.

Now, the process

$$M_t = N_t - \int_0^{t \wedge \tau} h_s \, ds$$

$$= N_t - \int_0^t h_s \mathbf{1}_{s < \tau} \, ds$$

$$= N_t - \int_0^t h_s \, (1 - N_s) \, ds \tag{6.9}$$

is a $(\mathbb{Q}, \mathcal{G}_t)$ martingale.

The following result will allow us to eliminate the jump process N_t from the evaluation of any derivative payoff.

LEMMA 6.2.1 *We admit the following result:*

$$E_{\mathbb{Q}} \left(1 - N_t | \mathcal{F}_t \right) = \exp \left(- \int_0^t h_s ds \right) \tag{6.10}$$

Let us define $S(t, T)$ the probability of no default (or survival probability). It can be expressed as

$$S(t, T) = E_{\mathbb{Q}} \left(\mathbf{1}_{\tau > T} \cap \mathbf{1}_{\tau > t} | \mathcal{F}_t \cup \mathbf{1}_{\tau > t} \right)$$

A direct application of Bayes's theorem gives

$$S(t, T) = \frac{E_{\mathbb{Q}} \left(\mathbf{1}_{\tau > T} \cap \mathbf{1}_{\tau > t} | \mathcal{F}_t \right)}{E_{\mathbb{Q}} \left(\mathbf{1}_{\tau > t} | \mathcal{F}_t \right)}$$

$$= \frac{E_{\mathbb{Q}} \left(E_{\mathbb{Q}} \left(1 - N_T | \mathcal{F}_T \right) | \mathcal{F}_t \right)}{E_{\mathbb{Q}} \left(1 - N_t | \mathcal{F}_t \right)}$$

$$= E_{\mathbb{Q}} \left(\exp \left(- \int_t^T h_s ds \right) | \mathcal{F}_t \right) \tag{6.11}$$

where the last equality directly follows from (6.10).

This important result generalizes the results of the previous section, allowing now the hazard-rate function to be stochastic.

Construction of a Default Time In this section, we give a background on how to construct a default time.

Let $(\Omega, \mathcal{G}, (\mathcal{G}_t), \mathbb{Q})$ be a filtered probability space, and Z_t a diffusion process on this space. Let θ be an exponential random variable with intensity 1 independent from Z_t.

We define the default time τ as the first time when the process $\int_0^t h(Z_u)\,du$ is above the random variable θ :

$$\tau = \inf\left\{t, \int_0^t h(Z_u)\,du \geq \theta\right\},$$

where h is a positive function. An equivalent way of defining τ is

$$\tau = \inf\left\{t, N_{\int_0^t h(Z_u)\,du} = 1\right\}$$

where N_t is a Poisson process with intensity 1 independent of $\mathcal{F} = \sigma(Z_t, t \geq 0)$.

Therefore, the conditional distribution of the default time τ given $\mathcal{F}_t$ ($\mathcal{F}_t = \sigma(Z_s, t \geq s)$) is given by

$$\mathbb{Q}(\tau > t|\mathcal{F}_t) = \exp\left(-\int_0^t h(Z_u)\,du\right). \tag{6.12}$$

We introduce the filtration $\mathcal{G}_t = \mathcal{F}_t \vee \sigma\left(1_{\tau \leq s}, t \geq s\right)$, the enlarged filtration with respect to which τ is a stopping time. Indeed, τ is not stopping time with respect to the filtration[1] $\mathcal{F}_t$; otherwise, we would have $\mathbb{Q}(\tau \leq t|\mathcal{F}_t) = 1_\tau \leq t$ and not (6.12).

For the pricing of contingent claims on defaultable securities, the following theorem is essential:

THEOREM 6.2.1 *Let X be an integrable random variable; we have the following result:*

$$E_\mathbb{Q}\left(1_{\tau \geq t}X|\mathcal{G}_t\right) = 1_{\tau \geq t}Y_t$$

where

$$Y_t = \frac{E_\mathbb{Q}\left(1_{\tau \geq t}X|\mathcal{F}_t\right)}{E_\mathbb{Q}\left(1_{\tau \geq t}|\mathcal{F}_t\right)}.$$

Modeling a hazard-rate function provides us information on the immediate default risk of each entity known to be alive at a given time t and facilitates comparisons with other entities. Also, as we will see, this kind of modeling can be easily adapted to the stochastic default case. Linked to this point, the strong similarities between the hazard-rate function and the short rate allow us to borrow some modeling techniques from the short-rate world.

---

[1] In the structural model approach, τ is a stopping time with respect to $\mathcal{F}_t$.

6.3 MODELING EQUITY CREDIT HYBRIDS

We are given a filtered probability space $(\Omega, \mathcal{G}, (\mathcal{G}_t), \mathbb{Q})$ where all processes are assumed to be defined and adapted to the filtration $(\mathcal{G}_t)$. We will be working in an arbitrage-free setting, and we will be considering the dynamics of the involved processes directly under the risk-neutral measure $\mathbb{Q}$.

6.3.1 Dynamics of the Hazard Rate

We will exploit the results of the previous sections to choose a stochastic diffusion for the hazard-rate process. The similarities between the hazard rate and the short rate legitimate the use of some modeling techniques proper to the short rate. Two kind of diffusion could be employed to model the dynamics of the hazard rate: affine diffusions and mixed diffusions.

Affine Diffusion Models   The tractability of affine diffusion models [132] makes them prime candidates for the modeling of the hazard rate process. Indeed, we can easily obtain closed-form solutions for the survival (default) probabilities in some cases, and we only need to solve an ordinary differential equation in some other cases.

An affine diffusion model is given by the following stochastic differential equation:

$$dh_t = \mu\left(t, h_t\right) dt + \sigma\left(t, h_t\right) dW_t,$$

where μ and σ^2 are affine functions of h_t; that is, $\mu\left(t, h_t\right) = a_1\left(t\right) + b_1\left(t\right) h_t$ and $\sigma^2\left(t, h_t\right) = a_2\left(t\right) + b_2\left(t\right) h_t$. The survival probability (the equivalent of a zero-coupon bond) is given by

$$S\left(0, T\right) = \exp\left(m(T) - h_0 n(T)\right),$$

where $m(T)$ and $n(T)$ are deterministic functions of $T, a_1, a_2, b_1,$ and b_2.

Note that the affine diffusions models remain tractable and yield similar expression for the survival probabilities in the multidimensional case.

Mixed Diffusion Models   This class of models contains the CEV kind diffusion given by

$$dh_t = a_t h_t dt + \sigma_t h_t^{\gamma} dW_t. \tag{6.13}$$

These models have the drawback of being computationally unattractive (except for $\gamma = 0$ or $\gamma = 0.5$, because we end up with an affine diffusion).

The model choices we make in the remainder of this chapter are based on affine models. Precisely, the dynamics we will study for the hazard-rate function are the Hull-White diffusion in the first stage. An extension to include jumps is studied later.

6.3.2 Model Choice

Assuming Hull-White-type diffusions for the hazard rate and short rate, we end with the following system of SDEs:

$$
\begin{cases}
\frac{dS_t}{S_t} = (r_t - y_t)\,dt + \sigma_t^S dW_t^S - (dN_t - h_t dt) \\
dr_t = \left(\theta_t^r - \beta_t^r r_t\right) dt + \sigma_t^r dW_t^r \\
dh_t = \left(\theta_t^h - \beta_t^h h_t\right) dt + \sigma_t^h dW_t^h
\end{cases}
$$

with

$$
\begin{cases}
d\langle W^S, W^h\rangle_t = \rho^{Sh}\,dt \\
d\langle W^r, W^h\rangle_t = \rho^{rh}\,dt \\
d\langle W^S, W^r\rangle_t = \rho^{Sr}\,dt
\end{cases}
$$

where $N_t = 1_{\tau \leq t}$, with τ being the inaccessible default time. N_t is taken to be independent of all the Brownian motions, W^S, W^h, and W^r. $y_t = \mu_t + \delta_t$, where μ_t and δ_t are the dividend yield and repo rate, respectively.

Initially, and in order to allow for a more tractable model, instantaneous short rate is taken to be deterministic. The extension to stochastic interest rates is straightforward and will be discussed later.

Study of the Hazard Rate Dynamics   As specified above, the dynamics of the hazard rate are given by

$$
dh_t = \left(\theta_t^h - \beta_t^h h_t\right) dt + \sigma_t^h dW_t^h \tag{6.14}
$$

The solution to (6.14) is given by

$$
h_t = h_0 \exp\left(-\int_0^t \beta_u^h du\right) + \exp\left(-\int_0^t \beta_u^h du\right) \left[\int_0^t \exp\left(\int_0^u \beta_s^h ds\right) \theta_u^h du \right.
$$
$$
\left. + \int_0^t \exp\left(\int_0^u \beta_s^h ds\right) \sigma_u^h dW_u^h \right];
$$

We have

$$
S(t, T) \equiv S(h_t, t, T)
$$
$$
= \exp\left(m(t, T) - n(t, T)h_t\right) \tag{6.15}
$$

with

$$
\begin{cases}
m(T, T) = 0 \\
n(T, T) = 0.
\end{cases}
$$

This is true for all affine-type diffusions as mentioned earlier, that is, for all diffusions for which the drift term and the square of volatility are linear functions of h_t.

Furthermore, the survival probability $S(t, T)$ satisfies the PDE below:

$$\frac{\partial S}{\partial t}(h, t) + \frac{1}{2}\left(\sigma_t^h\right)^2 \frac{\partial^2 S}{\partial h^2}(h, t) + \left[\theta_t^h - \beta_t^h h_t\right]\frac{\partial S}{\partial h}(h, t) = h_t S(t, T)$$

with the terminal condition

$$S(T, T) = 1.$$

Replacing the expression of the survival probability (6.15) in the PDE, we obtain

$$m_t(t, T) - \theta_t^h n(t, T) + \frac{1}{2}\left(\sigma_t^h\right)^2 n(t, T)^2 - \left[1 + n_t(t, T) - \beta_t^h n(t, T)\right]h_t = 0,$$

where $m_t(t, T)$ and $n_t(t, T)$ are the first derivatives of $m(t, T)$ and $n(t, T)$ with respect to t.

By separating terms that do not depend on h_t and those that do depend on h_t, we get a polynomial of degree one with respect to the variable h_t; both coefficients will be equal to zero. We therefore have the following system of differential equations:

$$\begin{cases} n_t(t, T) &= \beta_t^h n(t, T) - 1 \\ n(T, T) &= 0 \end{cases}$$

and

$$\begin{cases} m_t(t, T) &= \theta_t^h n(t, T) - \frac{1}{2}\left(\sigma_t^h\right)^2 n(t, T)^2 \\ m(T, T) &= 0 \end{cases}$$

Integrating these equations, we get

$$m(t, T) = \frac{1}{2}\int_t^T \left(\sigma_u^h\right)^2 n(u, T)^2 du - \int_t^T \theta_u^h n(u, T) du \qquad (6.16)$$

$$n(t, T) = \int_t^T \exp\left(-\int_t^u \beta_s^h ds\right) du. \qquad (6.17)$$

Let us define the T-maturity instantaneous forward hazard rate by

$$fh(0, T) = -\frac{\partial \log S(0, T)}{\partial T} \qquad (6.18)$$

with

$$S(0, T) = \exp\left(m(0, T) - n(0, T)h_0\right)$$

We have

$$fh(0, T) = n_T(0, T)h_0 - m_T(0, T)$$

where

$$n_T(0, T) = \exp\left(-\int_0^T \beta_u^h du\right)$$

and

$$m_T(0, T) = \int_0^T \left(\sigma_u^h\right)^2 n(u, T) n_T(u, T) du - \int_0^T \theta_u^h n_T(u, T) du$$

$$= \int_0^T \left(\sigma_u^h\right)^2 \Lambda^h(u, T) \left(\int_u^T \Lambda^h(u, v) dv\right) du - \int_0^T \theta_u^h \Lambda^h(u, T) du$$

where

$$\Lambda^h(t, T) = \exp\left(-\int_t^T \beta_u^h du\right).$$

Thus,

$$fh(0, T) = \Lambda^h(0, T) h_0 + \int_0^T \theta_u^h \Lambda^h(u, T) du$$

$$- \int_0^T \left(\sigma_u^h\right)^2 \Lambda^h(u, T) \left(\int_u^T \Lambda^h(u, v) dv\right) du.$$

This expression can be rewritten as

$$fh(0, T) = g(T) - h(T)$$

with

$$\begin{cases} g(T) & = \Lambda^h(0, T) h_0 + \int_0^T \theta_u^h \Lambda^h(u, T) du \\ h(T) & = \int_0^T \left(\sigma_u^h\right)^2 \Lambda^h(u, T) \left(\int_u^T \Lambda^h(u, v) dv\right) du \end{cases}$$

such that

$$\begin{cases} g'(T) & = \theta_T^h - \beta_T^h g(T). \\ g(0) & = h_0. \end{cases}$$

Consequently,

$$\theta_T^h = g'(T) + \beta_T^h g(T)$$

and

$$\begin{cases} \theta_T^h & = fh_T(0, T) + h'(T) + \beta_T^h \left[fh(0, T) + h(T)\right] \\ h(T) & = \int_0^T \left(\sigma_u^h\right)^2 \Lambda^h(u, T) \left(\int_u^T \Lambda^h(u, v) dv\right) du. \\ h'(T) & = -\beta_T h(T) + \int_0^T \left(\sigma_u^h\right)^2 \Lambda^h(u, T)^2 du \end{cases}$$

Finally, the parameter θ^b is uniquely determined and given by

$$\theta_T^b = fb_T(0, T) + \int_0^T \left(\sigma_u^b\right)^2 \Lambda^b(u, T)^2 du + \beta_T^b fb(0, T).$$

However, in practice, we do not need to calibrate θ_T^b, as it is implied by today's credit curve. The above result has only a theoretical interest in showing that θ_T^b is uniquely specified. Note also that the expression of the survival probability could be derived by simply computing the expectation $E_Q\left(\exp\left(-\int_t^T h_s ds\right) | \mathcal{F}_t\right)$, which is easy given that $\exp\left(-\int_t^T h_s ds\right) | \mathcal{F}_t$ is a log normal variable.

Dynamics of the Survival Probability The expression of the survival probability under the risk-neutral measure $\mathbb{Q}$ is given by

$$S(t, T) = E_\mathbb{Q}\left(\exp\left(-\int_t^T h_s ds\right) | \mathcal{F}_t\right).$$

Given this expression, we show that its dynamics under $\mathbb{Q}$ is given by

$$\frac{dS(t, T)}{S(t, T)} = h_t dt - \sigma^{SP}(t, T) dW_t^b, \tag{6.19}$$

where

$$\sigma^{SP}(t, T) = \sigma_t^b \times \Psi^b(t, T)$$

with

$$\Psi^b(t, T) = \int_t^T \Lambda^b(t, u) du.$$

Furthermore, we have that

$$\int_t^T h_s ds = \Psi^b(t, T) h_t + \int_t^T \Psi^b(u, T) \theta_u^b du + \int_t^T \Psi^b(u, T) \sigma_u^b dW_u^b.$$

This is going to be very useful when pricing various derivatives as we discount with $\exp\left(-\int_t^T h_s ds\right)$. The above results are very similar to the ones obtained in the case of short-rate models.

6.4 PRICING

6.4.1 Credit Default Swap

A credit default swap (CDS) is a financial agreement between two counterparties in which the protection buyer makes regular fixed payments during its term, whereas the protection seller is binded to making a payment upon the default of a reference entity. The default event definition could range from the failure of making a simple interest payment to complete bankruptcy. The default payment could be made at maturity (standard or European type) or at time of default (American type).

The CDS price (spread) is the premium value that makes the agreement a fair contract, that is, the default leg is equal to the premium leg. As mentioned above, we assume that the interest rates are deterministic (independence between the default process and the interest rates yield exactly the same results), and the default payment is made at the time of default (American case).

Premium Leg The premium leg is the price of a risky coupon bond with notional equal to the one of the CDSs and where all the payments are discounted using risky zero rates (default-free zero bond times the survival probability). Let $(t_1, t_2, \cdots, t_n = T)$ be the set of payment dates where T is the maturity of the CDS, N is the notional of the swap, and R is the recovery rate of the reference entity assumed to be constant.

$$
\begin{aligned}
PL &= N \sum_{i=1}^{n} c \Delta t_i B\left(0, t_i\right) E_{\mathbb{Q}}\left[\mathbf{1}_{\tau > t_i}\right] \\
&= N \sum_{i=1}^{n} c \Delta t_i B\left(0, t_i\right) S\left(0, t_i\right) \\
&= N \sum_{i=1}^{n} c \Delta t_i B^d\left(0, t_i\right)
\end{aligned}
$$

where Δt_i is the day count fraction for the period $[t_{i-1}, t_i]$, $t_0 = 0$ and $B^d\left(0, t_i\right)$ is the risky zero coupon bond defined as follows:

$$
B^d\left(0, t_i\right) = B\left(0, t_i\right) S\left(0, t_i\right) \tag{6.20}
$$

Note that this expression is not true if we have correlated hazard rate and short-rate processes.

Default Leg The default leg is the expected value of the default payment (DP) minus the accrual premium payment (AP). These two quantities are computed as follows:

$$
\begin{aligned}
DP &= N E_{\mathbb{Q}}\left[(1 - R) B\left(0, \tau\right) \mathbf{1}_{\tau < T}\right] \\
&= N\left(1 - R\right) E_{\mathbb{Q}}\left[B\left(0, \tau\right) \mathbf{1}_{\tau < T}\right]
\end{aligned}
$$

$$= N(1-R) \int_0^T B(0,u)\, dF(u)$$

$$= N(1-R) \left[1 - B^d(0,T) - \int_0^T f(0,u)\, B^d(0,u)\, du \right]$$

where $f(0,T)$ is the instantaneous forward rate given by: $f(0,T) = \frac{-\partial \log B(0,T)}{\partial T}$ and

$$AP = N \sum_{i=1}^n E_{\mathbb{Q}} \left[c\,(\tau - t_{i-1})\, B(0,\tau)\, 1_{t_{i-1} < \tau \le t_i} \right]$$

$$= Nc \sum_{i=1}^n \left[-\Delta t_i B^d(0,t_i) + \int_{t_{i-1}}^{t_i} B^d(0,u)\, du - \int_{t_{i-1}}^{t_i} (u - t_{i-1})\, f(0,u)\, B^d(0,u)\, du \right].$$

The spread of the credit default swap is the value of c that makes the default leg equal to the premium leg, hence:

$$\text{Spread} = \frac{(1-R)\left[1 - B^d(0,T) - \int_0^T f(0,u)\, B^d(0,u)\, du \right]}{\int_0^T B^d(0,u)\, du - \sum_{i=1}^n \int_{t_{i-1}}^{t_i} (u - t_{i-1})\, f(0,u)\, B^d(0,u)\, du} \tag{6.21}$$

Note that credit default swaps are quoted in spread in the marketplace.

6.4.2 Credit Default Swaption

Let's call $CDS_{S,N}(t)$, the value at time t of a CDS contract starting at time T_S and maturing at time T_N, with notional N and recovery rate R.

Similar to a CDS starting today (6.21), the expression of $CDS_{S,N}(t)$ is given as follows:

$$CDS_{S,N}(t) = N \times c \left(\sum_{i=S+1}^N \Delta t_i B^d(t,T_i) + \int_{T_{i-1}}^{T_i} (u - T_{i-1}) B(t,u) \left(-dS(t,u) \right) \right)$$

$$- N \times (1-R) \int_{T_S}^{T_N} B(t,u) \left(-dS(t,u) \right)$$

where

- $S(t,u)$ is the survival probability from t to u conditional to no default at time t.
- Δt_i is the length of time expressed in fraction of years between T_{i-1} and T_i.
- $B(t,u)$ ($B^d(t,u)$) is the default-free (risky or defaultable) discount factor from t to time u.
- c is the premium paid at every payment date by the protection buyer.

The CDS par spread s_N is defined as the rate c that cancels the present value of the swap, and is given as follows:

$$s_N(t) = \frac{(1-R) \int_{T_S}^{T_N} B(t,u) \left(-dS(t,u) \right)}{\sum_{i=S+1}^N \Delta t_i B^d(t,T_i) + \int_{T_{i-1}}^{T_i} (u - T_{i-1}) B(t,u) \left(-dS(t,u) \right)}$$

CDS Option Price Let's call $C_{S,N}(t) \equiv C_{S,N}(t, T_S, K)$ the value at time t of a call option maturing at time T_S and struck at K written on the CDS spread contract $CDS_{S,N}(t)$.

If the default occurs before the option maturity T_S, two different treatments are possible: either the option is knocked out and its value drops to zero or the option remains valid and pays the default protection at maturity.

We focus here on the pricing of the knock-out CDS whose price at time T_S is given by

$$
C_{S,N}(T_S) = N \times \left[(s_N - K)^+ \sum_{i=S+1}^{N} \left(\Delta t_i B^d(T_S, T_i) \right. \right.
$$
$$
\left. \left. + \int_{T_{i-1}}^{T_i} (u - T_{i-1}) fh(T_S, u) B^d(T_S, u) du \right) \right],
$$

where $B^d(t, T)$ is given by (6.20).
The payoff of the option can be rewritten as

$$
C_{S,N}(T_S) = \begin{bmatrix} N \times (1 - R) \sum_{i=S+1}^{N} \int_{T_{i-1}}^{T_i} fh(T_S, u) B^d(T_S, u) du \\ -N \times K \sum_{i=S+1}^{N} \left(\Delta t_i B^d(T_S, T_i) \right. \\ \left. + \int_{T_{i-1}}^{T_i} (u - T_{i-1}) fh(T_S, u) B^d(T_S, u) du \right) \end{bmatrix}^+ .
$$

Let us define the level of the swap at time t, $LVL_{S,N}(t)$ as

$$
LVL_{S,N}(t) = N \times \sum_{i=S+1}^{N} \left(\Delta t_i B^d(t, T_i) + \int_{T_{i-1}}^{T_i} (u - T_{i-1}) fh(t, u) B^d(t, u) du \right). \quad (6.22)
$$

Writing the expression of the call price under Q^{LVL}, we get

$$
C_{S,N}(t) = LVL_{S,N}(t) E_{\mathbb{Q}_{LVL}} \left[[s_N - K]^+ \mid \mathcal{F}_t \right].
$$

Under $\mathbb{Q}^{LVL}$, the CDS spread, s_N, is a martingale. Its diffusion is assumed to be log normal and can be written as

$$
\frac{ds_N(t)}{s_N(t)} = \sigma_t^{s_N} \, dW_t^{S,N}.
$$

The CDS option price is therefore given by the Black formula as follows:

$$
C_{S,N}(t) = LVL_{S,N}(t) \times \left(s_N(t) \mathcal{N}(d_1) - K \mathcal{N}(d_2) \right),
$$

where d_1 and d_2 are given by

$$
d_1 = \frac{\log\left(\frac{s_N(t)}{K}\right)}{\sigma(t, T_S)\sqrt{T_S - t}} + \frac{\sigma(t, T_S)\sqrt{T_S - t}}{2}
$$
$$
d_2 = d_1 - \sigma(t, T_S)\sqrt{T_S - t}
$$
$$
\sigma(t, T_S) = \frac{1}{T_S - t} \int_t^{T_S} \left(\sigma_u^{s_N} \right)^2 du.
$$

Link between CDS Spread Volatility and Hazard Rate Volatility   The objective of this section is to express the CDS spread volatility $\sigma_t^{s_N}$ as a function of the hazard rate volatility σ_t^h. For the ease of the computations we set $N = 1$.

At time t, the CDS spread, $s_N(t)$, is defined as

$$s_N(t) = (1 - R) \times \frac{\sum_{i=S+1}^{N} \int_{T_{i-1}}^{T_i} B(t, u) \left(-dS(t, u)\right)}{LVL_{S,N}(t)}$$

where $LVL_{S,N}(t)$ is given by (6.22).

Recall the diffusions of the survival probability $S(t, T)$ and the instantaneous forward hazard rate $fh(t, T)$ under the risk-neutral measure $\mathbb{Q}$:

$$\frac{dS(t, T)}{S(t, T)} = h_t dt - \sigma^{SP}(t, T) dW_t$$

and

$$dfh(t, T) = \sigma^{SP}(t, T) \sigma^{fh}(t, T) dt + \sigma^{fh}(t, T) dW_t,$$

where $\sigma^{SP}(t, T)$ and $\sigma^{fh}(t, T)$ are given by

$$\sigma^{SP}(t, T) = \sigma_t^h \int_t^T \Lambda^h(t, u) du \tag{6.23}$$

$$\sigma^{fh}(t, T) = \sigma_t^h \Lambda^h(t, T). \tag{6.24}$$

Applying Ito to the process $s_N(t)$, we get

$$ds_N(t) = \frac{1 - R}{LVL_{S,N}(t)} d\underbrace{\left[\sum_{i=S+1}^{N} \int_{T_{i-1}}^{T_i} fh(t, u) B^d(t, u) \, du \right]}_{A}$$

$$- \frac{(1 - R) \sum_{i=S+1}^{N} \int_{T_{i-1}}^{T_i} fh(t, u) B^d(t, u) \, du}{LVL_{S,N}(t)^2} \underbrace{d\left[LVL_{S,N}(t) \right]}_{B},$$

$$+ \dots$$

where the remaining terms are drift related.

The expansion of the terms A and B gives

$$A = \left(\sum_{i=S+1}^{N} \int_{T_{i-1}}^{T_i} B^d(t, u) \left[\sigma^{fh}(t, u) - fh(t, u) \sigma^{SP}(t, u) \right] du \right) dW_t + (\cdots) dt$$

$$B = -\left(\sum_{i=S+1}^{N} \Delta t_i B^d(t, T_i)\sigma^{SP}(t, T_i)\right) dW_t$$

$$+ \left(\sum_{i=S+1}^{N} \int_{T_{i-1}}^{T_i} (u - T_{i-1})B^d(t, u)\left[\sigma^{fh}(t, u) - fh(t, u)\sigma^{SP}(t, u)\right] du\right) dW_t + (\cdots) dt.$$

We can now relate the CDS spread volatility $\sigma_t^{S_N}$ to the hazard rate volatility σ_t^h, through $\sigma^{fh}(t, u)$ and $\sigma^{SP}(t, u)$, as follows:

$$\sigma_t^{S_N} = \frac{\sum_{i=S+1}^{N} \int_{T_{i-1}}^{T_i} B^d(t, u)\left[\sigma^{fh}(t, u) - fh(t, u)\sigma^{SP}(t, u)\right] du}{\sum_{i=S+1}^{N} \int_{T_{i-1}}^{T_i} fh(t, u)B^d(t, u)\, du} \tag{6.25}$$

$$+ \frac{\sum_{i=S+1}^{N} \left(\begin{array}{c} \Delta t_i B^d(t,T_i)\sigma^{SP}(t,T_i) \\ -\int_{T_{i-1}}^{T_i}(u-T_{i-1})B^d(t,u)\left[\sigma^{fh}(t,u)-fh(t,u)\sigma^{SP}(t,u)\right] du \end{array}\right)}{LVL_{S,N}(t)}$$

6.4.3 European Call

Deterministic Interest Rates Case At a given time t, the price of a standard call option struck at K and maturing at T is given by

$$\begin{aligned} C(t) &= B(t, T) \times E_{\mathbb{Q}}\left((S_T^* \mathbf{1}_{\tau>T} - K)^+ | \mathcal{G}_t\right) \\ &= B(t, T) \times E_{\mathbb{Q}}\left(\left[(S_T^* - K)^+ \mathbf{1}_{\tau>T}\right] | \mathcal{G}_t\right) \\ &= \mathbf{1}_{\tau>t} B(t, T) \times E_{\mathbb{Q}}\left(\exp\left(-\int_t^T h_s ds\right)(S_T^* - K)^+ | \mathcal{F}_t\right) \end{aligned}$$

where S_T^* is the nondefaultable stock and its diffusion is given as follows:

$$\frac{dS_t^*}{S_t^*} = (r_t + h_t - y_t)\, dt + \sigma_t^S dW_t^S$$

and we have

$$S_t = S_t^* \mathbf{1}_{\tau>t}.$$

On the other hand, $B(t, T)$ is the nondefaultable zero-coupon bond of maturity T. After some calculations, we obtain

$$C(t) = \mathbf{1}_{\tau>t} B(t, T)S(t, T) \times \left(\frac{F_t^T}{S(t, T)}\mathcal{N}(d_1) - K\mathcal{N}(d_2)\right) \tag{6.26}$$

where F_t^T is the T-forward value of the asset.

The expressions of d_1, d_2 and $\overline{\sigma}$ are given by

$$d_1 = \frac{\log\left(\frac{F_t^T}{KS(t,T)}\right) + \frac{1}{2}\int_t^T \overline{\sigma}_u^2 du}{\sqrt{\int_t^T \overline{\sigma}_u^2 du}}$$

$$d_2 = d_1 - \sqrt{\int_t^T \overline{\sigma}^2(u,T)\,du}$$

$$\overline{\sigma}^2(t,T) = \left(\sigma_t^S\right)^2 + \left(\sigma^{SP}(t,T)\right)^2 + 2\rho^{Sh}\sigma^{SP}(t,T)\sigma_t^S.$$

Stochastic Interest Rates Case Under the risk-neutral measure, the dynamics of the asset S_t, the survival probability $S(t,T)$ and the nondefaultable zero-coupon bond $B(t,T)$ are respectively given by

$$\begin{cases} \dfrac{dS_t}{S_t} &= (r_t - y_t)\,dt + \sigma_t^S dW_t^S - \left(dN_t - h_t dt\right) \\[2mm] \dfrac{dS(t,T)}{S(t,T)} &= h_t dt - \sigma^{SP}(t,T)dW_t^h \\[2mm] \dfrac{dB(t,T)}{B(t,T)} &= r_t dt - \sigma^B(t,T)dW_t^r \end{cases}$$

where r_t is the instantaneous short rate and

$$\begin{cases} d\langle W^S, W^h\rangle_t &= \rho^{Sh}\,dt \\ d\langle W^r, W^h\rangle_t &= \rho^{rh}\,dt \\ d\langle W^S, W^r\rangle_t &= \rho^{Sr}\,dt \end{cases}$$

As for the survival probability, the diffusion parameter of the zero-coupon bond is defined as

$$\sigma^B(t,T) = \sigma_t^r \times \int_t^T \Lambda^r(t,T),$$

where

$$\Lambda^r(t,T) = \exp\left(-\int_t^T \beta_u^r du\right).$$

N_t being independent of the rest of the random terms (Brownian motions), we will focus on the nondefaultable stock. The price of a European call option is given as follows:

$$C(t) = E_{\mathbb{Q}}\left(\exp\left(-\int_t^T r_s ds\right)(S_T^* \mathbf{1}_{\tau>T} - K)^+ |\mathcal{G}_t\right)$$

$$= \mathbf{1}_{\tau>t} E_{\mathbb{Q}}\left(\exp\left(-\int_t^T (r_s + h_s)\,ds\right)(S_T^* - K)^+ |\mathcal{F}_t\right)$$

$$= 1_{\tau > t} S_t \times \exp\left(-\int_t^T y_u du\right) \mathcal{N}(d_1) \tag{6.27}$$

$$- 1_{\tau > t} B(t, T) S(t, T) K \exp\left(\int_t^T \rho^{rh} \sigma^{SP}(u, T) \sigma^B(u, T) du\right) \mathcal{N}(d_2)$$

The expressions of d_1, d_2 and $\overline{\sigma}$ are given by

$$d_1 = \frac{\log\left(\dfrac{S_t \times \exp\left(-\int_t^T y_u du\right)}{KS(t, T) B(t, T)}\right) - \int_t^T \left[\rho^{rh} \sigma^B(u, T) \sigma^{SP}(u, T)\right] du}{\sqrt{\int_t^T \overline{\sigma}(u, T)^2 du}}$$

$$+ \frac{\sqrt{\int_t^T \overline{\sigma}(u, T)^2 du}}{2}$$

$$d_2 = d_1 - \sqrt{\int_t^T \overline{\sigma}(u, T)^2 du},$$

where

$$\overline{\sigma}(u, T) = \sqrt{\begin{array}{l} \left(\sigma_u^S\right)^2 + \sigma^B(u, T)^2 + \sigma^{SP}(u, T)^2 + 2\rho^{Sr} \sigma_u^S \sigma^B(u, T). \\ + 2\rho^{Sh} \sigma_u^S \sigma^{SP}(u, T) + 2\rho^{rh} \sigma^{SP}(u, T) \sigma^B(u, T) \end{array}}$$

Case Studied   To minimize the number of parameters to estimate, we chose to work within a deterministic interest rate framework. As shown above, the extension to a stochastic interest rate framework is straightforward, but requires some estimation of the correlation between the short rate and the hazard rate.

In the next section, we are going to focus on the calibration of the model's parameters exploiting the above results on the pricing of some derivatives products within the modeling framework.

6.5   CALIBRATION

6.5.1   Stripping of Hazard Rate

Calibration of Default Probabilities   Credit default swaps are the most liquid credit derivative instruments on a reference entity; therefore, we can use them to back out default probabilities. This is done by discretizing the integrals in the CDS price formula given by (6.21). Indeed, we can write the default and accrual payments as follows:

$$DP \simeq N(1 - R) \sum_{k=1}^{n_d} B(0, t_k) \left(F(0, t_k) - F(0, t_{k-1})\right)$$

$$AP \simeq Nc \sum_{k=1}^{n_d} \left(t_k - t_{\varphi(t_k) - 1}\right) B(0, t_k) \left(F(0, t_k) - F\left(0, t_{\varphi(t_k) - 1}\right)\right)$$

where n_d is the number of discretization dates, $\varphi(t_k)$ is the next coupon date after t_k, and $F(0, t_k) = \mathbb{Q}(\tau < t_k)$ is the default probability. The premium leg, on the other hand, as a function of default probabilities, is equal to

$$PL = Nc \sum_{i=1}^{n} \Delta t_i B(0, t_i)(1 - F(0, t_i)).$$

By bootstrapping we can we get back the default probabilities $F(0, t_k)$, $k = 1, \cdots, n_d$.

Hazard Rate Curve Estimation The hazard function is assumed to be a piecewise constant function, between the maturity dates of the credit default swaps on the reference entity, and is given as follows:

$$h_t = \sum_{i=1}^{m} h_i \mathbf{1}_{t_{i-1} \le t < t_i}$$

The default probability is therefore given as follows:

$$F(t) = 1 - \exp\left(-\int_0^t h_u du\right)$$

$$= 1 - \exp\left(-\sum_{i=1}^{i^*} h_i(t_i - t_{i-1}) + h_{i^*}(\varphi(t) - t)\right),$$

where as before $\varphi(t)$ is the next date (in the sequence $t_1, t_2, \cdots t_m$) after t, and i^* is the corresponding index ($i^* \in \{1, \cdots, m\}$). The hazard rate h_i is then given by

$$h_i = \frac{-1}{t_i - t_{i-1}} \log\left(\frac{1 - F(0, t_i)}{1 - F(0, t_{i-1})}\right)$$

$$= \frac{-1}{t_i - t_{i-1}} \log\left(\frac{S(0, t_i)}{S(0, t_{i-1})}\right),$$

where $S(0, t_i)$ is the survival probability up to date t_i.

6.5.2 Calibration of the Hazard Rate Process

As discussed above, we can back out the default probabilities and hazard rate curve seen from today using credit default swaps. Similarly to interest rate models (see chapter 3), the function θ_t^h does not need to be calibrated and is fully determined by today's survival (default) probabilities. Therefore, we only need to calibrate the volatility and mean reversion parameters σ_t^h and β_t^h which we can do using the credit default swaption prices and the relationship given in (6.25).

Recall the relationship between the CDS option implied volatility and the CDS spread local volatility $\sigma_t^{S_N}$ given by the following expression:

$$\sigma(t_0, t_S) = \frac{1}{t_S - t_0} \int_{t_0}^{t_S} \left(\sigma_u^{S_N}\right)^2 du$$

The main assumption relies on the log-normal distribution of the CDS spread under its natural measure. Therefore, we can rewrite (6.25) such that we can have an explicit dependency between $\sigma_t^{S_N}$ and σ_t^h, by replacing σ^{fh} and σ^{SP} by the expressions given in (6.24) and (6.23). We can therefore use a least square minimization to compute a piecewise constant σ_t^h and β_t^h.

6.5.3 Calibration of the Equity Volatility

The calibration of the equity diffusion consists of the calibration of the local volatility parameter σ^S to standard market option prices. To this end, we will use the formula (6.26) derived before for the price of a European call option in the framework where the stock jumps to zero as the default event happens.

Given that equity option prices are more liquid than their CDS counterpart, we will use the former to calibrate σ_t^S and ρ^{Sh} simultaneously.

6.5.4 Discussion

For most names, and due to the lack of liquid credit default swaptions available on the credit market, the parameters β^h and σ^h could be calibrated bond options. If none of these is liquid enough, calibration to historical data is sometimes done and the adjustment of these parameters (historical vs. risk-neutral) is left to the discretion of the trader.

Sending β^h to 0^+ in (6.14), we get a Ho-Lee kind diffusion for the hazard rate such that the mean reversion effect disappears. This property may prove to be useful when dealing with a credit quality with no particular mean-reverting behavior or with historical data too limited to be used to assess a value for this parameter.

The introduction of defaultable bonds written on the same credit name into the set of calibration instruments could allow us to calibrate the hazard-rate parameters to the market. Note that the presence of these instruments in the hedging strategy legitimates their use in the calibration. Furthermore, despite their close link to the CDS product, their difference in liquidity reflects the different nature of the risk they bear. Convertible bonds, provided some liquidity, could also be added as calibration instruments.

In the following section, we are going to present an extension to this framework by introducing jumps in the stock diffusion and hazard-rate diffusion. This will enable us to capture correctly the movements of the credit spreads. Indeed, when a downgrade is announced by a rating agency, the spreads widen in a jumpy way.

6.6 INTRODUCTION OF DISCONTINUITIES

A natural extension of the model consists of introducing jump processes within the previous framework to account for the spread-widening effects. The objective is threefold: First, the presence of jumps in the equity process allows us to capture the equity smile that is not explained by the introduction of the credit component. Second, adding some discontinuities to the hazard-rate process will allow us to capture, as said above, the spread movements observed in the market. Last, by describing the jumps in both processes, equity and hazard rate, with the same jump processes, we capture better the joint behavior of the hazard rate and the equity. Indeed, the same jump happens at the same time in both quantities with different amplitudes, which allows to capture the correlation between extreme events.

6.6.1   The New Framework

We model the discontinuities in both processes, equity and hazard rate, with the same Poisson processes N_t^1 and N_t^2 with deterministic intensities λ_t^1 and λ_t^2. The jump sizes J_1^S, J_2^S for the equity and J_1^h, J_2^h for the hazard rate are constant. The reason we introduce two jump processes is to account for downgrades and upgrades where the jump sizes account for the average downgrade and upgrade effects. The three Poisson processes N, N^1 and N^2 are taken to be independent:

$$\frac{dS_t}{S_{t-}} = (r_t - y_t)\, dt + \sigma_t^S dW_t^S + (J - 1)\,(dN_t - h_t dt)$$

$$+ J_1^S \left(dN_t^1 - \lambda_t^1 dt \right) + J_2^S \left(dN_t^2 - \lambda_t^2 dt \right)$$

and the hazard rate process is given by

$$dh_t = \left(\theta_t^h - \beta_t^h h_t \right) dt + \sigma_t^h dW_t^h \tag{6.28}$$

$$+ J_1^h dN_t^1 + J_2^h dN_t^2,$$

where W_t^h and W_t^S are correlated as before with the correlation ρ_t^{Sh}. We set $J = 0$ such that when the default event occurs, the equity process drops to zero and stays there.

6.6.2   Dynamics of the Survival Probability

We integrate the SDE (6.28) to get the expression of the hazard rate:
  For $t \geq s$,

$$h_t = h_s \Lambda^h(s,t) + \int_s^t \theta_u^h \Lambda^h(s,u)\, du + \int_s^t \sigma_u^h \Lambda^h(s,u)\, dW_u^h$$

$$+ \int_s^t J_1^h \Lambda^h(s,u)\, dN_u^1 + \int_s^t J_2^h \Lambda^h(s,u)\, dN_u^2.$$

Integrating between t, and T, we have :

$$\int_t^T h_u du = \Psi^h(t,T) h_t + \int_t^T \Psi^h(u,T) \theta_u^h du + \int_t^T \Psi^h(u,T) \sigma_u^h dW_u^h$$

$$+ \int_t^T J_1^h \Psi^h(u,T) dN_u^1 + \int_t^T J_2^h \Psi^h(u,T) dN_u^2.$$

The survival probability is therefore given by the following expression:

$$S(t,T) = E_{\mathbb{Q}}\left[\exp\left(-\int_t^T h_u du\right) | \mathcal{F}_t\right]$$

$$= \exp\left(-\Psi^h(t,T)h_t - \int_t^T \Psi^h(u,T)\theta_u^h du + \frac{1}{2}\int_t^T (\Psi^h(u,T)\sigma_u^h)^2 du\right)$$

$$\times E_{\mathbb{Q}}\left[\exp\left(-J_1^h \int_t^T \Psi^h(u,T)dN_u^1\right) | \mathcal{F}_t\right]$$

$$\times E_{\mathbb{Q}}\left[\exp\left(-J_2^h \int_t^T \Psi^h(u,T)dN_u^2\right) | \mathcal{F}_t\right]$$

$$= \exp\left(-\Psi^h(t,T)h_t - \int_t^T \Psi^h(u,T)\theta_u^h du + \frac{1}{2}\int_t^T (\Psi^h(u,T)\sigma_u^h)^2 du\right)$$

$$\times \exp\left(\int_t^T \lambda_u^1 \left[\exp(-J_1^h \Psi^h(u,T)) - 1\right] du\right)$$

$$\times \exp\left(\int_t^T \lambda_u^2 \left[\exp(-J_2^h \Psi^h(u,T)) - 1\right] du\right)$$

In the above expression, we have made use of the independence between all the random processes involved in the diffusion of the hazard rate (the two Poisson processes and the Brownian motion).

We can also write the expression for $\exp\left(\int_t^T h_u du\right)$ (the equivalent of the cash bond in interest rate):

$$\exp\left(\int_t^T h_u du\right) = \frac{1}{S(t,T)} \exp\left(\int_t^T \Psi^h(u,T)\sigma_u^h dW_u^h + \frac{1}{2}\int_t^T (\Psi^h(u,T)\sigma_u^h)^2 du\right)$$

$$\times \exp\left(J_1^h \int_t^T \Psi^h(u,T)dN_u^1 + \int_t^T \left[\exp(-J_1^h\Psi^h(u,T))-1\right]\lambda_u^1 du\right)$$

$$\times \exp\left(J_2^h \int_t^T \Psi^h(u,T)dN_u^2 + \int_t^T \left[\exp(-J_2^h\Psi^h(u,T))-1\right]\lambda_u^2 du\right)$$

6.6.3   Pricing of European Options

The price of a European call option with a strike K and maturity T is given by

$$C_t = B(t,T) E_{\mathbb{Q}}\left([S_T^* 1_{\tau > T} - K]^+ | \mathcal{G}_t\right)$$

$$= B(t,T) E_{\mathbb{Q}}\left(1_{\tau > T}[S_T^* - K]^+ | \mathcal{G}_t\right)$$

$$= \mathbf{1}_{\tau > t} B\left(t, T\right) E_{\mathbb{Q}} \left(\underbrace{E_{\mathbb{Q}} \left(\exp\left(- \int_t^T h_u du\right) \left[S_T^* - K\right]^+ | \sigma\left(N^1, N^2\right)\right)}_{C_t^n} | \mathcal{F}_t \right),$$

where $B\left(t, T\right)$ is the nondefaultable zero-coupon bond maturing at time T.

$$C_t^n = E_{\mathbb{Q}} \left(\exp\left(- \int_t^T h_u du\right) \left[Z_T - K\right]^+ | \sigma\left(N^1, N^2\right)\right)$$

$$Z_T = F_{t,T}^S \times \exp\left(\int_t^T h_u du\right)$$

$$\times \exp\left(\int_t^T \sigma_u^S dW_u^h - \int_t^T \frac{1}{2}\left(\sigma_u^S\right)^2 du\right)$$

$$\times \exp\left(-\int_t^T \lambda_u^1 J_1^S du\right) \prod_{n_1=1}^{N_{T-t}^1}\left(1 + J_1^S\right) \times \exp\left(-\int_t^T \lambda_u^2 J_2^S du\right) \prod_{n_2=1}^{N_{T-t}^2}\left(1 + J_2^S\right).$$

Therefore,

$$C_t = \mathbf{1}_{\tau > t} B\left(t, T\right) \sum_{n_1=0}^{+\infty} \sum_{n_2=0}^{+\infty} \mathbb{Q}\left(N_{T-t}^1 = n_1\right) \mathbb{Q}\left(N_{T-t}^2 = n_2\right)$$

$$E_{\mathbb{Q}} \left[E_{\mathbb{Q}} \left[\exp\left(-\int_t^T h_u du\right)\left(Z_T - K\right)^+ | N_{T-t}^1 = n_1, N_{T-t}^2 = n_2 \right] | \mathcal{F}_t \right]$$

$$\mathbb{Q}\left(N_{T-t}^i = k\right) = \exp\left(-\int_t^T \lambda_u^i du\right) \frac{\left(\int_t^T \lambda_u^i du\right)^k}{k!}, \ i = 1, 2.$$

Conditionally to $\{N_{T-t} = k\}$, the jump times $(T_1, T_2, \ldots, T_k)$ have the following law:

$$\frac{1}{\left(\int_t^T \lambda_u du\right)^k} \mathbf{1}_{t < t_1 < t_2 < \cdots < t_k < T} \lambda_{t_1} \lambda_{t_2} \cdots \lambda_{t_k} dt_1 dt_2 \cdots dt_k$$

Define

$$H\left(t, T\right) = \exp\left(\int_t^T h_u du\right), \quad \Gamma_{t,T}^i = \int_t^T \lambda_u^i du$$

and

$$\left\{ \begin{array}{c} H^{n_1, n_2}\left(t, T\right) = H\left(t, T\right) |_{N_{T-t}^1 = n_1, N_{T-t}^2 = n_2} \\ Z_T^{n_1, n_2} = Z_T|_{N_{T-t}^1 = n_1, N_{T-t}^2 = n_2} \end{array} \right\}.$$

The call price computation requires computing a double summation. Indeed, we have

$$C_t = 1_{\tau > t} B(t, T)$$

$$\times \sum_{n_1=0}^{+\infty} \sum_{n_2=0}^{+\infty} \frac{1}{n_1!} \frac{1}{n_2!} \int_t^T \cdots \int_t^T E_{\mathbb{Q}} \left[H^{n_1,n_2}(t,T)^{-1} \left(Z_T^{n_1,n_2} - K \right)^+ | \mathcal{F}_t \right]$$

$$\times \lambda_{t_1}^1 \lambda_{t_2}^1 \cdots \lambda_{t_k}^1 \lambda_{t_1}^2 \lambda_{t_2}^2 \cdots \lambda_{t_k}^2 dt_1^1 dt_2^1 \cdots dt_k^1 dt_1^2 dt_2^2 \cdots dt_k^2$$

$$\times \exp\left(-\Gamma_{t,T}^1\right) \exp\left(-\Gamma_{t,T}^2\right),$$

where the expressions of $H^{n_1,n_2}(t,T)$ and $Z_T^{n_1,n_2}$ are respectively given by

$$H^{n_1,n_2}(t,T)^{-1} = \frac{1}{S(t,T)} \exp\left(\sum_{i_1=1}^{n_1} \Psi^b(t_{i_1}^1, T) J_1^b + \sum_{i_2=1}^{n_2} \Psi^b(t_{i_2}^2, T) J_2^b \right)$$

$$\times \exp\left(\int_t^T \left[\exp(-J_1^b \Psi^b(u,T)) - 1 \right] \lambda_u^1 du \right)$$

$$\times \exp\left(\int_t^T \left[\exp(-J_2^b \Psi^b(u,T)) - 1 \right] \lambda_u^2 du \right)$$

$$\times \exp\left(\int_t^T \Psi^b(u,T) \sigma_u^b dW_u^b + \frac{1}{2} \int_t^T (\Psi^b(u,T) \sigma_u^b)^2 du \right)$$

$$Z_T^{n_1,n_2} = F_{t,T}^S H^{n_1,n_2}(t,T) \left(1 + J_1^S \right)^{n_1} \left(1 + J_2^S \right)^{n_2}$$

$$\times \exp\left(-\int_t^T J_1^S \lambda_u^1 du \right) \times \exp\left(-\int_t^T J_2^S \lambda_u^2 du \right)$$

$$\times \exp\left(\int_t^T \sigma_u^S dW_u^S - \frac{1}{2} \int_t^T \left(\sigma_u^S \right)^2 du \right).$$

To simplify these expression, we introduce the new quantities:

$$\overline{H}^{n_1,n_2}(t,T) = \exp\left(\sum_{i_1=1}^{n_1} \left(T - t_{i_1}^1 \right) J_1^b + \sum_{i_2=1}^{n_2} \left(T - t_{i_2}^2 \right) J_2^b \right)$$

$$\times \exp\left(\int_t^T \left[\exp(-J_1^b \Psi^b(u,T)) - 1 \right] \lambda_u^1 du \right)$$

$$\times \exp\left(\int_t^T \left[\exp(-J_2^b \Psi^b(u,T)) - 1 \right] \lambda_u^2 du \right)$$

$$\overline{Z}_T^{n_1,n_2}(t,T) = \left(1 + J_1^S\right)^{n_1}\left(1 + J_2^S\right)^{n_2}$$

$$\times \exp\left(-\int_t^T J_1^S \lambda_u^1 du\right) \times \exp\left(-\int_t^T J_2^S \lambda_u^2 du\right)$$

such that

$$H^{n_1,n_2}(t,T) = \frac{1}{\overline{H}^{n_1,n_2}(t,T)\,S(t,T)}$$

$$\times \exp\left(\int_t^T \Psi^b(u,T)\sigma_u^b dW_u^b + \frac{1}{2}\int_t^T (\Psi^b(u,T)\sigma_u^b)^2 du\right)$$

$$Z_T^{n_1,n_2} = F_{t,T}^S \frac{\overline{Z}_T^{n_1,n_2}(t,T)}{\overline{H}^{n_1,n_2}(t,T)\,S(t,T)}$$

$$\times \exp\left(\int_t^T \Psi^b(u,T)\sigma_u^b dW_u^b + \frac{1}{2}\int_t^T (\Psi^b(u,T)\sigma_u^b)^2 du\right)$$

$$\times \exp\left(\int_t^T \sigma_u^S dW_u^S - \frac{1}{2}\int_t^T \left(\sigma_u^S\right)^2 du\right).$$

Therefore,

$$E_{\mathbb{Q}}\left[H^{n_1,n_2}(t,T)\left(Z_T^{n_1,n_2} - K\right)^+ |\mathcal{F}_t\right] = F_{t,T}^S \overline{Z}_T^{n_1,n_2}(t,T)\,\mathbb{Q}_1\left[Z_T^{n_1,n_2} > K|\mathcal{F}_t\right]$$

$$- K\overline{H}^{n_1,n_2}(t,T)\,S(t,T)\mathbb{Q}_2\left[Z_T^{n_1,n_2} > K|\mathcal{F}_t\right],$$

where $\mathbb{Q}_1$ and $\mathbb{Q}_2$ are given as follows:

$$\frac{d\mathbb{Q}_1}{d\mathbb{Q}} = \exp\left(\int_t^T \sigma_u^S dW_u^S - \frac{1}{2}\int_t^T \left(\sigma_u^S\right)^2 du\right)$$

$$\frac{d\mathbb{Q}_2}{d\mathbb{Q}} = \exp\left(-\int_t^T \Psi^b(u,T)\sigma_u^b dW_u^b - \frac{1}{2}\int_t^T (\Psi^b(u,T)\sigma_u^b)^2 du\right)$$

We can therefore write the price C_t as follows:

$$C_t = \mathbf{1}_{\tau > t} B(t,T) \exp\left(-\Gamma_{t,T}^1\right)\exp\left(-\Gamma_{t,T}^2\right) \tag{6.29}$$

$$\times \sum_{n_1=0}^{+\infty}\sum_{n_2=0}^{+\infty} \frac{1}{n_1!}\frac{1}{n_2!}\int_t^T \cdots \int_t^T P^{n_1,n_2}(t,T)$$

$$\times \lambda_{t_1}^1 \lambda_{t_2}^1 \cdots \lambda_{t_k}^1 \lambda_{t_1}^2 \lambda_{t_2}^2 \cdots \lambda_{t_k}^2\, dt_1^1 dt_2^1 \cdots dt_k^1 dt_1^2 dt_2^2 \cdots dt_k^2,$$

where

$$P^{n_1,n_2}(t,T) = F^S_{t,T} \overline{Z}^{n_1,n_2}_T(t,T) \mathcal{N}(d^{n_1,n_2}_1) - K\overline{H}^{n_1,n_2}(t,T) S(t,T) \mathcal{N}(d^{n_1,n_2}_2)$$

$$d^{n_1,n_2}_1 = \frac{\log\left(\dfrac{F^S_{t,T}\overline{Z}^{n_1,n_2}_T(t,T)}{K\overline{H}^{n_1,n_2}(t,T)S(t,T)}\right) + \frac{1}{2}\overline{\sigma}(t,T)^2}{\overline{\sigma}(t,T)}$$

$$d^{n_1,n_2}_2 = \frac{\log\left(\dfrac{F^S_{t,T}\overline{Z}^{n_1,n_2}_T(t,T)}{K\overline{H}^{n_1,n_2}(t,T)S(t,T)}\right) - \frac{1}{2}\overline{\sigma}(t,T)^2}{\overline{\sigma}(t,T)}$$

$$\overline{\sigma}(t,T) = \sqrt{\frac{1}{2}\int_t^T \left[(\sigma^S_u)^2 + (\Psi^h(u,T)\sigma^h_u)^2 + 2\rho^{Sh}_u \sigma^S_u \sigma^h_u \Psi^h(u,T)\right] du}.$$

It is clear from (6.29) that a direct computation of the price of a European call option is time consuming and a better alternative is needed. In the following section, we apply the Fourier method in order to speed the pricing.

6.6.4 Fourier Pricing

Applying the Carr-Madan technique, we define the dampened call price as follows:

$$C^\alpha_t(k) = \exp(\alpha k)\, C(t,T,k), \ \text{with } \alpha > 0 \ \text{and} \ k = \log K$$

$C(t,T,k)$ is the price of a European option with strike K and maturity T. The Fourier transform of $C^\alpha_t(k)$ is given by

$$\Psi(\zeta) = \int_{-\infty}^{+\infty} e^{i\zeta k} C^\alpha_t(k)\, dk$$

$$= B(t,T) \int_{-\infty}^{+\infty} e^{i\zeta k} e^{\alpha k} E_\mathbb{Q}\left[\exp\left(-\int_t^T h_u du\right)\left(e^{s_T} - e^k\right)^+ |\mathcal{F}_t\right],$$

where $S^*_T = e^{s_T}$ is the nondefaultable stock.

$$\Psi(\zeta) = B(t,T) E_\mathbb{Q}\left[\exp\left(-\int_t^T h_u du\right)\int_{-\infty}^{+\infty} e^{i\zeta k} e^{\alpha k} dk \left(e^{s_T} - e^k\right)^+ |\mathcal{F}_t\right]$$

$$= B(t,T) E_\mathbb{Q}\left[\exp\left(-\int_t^T h_u du\right)\int_{-\infty}^{s_T} e^{i\zeta k} e^{\alpha k} dk \left(e^{s_T} - e^k\right) |\mathcal{F}_t\right]$$

$$= \frac{B(t,T) S(t,T)}{(i\zeta + \alpha)(i\zeta + \alpha + 1)} \overline{\Psi}(\zeta)$$

with

$$
\overline{\Psi}(\zeta) = E_{\mathbb{Q}}\left[\frac{1}{S(t,T)} \exp\left(-\int_t^T h_u du \right) e^{(i\zeta+\alpha+1)s_T} | \mathcal{F}_t \right]
$$

$$
= \left(\frac{F_{t,T}^S}{S(t,T)} \right)^{\omega} E_{\mathbb{Q}}\left[\exp\left(\omega \int_t^T \sigma_u^S \overline{\rho}_u^{Sh} dZ_u^S \right) | \mathcal{F}_t \right]
$$

$$
\times E_{\mathbb{Q}}\left[\exp\left(\int_t^T \left[\omega \sigma_u^S \rho_u^{Sh} + (\omega-1) \Psi^h(u,T)\sigma_u^h \right] dW_u^h \right) | \mathcal{F}_t \right]
$$

$$
\times E_{\mathbb{Q}}\left[\exp\left(\int_t^T \left[\omega \log\left(1+J_1^S \right) + (\omega-1) \Psi^h(u,T)J_1^h \right] dN_u^1 \right) | \mathcal{F}_t \right]
$$

$$
\times E_{\mathbb{Q}}\left[\exp\left(\int_t^T \left[\omega \log\left(1+J_2^S \right) + (\omega-1) \Psi^h(u,T)J_2^h \right] dN_u^2 \right) | \mathcal{F}_t \right]
$$

$$
\times \exp\left(\frac{-\omega}{2} \int_t^T \left(\sigma_u^S \right)^2 du \right) \times \exp\left(\frac{-(\omega-1)}{2} \int_t^T \left(\Psi^h(u,T)\sigma_u^h \right)^2 du \right)
$$

$$
\times \exp\left(-\int_t^T \left[\omega J_1^S - (\omega-1) \left(e^{-J_1^h \Psi^h(u,T)} - 1 \right) \right] \lambda_u^1 du \right)
$$

$$
\times \exp\left(-\int_t^T \left[\omega J_2^S - (\omega-1) \left(e^{-J_2^h \Psi^h(u,T)} - 1 \right) \right] \lambda_u^2 du \right)
$$

where $\omega = i\zeta + \alpha + 1$, and Z^S is independent from W^h such that: $W_t^S = \rho_t^{Sh} W_t^h + \overline{\rho}_t^{Sh} Z_t^S$. The above expression is simplified as follows:

$$
\overline{\Psi}(\zeta) = \left(\frac{F_{t,T}^S}{S(t,T)} \right)^{\omega} \exp\left(\frac{\omega(\omega-1)}{2} \int_t^T \left[\left(\sigma_u^S \rho_u^{Sh} \right)^2 + 2\sigma_u^S \rho_u^{Sh} \sigma_u^h \Psi^h(u,T) \right] du \right)
$$

$$
\times \exp\left(\frac{(\omega-1)(\omega-2)}{2} \int_t^T \left(\Psi^h(u,T)\sigma_u^h \right)^2 du \right)
$$

$$
\times \exp\left(-\int_t^T \left[\left(1+J_1^S \right)^{\omega} e^{-(\omega-1)J_1^h \Psi^h(u,T)} - \omega \left(1+J_1^S \right) \right. \right.
$$

$$
\left. + (\omega-1) e^{-J_1^h \Psi^h(u,T)} \right] \lambda_u^1 du \bigg)
$$

$$
\times \exp\left(-\int_t^T \left[\left(1+J_2^S \right)^{\omega} e^{-(\omega-1)J_2^h \Psi^h(u,T)} - \omega \left(1+J_2^S \right) \right. \right.
$$

$$
\left. + (\omega-1) e^{-J_2^h \Psi^h(u,T)} \right] \lambda_u^2 du \bigg)
$$

We can therefore compute the call price by inverting the Fourier transform computed above.

$$C\left(t,T,k\right) = e^{-k\alpha} C_t^{\alpha}\left(k\right) = B\left(t,T\right) S\left(t,T\right) \frac{e^{-k\alpha}}{\pi}$$
$$\times \int_0^{+\infty} \frac{1}{(i\zeta + \alpha)(i\zeta + \alpha + 1)} e^{-i\zeta k} \overline{\Psi}\left(\zeta\right) d\zeta$$

This technique is computationally very quick, which is very important for the calibration.

6.7 EQUITY DEFAULT SWAPS

The *equity default swap*, or EDS, is an instrument whose definition intentionally reflects that of the much-better-known credit default swap (CDS).

The two counterparties to the EDS transaction are the *protection buyer* and *protection seller*. The protection that is traded is protection against a stock's reaching a level that is relatively low compared to the *reference price* (the stock's traded price at the inception of the trade). This level, the barrier, might be 70%, perhaps 50%, or even 30% of the reference price, that is, low compared to barriers typically seen in standard down-barrier options.

The key difference between the EDS and CDS is that the CDS protection is triggered only on a default event, doubtless accompanied by a precipitous drop in the share price of the defaulting company, perhaps to near zero, whereas the EDS protection pays out if the stock drops below a level that is still far from zero, whether or not this is accompanied by a default. (It is perfectly possible for the share price of a company to fall, over a reasonably long period, by a factor of three with no suggestion that the company is close to default nor with necessarily a corresponding fall in its dividend payment.)

This breach of the barrier is known as the *knock-in event*. We may immediately distinguish two cases: the knock-in event being caused by the stock diffusing across the barrier in the ordinary way (the mechanism by which barriers are breached when barrier options are priced, as they frequently are, in a pure diffusion model such as local volatility); and the event being caused by a default causing the share price to "gap" to below the barrier (perhaps to near zero).

Note that although we distinguish these cases within the context of a diffusion model with jump-to-default, there is no such distinction written into the definition of the structure. Nor, for that matter, is it generally clear from market information what is causing any given move in the stock. An advantage often claimed for EDS over CDS is that the determination of a credit event is less transparent than an observation of a share price, as the latter is based on public market information.

As its name suggests, the EDS is structured as a swap having two legs: the *fixed* leg and the *protection* leg, sometimes known as the *equity* leg. Each leg, of course, is written on the same notional amount N_0. The protection buyer is short the fixed leg: he pays a predetermined coupon stream to the protection seller. This might be $x\% \times N_0$ quarterly, for example. The protection seller pays a predetermined amount to the protection buyer in the event of the barrier's being breached. This amount will be $y\% \times N_0$ less the accrued on the fixed leg at the time of the knock-in event.

Another variant replaces the fixed coupons with floating, so the payments might be calculated using a LIBOR rate plus a spread. Again, the floating leg payment in the event of a knock-in event is the appropriate accrued amount.

It is possible to extend the equity default swap concept to so-called *multiname* structures, in which the protection traded, and therefore the definition of the knock-in event, relates to the *first* of several underlyings to hit its corresponding barrier (compare first-to-default structures in the credit market); all barriers being set at the same level relative to their spot values at the inception of the trade. We will not explicitly describe these here; it is a straightforward generalization. At the time of writing, in the authors' experience, multiname EDSs trade less frequently than single name.

Structuring an EDS   EDSs as described above trade in the interbank market. For wider distribution, however, it is common to structure the product as a *note*.

The buyer pays 100 on entering the position, and receives this amount back from the issuer at maturity unless there has been a *knock-in event* prior to this. The knock-in event is defined as the first date on which the closing price of the underlying share on the relevant exchange is at or below the barrier. (It is precisely this transparency and simplicity of definition that is the feature argued in favor of the EDS.) The buyer of the note receives a coupon stream, or else it may be a *zero-coupon* instrument, in which case he receives only a coupon at maturity, in addition to the redemption payment.

In the event of a knock-in, the note is said to *accelerate* (i.e., terminate early), and the holder receives an early redemption payment much less than 100: only 50, say. He also receives the accrued on the coupon accruing at the time of the knock-in event.

The holder therefore stands to lose a substantial fraction of his investment if the underlying share breaches the barrier. If default were the only process that could trigger this, he would be accepting simple credit risk and would have sold the protection against that risk. Of course, in a model with default and diffusion, either process can cause the knock-in event to trigger. In exchange for accepting this risk, he is compensated with an above-risk-free coupon stream.

This trade can be decomposed into an EDS as defined above, whose protection leg pays 50, plus a bond that knocks out under the same conditions as the knock-in event of the note.

The protection seller (note holder) may also enter into a cancelable swap to mitigate his interest rate risk. Thus, he may agree to exchange his fixed-coupon payment for a sequence of floating payments plus a spread. He would then have interest rate risk only on the spread (the floating payments plus final redemption payment value exactly to 100, irrespective of rates). The cancellation clause would, of course, be precisely the knock-in event of the note.

6.7.1   Modeling Equity Default Swaps

For a general-case multiname EDS priced under stochastic hazard rates, any of the choices for the hazard-rate diffusion given in section 6.3.1 may be realized by brute-force Monte Carlo. There are a number of issues with this:

■ Each time step of each path of each underlying requires an interpolation to be made on a local volatility surface, which can be slow. That said, careful implementation techniques can considerably alleviate this problem.

■ Structures having many underlyings are computationally intensive to risk manage: for N underlyings, there are obviously N deltas, gammas, and vegas, and $\frac{1}{2}N(N-1)$ off-diagonal gammas. Clearly, this is not limited to multiname EDSs, nor is it specific to Monte Carlo as a numerical technique, but it is a significant issue in modeling and risk managing these positions. Combined with the instability of simple finite difference approximations for the gammas of barrier-type products valued by Monte Carlo, there is a real issue in obtaining this risk for multiname EDS. Exactly the same issue is addressed in section 7.4.1 as applied to another multiunderlying structure type: the Altiplano.

■ The simulation requires as parameters the correlations between all pairs of equities and hazard rates. In particular, it requires equity-equity correlations, which we take to be given. It requires also the correlations between equities and their corresponding hazard rates; the calibration of the hazard-rate process provides these. But it also needs correlations between pairs of hazard rates and between hazard rates and other stocks: We have to make assumptions about these categories of data.

Furthermore, it is found that the EDS is not especially sensitive to the volatility of the hazard rate. Accordingly, it is reasonable to model it under deterministic hazard rates, which is usually done.

6.7.2   Single-Name EDSs in a Deterministic Hazard Rate Model

In the case of single-name EDSs, we can do significantly better than Monte Carlo by treating the structure as a sort of barrier option. The usual approach to these types is to use a finite difference or finite element scheme to discretize the PDE, and to apply a Dirichlet condition at the barrier. Chapter 9 gives an account of numerical solution of the PDEs of finance using finite element methods, and there are many accounts of the application of finite difference techniques to these PDEs.

If the protection amount is $y\% \times N_0$ less the accrued on the fixed leg at the time of the knock-in event, then the Dirichlet condition is a sawtooth function of time, whose discontinuities are the coupon dates. This should not cause a problem in practice, as the scheme will in any event place time steps exactly on the coupon dates in order to adjust the node values by the coupon payments.

One natural corollary to using a PDE approach instead of a Monte Carlo is that the barrier is assumed to be observed continuously, whereas in a simple Monte Carlo, the observations are necessarily discrete at the step dates. In the case of our example above, the observation of exchange closing prices implies that the Monte Carlo approach is exact. Accordingly, in adopting a PDE approach we are trading

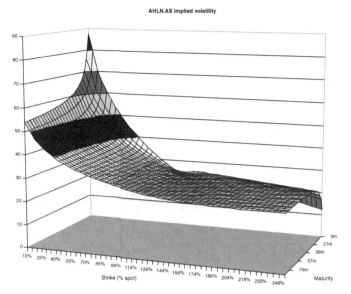

FIGURE 6.1 Ahold implied volatility as of December 2005, across a wide range of strikes and up to 7y maturity.

a slight bias in the pricing for an improvement in speed and in the stability of the greeks.[2]

We therefore have a PDE in one spatial variable to solve for the single-name EDS. For a time-dependent protection payment $R(t)$, the PDE we solve in a local volatility model with deterministic default risk is

$$\frac{\partial V}{\partial t} = \frac{1}{2}\sigma(S,t)S^2\frac{\partial^2 V}{\partial S^2} + (r(t) + \lambda(t))S\frac{\partial V}{\partial S} - (r(t) + \lambda(t))V + \lambda(t)R(t). \quad (6.30)$$

The significant term in this is, of course, the inhomogeneous source term introduced by the presence of jumps.

A Worked Example: Ahold As an example, we select for study a five-year EDS written on Ahold (Reuters code AHLN.AS) with a barrier at 50% (of the share's traded price at the inception of the trade). (Ahold is a group of food retail and food service operators listed on Euronext and other exchanges.) As of December 2005, the credit default swap curve for this company was rising steeply from around 20bps for a one-year CDS to around 110bps at five years. With this information and market implied volatilities (shown in figure 6.1), we can calibrate a local volatility for the stock, given the possibility of jump to zero, using the procedures of chapter 8. The results of the calibration procedure are shown in figure 6.2.

The figure shows the relative error in European option prices after the calibration, that is, the difference between prices calculated in a local volatility model and market prices inferred from implied volatilities, divided by the price of the stock:

$$\text{Error} = \frac{P_{LV} - P_{Mkt}}{S}$$

---

[2]A *barrier shift* can approximately compensate for this.

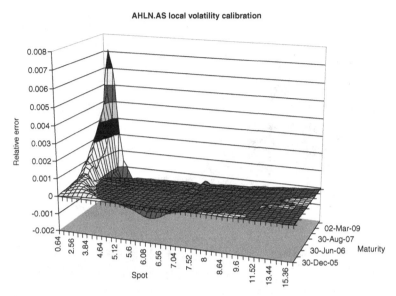

AHLN.AS local volatility calibration

FIGURE 6.2 The local volatility calibration error on European option prices as a fraction of spot. The peak indicates the onset of arbitrage in the data.

The graph indicates that the majority of the region displayed calibrates to within ±10 basis points, regarded as reasonably acceptable. However, there is a pronounced peak at longer maturities and at spot prices below about 50% of the prevailing traded price. This is not an error in the calibration: It indicates the onset of arbitrage between the implied volatilities and the CDS curve used in the calibration. We can think of this in the following way:

For a constant volatility of the diffusion process, the presence of default risk makes puts more expensive as it raises the conditional (on no default) forward while at the same time introducing a likelihood of a maximum payout from the put. (The calibration options are taken to be riskless, perhaps exchange-traded, options on a risky share.) It also raises the call price: the increased forward contributing positively to the price while the probability of default before maturity resulting in a zero payout acts in the opposite way. Call-put parity is still required to hold, as the effect of default risk on the distribution at maturity is simply to change its form by introducing a peak at $S_T = 0$. (Throughout, we are considering that default results in the share price dropping to zero.) The local volatility calibration tries to compensate for this price-increasing effect of the credit by lowering the diffusion volatility to preserve the observed market price. If a near-zero local volatility cannot reproduce the calibration prices, then the data are arbitrageable.

We may value the EDS in a finite difference lattice scheme and use this to look at the price as a function of spot at the $t = 0$ time step of the grid.[3] In the interests of simplicity, we will, in the following, drop the time variation of the protection payment caused by the accrued coupon. No essential features of the protection leg are lost.

---

[3]The barrier of 50% keeps the lattice clear of the arbitrageable region.

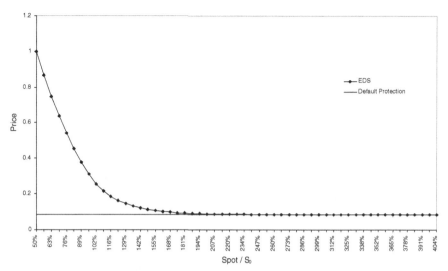

EDS Approach to Default Protection

FIGURE 6.3 A 5y EDS on AHLN.AS vs. share price. The asymptote is the value of a default protection written on the stock.

Figure 6.3 plots only the protection leg of the EDS. Note that, since the plot is taken from a single FD grid, the local volatility model is assumed valid, inasmuch as the local volatility surface is held constant rather than the implied surface. (See section 1.2.1 and remark 1.2.1 for reasons why keeping the implied surface constant between plots, and recalibrating local volatility each time, is inappropriate.) The graph shows an asymptote, which is the value of a pure *default protection* calculated according to

$$\text{Default Protection} := \mathbb{E}\left[\,1_{0<\tau\leq T} \cdot \text{DF}(\tau)\,\right]$$

$$= \int_0^\infty 1_{0<t\leq T} \cdot \exp\{-\int_0^t r_s\,ds\} \cdot h_t \cdot \exp\{-\int_0^t h_s\,ds\}\,dt$$

$$= \int_0^T h_t \cdot \exp\{-\int_0^t h_s\,ds\} \cdot \exp\{-\int_0^t r_s\,ds\}dt,$$

this being the value of a payment of one at the time of default, if default occurs before a maturity T.[4] Although not visible in the graph, there is a small offset between the analytic default protection value and the limiting EDS leg value. This decreases slowly with increasing the number of time steps in the FD grid.

Were we to model the protection leg of the EDS on a default-free underlying, we would call it a deep out-of-the-money American Digital put,[5] and the asymptotic

---

[4]In evaluating the default protection, a quantity completely independent of spot price, the same interest rates and hazard rates were used as for the EDS.

[5]This is just a matter of language. The contract terms are (apart from the accrued coupon) identical between an American Digital put and the protection leg of an EDS. The only distinction is whether we are considering the underlying to be risky or not.

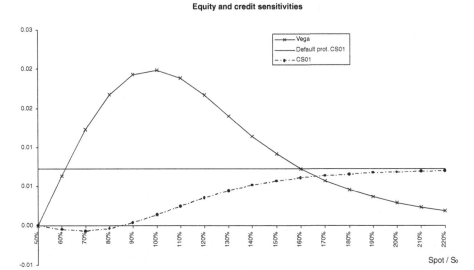

FIGURE 6.4 The vega and CDS curve sensitivity of the protection leg across a reasonably wide range of spot prices, showing regions of predominant equity sensitivity and credit sensitivity. The asymptote is the CS01 of the pure default protection.

value as $S \to \infty$ would be zero, in contrast to figure 6.3. The only way in which such a structure can yield value to the holder, in the default-free model, is by the stock diffusing across the barrier. Contrast this with the EDS default protection leg on a risky underlying where the protection buyer can receive a payout either if diffusion carries the stock to the barrier or if default carries the stock clean through the barrier. Both possibilities contribute value to the structure, in amounts according to the distance of the asset from the barrier relative to the general level of its volatility and to its hazard rates. Accordingly, we can identify the two regimes in which the EDS can exist, and call them *diffusion dominated* and *default dominated*, corresponding to the cases where most of the value comes from the possibility of the stock diffusing to the barrier, and to the converse case where it mostly comes from the possibility of default.

We can quantify these notions by looking at the equity and credit sensitivities of the protection leg. We do so for our example Ahold EDS.

Figure 6.4 shows the vega and CDS curve sensitivity of the protection leg, in isolation, over a wide range of share prices around the prevailing traded price. The vega looks qualitatively very similar to the American Digital: necessarily zero at the barrier, positive elsewhere, and tending to zero as $S \to \infty$ and the probability of diffusion to the barrier consequently vanishes. The sensitivity to CDS rates (known as *CS01*) tends to a nonzero asymptote as $S \to \infty$: this is the CS01 of the pure default protection, as expected. The regions in which one sensitivity is substantial and the other negligible serve to identify the diffusion dominated and default dominated regions.

The negative CS01 near the barrier is at first sight counterintuitive: We plot it on an expended horizontal scale and a greatly expanded vertical scale in figure 6.5. The expectation is that increased CDS rates implies increased probability of default before maturity, increased value and positive CS01. This is indeed the case far from the barrier.

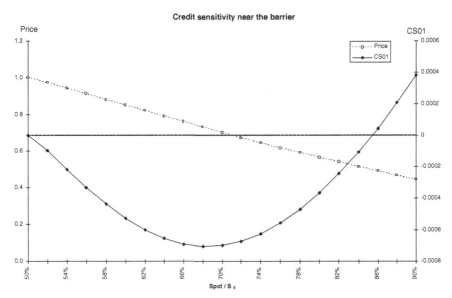

FIGURE 6.5 The CDS curve sensitivity of the EDS protection leg in the diffusion-dominated region near the barrier.

We can, however, understand how this intuition fails by noting that increased hazard rates increase the drift of the asset (the convection term in (6.30)) and so tend to bring it further from the barrier early in the lifetime of the structure. It is precisely in the diffusion-dominated region near the barrier that this is critical, where the likelihood is that the asset will diffuse to the barrier before it defaults. Increased drift lessens this likelihood, or lengthens the expected time before the barrier is breached. The negative CS01 indicates that this is more significant than the increase in the probability of breaching the barrier due to a default given that in this region any default is likely to occur after the barrier is hit.

6.8 CONCLUSION

In this chapter we have presented a modeling framework suitable for equity- and credit-sensitive structures. The main problem we face when it comes to pricing these structures is liquidity. Indeed, the scarcity of the data especially from the credit point of view makes it difficult to calibrate any model no matter how good that model.

While convertible bonds (see chapter 4, in the context of equity-interest rate hybrids) remain the most liquid and popular hybrid structure, we have witnessed lately a surge in new hybrid structures, such as the equity default swap.

Advanced Pricing Techniques

Copulas Applied to Derivatives Pricing

7.1 INTRODUCTION

In this chapter, we highlight the importance that copulas have gained in derivatives pricing in the last decade. This is due mainly to the growth seen in the credit derivatives markets. Indeed, basket default swaps, CDO tranches, and all correlation structures are often priced and risk managed using the copula technology. Copulas have been used widely in the insurance business, and the transition to the credit derivatives world was natural, as the latter is often thought of as an insurance business on the default of companies.

This chapter is organized as follows: First, we tackle copulas from a theoretical point of view by presenting various properties and families of copulas. We present as well the copula of a stochastic process highlighting the time dependency, or autocorrelation, induced by a process. Second, we look at some applications to derivatives pricing. We start by presenting the factor copula technique, which enables us to reduce dimensionality of the problem and find semiclosed-form solutions for various derivatives contracts. Last, we apply the previous approach to the pricing not only of credit derivatives but some popular multiunderlying equity derivatives, precisely collateralized debt obligations, basket default swaps, and Altiplanos.

7.2 THEORETICAL BACKGROUND OF COPULAS

7.2.1 Definitions

Definition and Sklar Theorem

DEFINITION 7.2.1 *A copula is an n-dimensional function* $C: [0,1]^n \longrightarrow [0,1]$, *which has the following properties:*

- C is increasing in each of its coordinates u_k for $k \in \{1, 2, \ldots, n\}$.
- $C(u) = 0$ if at least one of the coordinates of the vector u is equal to 0.
- $C(u) = u_k$ if all the coordinates of u but u_k are equal to 1.
- for every $x, y \in [0,1]^n$, such that $x \leq y^1$. The volume of the hypercube $H = [x_1, y_1] \times [x_2, y_2] \times \cdots \times [x_n, y_n]$, $V_C(H)$ is non-negative, where

---

[1] $x \leq y$ means that $x_k \leq y_k$ for $k \in \{1, \ldots, n\}$.

$$V_C(H) = \sum_{i_1=1}^{2} \sum_{i_2=1}^{2} \cdots \sum_{i_n=1}^{2} (-1)^{i_1+i_2+\cdots+i_n} C(z_{i_1}, \ldots, z_{i_n})$$

where $z_{i_j} = x_j$ if $i_j = 1$ and $z_{i_j} = y_j$ if $i_j = 2$ for $j \in \{1, \ldots, n\}$.

From the above definition, we can conclude that a copula is a multidimensional distribution with uniform marginals. The following theorem proves to be at the heart of the copula theory and its applications.

THEOREM 7.2.1 *(Sklar) Let F be an n-dimensional distribution function with marginals $F_1, F_2, \ldots, F_n$, then there exist an n-dimensional copula C, such that*

$$F(x_1, x_2, \ldots, x_n) = C(F_1(x_1), F_2(x_2), \ldots, F_n(x_n)) \text{ for all } (x_1, x_2, \ldots, x_n) \in \mathcal{R}^n.$$

And if $F_1, F_2, \ldots, F_n$ are continuous, then C is unique.

REMARK 7.2.1 *Let C be the copula of the random variables X and Y. Any increasing transformation of (X, Y) has the same copula C.*

Frechet Bounds

THEOREM 7.2.2 *Let C be a two-dimensional copula; we have the following result:*

$$\max(u + v - 1, 0) \leq C(u, v) \leq \min(u, v) , \ (u, v) \in [0, 1]^2$$

This result is straightforward: Due to monotonicity we have $C(u, v) \leq C(u, 1) = u$ and $C(u, v) \leq C(1, v) = v$. On the other hand, let $H = [u, 1] \times [v, 1]$; we have $V_C(H) \geq 0$, which implies $C(u, v) \geq u + v - 1$, the positivity of C completes the proof.

$W(u, v) = \max(u + v - 1, 0)$ and $M(u, v) = \min(u, v)$ are called Frechet bounds. The Frechet bounds also exist in the multidimensional case and are given as follows:

$$W(u_1, \ldots, u_n) = \max\left(\sum_{i=1}^{n} u_i - n + 1, 0\right)$$

$$M(u_1, \ldots, u_n) = \min(u_1, \ldots, u_n)$$

$(u_1, \ldots, u_n) \in [0, 1]^n$, $n \geq 2$.

Another well-known and useful copula is the independence copula defined as follows:

$$\pi(u_1, \ldots, u_n) = \prod_{i=1}^{n} u_i, (u_1, \ldots, u_n) \in [0, 1]^n, n \geq 2.$$

REMARK 7.2.2 *W is not a copula for $n \geq 3$. Indeed, consider $H = \left[\frac{1}{2}, 1\right]^n$, $V_W(H) = 1 - \frac{n}{2} \leq 0$. This means that condition 4 in the definition above is violated.*

Conditional Distributions and Partial Derivatives
The partial derivatives of a copula function are closely linked to the concept of conditional expectations. This proves to

be very useful when sampling random variables whose dependency is described by a copula function. The heuristic argument comes from the following computation: Consider the probability measure $\mathbf{Q}$ and two random variables x_1 and x_2 with distribution functions F_1 and F_2 respectively and a joint distribution F.

$$
\begin{aligned}
\mathbf{Q}\left(X_1 \leq x_1 | X_2 = x_2\right) &= \lim_{\Delta x_2 \to 0} \mathbf{Q}\left(X_1 \leq x_1 | x_2 \leq X_2 \leq x_2 + \Delta x_2\right) \\
&= \lim_{\Delta x_2 \to 0} \frac{F\left(x_1, x_2 + \Delta x_2\right) - F\left(x_1, x_2\right)}{F_2\left(x_2 + \Delta x_2\right) - F_2\left(x_2\right)} \\
&= \lim_{\Delta x_2 \to 0} \frac{C\left(F_1\left(x_1\right), F_2\left(x_2 + \Delta x_2\right)\right) - C\left(F_1\left(x_1\right), F_2\left(x_2\right)\right)}{F_2\left(x_2 + \Delta x_2\right) - F_2\left(x_2\right)} \\
&= \frac{\partial C}{\partial v}\left(u, v\right)|_{F_1(x_1), F_2(x_2)}
\end{aligned}
$$

The multidimensional density[2] f is linked to the copula function as follows:

$$
\begin{aligned}
f\left(x_1, x_2, \ldots, x_n\right) &= \frac{\partial C}{\partial u_1 \ldots \partial u_n}\left(u_1, u_2, \ldots, u_n\right)|_{(F_1(x_1), F_2(x_2), \ldots, F_n(x_n))} \prod_{i=1}^{n} f_i\left(x_i\right) \\
&= c\left(F_1\left(x_1\right), F_2\left(x_2\right), \ldots, F_n\left(x_n\right)\right) \times \prod_{i=1}^{n} f_i\left(x_i\right)
\end{aligned}
$$

where $c\left(u_1, u_2, \ldots, u_n\right)$ is the copula density.

7.2.2 Measures of Dependence

Concordance

DEFINITION 7.2.2 *The realizations (x_1, y_1), and (x_2, y_2) of two random variables X, Y are said to be concordant if $(x_1 - x_2) \times (y_1 - y_2) \geq 0$, and discordant if $(x_1 - x_2) \times (y_1 - y_2) \leq 0$.*

Kendall's Tau

DEFINITION 7.2.3 *In a discrete space, if we call $(x_1, y_1), (x_2, y_2) \ldots . (x_n, y_n)$ the possible realizations of two random variables X, Y. Let note c be the number of concordant pairs and d the number of discordant pairs. The Kendall's τ for this sample is defined as follows:*

$$
\tau = \frac{c - d}{c + d}
$$

In the general case, Kendall's τ is defined as the probability of concordance minus the probability of discordance. Indeed, let (X_1, Y_1) and (X_2, Y_2) be two

---

[2] $f\left(x_1, x_2, \ldots, x_n\right) = \frac{\partial F}{\partial x_1 \ldots \partial x_n}\left(x_1, x_2, \ldots, x_n\right)$ where F is the cumulative distribution function.

independent vectors with the same joint distribution function as (X, Y); we have

$$\tau = \mathbf{Q}\left((X_1 - X_2)(Y_1 - Y_2) > 0\right) - \mathbf{Q}\left((X_1 - X_2)(Y_1 - Y_2) < 0\right).$$

THEOREM 7.2.3 *Let (X_1, Y_1) and (X_2, Y_2) be independent vectors with continuous random variables with joint distributions F_1 and F_2, respectively, with common marginals for F_X and F_Y. Denote C_1 and C_2 the corresponding copulas such that $F_1(x, y) = C_1(F_X(x), F_Y(y))$ and $F_2(x, y) = C_2(F_X(x), F_Y(y))$. If we define Υ as the difference between the probabilities of concordance and discordance of (X_1, Y_1) and $(X_2, Y_2) : \Upsilon = \mathbf{Q}\left((X_1 - X_2)(Y_1 - Y_2) > 0\right) - \mathbf{Q}\left((X_1 - X_2)(Y_1 - Y_2) < 0\right)$, then*

$$\Upsilon = \Upsilon(C_1, C_2) = 4 \iint_{[0,1]^2} C_2(u, v)\, dC_1(u, v) - 1.$$

In the case of two continuous random variables X, Y whose copula is C, the Kendall's τ is given by

$$\tau_{XY} = \Upsilon(C, C) = 4 \iint_{[0,1]^2} C(u, v)\, dC(u, v) - 1.$$

Spearman's Rho   The Spearman's rho dependence measure is also based on concordance and discordance concepts.

DEFINITION 7.2.4 *If we take now three independent random vectors (X_1, Y_1), (X_2, Y_2), and (X_3, Y_3) with the same joint distribution F, the Spearman's rho is defined as the difference between the probability of concordance and the probability of discordance of the two random vectors (X_1, Y_1) and (X_2, Y_3):*

$$\rho = \mathbf{Q}\left((X_1 - X_2)(Y_1 - Y_3) > 0\right) - \mathbf{Q}\left((X_1 - X_2)(Y_1 - Y_3) < 0\right)$$

THEOREM 7.2.4 *For continuous random variables X and Y whose copula is C, the Spearman's rho is given by*

$$\rho_{XY} = 3\Upsilon(C, \pi) = 12 \iint_{[0,1]^2} uv\, dC(u, v) - 3$$

$$= 12 \iint_{[0,1]^2} C(u, v)\, du\, dv - 3,$$

where π is the independence copula introduced previously.

Tail Dependence   It is well known that the Gaussian copula, the most used one in the financial industry, fails to capture tail dependencies as its tails flatten very quickly.

On the other hand, when dealing with fat-tailed distributions we want to know how well we capture the dependency between those extreme values. The two concepts of *low tail dependency* and *up tail dependency* have been introduced in order to measure the extreme values dependency as the number of financial contingent claims that depend on these values has risen dramatically in the last years. This has been triggered by the markets being marked with few extreme events, from the technology bubble to the corporate scandals and of course the terrorist attacks.

DEFINITION 7.2.5 *Let X and Y be two random variables with cumulative distribution functions F_X and F_Y. The coefficients of upper and lower dependency are defined as follows:*

$$\lambda_L = \lim_{u \to 0} Q\left(Y \leq F_Y^{-1}(u) | X \leq F_X^{-1}(u)\right)$$

$$\lambda_U = \lim_{u \to 1} Q\left(Y > F_Y^{-1}(u) | X > F_X^{-1}(u)\right),$$

provided, of course, that these limits exist.

If $\lambda_L \in]0,1]$ ($\lambda_U \in]0,1]$) then X and Y are said to be asymptotically dependent in the lower tail (upper tail), and if $\lambda_L = 0$ ($\lambda_U = 0$), they are said to be asymptotically independent in the lower tail (upper tail).

We can show using the Base rule and the relationship between the survival function[3] $S(x,y)$ of (X,Y) and the cumulative distribution functions of X, Y and (X,Y) that

$$\lambda_L = \lim_{u \to 0} \frac{C(u,u)}{u}$$

$$\lambda_U = \lim_{u \to 1} \frac{1 + C(u,u) - 2u}{1 - u}.$$

7.2.3 Copulas and Stochastic Processes

Some properties of stochastic processes can be characterized by their finite-dimensional distributions and therefore by copulas. Unfortunately, many of the stochastic process concepts are stronger than the finite dimensional distributions. In this paragraph, we focus on some well-known Markov[4] processes. We define the copula of a Markov process X as being the copula $C^{s,t}$ of X_t and X_s.

The Copula of a Brownian Motion From the definition of a Brownian motion we know that for $t > s$ and x, y real numbers, we have

$$Q(W_t \leq x | W_s = y) = \mathcal{N}\left(\frac{x - y}{\sqrt{t - s}}\right)$$

---

[3]It is defined as follows: $S(x,y) = Q(X \geq x, Y \geq y)$.
[4]A process X_t is said to be Markov if $Q(X_t \leq x | \mathcal{F}_s) = Q(X_t \leq x | X_s)$ where $\mathcal{F}_s = \sigma(X_u, u \leq s)$.

where $\mathcal{N}$ is the cumulative distribution function of a standard normal distribution variable.

Exploiting the relationship between the conditional expectation and partial derivatives of a copula we can write

$$C_W^{s,t}\left(F_s\left(x\right), F_t\left(y\right)\right) = \int_{-\infty}^x \frac{\partial C}{\partial v}\left(u, v\right)|_{F_s(w), F_t(y)} f_s\left(w\right) dw$$

where F_s and F_t are the cumulative distribution functions of W_s and W_t, respectively, and f_s is the density of W_s. Hence

$$
\begin{aligned}
C_W^{s,t}\left(F_s\left(x\right), F_t\left(y\right)\right) &= \int_{-\infty}^x \mathcal{N}\left(\frac{y-w}{\sqrt{t-s}}\right) f_s\left(w\right) dw \\
&= \int_{-\infty}^{F_s^{-1}(F_s(x))} \mathcal{N}\left(\frac{F_t^{-1}\left(F_t\left(y\right)\right) - F_s^{-1}\left(F_s\left(w\right)\right)}{\sqrt{t-s}}\right) f_s\left(w\right) dw \\
&= \int_{-\infty}^{F_s(x)} \mathcal{N}\left(\frac{F_t^{-1}\left(F_t\left(y\right)\right) - F_s^{-1}\left(w\right)}{\sqrt{t-s}}\right) dw.
\end{aligned}
$$

We therefore can express the copula $C_W^{s,t}$ as follows:

$$C_W^{s,t}\left(u, v\right) = \int_{-\infty}^u \mathcal{N}\left(\frac{\sqrt{t}\mathcal{N}^{-1}\left(v\right) - \sqrt{s}\mathcal{N}^{-1}\left(w\right)}{\sqrt{t-s}}\right) dw.$$

We have used $F_t^{-1}\left(x\right) = \sqrt{t}\mathcal{N}^{-1}\left(x\right)$. The copula density is then given by

$$c_W^{s,t}\left(u, v\right) = \sqrt{\frac{t}{t-s}} \frac{\varphi\left(\frac{\sqrt{t}\mathcal{N}^{-1}(v) - \sqrt{s}\mathcal{N}^{-1}(u)}{\sqrt{t-s}}\right)}{\varphi\left(\mathcal{N}^{-1}\left(v\right)\right)}, \quad \left(u, v\right) \in [0,1]^2,$$

where φ is the density of a standard normal variable.

REMARK 7.2.3 *A geometric Brownian motion is an increasing transformation of its underlying arithmetic Brownian motion; therefore, they have the same copula.*

Copula of a Continuous Martingale By employing a time change we can link the copula of a martingale to that of a Brownian motion. This is possible only for martingales whose bracket goes to infinity when time goes to infinity.

THEOREM 7.2.5 *Let X_t be a $(Q, \mathcal{F}_t)$ local martingale with deterministic bracket such that $X_0 = 0$ and $\lim_{t \to +\infty} <X>_t = +\infty$ a.s. Define T_t and B_t as follows:*

$$T_t := \inf\{u, \ <X>_u > t\}, \ B_t = X_{T_t}$$

B_t is an $\mathcal{F}_{T_t}$ Brownian motion and $X_t = B_{<X>_t}$, and its copula is given by

$$C_X^{s,t}\left(u, v\right) = \int_{-\infty}^u \mathcal{N}\left(\frac{\sqrt{<X>_t}\mathcal{N}^{-1}\left(v\right) - \sqrt{<X>_s}\mathcal{N}^{-1}\left(w\right)}{\sqrt{<X>_t - <X>_s}}\right) dw \text{ for } t > s.$$

The Copula of an Ornstein-Uhlenbeck Process: The OU process is defined on $(Q, \mathcal{F}_t)$ as follows:

$$dr_t = -\lambda r_t dt + \sigma \, dW_t$$

where W_t is standard $\mathcal{F}_t$ Brownian motion and $\lambda, \sigma > 0$. Solving the above SDE we get

$$r_t = r_s e^{-\lambda(t-s)} + \sigma \int_s^t e^{-\lambda(t-u)} dW_u, \ t > s.$$

We can apply the above theorem to $m_t = r_t e^{\lambda t} - r_0$. We have $<m>_t = \sigma^2 \frac{e^{2\lambda t}-1}{2\lambda}$, and the copula of the process m_t is given by

$$C_m^{s,t}(u,v) = \int_{-\infty}^u \mathcal{N}\left(\frac{\sqrt{\frac{e^{2\lambda t}-1}{2\lambda}} \mathcal{N}^{-1}(v) - \sqrt{\frac{e^{2\lambda s}-1}{2\lambda}} \mathcal{N}^{-1}(w)}{\sqrt{\frac{e^{2\lambda t}-1}{2\lambda} - \frac{e^{2\lambda s}-1}{2\lambda}}} \right) dw.$$

m_t is a monotone transformation of r_t and therefore has the same copula. We can note that the OU copula depends on λ but not on σ. On the other hand, when λ goes to zero, the OU copula is reduced to the Brownian motion copula. This is not surprising, as the process itself reduces to a Brownian motion. Whereas when λ goes to infinity, the OU copula tends to the independence copula π.

7.2.4 Some Popular Copulas

In this section, we present some copulas widely used in practice. They are appealing for their analytical and numerical tractability. Indeed, the Gaussian copula is used almost everywhere in the financial literature even if its use is most of the time implicit as we mention geometric Brownian motions and multidimensional log-normal distributions without using the word copula. It belongs to the family of elliptic copulas. Another family of widely used copulas is the Archimedean copulas.

Elliptic Copulas

Gaussian Copula

DEFINITION 7.2.6 *The Gaussian copula is defined as follows:*

$$C(u_1, u_2, u_3, \ldots, u_n) = \mathcal{N}_{n,\Sigma}\left(\mathcal{N}^{-1}(u_1), \mathcal{N}^{-1}(u_2), \ldots, \mathcal{N}^{-1}(u_n) \right)$$

where Σ is a correlation matrix, $\mathcal{N}_{n,\Sigma}$ is the standard n-dimensional normal distribution with correlation matrix Σ, and $\mathcal{N}^{-1}$ is the inverse cumulative distribution function of a standard one-dimensional normal variable.

The corresponding copula density is given by

$$c\left(\mathcal{N}(x_1), \mathcal{N}(x_2), \ldots, \mathcal{N}(x_n)\right) = \frac{\frac{1}{\sqrt{(2\pi)^n \det(\Sigma)}} \exp\left[-\frac{1}{2} X^t \Sigma^{-1} X\right]}{\prod\limits_{i=1}^{i=n} \frac{1}{\sqrt{2\pi}} \exp\left[-\frac{x_i^2}{2}\right]}$$

with $X^t = (x_1, x_2, \ldots, x_n)$. This leads to $(\mathcal{N}(x_i) = u_i)$

$$c(u_1, u_2, \ldots, u_n) = \frac{1}{\sqrt{\det(\Sigma)}} \exp\left[-\frac{1}{2} U^t \left(\Sigma^{-1} - I_n\right) U\right]$$

where $U^t = \left(\mathcal{N}^{-1}(u_1), \mathcal{N}^{-1}(u_2), \ldots, \mathcal{N}^{-1}(u_n)\right)$ and I_n is the identity matrix.
The tail dependency parameters in the two-dimensional case are given as follows:

$$\lambda_L = 0$$

$$\lambda_U = 0$$

This concludes that the bivariate Gaussian copula does not exhibit tail dependency.

Student Copula (t-Copula)

DEFINITION 7.2.7 *The t-copula is characterized by a correlation matrix Σ and a parameter v called degree of freedom. It is defined as follows:*

$$C(u_1, u_2, u_3, \ldots, u_n) = T_{v,n,\Sigma}\left(T_v^{-1}(u_1), T_v^{-1}(u_2), \ldots, T_v^{-1}(u_n)\right)$$

where $T_{v,n,\Sigma}$ is the n-dimensional student distribution with correlation matrix Σ and number of degrees of freedom v, and T_v^{-1} is the inverse cumulative distribution of a student random variable with v degrees of freedom.
The corresponding copula density is given by

$$c\left(T_v(x_1), T_v(x_2), \ldots, T_v(x_n)\right) = \frac{\frac{\Gamma(\frac{n+v}{2})}{\Gamma(\frac{v}{2})} \frac{1}{\sqrt{(\pi v)^n \det(\Sigma)}} \left[1 + \frac{X^t \Sigma^{-1} X}{v}\right]^{-\frac{n+v}{2}}}{\prod\limits_{i=1}^{i=n} \frac{\Gamma(\frac{1+v}{2})}{\Gamma(\frac{v}{2})} \frac{1}{\sqrt{\pi v}} \left[1 + \frac{x_i^2}{v}\right]^{-\frac{1+v}{2}}}.$$

Changing variables and denoting $T_v(x_i) = u_i$ and $U^t = (T_v^{-1}(u_1), T_v^{-1}(u_2), \ldots, T_v^{-1}(u_n))$ leads to

$$c\left(T_v(u_1), T_v(u_2), \ldots, T_v(u_n)\right) = \frac{\frac{\Gamma(\frac{n+v}{2})}{\Gamma(\frac{v}{2})} \left(\frac{\Gamma(\frac{v}{2})}{\Gamma(\frac{1+v}{2})}\right)^n \frac{1}{\sqrt{\det(\Sigma)}} \left[1 + \frac{U^t \Sigma^{-1} U}{v}\right]^{-\frac{n+v}{2}}}{\prod\limits_{i=1}^{i=n} \left[1 + \frac{(T_v^{-1}(u_i))^{v2}}{v}\right]^{-\frac{1+v}{2}}},$$

where the Γ function is defined as follows:

$$\Gamma(y) = \int_0^\infty e^{-x} x^{y-1} dx.$$

The tail dependency parameters for the bivariate t-copula with linear correlation ρ can be shown to be:

$$\lambda_L = 2 - 2T_{\nu+1}\left(\sqrt{\frac{(\nu+1)(1-\rho)}{1+\rho}}\right)$$

$$\lambda_U = 2 - 2T_{\nu+1}\left(\sqrt{\frac{(\nu+1)(1-\rho)}{1+\rho}}\right)$$

It can be seen that a bivariate t-distribution exhibits tail dependency, in contrast with the bivariate Gaussian copula.

Archimedean Copulas

DEFINITION 7.2.8 *Let φ be a strictly decreasing continuous function from $[0,1]$ to $[0,+\infty]$ such that $\varphi(1) = 0$. $\varphi^{[-1]}$, the pseudo inverse of φ, is defined as follows:*

$$\varphi^{[-1]}(x) = \begin{cases} \varphi^{-1}(x), & 0 \leq x \leq \varphi(0) \\ 0, & \varphi(0) \leq x \leq +\infty \end{cases}$$

if $\varphi(0) = +\infty$, we have $\varphi^{[-1]} = \varphi^{-1}$.

THEOREM 7.2.6 *Define the function C from $[0,1]^2$ to $[0,1]$ such that $C(u,v) = \varphi^{[-1]}(\varphi(u) + \varphi(v))$. C is a copula if, and only if, φ is convex.*

For a proof of this theorem, please refer to Nelson [133].
A generalization of this result defines the Archimedean[5] copula in the multidimensional case.
The function φ is called the generator of the copula, and if $\varphi(0) = +\infty$, φ is called a strict generator and the corresponding copula a strict Archimedean copula.

Examples:

- The independence copula Π is a strict Archimedean copula: indeed, $\pi(u,v) = uv = \exp\left(-[-\ln u - \ln v]\right)$, so define $\varphi(x) = -\ln(x)$ for $x \in [0,1]$. We therefore have $\varphi(0) = +\infty$ and $\pi(u,v) = \varphi^{-1}(\varphi(u) + \varphi(v))$.
- Similarly, we can show that the Frechet boundary W, in the two-dimensional case, is also an Archimedean copula with $\varphi(x) = 1 - x$ for $x \in [0,1]$.
- Considering $\varphi(x) = \frac{(x^{-\alpha}-1)}{\alpha}$ with $\alpha \in [-1,+\infty[\backslash\{0\}$ we have $C(u,v) = \varphi^{[-1]}$ $(\varphi(u) + \varphi(v)) = \max[(u^{-\alpha} + v^{-\alpha} - 1)^{-\frac{1}{\alpha}}, 0]$, which is called the Clayton copula, and it is a strict copula if $\alpha > 0$.

---

[5]The word *Archimedean* is used because the Archimedean axiom is satisfied by these copulas.

MinMax Copula In this section, we derive the copula of the minimum and maximum of n iid random variables $X_1, X_2 \ldots, X_n$ with a distribution function F. We know that the distribution function of the order r (meaning that we order the variables from 1 to n and select the one of order r, which is similar to what we do with default times when trying to price an r-to-default basket) is given by

$$F_r(x) = \sum_{i=r}^{n} \binom{n}{i} F^i(x)(1 - F(x))^{n-i}.$$

The minimum m_X and maximum M_X therefore have the following distributions:

$$F_{m_X}(x) = \sum_{i=1}^{n} \binom{n}{i} F^i(x)(1 - F(x))^{n-i} = 1 - (1 - F(x))^n$$

$$F_{M_X}(x) = F^n(x)$$

On the other hand, we have the joint distribution of m_X and M_X given as follows:

$$
\begin{aligned}
F_{m,M}(x,y) &= Q(m_X \leq x, M_X \leq y) \\
&= Q(m_X \leq x, M_X \leq y) 1_{x<y} + Q(M_X \leq y) 1_{x \geq y} \\
&= \sum_{i=1}^{n} \binom{n}{i} F^i(x)(F(y) - F(x))^{n-i} 1_{x<y} + F^n(y) 1_{x \geq y}
\end{aligned}
$$

By solving the equation $C_{m_M}\left(F_{m_X}(x), F_{M_X}(y)\right) = F_{m,M}(x,y)$ we get to the following expression for the MinMax copula of n iid random variables:

$$
C_{m_M}(u,v) = \left\{
\begin{array}{ll}
v - \left[v^{\frac{1}{n}} + (1-u)^{\frac{1}{n}} - 1 \right]^n, & 1 - \left(1 - u^{\frac{1}{n}}\right) < v^{\frac{1}{n}} \\
v, & 1 - \left(1 - u^{\frac{1}{n}}\right) \geq v^{\frac{1}{n}}
\end{array}
\right\}
$$

This copula is linked to the Clayton copula mentioned above. Indeed, if we consider the Clayton copula C_α with $\alpha = \frac{-1}{n}$, we can write

$$v - C_{m_M}(1 - u, v) = C_\alpha(u, v).$$

We can also note that when n goes to $+\infty$, the MinMax copula approaches the independence copula π. Moreover, the Kendall's τ and Spearman's ρ for the MinMax copula are given by

$$\tau_{mM} = \frac{1}{2n-1},$$

$$\rho_{mM} = 3 - \frac{12n}{\binom{2n}{n}} \sum_{i=0}^{n} \frac{(-1)^i}{2n-i} \binom{2n}{n+k} + 12(-1)^n \frac{(n!)^3}{(3n)!}.$$

7.3   FACTOR COPULA FRAMEWORK

The copula is only a way to separate the dependency structure (the copula) from the distribution of each random variable (the marginals). When it comes to pricing multiasset derivatives in practice, the dimension of the distribution of the copulated assets is generally high, and Monte Carlo simulation is the only applicable numerical method. There is nothing wrong with using Monte Carlo to price multiasset structures; however, as these structures become commoditized and traded in large volumes, the need for quicker methods becomes a necessity in order to deal with the volume. Another interest in faster pricers is the fact that they enable us to extract much more useful information from these structures such as greeks.

In order to tackle the dimensionality problem, factor copulas have been introduced. The idea is to factor the correlation matrix such that it depends only on few factors that explain a large percentage of the whole variance. This is similar to performing a Principal Component Analysis (PCA) on the correlation matrix.

The approach presented below is the one-factor Gaussian copula framework, a setting that is particularly well suited for high dimensional problems. The idea is that we choose a common factor that explains the dependency between n random variables such that they are independent conditionally on the common factor.

Let's define a series of hitting times τ^k with $k \in \{1, \ldots, n\}$, and n being the number of assets. The hitting time could be the time to default of a credit name or the first time a stock hits certain level:

$$\tau^k \equiv \inf\{t \geq 0 / S_t^k \leq L^k\}$$

where L^k is the barrier related to the asset S^k that prevails at time t.
The joint distribution function of the hitting times is

$$F(t_1, \ldots, t_n) \equiv Q\left(\tau^1 < t_1, \ldots, \tau^n < t_n\right), \qquad (7.1)$$

which can be modeled using the Gaussian copula thus:

$$F(t_1, \ldots, t_n) \equiv \mathcal{N}_{n,\Sigma}\left(\mathcal{N}^{-1}(F_1(t_1)), \ldots, \mathcal{N}^{-1}(F_n(t_n))\right) \qquad (7.2)$$

where $\mathcal{N}_{n,\Sigma}$ is the n-dimensional Gaussian distribution with correlation matrix Σ, and $F_i(t_i) = Q(\tau^i < t_i)$ is the distribution function of τ^i for $i \in \{1, \ldots, n\}$. Note that we have here chosen the copula function for the hitting times to be a Gaussian copula. It is a modeling choice and not something that could be derived. By construction, the vector $\left(\mathcal{N}^{-1}(F_1(\tau^1)), \ldots, \mathcal{N}^{-1}(F_n(\tau^n))\right)$ is a Gaussian vector with a correlation matrix Σ.

Let $(X_1, \ldots, X_n)$ be a Gaussian vector, where $X_k \equiv \mathcal{N}^{-1}(F_k(\tau^k))$, $k = 1, \ldots, n$. In the following, we consider a special case of a one factor copula representation, where

$$X_k = \rho_k Z + \sqrt{1 - \rho_k^2}\, \overline{Z}_k$$

and Z, $\overline{Z}_k$, $k = 1, \ldots, n$ are independent standard Gaussian random variables. On the other hand, $\rho_k \in [-1, 1]$, $k = 1, \ldots, n$ are calibrated to the initial correlation matrix Σ.

Denoting by $p_t^{k/Z} = Q\left(\tau^k < t | Z\right)$, and exploiting the independence assumption, we readily get

$$p_t^{k/Z} = \mathcal{N}\left(\frac{\mathcal{N}^{-1}(F_k(t)) - \rho_k Z}{\sqrt{1 - \rho_k^2}}\right).$$

The joint distribution and copula functions are then given by

$$F(t_1, \ldots, t_n) = \int_{-\infty}^{+\infty} \left(\prod_{k=1}^{n} \mathcal{N}\left(\frac{\mathcal{N}^{-1}(F_k(t_k)) - \rho_k z}{\sqrt{1 - \rho_k^2}}\right)\right) \varphi(z) dz$$

$$C(u_1, \ldots, u_n) = \int_{-\infty}^{+\infty} \left(\prod_{k=1}^{n} \mathcal{N}\left(\frac{\mathcal{N}^{-1}(u_k) - \rho_k z}{\sqrt{1 - \rho_k^2}}\right)\right) \varphi(z) dz$$

where $\varphi(z) = \frac{1}{\sqrt{2\pi}} e^{-z^2/2}$ is the Gaussian density.

In the following section we are going to take advantage of source of the foregoing results in order to price semianalytically some complex structures that otherwise require lengthy Monte Carlo simulations to price and risk manage. We have chosen a well-known equity derivative structure named Altiplano, a very popular credit derivatives structures called collateralized debt obligations (CDOs), and basket default swaps.

7.4 APPLICATIONS TO DERIVATIVES PRICING

7.4.1 Equity Derivatives: The Altiplano

A family of equity derivatives structures called mountain range options arose during the 1990s and subsequent years. They are a series of path-dependent options on a basket of underlying assets. Exotic mountain names have been assigned to these structures like Altiplano, Himalaya, Atlas, Everest, Annapurna, Etna, and many more.

These structures are usually written on many underlying assets, and Monte Carlo simulation is the only suitable numerical method to price them. Unfortunately, this method shows its limits when it comes to live risk management. Indeed, because of the large dimension of the portfolio, the number of computed quantities, that is, price, and different greeks grows rapidly, it becomes intractable to have quick and accurate results.

In the remainder of this section, we focus on the pricing of the Altiplano structures using the factor copula framework presented before. We therefore start with a quick reminder of an Altiplano payoff, then prepare the ingredients for the factor copula approach by computing the cumulative distribution functions for a currently running period and a period starting in the future. A semianalytical solution is derived for the price of this structure.

The structure we are interested in is a multiasset, multibarrier option that pays a series of coupons depending on the number of assets crossing the barriers and on the barrier period. No underlying is removed throughout the life of the product.[6]

We are given

- n starting assets prices

$$S_0^i, i \in \{1, 2, \ldots n\}$$

- The corresponding correlation matrix Σ of these assets
- A set of m monitoring periods $[T_0, T_1] \ldots [T_{m-1}, T_m]$

- A barrier matrix $K = \begin{pmatrix} K_1^1 & K_2^1 & & K_n^1 \\ \cdot & \cdot & & \cdot \\ \cdot & & \cdot & \cdot \\ \cdot & & & \cdot \\ \cdot & & & \cdot \\ K_1^m & K_2^m & & K_n^m \end{pmatrix}$ being the barriers applying to each

asset serving each monitoring period
- A maturity date T

- A matrix $C = \begin{pmatrix} C_0^1 & C_1^1 & & C_n^1 \\ \cdot & \cdot & & \cdot \\ \cdot & & \cdot & \cdot \\ \cdot & & & \cdot \\ \cdot & & & \cdot \\ C_0^m & C_1^m & & C_n^m \end{pmatrix}$ of coupon payments, the structure pays at

T_i the coupon C_j^i where j is the number of assets which breached their respective barriers during the period $[T_{i-1}, T_i]$.
Normally, one has $C_0^i > C_1^i > C_2^i > 0$ and $C_3^i = C_4^i = \ldots = C_n^i = 0$.

The coupon payments are made at the end of each barrier period.
We define the n stopping times for each period l,
hence τ_i^l is the first time when asset S^i hits the barrier K_i^l for the period l.
Let N^l be the number of assets that hit the given barriers, that is,

$$N^l(T) = \sum_{i=1}^{n} 1_{T_{l-1} \leq \tau_i^l \leq T}.$$

---

[6]Other variants of the Altiplanos structure remove poorly performing assets from the basket during the lifetime of the structure.

Therefore, the value at time 0 of an m period, n-underlying Altiplano that pays at maturity is

$$price = \sum_{l=\lambda}^{m} \sum_{i=0}^{n} B\,(0, T_l)\, C_i^l \mathbf{Q}(N^l = i). \qquad (7.3)$$

In order to use the factor copula approach, we will need to compute the marginal distribution functions of the hitting time, and this is the subject of the next section.

Cumulative Distribution Functions of the Hitting Times

Current period The current period is a barrier period that contains the valuation sale. We are working in the n-dimensional correlated Black-Scholes model, that is,

$$\frac{dS_t^i}{S_t^i} = (r_t^i - d_t^i)dt + \sigma_t^i dW_t^i.$$

The hitting time, of a certain barrier LS_0, for an underlying S_t is defined as follows:

$$\tau = \inf_{0 \le t}\{S_t < L \times S_0\}$$

We have to compute the following quantity $F(T_1) = \mathbf{Q}\,(\tau < T_1)$:

$$F(T_1) = \mathbf{Q}\left(\inf_{0 \le t}\{t,\, S_t < L \times S_0\} \le T_1\right) = \mathbf{Q}\left(\inf_{0 \le t}\{(S_t/S_0) < L\} \le T_1\right)$$

$$= \mathbf{Q}\left(\inf_{0 \le t}\left\{t,\, \int_0^t \alpha_s ds + \int_0^t \sigma_s dW_s < L\right\} \le T_1\right)$$

$$= E_{\mathbf{Q}_1}\left(L_{T_1} \times \mathbf{1}_{\inf_{0 \le t}\left\{t,\, \int_0^t \sigma_s dB_s < L\right\} \le T_1}\right)$$

α_s is defined as follows:

$$\alpha_s = r_s - d_s - \frac{1}{2}\sigma_s^2, \beta_s = W_s + \int_0^s \frac{\alpha_u}{\sigma_u} du$$

where r_s is the short rate and d_s is the dividend and repo rates and σ_s is the volatility function of S_t.

L_t is defined as follows:

$$L_t = \exp\left(\int_0^t -\frac{1}{2}\left(\frac{\alpha_s}{\sigma_s}\right)^2 ds + \int_0^t \frac{\alpha_s}{\sigma_s} dB_s\right)$$

and

$$\frac{d\mathbf{Q}_1}{d\mathbf{Q}} = \exp\left(\int_0^t -\frac{1}{2}\left(\frac{\alpha_s}{\sigma_s}\right)^2 ds - \int_0^t \frac{\alpha_s}{\sigma_s} dW_s\right)$$

Girsanov theorem tells us that $B_t = W_t + \int_0^t \frac{\alpha_s}{\sigma_s}$ is a Brownian motion under $\mathbf{Q}_1$. Define the following quantities:

$$\eta_t = \int_0^t \left(\frac{\alpha_s}{\sigma_s}\right)^2 ds \text{ and } V_t = \int_0^t \sigma_s^2 ds$$

Assuming that α_s has the same sign $\varepsilon = sign(\alpha_s)$, either positive or negative $\underset{0 \leq s \leq T_1}{}$ throughout the period (the same assumption is made for forward periods), we have the following result:

$$F(T_1) = E_{\mathbf{Q}_1}\left(L_{T_1} \times \mathbf{1}_{\inf_{0 \leq t}\left\{t, \int_0^t \sigma_s dB_s < L\right\} \leq T_1}\right)$$

$$\approx \mathcal{N}\left(\frac{\ln(L) - \varepsilon \eta_{T_1} V_{T_1}}{\sqrt{V_{T_1}}}\right) + L^{2\varepsilon \eta_{T_1}} \mathcal{N}\left(\frac{\ln(L) + \varepsilon \eta_{T_1} V_{T_1}}{\sqrt{V_{T_1}}}\right)$$

Forward period For a forward period $[T_i, T_{i+1}]$, the computation is similar.

$$F(T_i, T_{i+1}) = \mathbf{Q}\left(\inf_{T_i \leq t}\{S_t < L \times S_0\} \leq T_{i+1}\right)$$

$$= \mathbf{Q}\left(\inf_{T_i \leq t}\{S_t < L \times S_0\} \leq T_{i+1}, S_{Ti} > L \times S_0\right)$$

$$+ \mathbf{Q}\left(\inf_{T_i \leq t}\{S_t < L \times S_0\} \leq T_{i+1}, S_{Ti} < L \times S_0\right)$$

$$= \underbrace{\mathbf{Q}\left(\inf_{T_i \leq t}\{S_t < L \times S_0\} \leq T_{i+1}, S_{Ti} > L \times S_0\right)}_{A} + \underbrace{\mathbf{Q}\left(S_{Ti} < L \times S_0\right)}_{B}$$

The second term B is easy to compute:

$$B = \mathcal{N}\left(\frac{\ln(L) - \mu_{T_i}}{\sqrt{V_{T_i}}}\right) \text{ where } \mu_{T_i} = \int_0^{T_i} \alpha_s ds$$

Following the same steps of the computation in the previous paragraph we have:

$$A \approx \mathcal{N}_2(x_1, y_1, \rho) + fact \times \mathcal{N}_2(x_2, y_2, \rho)$$

where $\mathcal{N}_2$ is the bivariate normal distribution function and x_1, y_1, x_2, y_2, ρ and *fact* are given by

$$x_1 = \frac{\mu_{T_i} - \ln(L)}{\sqrt{V_{T_i}}}, \quad y_1 = \frac{\ln(L) - \mu_{T_i} - \varepsilon_{i,i+1} V_{T_i,T_{i+1}} \eta_{T_i,T_{i+1}}}{\sqrt{V_{T_{i+1}}}}$$

$$x_2 = \frac{\mu_{T_i} - \ln(L) - 2\varepsilon_{i,i+1}\eta_{T_i,T_{i+1}} V_{T_i}}{\sqrt{V_{T_i}}},$$

$$y_2 = \frac{\ln(L) - \mu_{T_i} + \varepsilon_{i,i+1}\eta_{T_i,T_{i+1}}(V_{T_i} + V_{T_{i+1}})}{\sqrt{V_{T_{i+1}}}}$$

$$\rho = -\sqrt{\frac{V_{T_i}}{V_{T_{i+1}}}}$$

$$fact = L^{2\varepsilon_{i,i+1}\eta_{T_i,T_{i+1}}} * e^{2\eta_{T_i,T_{i+1}}\left(\eta_{T_i,T_{i+1}}V_{T_i} - \mu_{T_i}\varepsilon_{i,i+1}\right)}$$

where

$$\eta_{T_i,T_{i+1}} = \int_{T_i}^{T_{i+1}} \left(\frac{\alpha_s}{\sigma_s}\right)^2 ds$$

$$\varepsilon_{i,i+1} = \varepsilon = \underset{T_i \le s \le T_{i+1}}{sign(\alpha_s)}$$

$$V_{T_i,T_{i+1}} = \int_{T_i}^{T_{i+1}} \sigma_s^2 ds$$

Up to this point we have prepared the main ingredients for the copula approach. In the next paragraph, we apply this in order to derive a semiclosed solution for the structure presented above.

Pricing of Altiplanos In order to compute the price in (7.3), all we need to do is to compute the probabilities $Q\left(N^l(t) = k\right)$ (k hits for the period l).

Recall that $N^l(t) = \sum_{i=1}^n 1_{T_{l-1} \le \tau_i^l \le t}$, the counting process associated with the number of hits up to time t for the period l.

The probability generating function of $N^l(t)$ is given by

$$\Psi_{N^l(t)} = E_Q\left(u^{N^l(t)}\right) \tag{7.4}$$

$$= \sum_{k=0}^n Q\left(N^l(t) = k\right) u^k. \tag{7.5}$$

Recall

$$p_t^{k/Z} = \mathcal{N}\left(\frac{\mathcal{N}^{-1}(F_k(t)) - \rho_k Z}{\sqrt{1 - \rho_k^2}}\right).$$

Using the iterated expectations theorem, $\Psi_{N^l(t)}$ can be rewritten as

$$\Psi_{N^l(t)} = E_Q\left(\prod_{k=1}^n \left(1 - p_t^{i/Z} + p_t^{i/Z} \times u\right)\right) \tag{7.6}$$

$$= \int_{-\infty}^{+\infty} \prod_{k=1}^n \left(1 - p_t^{i/Z=z} + p_t^{i/Z=z} \times u\right) \varphi(z) dz \tag{7.7}$$

$$= \int_{-\infty}^{+\infty} \sum_{k=0}^n u^k \mu_k^l(z)\varphi(z) dz \tag{7.8}$$

where the last equality stems from a formal expansion of $\prod_{i=1}^{n} \left(1 - p_t^{i/Z} + p_t^{i/Z} \times u \right)$.

Note that we have dropped the index l from the probabilities $p_t^{i/Z}$ to ease the notation.

Using the vieta's formulas, which link the roots of a polynomial to its coefficients, we can express $\mu_k(z)$ as a function of $p_t^{i/Z=z}$, $i \in \{1, \ldots, n\}$.

$$\mu_k^l(z) = (-1)^{n-k} \mu_n^l(z) \sum_{1 \le i_1 < i_2 < \ldots < i_{n-k} \le n} r_{i_1}^l(z) \, r_{i_2}^l(z) \ldots r_{i_{n-k}}^l(z)$$

where

$$r_k^l(z) = \frac{-1 + p_t^{i/Z=z}}{p_t^{i/Z=z}}$$

$$\mu_n^l(z) = \prod_{i=1}^{n} p_t^{i/Z=z}$$

The probability of k hits by time t is thus given by

$$Q\left(N^l(t) = k \right) = \int_{-\infty}^{+\infty} \mu_k^l(z)\varphi(z)dz$$

and the price in (7.3) is given as follows:

$$price = \sum_{l=\lambda}^{m} \sum_{i=0}^{n} B\left(0, T_l\right) C_i^l \int_{-\infty}^{+\infty} \mu_i^l(z)\varphi(z)dz$$

This integral maybe evaluated using a simple quadrature and it reduces the computation time massively.

In the following section, we focus on the application of the above approach to multiname credit derivatives, specifically CDOs and basket default swaps.

7.4.2 Credit Derivatives: Basket and Tranche Pricing

The extensive application of copulas in the financial industry is in large part due to the development of the credit derivatives market. In this section, we present an approach to pricing the well-known CDOs and basket default swaps in the factor copula framework presented above in the same way we did for Altiplano.

Pricing of CDO Tranches

Introduction Collateralized Debt Obligations belong to a class of securitized products called *Asset Backed Securities* (ABS). These are securities backed by pools of assets which range from corporate bonds, bank loans, catastrophe bonds, emerging market securities, credit cards, or various types of mortgage securities. These securities are the property of a special purpose vehicle (SPV) which issues a variety of equity and debt notes (tranches). Typically, the SPV issues an equity, junior, mezzanine, and senior tranches plus sometimes a super-senior tranche. The fundamental difference of these tranches lies in the risk they bear as the repayment of both interests and principal is done in a given order and the first losses are borne by the equity tranche.

The SPV is called a CDO which also refers to the various notes issued by the SPV, this leads to the known circular phrase "a CDO issues CDOs." These are bought by investors looking to gain an exposure to a diversified portfolio of underlying assets without having to buy each asset individually, and to obtain a higher return than is available on other securities of equivalent credit rating.

The motivations behind participating in the CDO market are different for both the originator and the investor. Banks for example, or any other holder of assets, aim at shrinking the balance sheet, therefore reducing the required regulatory capital, or economic capital. Investors, on the other hand, are looking for both investment and arbitrage opportunities. These motivations coupled with the source of the underlying assets allow for a classification of CDOs into Balance Sheet and Arbitrage CDOs.

Synthetic CDOs   Synthetic CDOs are similar to ordinary CDOs, or cash CDOs, except that their portfolios are constituted of Credit Default Swaps ("CDS") rather than actual bonds or loans. In a CDS, one counterparty pays a premium to a second counterparty in exchange for a contingent payment should a defined credit event occur such as the reference entity going into default. This way the CDO gains exposure synthetically to a reference credit entity without purchasing a bond or a loan. An analogy can be drawn with insurance where one party pays regular premiums against the protection, by the other party, against potential coverage losses.

The sophistication of synthetic CDOs has reached another level as the underlying portfolio is customized to include CDO notes (CDO^2, CDO squared), and this works in the same way as a standard CDO structure. Leveraged super senior and CPPI on CDO tranches constitute the latest innovations in the field of CDOs.

Synthetic CDOs offer access to a more diversified portfolio of assets and a larger number of assets than Cash CDOs. They also create a cheaper capital structure, leading to higher equity returns and higher portfolio quality.

Default Leg of a CDO   Given a pool of n credit names with recovery rates R_i and nominals $N_i, i \in \{0, \ldots, n\}$. We denote by τ_i the default time of credit name i. We assume the recovery rates are known beforehand. Define L_t the cumulative loss of the portfolio at the time t:

$$L_t = \sum_{i=1}^{n} L^i \mathbf{1}_{\tau_i \leq t},$$

where L_t^i is the loss if the name i defaults before time t, and $L^i = (1 - R_i) N_i$. We assume that interest rates are deterministic.

We consider a CDO tranche where the default leg pays losses borne by the above portfolio and which are in excess of K_1 and not more than K_2 ($K_1 < K_2$). The payoff of the tranche is therefore given as follows:

$$P_t = (L_t - K_1) \mathbf{1}_{K_1 \leq L_t \leq K_2} + (K_2 - K_1) \mathbf{1}_{K_2 \leq L_t}$$

$K_1 = 0$ corresponds to the equity tranche, $K_2 = \sum_{i=1}^{n} L^i$ corresponds to the senior tranche and finally $K_1 > 0$ and $K_2 < \sum_{i=1}^{n} L^i$ corresponds to the mezzanine tranche.

For a maturity T, the price of the default leg is the expectation of the sum of all default payments before T. It is given as follows[7]:

$$DefaultLeg = E_Q \left[\sum_{t \leq T} B(0,t)(P_{t^+} - P_t) \right] = E_Q \left[\int_0^T B(0,t) \, dP_t \right] \quad (7.9)$$

Using integration by parts we have:

$$DefaultLeg = B(0,T) E_Q[P_T] + \int_0^T f(0,t) B(0,t) E_Q(P_t) \, dt$$

where $f(0,t)$ is the instantaneous forward rate defined as follows: $f(0,t) = -\frac{\partial \log B(0,t)}{\partial t}$.

For simplification we consider the case where all the names have the same nominal and recovery rate; this is called a homogeneous portfolio ($L^i = L$, for all i's). Denote by k_1 and k_2 the number of defaults that correspond to the losses K_1 and K_2, respectively.

$$E_Q(P_t) = \sum_{k=k_1}^{k_2-\lambda} (kL - K_1) Q(L_t = kL) + (K_2 - K_1) \sum_{k=k_2}^{n} Q(L_t = kL) \quad (7.10)$$

Within the one-factor Gaussian copula framework presented above, we have

$$Q(L_t = kL) = Q(N(t) = k) = \int_{-\infty}^{+\infty} \mu_k(z)\varphi(z)dz \quad (7.11)$$

where μ_k is the coefficient of u^k in the moment-generating function.

Fixed Leg The fixed leg is a risky coupon-bearing bond with a notional equal to the notional of the tranche K_1, K_2. Hence, we have the following expression:

$$FL = E_Q \left[\sum_{i=1}^{p} s\Delta t_i B(0,t_i) \left[(K_2 - K_1) - \left(\underbrace{(L_{t_i} - K_1)^+ - (L_{t_i} - K_2)^+}_{=P_{t_i}} \right) \right] \right]$$

$$= \sum_{i=1}^{p} s\Delta t_i B(0,t_i) \left[(K_2 - K_1) - E_Q(P_{t_i}) \right],$$

where $t_i s$, $i \in \{1, \ldots, p\}$, are the payment dates and s is the fixed premium paid at each payment date.

---

[7] We are able to write 7.9 because P_t is an increasing pure jump process.

The CDO spread is the value of s that makes the default leg equal to the fixed led and is given by

$$spread = \frac{B(0,T) E_Q[P_T] + \int_0^T f(0,t) B(0,t) E_Q(P_t) dt}{\sum_{i=1}^p \Delta t_i B(0,t_i) [(K_2 - K_1) - E_Q(P_{t_i})]} \qquad (7.12)$$

Note that in the above computation we have omitted for simplicity the accrual payment that could be added to the fixed leg in the event that the default happens between two premium dates.

This comes down again to the computation of the probabilities $Q(N_t = m)$, which is, as explained before, very easy to compute within the factor copula framework.

We can therefore compute the prices of different tranches in a CDO by numerical integration. The generalization to a nonhomogenous portfolio is straightforward.

Pricing of Basket Default Swaps Another structure that provides similar credit protection to CDO tranches is a Basket Default Swap. A basket swap is similar to single name credit default swap except that it offers protection against a number of credit entities (2 to 25 or 30 names) rather than a single entity. These can be structured in a way that offers investors access to different risk profiles depending on their risk appetite, and protects against different ranges of portfolio losses.

In a First to Default (FTD) swap, the protection buyer is only protected against the losses incurred on the first default and the contract is terminated after this event. In a Second to Default swap, the protection buyer is protected against the losses incurred on the first and second defaults but not the third with the contract being terminated after the second default. In a Ninth to Default swap, the protection buyer is protected against the losses incurred on the first nine defaults but not the tenth. These structures would be similar to the equity tranche, mezzanine tranche, and senior tranche of a CDO, respectively.

The success of these structures stems from the fact that they offer the investor higher spreads than the underlying single name credit default swaps. However, this spread depends on the level of correlation between the reference credits constituting the basket.

Pricing a kth to Default Basket As in the case of CDOs, we consider a pool of n credit names with recovery rates R_i and nominals $N_i, i \in \{0, \ldots, n\}$. We denote by τ_i the default time of credit name i. We assume the recovery rates are known beforehand. Let N_t be the counting process:

$$N_t = \sum_{i=1}^n \mathbf{1}_{\tau_i \leq t}$$

We also assume for simplicity that we have a homogeneous portfolio ($R_i = R$, and $N_i = N$), and we have therefore $L^i = (1 - R) N = L$ where L^i is the loss incurred if the name i defaults. We also assume that interest rates are deterministic.

As mentioned before, the kth to default basket is swap that provides a protection against defaults up to the kth. We therefore are interested in the distribution of $\tau^{(k)}$, which is the kth default time.

We can write:

$$F^{\tau^{(k)}}(t) = Q\left(\tau^{(k)} \leq t\right) = Q\left(N_t \geq k\right)$$

$$= \sum_{m=k}^{n} Q\left(N_t = m\right)$$

The Default Leg The default leg denoted DL is computed as follows:

$$DL = L \times E_Q\left[B\left(0, \tau^{(k)}\right) \mathbf{1}_{\tau^{(k)} \leq T}\right] = L \int_0^T B\left(0, t\right) f^{\tau^{(k)}}(t)dt, \tag{7.13}$$

where $f^{\tau^{(k)}}(t)$ is the density function of $\tau^{(k)}$ given by $f^{\tau^{(k)}}(t) = \frac{dF^{\tau^{(k)}}(t)}{dt}$.

Within the one factor Gaussian copula framework, $F^{\tau^{(k)}}(t)$ is given as a sum of $Q\left(N_t = m\right)$, $k \leq m \leq n$, where, as explained before:

$$Q\left(N_t = m\right) = \int_{-\infty}^{+\infty} \mu_k(z)\varphi(z)dz$$

where μ_k is the coefficient next to u^k in the moment-generating function.

Note that (7.13) could be written as follows:

$$DL = L \times E_Q\left[B\left(0, \tau^{(k)}\right) \mathbf{1}_{\tau^{(k)} \leq T}\right] = -L \int_0^T B\left(0, t\right) s^{\tau^{(k)}}(t)dt$$

Integrating by parts we get:

$$DL = L\left[1 - S^{\tau^{(k)}}(T) B\left(0, T\right) - \int_0^T f\left(0, t\right) B\left(0, t\right) S^{\tau^{(k)}}(t)dt\right],$$

where $s^{\tau^{(k)}}(t)$ is the survival probability density given by

$$s^{\tau^{(k)}}(t) = -\frac{dF^{\tau^{(k)}}(t)}{dt} = \frac{dS^{\tau^{(k)}}(t)}{dt}$$

and $S^{\tau^{(k)}}(t)$ by

$$S^{\tau^{(k)}}(t) = Q\left(\tau^{(k)} > t\right) = Q\left(N_t < k\right)$$

$$= \sum_{m=0}^{k-1} Q\left(N_t = m\right).$$

Therefore, depending on the number of terms in the sum, we can use one or the other (survival or default) to ease computations.

The Fixed Leg As with the CDO, the fixed leg of a basket default swap is basically a risky coupon bond. Hence, we have the following expression:

$$FL = N \times E_Q \left[\sum_{i=1}^{p} s \Delta t_i B (0, t_i) \mathbf{1}_{\tau^{(k)} > t_i} \right]$$

$$= N \times \sum_{i=1}^{p} s \Delta t_i B (0, t_i) S^{\tau^{(k)}} (t_i)$$

where $t_i s$, $i \in \{1, \dots, p\}$, are the payment dates, $\Delta t_i = t_i - t_{i-1}$, and s is the fixed premium paid at each payment date.

As with the CDO, the kth to default basket default swap spread is the value of s that makes the default leg equal to the fixed led and is given by

$$spread = \frac{(1 - R) \left[1 - S^{\tau^{(k)}} (T) B (0, T) - \int_0^T f (0, t) B (0, t) S^{\tau^{(k)}}(t) dt \right]}{\sum_{i=1}^{p} \Delta t_i B (0, t_i) S^{\tau^{(k)}} (t_i)}.$$

Again, we have omitted for simplicity the accrual payment that could be added to the fixed leg in case the default happens between two premium dates.

This comes down again to the computation of the probabilities $\mathbf{Q} (N_t = m)$, which is, as explained before, very easy to compute within the factor copula framework.

7.5   CONCLUSION

Copulas have found many applications within the field of financial derivatives. Their application is not limited to equity or credit derivatives. Copulas are also used for risk management purposes as the calculation of risk limits for large portfolios poses problems similar to the pricing of CDOs and Altiplanos. They we also applied in interest rates derivatives for structures like CMS spread options, and the field of hybrid derivatives.

CHAPTER 8

Forward PDEs and Local Volatility Calibration

8.1 INTRODUCTION

8.1.1 Local and Implied Volatilities

In the Black-Scholes model ([134]), the stock price follows geometric Brownian motion with a constant volatility σ:

$$\frac{dS_t}{S_t} = (r_t - v_t)dt + \sigma dW_t, \tag{8.1}$$

where r_t is the short interest rate and v_t contains the repo rate and a dividend yield. This is discussed in more detail in chapter 1. Under this assumption, the price of a European call option with strike K and maturity T is given by the Black-Scholes formula

$$C(K, T) = P(0, T)(F_T N(d^+) - K N(d^-))$$

where $P(t, T)$ is the price at time t of a zero-coupon bond with maturity T, F_T is the stock forward, and

$$d^{\pm} = \frac{\ln(K/F_T) \pm \frac{1}{2}\sigma^2(T - t)}{\sigma\sqrt{T - t}}.$$

Now that the European options themselves form a liquid market, prices are available for many options on many stocks and indices. The implied volatility of an option is the constant volatility that when used in the above equations recovers the market price of the option. Figure 8.1 shows the dependence of the implied volatility of the Stoxx50 index on the maturity and strike of the options.

Since the implied volatility is a function of the strike price, the volatility that we use in equation (8.1) cannot be constant. If we want our stock model to be Markovian in just one factor, we must make the volatility of the stock a deterministic function of both the stock price and time. This is referred to as the local volatility. In reality, though, there is not such a simple relationship between volatility and stock price. Studies of historical market data show that the volatility is stochastic and can be modeled well by mean-reverting processes such as Heston's model [135].

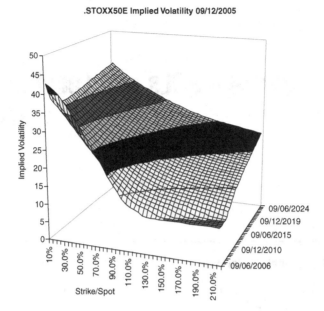

FIGURE 8.1 Implied volatility surface for the Stoxx50 index.

A local volatility model has the benefit over a stochastic volatility model that it is Markovian in only one factor (and therefore more tractable). It is also possible to calibrate a local volatility model to a complete implied volatility surface (assuming there is no arbitrage). It has the drawback that it predicts unrealistic dynamics for the stock volatility and therefore the implied volatility surface. However, a local volatility model is sufficient for pricing some products—particularly ones with European payoffs, which can be hedged perfectly with a static set of positions in European calls and puts.

In a simple one-factor model with no extra sources of randomness, Dupire [136] showed that we can express a local volatility in terms of the implied volatility surface and its derivatives. However, this formula can be difficult to use in practice. If we add more sources of randomness to our model—for example, stochastic interest rates, hazard rates, or dividends—Dupire's formula no longer applies and we must find another way to create a local volatility surface from an implied volatility surface.

Tied in with the problem of calibrating a local volatility surface is the problem of pricing options with European payoffs (where the payoff depends on the value of the stock on a single maturity) where no closed form solutions exist. This can obviously be done by Monte Carlo simulation or backwards induction using a tree or numerical PDE solver. However, simulation methods suffer from a slow rate of convergence, while backward PDE methods and trees have better convergence but can price only one option at a time.

In this chapter, we demonstrate the powerful technique of using forward PDEs to price multiple European options very efficiently. We then go on to discuss how to use this technique to calibrate a local volatility surface to an implied volatility surface in single- and multifactor models.

8.1.2   Dupire's Formula and Its Problems

Dupire [136] showed that the local volatility (which we shall denote by σ^l) can be expressed in terms of the implied volatility surface, or more simply in terms of European call prices. We derive his full result in section 8.3, equation (8.18), but for the purposes of this section, we can ignore the effects of interest rates and dividends. Letting $r_t = v_t = 0$, Dupire's formula becomes

$$\sigma^l(K,T)^2 = \frac{2\frac{\partial C}{\partial T}(K,T)}{K^2 \frac{\partial^2 C}{\partial K^2}(K,T)}. \tag{8.2}$$

The drawback of this equation in practice is that it requires the knowledge of call prices for all strikes and maturities, whereas in reality there will be data for only call prices at a discrete set of strikes and maturities. We must therefore interpolate the call prices (or implied volatilities) between the market data points if we are to use equation (8.2). For the local volatility to be continuous in the stock price (which is necessary for good convergence of any numerical scheme) we need the second derivatives of the call prices with respect to strike to be continuous. We also need the call prices to be once differentiable with respect to time. Additionally, the call prices must obey the following no-arbitrage conditions:

$$C(K,T) > (S_0 - K)^+$$

$$\frac{\partial C}{\partial T} \geq 0,$$

$$-1 < \frac{\partial C}{\partial K} < 0$$

and

$$\frac{\partial^2 C}{\partial K^2} > 0,$$

as well as the boundary conditions

$$C(K,T) \to S_0 - K \quad \text{as} \quad K \to 0$$

and

$$C(K,T) \to 0 \quad \text{as} \quad K \to \infty.$$

The equivalent conditions when expressed in terms of implied volatilities are even more complicated to evaluate.

Occasionally, the market data may include regions of arbitrage owing to large bid-offer spreads on illiquid options or the difficulty of extrapolating into regions where there is no data. However, it is necessary to remove all arbitrageability from the implied volatility surface as Dupire's formula is only valid up to the first time when the above conditions are violated. If, instead of trying to fit a smooth implied volatility surface to a discrete set of European options, we assume a local volatility surface $\sigma^l(S, t)$, then our arbitrage and boundary conditions become that $\sigma^l(S, t)$ is greater than zero and $S\sigma^l(S, t)$ is Lipschitz continuous [137]. Finding a local volatility surface that satisfies these no-arbitrage conditions is much simpler than finding an implied volatility surface. The only difficulty is how to fit the local volatility surface to the market call prices, and this will be addressed in the rest of the chapter.

8.1.3   Dupire-like Formula in Multifactor Models

Another reason for looking for an alternative to Dupire's formula is that to the authors' knowledge there is no equivalent formula in higher-dimensional models.

To demonstrate the difficulty of finding a two-factor version, we can consider a simple non-dividend-paying stock with interest rates following the Hull-White model [61]. We have

$$dr_t = (\theta_t - \kappa r_t)dt + \sigma_t^r dW_t^r$$

$$\frac{dS_t}{S_t} = r_t dt + \sigma^l(S, t)dW_t^S.$$

Borrowing equation (8.33) from section 8.6, we have

$$\sigma_{\text{imp}}(T)^2 = \frac{1}{T} \int_0^T \left((\sigma_t^l)^2 + 2\rho\sigma_t^l\sigma_t^r \hat{B}(\kappa, t, T) + \hat{B}(\kappa, t, T)^2(\sigma_t^r)^2 \right) dt$$

(see section 8.6 for details). The local volatility at time T depends not just on the implied volatility and its derivatives at T, but also on the implied volatility at all times $t < T$. We cannot then hope to find a simple expression like Dupire's formula, even in the simplest case we can study.

When we follow the steps that lead to Dupire's formula, but with stochastic interest rates (see section 8.4), we arrive at the following expression (see equation (8.27)):

$$\sigma^l(K, T)^2 = \frac{2\dfrac{\partial c}{\partial T} - 2\exp(k) \displaystyle\int_{-\infty}^{\infty} \int_k^{\infty} g_T(y)\phi(x, y, T)dxdy}{\dfrac{\partial^2 c}{\partial k^2} - \dfrac{\partial c}{\partial k}}, \tag{8.3}$$

where c, x, y, and k are transformed call prices, stock prices, interest rates, and strikes, respectively, and ϕ is the joint probability distribution of x and y. (See section 8.4 for more details.) The integral in equation (8.2) involves the expectation of r at fixed S and cannot be uniquely determined by the implied volatility locally to S and t (as we have shown above in the simplified case).

An alternative might be to find a liquid derivative that is sensitive to this unknown integral. The problem with this is that we know there is enough information to calibrate the local volatility given just the call prices. If we introduce more instruments, we then have an over-specified problem.[1] We could use the new

---

[1]This is if we assume the volatility is just a function of the stock price and time. If we let the volatility depend on the short rate as well, then we could use the extra liquid instruments—if they existed! See Gyöngy [138].

instruments to come up with a local volatility surface, but it would price neither the new instruments nor the European calls correctly (unless by some accident we had a model that exactly described the behavior of the market, which is very unlikely).

Equation (8.3) shows that we can find the local volatility if we know the joint probability distribution for S and r. The approach we present in section 8.5 is to bootstrap both the local volatility and the probability distribution together. First, we derive the PDEs satisfied by the probability distributions in the one-factor (section 8.3) and two-factor (section 8.4) cases.

8.2   FORWARD PDEs

By forward/backward PDE, we mean the direction in time in which the PDE is solved. In a forward PDE, we specify the solution at the evaluation date and propagate it forward in time; all of the forward PDEs we discuss here solve for the present value of some European derivative as a function of its maturity T and strike K. In a backward PDE, such as the familiar Black-Scholes PDE, we solve for the value of a particular derivative as seen from a time t and a stock level S. A forward PDE, where applicable, has the advantage that we can use the solution to price many different options. To price different options using backward PDEs, we must solve the PDE once per option as each option has a different final payoff.

In this section, we derive forward PDEs for the probability distribution arising from some general risk-neutral processes:

$$\mathrm{d}x_i = \mu_i(\mathbf{x}_t, t)\mathrm{d}t + \sigma_i(\mathbf{x}_t, t)\mathrm{d}W_t^i \tag{8.4}$$

for $1 \leq i \leq n$, with

$$\mathrm{d}\langle W_t^i, W_t^j \rangle = \rho_{ij}\mathrm{d}t.$$

Any derivative price $V(\mathbf{x}, t)$, discounted by the money market account

$$B_t = \exp\left(\int_0^t r_s \mathrm{d}s\right)$$

must be a martingale in the risk-neutral measure. Hence, applying Ito, we have

$$\mathrm{d}\left(\frac{V}{B}\right) = \frac{1}{B}\left(\frac{\partial V}{\partial t} - r_t V + \sum_i \mu_i \frac{\partial V}{\partial x_i} + \frac{1}{2}\sum_{i,j} \rho_{ij}\sigma_i\sigma_j \frac{\partial^2 V}{\partial x_i \partial x_j}\right)\mathrm{d}t$$

$$+ \frac{1}{B}\sum_i \sigma_i \frac{\partial V}{\partial x_i}\mathrm{d}W_t^i,$$

and so setting the drift to zero gives the PDE for V:

$$\frac{\partial V}{\partial t} - r_t V + \sum_i \mu_i \frac{\partial V}{\partial x_i} + \frac{1}{2}\sum_{i,j} \rho_{ij}\sigma_i\sigma_j \frac{\partial^2 V}{\partial x_i \partial x_j} = 0. \tag{8.5}$$

Next, we define the Arrow-Debreu price $\psi(\mathbf{x}', t)$ as the present value of a derivative that pays off $\delta(\mathbf{x_t} - \mathbf{x}')$ at time t. This is related to the t-forward measure probability density of $\mathbf{x}$, $\phi(\mathbf{x}, t)$ by

$$\psi(\mathbf{x}, t) = P(0, t)\phi(\mathbf{x}, t), \tag{8.6}$$

as can be seen from the defining equations for ψ and ϕ:

$$V(\mathbf{x}_0, 0) = \int V(\mathbf{x}, t)\psi(\mathbf{x}, t)\mathrm{d}\mathbf{x} \tag{8.7}$$

$$= P(0, t) \int V(\mathbf{x}, t)\phi(\mathbf{x}, t)\mathrm{d}\mathbf{x}. \tag{8.8}$$

The latter follows by noting that $P(s, t)$ is the numeraire of the t-forward measure, $\mathbb{Q}_t$, so

$$\frac{V(\mathbf{x}_0, 0)}{P(0, t)} = \mathbb{E}^{\mathbb{Q}_t}\left[\frac{V(\mathbf{x}_t, t)}{P(t, t)}\right] = \mathbb{E}^{\mathbb{Q}_t}\left[V(\mathbf{x}_t, t)\right].$$

To derive the forward PDE for ψ, we note that the left-hand side of equation (8.7) is independent of t. Differentiating both sides with respect to t, and using equation (8.5), gives

$$0 = \int \left[V\frac{\partial \psi}{\partial t} + \psi\left(r_t V - \sum_i \mu_i \frac{\partial V}{\partial x_i} - \frac{1}{2}\sum_{i,j} \rho_{ij}\sigma_i\sigma_j \frac{\partial^2 V}{\partial x_i \partial x_j}\right)\right]\mathrm{d}\mathbf{x}.$$

Integrating by parts, we get

$$0 = \int V\left(\frac{\partial \psi}{\partial t} + r_t\psi + \sum_i \frac{\partial(\mu_i\psi)}{\partial x_i} - \frac{1}{2}\sum_{i,j} \frac{\partial^2(\rho_{ij}\sigma_i\sigma_j\psi)}{\partial x_i \partial x_j}\right)\mathrm{d}\mathbf{x}$$

$$+ \text{ boundary terms.} \tag{8.9}$$

These boundary terms depend on the specific problem. In all the cases we will discuss, μ_i and σ_i are well behaved everywhere, including infinity, so these boundary terms can be ignored. The above equation holds for all payoffs $V(\mathbf{x}, t)$, and so the only way in which it can hold generally is by setting

$$\frac{\partial \psi}{\partial t} + r_t\psi + \sum_i \frac{\partial(\mu_i\psi)}{\partial x_i} - \frac{1}{2}\sum_{i,j} \frac{\partial^2(\rho_{ij}\sigma_i\sigma_j\psi)}{\partial x_i \partial x_j} = 0.$$

This is the PDE that we have been seeking for ψ.

We can remove the effect of deterministic interest rates or reduce the effect of jumps in the forward curve for stochastic interest rates by working with ϕ rather than ψ. If we let the forward short rate with maturity T, observed at t, be $f(t, T)$, then

$$f(t, T) \equiv -\frac{\partial}{\partial T} P(t, T).$$

Using equation (8.6), we can show that ϕ obeys

$$\frac{\partial \phi}{\partial t} + (r_t - f(0, t))\phi + \sum_i \frac{\partial(\mu_i \phi)}{\partial x_i} - \frac{1}{2} \sum_{i,j} \frac{\partial^2(\rho_{ij}\sigma_i\sigma_j\phi)}{\partial x_i \partial x_j} = 0. \qquad (8.10)$$

The above equation demonstrates why it can be better in practice to work with ϕ rather than ψ. When interest rates are deterministic, $r_t - f(0, t) = 0$, so the reaction term vanishes; when we use a Vasicek/Hull-White model for interest rates [61], [62], $r_t - f(0, t)$ is continuous, even if $f(0, t)$ has discontinuities (which can happen if the yield curve is not interpolated smoothly). For more complicated rate models, such as Black-Karazinski ([63]), $r_t - f(0, t)$ will not be continuous, but its jumps will generally be much smaller than the ones in r_t alone.

The initial conditions for ϕ or ψ can be found by taking the limit of the SDEs in equation (8.4) as $t \to 0$. If the drift and volatility functions are bounded, then the equations reduce to

$$x_i(\delta t) \approx \mu_i(\mathbf{x}_0, 0)\delta t + \sigma_i(\mathbf{x}_0, 0)W^i(\delta t),$$

and so we can use an n-factor Gaussian as an initial condition at time δt. At time $t = 0$ the solution will be a delta function, so difficult to represent on a finite difference grid. An alternative approach is to rescale the coordinates near $t = 0$ so that the solution is a multifactor Gaussian is constant in the limit $t \to 0$. We discuss this further in section 8.4.

Once we have $\phi(\mathbf{x}, t)$, it is then easy to price any derivative with a European payoff at t by using equation (8.8). We can therefore price a whole series of European options with different strikes and maturities by propagating the solution for ϕ out to the latest maturity once. Note that this is only one example of a forward PDE. We show in section 8.3 that in a single-factor equity model (with no stochastic interest rates/hazard rates, etc.) we can derive a forward PDE for the call prices themselves as a function of their strikes and maturities.

8.3 PURE EQUITY CASE

In this section, we describe the equations governing the pure equity problem (by which we mean that there are no stochastic interest rates, credit, or volatility). We assume we have some stock S which pays a mixture of cash and proportional dividends as defined in section 1.1.1. Recall equation (1.6):

$$S_t = F_t^* X_t + A_t.$$

(F_t^* and A_t are defined in equations (1.7) and (1.8) of section 1.1.2.) We will use this to transform away the dividends and yield curve, leaving us with a martingale X, which we will assume follows the SDE

$$\frac{\mathrm{d}X_t}{X_t} = \sigma(X_t, t)\mathrm{d}W_t.$$

It will simplify the numerics (and in particular the boundary conditions that go into equation (8.9)) to work in log-space, so we define $x_t = \ln(X_t/X_0)$ and have

$$\mathrm{d}x_t = -\frac{1}{2}\sigma^2(x_t, t)\mathrm{d}t + \sigma(x_t, t)\mathrm{d}W_t. \tag{8.11}$$

We will use $\sigma(x_t, t)$ as shorthand notation for $\sigma(\exp(x_t), t)$. The meaning will always be clear from the context.

Using equation (8.10) from section 8.2, then provided σ is bounded as $x \to \pm\infty$, we can ignore the boundary terms and get that

$$\frac{\partial\phi}{\partial t} - \frac{1}{2}\frac{\partial(\sigma^2\phi)}{\partial x} - \frac{1}{2}\frac{\partial^2(\sigma^2\phi)}{\partial x^2} = 0. \tag{8.12}$$

If we have computed $\phi(x, t)$ for some t, we can use it to price call options using equation (8.8):

$$C(K, t) = P(0, t)\int_k^\infty \left(X_0 F_t^*\right)(\exp(x) - \exp(k))\phi(x, t)\mathrm{d}x,$$

where k is the strike transformed to log-space by

$$K = F_t^* X_0 \exp(k) + A_t.$$

We also define a normalized call price

$$c(k, t) = C(F_t^* X_0 \exp(k) + A_t, t)/(F_t^* X_0 P(0, t)),$$

and get that

$$c(k, t) = \int_k^\infty \left(\exp(x) - \exp(k)\right)\phi(x, t)\mathrm{d}x. \tag{8.13}$$

Obviously, we can price any European payoff using ϕ. However, if we are interested just in call prices (as is the case when calibrating a local volatility), we can instead write a PDE for $c(k, t)$ and solve for the call prices directly. To do this, we start by differentiating equation (8.13) twice with respect to k, giving

$$\frac{\partial c}{\partial k} = -\exp(k)\int_k^\infty \phi(x, t)\mathrm{d}x$$

and

$$\frac{\partial^2 c}{\partial k^2} = \frac{\partial c}{\partial k} + \exp(k)\phi(k,t). \tag{8.14}$$

This last equation allows us to convert from c to ϕ. Next, we differentiate c with respect to t, giving

$$\frac{\partial c}{\partial t} = \int_k^\infty \left(\exp(x) - \exp(k)\right) \left(\frac{1}{2}\frac{\partial}{\partial x}\left(1 + \frac{\partial}{\partial x}\right)\right)(\sigma^2 \phi)dx,$$

where we have used equation (8.12) to eliminate $\frac{\partial \phi}{\partial t}$. Integrating by parts gives

$$\frac{\partial c}{\partial t} = -\frac{1}{2}\int_k^\infty \exp(x)\left(1 + \frac{\partial}{\partial x}\right)(\sigma^2 \phi)dx \tag{8.15}$$

$$= -\frac{1}{2}\int_k^\infty \frac{\partial}{\partial x}\left(\exp(x)\sigma^2 \phi\right)dx \tag{8.16}$$

$$= +\frac{1}{2}\exp(k)\sigma^2(k,t)\phi(k,t). \tag{8.17}$$

By combining equations (8.14) and (8.17) we can eliminate $\phi(k,t)$, giving the desired PDE for $c(k,t)$:

$$\frac{\partial c}{\partial t} = \frac{1}{2}\sigma^2(k,t)\left(\frac{\partial^2 c}{\partial k^2} - \frac{\partial c}{\partial k}\right).$$

Rearranging this gives Dupire's formula in log-coordinates:

$$\sigma^2(k,t) = \frac{2\frac{\partial c}{\partial t}}{\frac{\partial^2 c}{\partial k^2} - \frac{\partial c}{\partial k}}. \tag{8.18}$$

Now we have two ways to price European call options efficiently: solving the PDE for ϕ or solving the PDE for c. Note that the initial condition for c, $c(k,0) = \left(\exp(k) - 1\right)^+$ is discontinuous in its first derivative in k, so for very short maturities we will have noise in the numerical solution. We can reduce this by taking smaller time steps and using a denser mesh near $t = 0$. Alternatively, we can solve for ϕ near $t = 0$, and switch to using the PDE for c at some larger t.

The initial condition for ϕ is even more pathological than the one for c, being a delta function. However, we can transform our x coordinate by $x_t = x_t'\overline{\sigma}_t\sqrt{t}$, where $\overline{\sigma}_t$ is some averaged implied volatility at time t, and work with $\phi'(x',t)$, where $\phi'(x',t)dx' = \phi(x,t)dx$. The initial condition for ϕ' is a Gaussian. Unfortunately, the coefficients of the transformed PDE become infinite as $t \to 0$. To get around this, we could start the PDE from a small time δt, but in practice a second-order Crank-Nicholson scheme where the coefficients are evaluated halfway through a time step works even if started at $t = 0$.

8.4   LOCAL VOLATILITY WITH STOCHASTIC INTEREST RATES

In this section, we derive the forward PDEs for a two-factor interest rate and equity model. As discussed in chapter 3, many short rate models can be expressed as follows:

$$r_t = f(0, t) + g(y_t, \overline{y}_t, t), \tag{8.19}$$

where y_t follows the Ornstein-Uhlenbeck process:

$$dy_t = -\kappa y_t dt + \sigma_t^r dW_t^r$$

in the risk-neutral measure. The function $\overline{y}_t$ is assumed to have been calibrated to fit the yield curve. If $g(y, \overline{y}, t) = y + \overline{y}$, we have the extended Vasicek/Hull-White model, whereas if $g(y, \overline{y}) = \exp(y_t + \overline{y}_t) - f(0, t)$ we have the Black-Karasinski model. Of course, we could have written $r_t = g(y_t, \overline{y}_t, t)$, and this would have been equivalent mathematically. However, with the definition of equation (8.19), the function g is generally smoother (it is continuous in the Vasicek model, whereas the paths of r_t may not be).

We have the stock price process in the risk-neutral measure:

$$\frac{dS_t}{S_t} = (r_t - v_t)dt + \sigma_t^S dW_t^S.$$

The term v_t encompasses all of the dividend/repo terms. To take these into account we change a variable, defining

$$x_t = \ln\left(S_t \exp\left(-\int_0^t v_s ds\right) P(0, t)\right)$$

$$= \ln\left(\frac{S_t}{F_t}\right), \tag{8.20}$$

where F_t is the stock forward with maturity t. This new variable follows the process

$$dx_t = \left(g_t(y_t) - \frac{1}{2}(\sigma_t^S)^2\right) dt + \sigma_t^S dW_t^S. \tag{8.21}$$

Note that the deterministic interest rate case corresponds to $g_t(y) = 0$, and equation (8.21) reduces to equation (8.11).

We have our SDEs for the two state variables, x and y, so we can apply equation (8.10) to get the PDE followed by the joint probability density $\phi(x, y, t)$:

$$0 = \frac{\partial \phi}{\partial t} + g_t(y_t)\left(\phi + \frac{\partial \phi}{\partial x}\right) - \frac{1}{2}\frac{\partial((\sigma^S)^2\phi)}{\partial x} - \frac{\partial}{\partial y}\left(\kappa y\phi + \frac{1}{2}(\sigma^r)^2\frac{\partial \phi}{\partial y}\right)$$

$$- \frac{1}{2}\frac{\partial^2((\sigma^S)^2\phi)}{\partial x^2} - \rho\sigma^r\frac{\partial^2(\sigma^S\phi)}{\partial x\partial y}. \tag{8.22}$$

In practice, this is a cumbersome PDE to solve: The initial condition at $t = 0$ is a two-dimensional delta function, and the distribution then spreads out as $\sqrt{t}$ while the peak decreases as $1/\sqrt{t}$. Taking advantage of this information, we can rescale the x and y coordinates as

$$x = x'a_t,$$

$$y = y'b_t,$$

where a_t and b_t scale as $\sqrt{t}$ as $t \to 0$, and also rescale ϕ as

$$\phi(x, y, t) = \frac{\phi'(x', y', t)}{a_t b_t}.$$

Note that we have

$$\int \phi(x, y, t)dxdy = \int \phi'(x', y', t)dx'dy',$$

so ϕ' is just the probability density associated with the new coordinates x' and y'.

We can use a_t and b_t to make our PDE grid cover just the region where the probability density is significant. In the interest rate direction, we know that the marginal probability distribution is Gaussian with variance

$$V_r(t) = \int_0^t \sigma^r(s)^2 \exp(2\kappa(s - t))ds,$$

and so we can define b_t as the square root of this:

$$b_t = \sqrt{\int_0^t \sigma^r(s)^2 \exp(2\kappa(s - t))ds} \,.$$

This makes y' the number of standard deviations that the short rate is away from the mean.

The problem is more complicated in the equity direction, where we do not have a normal marginal probability distribution because of the volatility skew. However, we can compute the actual marginal probability distribution from call prices and use some feature of it to determine a_T. One approach is to use the at-the-money implied volatility σ_{atm} and let

$$a_t = \sigma_{\text{atm}}(t)\sqrt{t}. \tag{8.23}$$

A better choice of a_t will allow us to distribute mesh points more efficiently in terms of speed of calculation for a given tolerance.

We get the following PDE for ϕ':

$$0 = \frac{\partial \phi'}{\partial t} + g_t(by')\left(\phi' + \frac{1}{a}\frac{\partial \phi'}{\partial x'}\right) - \frac{\partial}{\partial x'}\left[\left(\frac{(\sigma^S)^2}{2a} + \frac{\dot{a}}{a}x'\right)\phi'\right]$$

$$- \frac{(\sigma^r)^2}{2b^2}\frac{\partial}{\partial y'}\left(y\phi' + \frac{\partial \phi'}{\partial y'}\right) - \frac{1}{2a^2}\frac{\partial^2((\sigma^S)^2\phi')}{\partial x'^2} - \frac{\rho\sigma^r}{ab}\frac{\partial^2(\sigma^S\phi')}{\partial x'\partial y'}. \tag{8.24}$$

Note that the coefficients diverge as $t \to 0$. One approach is to move the initial condition to some small time δt; however, depending on the implementation of the PDE solver, this might not be necessary. The authors have obtained good results propagating from $t = 0$ with an ADI scheme where the coefficients are evaluated halfway through a time-step, hence avoiding the infinities at $t = 0$.

The initial condition for ϕ' is a two-factor Gaussian; for small t we have

$$\phi'(x',y',t) \approx \frac{ab}{2\pi\sqrt{1-\rho^2}\sigma^S\sigma^r t} \exp\left(-\frac{1}{2(1-\rho^2)}\left(\frac{x'^2 a^2}{(\sigma^S)^2 t} + \frac{y'^2 b^2}{(\sigma^r)^2 t} - \frac{2\rho x'y' ab}{\sigma^S\sigma^r t}\right)\right)$$

$$= \frac{1}{2\pi\sqrt{1-\rho^2}} \exp\left(-\frac{1}{2(1-\rho^2)}\left(x'^2 + y'^2 - 2\rho x'y'\right)\right)$$

if we use a and b as in equations (8.23) and (8.4).

Figure 8.2 show the results of propagating equation (8.24) for 18 years using the volatility surface of the Nikkei index and a Hull-White model for the JPY interest rates with an instantaneous correlation of zero (the terminal distribution shown in the figure actually has some positive correlation from the effect of rate shifts on the growth rate of the index; see section 4.1). The long tail to the left of the distribution comes from the skew of the implied volatility surface; the in-the-money options have higher implied volatilities than out-of-the-money ones. The marginal distributions of x and y are shown in figure 8.3; note that in the interest-rate direction, we have just a Gaussian, as we are using a Hull-White model. In the equity direction, we have the same distribution we would get from solving the one-factor problem in section 8.3.

The coordinate rescalings are useful for the solution of the PDE but cumbersome when discussing the method, so we now return to working with ϕ. Inverting equation (8.20), the stock price is given by

$$S_t = F_t \exp(x_t),$$

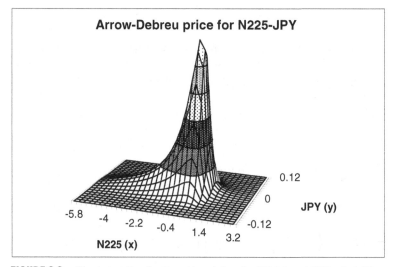

FIGURE 8.2 The joint distribution $\phi(x,y)$ for the N225 and JPY after 18 years, with zero instantaneous correlation.

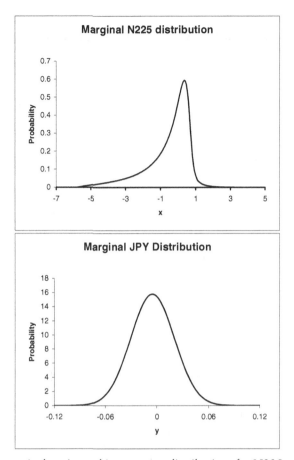

FIGURE 8.3 The marginal equity and interest rate distributions for N225 and JPY after 18 years.

and so the price of a European call is given by

$$C(K, T) = P(0, T) \int_{-\infty}^{\infty} \int_{k}^{\infty} F_T \left(\exp(x) - \exp(k)\right) \phi(x, y, T) dx dy,$$

where

$$K = F_t \exp(k).$$

In an attempt to get a Dupire-like result, we can differentiate this expression with respect to k and T respectively. As in the previous section, in order to simplify the equations, we first write

$$c(k, T) = \frac{C(K, T)}{P(0, T)F_T}$$

$$= \int_{-\infty}^{\infty} \int_{k}^{\infty} \left(\exp(x) - \exp(k)\right) \phi(x, y, T) dx dy. \qquad (8.25)$$

Working in terms of $c(k, T)$ rather than $C(K, T)$, we don't have to worry about dividends or the initial yield curve. Differentiating with respect to T and using equation (8.22) gives

$$\frac{\partial c}{\partial T} = \int_{-\infty}^{\infty} \int_{k}^{\infty} (\exp(x) - \exp(k)) \left(-g_T(y) \left[\phi + \frac{\partial \phi}{\partial x} \right] + \frac{\partial}{\partial x} \left[\frac{(\sigma^S)^2}{2} \phi \right] \right.$$

$$\left. + \frac{1}{2} \frac{\partial^2 ((\sigma^S)^2 \phi)}{\partial x^2} \right) \mathrm{d}x \mathrm{d}y.$$

Integrating by parts a few times gives

$$\frac{\partial c}{\partial T} = \frac{1}{2} \exp(k) \sigma^S(k, T)^2 \int_{-\infty}^{\infty} \phi(k, y, T) \mathrm{d}y$$

$$+ \exp(k) \int_{-\infty}^{\infty} \int_{k}^{\infty} g_T(y) \phi(x, y, T) \mathrm{d}y \mathrm{d}x. \qquad (8.26)$$

Differentiating equation (8.25) with respect to k gives

$$\frac{\partial c}{\partial k} = \int_{\infty}^{\infty} \int_{k}^{\infty} -\exp(k) \phi(x, y, T) \mathrm{d}x \mathrm{d}y$$

$$\frac{\partial^2 c}{\partial k^2} = \int_{\infty}^{\infty} \int_{k}^{\infty} -\exp(k) \phi(x, y, T) \mathrm{d}x \mathrm{d}y + \exp(k) \int_{-\infty}^{\infty} \phi(k, y, T) \mathrm{d}y$$

and so we can combine the last three equations to give

$$\frac{\partial c}{\partial T} = \frac{(\sigma^S)^2}{2} \left(\frac{\partial^2 c}{\partial k^2} - \frac{\partial c}{\partial k} \right) + \exp(k) \int_{-\infty}^{\infty} \int_{k}^{\infty} g_T(y) \phi(x, y, T) \mathrm{d}x \mathrm{d}y. \qquad (8.27)$$

This is almost, but not quite, the Dupire-like result we want. Indeed, if we let $g_t(y) = 0$ (which reduces the problem to the deterministic interest rate case), the above expression reduces to Dupire's formula. Unfortunately, there is no way to back out the second term on the right-hand side from just European option prices. However, if we have propagated ϕ up to time T, we can use the above expression to determine the local volatility between T and $T + \delta T$.

8.5   CALIBRATING THE LOCAL VOLATILITY

In the previous sections, we have shown how to use forward PDEs to price European options efficiently given a local volatility surface. It is then a standard inverse problem to find the local volatility surface that is consistent with an implied volatility surface. We can parameterize the local volatility in some way, then adjust the parameters until we correctly reprice a set of European options. Since the prices of European options with maturity T depend only on the local volatility surface at times $t < T$, we can bootstrap the calibration; that is, we can calibrate the surface up to some time T_i, then calibrate the surface from T_i to T_{i+1}, leaving the local volatility at

$t < T_i$ unchanged. We can also use $\phi(\mathbf{x}, T_i)$, found in the calibration up to T_i, as a starting point for the calibration from T_i to T_{i+1}.

Depending on the amount of detail in the implied volatility surface we are trying to fit, we might want to parameterize the local volatility by tens or hundreds of parameters in any given time slice. The number of iterations that any root-finding algorithm is likely to need will grow accordingly. It can therefore become a very slow process to solve the inverse problem where the forward problem involves solving for ϕ with a one- or two- (or potentially higher) factor PDE solver. However, a better approach is available.

Assuming that we have evolved ϕ up to time t, we can write the call prices consistent with our local volatility surface as integrals over ϕ (see, for example, equation (8.25) for the two-factor version). We can then find a relationship between our local volatility $\sigma(x, t)$ at this time and the rates of change of call prices with respect to maturity at fixed k. In one factor this is just equation (8.17) and in two factors it is equation (8.26). We can therefore express the call prices at time $t + \delta t$ in terms of $\phi(t)$ and the local volatility between t and $t + \delta t$.

As an example, in the two-factor case we have

$$
\begin{aligned}
c(k, T_{i+1}) \approx & \int_k^\infty \int_{-\infty}^\infty (\exp(x) - \exp(k))\phi(x, y, T_i)\mathrm{d}y\mathrm{d}x \\
& + \frac{1}{2} \exp(k)\sigma^S(k, T_i)^2 \int_{-\infty}^\infty \phi(k, y, T_i)\mathrm{d}y \\
& + \exp(k) \int_{-\infty}^\infty \int_k^\infty g_{T_i}(y)\phi(x, y, T_i)\mathrm{d}x\mathrm{d}y.
\end{aligned}
\tag{8.28}
$$

We want to find some function $\sigma(x)$ that when applied between T_i and T_{i+1}, gives the minimum discrepancy between the model call prices $c(k, T_{i+1})$ and the market call prices $c_m(k, T_{i+1})$. The above equation (and indeed the equivalent equation in the one-factor case) reduces to

$$
c_m(k, T_{i+1}) - c(k, T_{i+1}) = -a(k, T) + b(k, T)\sigma^S(k, T)^2,
$$

where a and b are known at time T. We can iteratively guess the parameters of $\sigma(x)$ until we minimize the above difference (in some norm). This is much faster than iterating the full problem, where $c(k, T_{i+1})$ is the result of an expensive PDE solution. Note that we could insist that the difference between the market and model call prices be zero, letting

$$
\sigma^S(k, T)^2 = \frac{a(k, T)}{b(k, T)}.
$$

The problems with doing this are that a might be negative (if the data are arbitrageable) and that at low/high strikes both a and b go to zero and the ratio of them cannot be computed with much confidence. A better approach is to minimize the difference between the model and the market call prices in some norm: $||c - c_m||$, plus some penalty function for nonsmooth $\sigma(x)$ functions. We might want to minimize

$$
F(\sigma^S) = \int_{-\infty}^\infty w(k) \left(c_m(k, T_{i+1}) - c(k, T_{i+1})\right)^2 + z(k) \left(\frac{\partial^2 \sigma}{\partial k^2}\right)^2 \mathrm{d}k
$$

for some weight functions $w(k)$ and $z(k)$. Realistically, we would choose some discretised version of the above such as

$$F(\sigma^S) = \sum_n w(k_n) \left(c_m(k_n, T_{i+1}) - c(k_n, T_{i+1}) \right)^2 + z(k_n) \left(\frac{\partial^2 \sigma}{\partial k_n^2} \right)^2.$$

This function can be easily evaluated given a local volatility curve and does not involve expensive finite-difference computations, so we can back out the best local volatility curve using some least-squares fitting routine. It is also much safer to use a simple functional form in a minimization routine: the numerical noise in propagating with a PDE solver could easily confuse a minimization algorithm.

We can now use our local volatility with our slow finite-difference solver to propagate ϕ from T_i to T_{i+1}. Note that equation (8.28) is equivalent to using an explicit finite difference step to propagate from T_i to T_{i+1}, and the predicted call prices at time T_{i+1} (and therefore the local volatility) are accurate only to $O(\delta T)$, where $\delta T = T_{i+1} - T_i$. However, while the call prices at T_{i+1} from our local volatility surface might differ from the market call prices by $O(\delta T)$, we know them to the same order of accuracy as our finite-difference solution. Any errors from the approximation will not accumulate but be corrected for on the next time step. The accuracy of our fit to the call prices is always $O(\delta T)$, regardless of how many steps we are using to propagate up to time T providing our finite difference solver is accurate to at least $O(\delta T^2)$.

8.6 SPECIAL CASE: VASICEK PLUS A TERM STRUCTURE OF EQUITY VOLATILITIES

In this section, we show a quicker way to find a term structure of equity volatilities when the interest rates follow a Vasicek/Hull-White model and the stock has no implied volatility skew.

We have the risk-neutral dynamics

$$dr_t = (\theta_t - \kappa r_t)dt + \sigma_t^r dW_t^r \tag{8.29}$$

and

$$\frac{dS_t}{S_t} = (r_t - v_t)dt + \sigma_t^S dW_t^S.$$

To remove the effects of the dividends, we define a new variable X_t by

$$X_t = S_t \exp\left(-\int_0^t v_u du \right) = \frac{S_t}{P(0, t)F_t},$$

which has the familiar dynamics

$$\frac{dX_t}{X_t} = r_t dt + \sigma_t^S dW_t^S.$$

X_t corresponds to the strategy of reinvesting the dividends in the stock and so is tradable.

We want to find the dynamics of X_t in the T−forward measure, $\mathbb{Q}_T$, in which the zero-coupon bond $P(t, T)$ is the numeraire; first, we must find the dynamics of $P(t, T)$ under the risk-neutral measure $\mathbb{P}$. Integrating equation (8.29) gives

$$r_s = \int_t^s \exp(\kappa(u - s))\sigma_u^r dW_u + \text{nonstochastic terms.}$$

The zero-coupon bond $P(t, T)$ has value

$$P(t, T) = \mathbb{E}^{\mathbb{P}}\left[\exp\left(-\int_t^T r_s ds\right)\right] \tag{8.30}$$

$$\propto \mathbb{E}^{\mathbb{P}}\left[\exp\left(-\int_t^T \int_t^s \exp(\kappa(u - s))\sigma_u^r dW_u^r ds\right)\right] \tag{8.31}$$

$$\propto \mathbb{E}^{\mathbb{P}}\left[\exp\left(-\int_t^T \hat{B}(\kappa, u, T)\sigma_u^r dW_u^r\right)\right], \tag{8.32}$$

where

$$\hat{B}(\kappa, u, T) = \frac{1 - \exp(\kappa(u - T))}{\kappa}.$$

Equation (8.32) gives us the volatility of the zero-coupon bond. We can find the drift using the fact that $P(t, T)$ is tradable, so $P(t, T)/B_t$ must be a $\mathbb{P}$−martingale and so we have

$$\frac{dP(t, T)}{P(t, T)} = r_t dt - \hat{B}(\kappa, t, T)\sigma_t^r dW_t^r.$$

Since X_t is tradable, $X_t/P(t, T)$ will be a $\mathbb{Q}_T$-martingale, so it follows that

$$\frac{d\left(\frac{X_t}{P(t,T)}\right)}{\frac{X_t}{P(t,T)}} = \sigma_t^S d\widetilde{W}_t^S + \hat{B}(\kappa, t, T)\sigma_t^r d\widetilde{W}_t^r,$$

where $\widetilde{W}_i$ are Brownian motions in $\mathbb{Q}_T$. It follows that under $\mathbb{Q}_T$, X_T is log-normally distributed with mean $1/P(0, T)$ (since $X_0 = 1$) and variance

$$V_T = \int_0^T \left((\sigma_t^S)^2 + 2\rho\sigma_t^S \hat{B}(\kappa, t, T)\sigma_t^r + \hat{B}(\kappa, t, T)^2(\sigma_t^r)^2\right) dt. \tag{8.33}$$

We can write

$$X_T = \frac{1}{P(0, T)}\mathcal{E}\left(\sqrt{\frac{V_T}{T}}\widetilde{W}_T\right),$$

where ε is the Doléans-Dade exponential:

$$\varepsilon\left(\sqrt{\frac{V_T}{T}}\,\widetilde{W}_T\right) = \exp\left(\sqrt{\frac{V_T}{T}}\,\widetilde{W}_T - \frac{V_T}{2}\right)$$

and so the stock price is given by

$$S_T = F_t\varepsilon\left(\sqrt{\frac{V_T}{T}}\,\widetilde{W}_T\right).$$

The price of a call with maturity T and strike K is

$$C(K,T) = P(0,T)\mathbb{E}^{\mathbb{Q}T}[(S_t - K)^+]$$

$$= P(0,T)\mathbb{E}^{\mathbb{Q}T}\left[\left(F_T\varepsilon\left(\sqrt{\frac{V_T}{T}}\,\widetilde{W}_T\right) - K\right)^+\right].$$

If we use the same assumptions that go into the definition of implied volatility (i.e., deterministic interest rates and a constant volatility), then we can identify

$$V_T = \sigma^2_{\mathrm{imp},T}T.$$

Substituting this into equation (8.33) gives the relationship between the implied volatility, σ_{imp} and the process volatilities, σ^S and σ^r:

$$\sigma^2_{\mathrm{imp}}(T) = \frac{1}{T}\int_0^T \left((\sigma_t^S)^2 + 2\rho\sigma_t^S\hat{B}(\kappa,t,T)\sigma_t^r + \hat{B}(\kappa,t,T)^2(\sigma_t^r)^2\right)\mathrm{d}t. \qquad (8.34)$$

To find σ^S from σ_{imp} and σ^r, we must invert the above expression. This can be done numerically by bootstrapping. Figure 8.4 shows the result for a constant implied

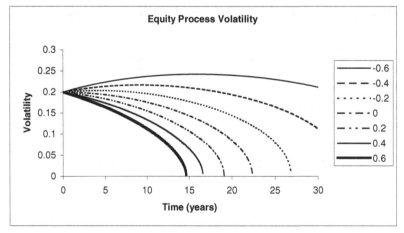

FIGURE 8.4 Equity process volatility for different correlations, with a fixed implied volatility of $\sigma_{\mathrm{imp}} = 20\%$, with $\kappa = 1\%$ and $\sigma_r = 1\%$.

volatility of $\sigma_{\text{imp}} = 20\%$, with $\kappa = 1\%$ and $\sigma_r = 2\%$, for a range of correlations. The larger the correlation, the more suppressed the local volatility becomes. Note that even with zero correlation, the process volatility is less than the implied volatility. Also note that we cannot fit a flat implied volatility beyond a certain maturity for each correlation.

CHAPTER 9

Numerical Solution of Multifactor Pricing Problems Using Lagrange-Galerkin with Duality Methods

9.1   INTRODUCTION

Many financial derivative products are conveniently modeled in terms of one or more factors, or stochastic spatial variables, and time. Based on the contingent claims analysis developed by Black and Scholes [72] and Merton [73], a partial differential equation (PDE) for the fair price of these derivatives can be obtained. Valuation PDEs for financial derivatives are usually parabolic and of second order. In the more general case, partial differential inequalities (PDIs) arise. The inequality comes when the option has some embedded early-exercise features and the price of the contingent claim must satisfy some inequality constraints in order to avoid arbitrage opportunities. In other words, if the price were to violate those constraints, the option would be exercised, since both the buyer and the seller of an option will try to maximize the value of their rights under the contract. Early-exercise features appear, for example, in American options and in the conversion, call, and put provisions of convertible bonds. These are so-called free boundary problems because there are (a priori) unknown boundaries separating the regions where inequalities are strict from those where they are saturated.

It is almost always impossible to find an explicit solution to a free boundary problem: we need numerical techniques. The extra complication in those problems comes from the fact that we do not know where the free boundary is; it is an extra unknown that we need to find as part of the solution procedure. The most common method of handling the early exercise condition is simply to advance the discrete solution over a time step, ignoring the restriction, and then to make a projection on the set of constraints (see, for example, Clewlow and Strickland [139]). This is very easy to implement but has the disadvantage that the solution is in an inconsistent state at the beginning of each time step (see Wilmott, Dewynne, and Howison [140]).

Rigorous methods to deal with free boundaries transform the original problem into a new one having a fixed domain from which the free boundary can be found a posteriori. The problem may be formulated in two ways: The first is as a linear complementary problem (a strong formulation), usually combined with finite difference methods; the second is as a variational inequality (a weak formulation), usually related to finite element methods. The latter has some advantages. First, variational inequalities are an excellent framework to deal with issues such as existence and uniqueness of the solution. Second, they are appropriate to analyze the error incurred in the numerical methods (numerical analysis). Finally, writing a weak formulation is a necessary step in using finite element methods for numerical solution.

In this chapter, we present a framework for solving multifactor option-pricing problems with early-exercise features. We first introduce a duality (or Langrange multiplier) method to deal with inequality constraints in the solution or its derivatives. Then the method of characteristics and finite elements is proposed for time and space discretization, respectively. The combination of these numerical methods has been applied to finance by Bermúdez and Nogueiras [107] and Vázquez [141].

There are three main issues when using PDE methods in contingent claim valuation: (1) how to account for early-exercise features; (2) how to discretize the model; and (3) how to deal with the convection-dominance problem. The main goal, of course, is to achieve the best trade-off between speed and accuracy according to the circumstances of our valuation problem.[1]

In order to deal with free boundary problems, we first reformulate them in a mixed form by means of a Lagrange multiplier. Then we propose an iterative algorithm in which the solution of the nonlinear problem, that is, the problem with constraints, is approximated by a sequence of solutions of linear (unconstrained) problems. This algorithm is a particular application of the one introduced by Bermúdez and Moreno [142] and has been used extensively in other fields. The algorithm provides great generality in the sense that it allows for any type of constraint to be imposed on the value function or its derivatives, which may depend on the spatial variables and time. It can be applied to either the weak or the strong problem; hence, it can be combined with either finite difference or finite element discretization. Moreover, since the solution of the nonlinear problem is approximated by a sequence of solutions of linear problems, any existing code for discretizing partial differential equations could be easily extended.

Sometimes in finance the effect of the volatility term is smaller than the effect of the drift term, giving rise to the so-called convection-dominated problems. Furthermore, the diffusive term may become degenerate in the following senses: We may distinguish between weak degeneration, as in Black-Scholes where the diffusion vanishes for zero spot, or strong degeneration of ultraparabolic type, as in Asian options in which there is no diffusion in one direction. In such situations second-order centered space-discretization schemes may lead to spurious oscillations. In the tree framework this is equivalent to saying that the local drift is so large relative to the diffusion that branching into the usual binomial or trinomial tree will lead to negative probabilities. Hull and White [143] have solved this with their alternative branching technique. In a PDE approach, one has to resort to first-order, one-sided space differencing or to the more recent Eulerian and characteristics techniques, such as the ones described in Ewing and Wang [144]. The method of characteristics for time discretization is a possible approach to deal with convection-dominated problems. Its main advantages are:

---

[1]Research, VAR, risk management, pricing.

- It is unconditionally stable even when applied to the transport equation (no diffusion). Hence, it copes well with degenerate diffusions.
- It yields discrete symmetrical linear systems, whose numerical solution is faster than nonsymmetrical ones.

The modified method of characteristics or semi-Lagrangian method was introduced in the 1990s by Pironneau [145] and Douglas and Russell [146]. It has been applied to convection-diffusion equations combined with space discretization using both finite differences (see [146]) and finite elements (see [147], [148], [149]). When combined with finite elements it is referred to as characteristics finite elements, or the Lagrange-Galerkin method. The classical method of characteristics is only first order accurate. However, higher order characteristic finite element methods have been proposed by Boukir et al. [150] and Rui and Tabata [151]. Bermúdez, Nogueiras, and Vázquez [152, 197] extended the method in Rui and Tabata and applied it to the valuation of American-Asian options. We describe the classical Lagrange-Galerkin method as well as the second-order scheme proposed in [152, 197].

While most papers and books on financial derivatives employ finite differences (FDs) for the numerical solution (see, for instance, Wilmott, Dewynne, and Howison [140]), the use of finite elements (FEs) has several advantages (see Ciarlet and Lions [153]):

- It can be used with domains of arbitrary geometries and arbitrary boundary conditions.
- It allows unstructured meshes, which can be convenient for making refinements in particular regions of the domain, such as around free boundaries or near barriers.
- It has a solid mathematical foundation. There is a well-developed theory about *a priori* and *a posteriori* error estimates, which allows a rigorous analysis and is a necessary tool for adaptive algorithms.
- It is well suited for modern computer architectures, particularly parallel processing.

This chapter is organized as follows: In section 9.2, we introduce the general modeling framework. In section 9.3, we describe the duality method to reduce the nonlinear problem to a sequence of linear problems. Section 9.4 describes the classical first-order Lagrange-Galerkin method, which can be used to solve the linear problem numerically. Section 9.5 introduces higher-order Lagrange-Galerkin schemes, and section 9.6 applies the classical Lagrange-Galerkin method to the valuation of convertible bonds.

9.2   THE MODELING FRAMEWORK: A GENERAL D-FACTOR MODEL

The fair price of many financial derivatives can be obtained by solving final-value problems for parabolic partial differential equations, eventually involving inequality constraints. These constraints could affect the option value, like in American-and Bermudan-style options or in convertible bonds, or may be imposed on the value of the spatial derivative of the solution, if we intend, for instance, to price a barrier option subject to a cap on the delta. Those are the so-called *free boundary problems* and are an example of nonlinear problems. Recall that free boundary problems may be mathematically formulated as linear complementary problems (strong formulation) or as variational inequalities (weak formulation). The terminology *weak–strong* refers to the regularity of the solution. Each solution of the strong formulation is a solution of the weak problem. Conversely, if a solution of the weak problem is smooth enough, then it is a solution of the original problem in the classical sense. Existence and uniqueness of a strong solution require the final and boundary conditions to be sufficiently smooth (payoff functions are generally not even differentiable). These constraints can be weakened when we use a weak formulation of the problem; the difficulties do not disappear, but solutions are sought in more general functional spaces (weighted Sobolev spaces).

In this section, we introduce a general *d*-factor pricing framework. First, we set the final-value linear problem in the absence of constraints. Then we formulate the nonlinear problem, both in strong and weak form. In order to use an iterative algorithm to deal with the free boundaries, we will need to reformulate the problem in a mixed form by means of a Lagrange multiplier. We will distinguish between the primal formulation, which involves only the unknown option price, and the mixed formulation, which involves the Lagrange multiplier as an extra unknown.

9.2.1   Strong Formulation of the Linear Problem: Partial Differential Equations

Let the value of a contingent claim ϕ be a function of time t and d spatial variables $\mathbf{x} = (x_1, ..., x_d)$. Very often, the value ϕ of the contingent claim can be found as the solution of a *parabolic partial differential* equation of the following form:

$$\frac{\partial \phi}{\partial t}(\mathbf{x}, t) + \sum_{i,j=1}^{d} A_{ij}(\mathbf{x}, t) \frac{\partial^2 \phi}{\partial x_i \partial x_j}(\mathbf{x}, t)$$

$$+ \sum_{j=1}^{d} B_j(\mathbf{x}, t) \frac{\partial \phi}{\partial x_j}(\mathbf{x}, t) + A_0(\mathbf{x}, t) \phi(\mathbf{x}, t)$$

$$= f(\mathbf{x}, t), \quad \text{in} \quad \Omega \times (0, T), \tag{9.1}$$

where Ω is the spatial domain and A_{ij}, B_i, A_0 and f are given measurable functions of $(\mathbf{x}, t)$. Typically, x_j represents quantities such as the value of an underlying asset or a stochastic interest rate. Therefore, they run either in the interval $[0, \infty)$ or in the whole real line $\mathbb{R}$. We also have to include the *final condition*, the payoff of the contract, which depends on the specific derivative product. In general, we will write

$$\phi(\mathbf{x}, T) = \Lambda(\mathbf{x}). \tag{9.2}$$

In order to obtain a weak formulation, we need to rewrite the equation in divergence form

$$
\frac{\partial \phi}{\partial t}(\mathbf{x}, t) - \sum_{i,j=1}^{d} \frac{\partial}{\partial x_i} \left(a_{ij}(\mathbf{x}, t) \frac{\partial \phi}{\partial x_j}(\mathbf{x}, t) \right)
$$

$$
+ \sum_{j=1}^{d} v_j(\mathbf{x}, t) \frac{\partial \phi}{\partial x_j}(\mathbf{x}, t) + a_0(\mathbf{x}, t) \phi(\mathbf{x}, t)
$$

$$
= f(\mathbf{x}, t) \qquad \text{in} \quad \Omega \times (0, T), \tag{9.3}
$$

where the new coefficients a_{ij}, b_i, a_0 are given by

$$
a_{ii} = -A_{ii}, \; a_{ij} = a_{ji} = -\frac{1}{2}\left(A_{ij} + A_{ji}\right), \tag{9.4}
$$

$$
v_i = \sum_{j=1}^{d} \frac{\partial a_{ij}}{\partial x_j} + B_i = -\frac{\partial A_{ii}}{\partial x_i} - \frac{1}{2} \sum_{j \neq i}^{d} \frac{\partial \left(A_{ij} + A_{ji}\right)}{\partial x_j} + B_i, \tag{9.5}
$$

$$
a_0 = A_0. \tag{9.6}
$$

Notice that we have imposed symmetry to the matrix $\mathbf{A} = \left(a_{ij}\right)$. Equation (9.3) is simply a d-dimensional *linear convection-diffusion-reaction equation*, with *diffusion matrix* $\mathbf{A} = (a_{ij})$, *velocity vector* $\mathbf{v} = (v_1, v_2, \cdots, v_d)$ *(convection)*, and *reaction coefficient* a_0.

It will be useful, for the following sections, to formulate the model using the *material* or *total derivative* of ϕ with respect to time t and the velocity field $\mathbf{v}$, namely,

$$
\frac{d\phi}{dt} = \dot{\phi}(\mathbf{x}, t) = \frac{\partial \phi}{\partial t}(\mathbf{x}, t) + \sum_{j=1}^{d} v_j(\mathbf{x}, t) \frac{\partial \phi}{\partial x_j}(\mathbf{x}, t). \tag{9.7}
$$

With this notation, equation (9.3) becomes

$$
\dot{\phi}(\mathbf{x}, t) - \sum_{i,j=1}^{d} \frac{\partial}{\partial x_i} \left(a_{ij}(\mathbf{x}, t) \frac{\partial \phi}{\partial x_j}(\mathbf{x}, t) \right) + a_0(\mathbf{x}, t) \phi(\mathbf{x}, t)
$$

$$
= f(\mathbf{x}, t). \tag{9.8}
$$

Denoting the differential operator by

$$
\mathcal{L}\left[\phi(\mathbf{x}, t)\right] = \dot{\phi}(\mathbf{x}, t)
$$

$$
- \sum_{i,j=1}^{d} \frac{\partial}{\partial x_i} \left(a_{ij}(\mathbf{x}, t) \frac{\partial \phi}{\partial x_j}(\mathbf{x}, t) \right)
$$

$$
+ a_0(\mathbf{x}, t) \phi(\mathbf{x}, t), \tag{9.9}
$$

the pricing problem (9.1)–(9.2) may be written as

PROBLEM 1 *Linear Problem (Strong Formulation)*
Find $\phi : \Omega \times [0, T] \to \mathbb{R}$ such that

$$
\begin{cases}
\mathcal{L}\left[\phi\left(\mathbf{x}, t\right)\right] = f\left(\mathbf{x}, t\right) & in \quad \Omega \times (0, T) & \text{(9.10a)} \\
\phi\left(\mathbf{x}, T\right) = \Lambda\left(\mathbf{x}\right) & in \quad \Omega. & \text{(9.10b)}
\end{cases}
$$

9.2.2 Truncation of the Domain and Boundary Conditions

Very often, the pricing problem is a pure Cauchy problem; that is, only an initial condition is needed to guarantee existence and uniqueness of solution. However, numerical discretization, by using either finite difference, finite elements, or finite volume methods, makes it necessary to cut the domain at finite distance and to introduce "artificial" *boundary conditions*. Those are generally obtained by financial arguments, but also by pure mathematical reasoning, and have to be included in the weak formulation. This process, called *localization*, often arises in numerical finance, and introduces a model error that has been studied, for instance, by Kangro and Nicolaides [154] and by Barles et al. [162].

Let us still call Ω the bounded domain, and Γ its boundary. We denote Γ_D (respectively Γ_R) the subset of Γ where *Dirichlet* (respectively *Robin*) *boundary conditions* are imposed. Specifically,

$$
\frac{\partial \phi}{\partial \mathbf{n}_A}\left(\mathbf{x}, t\right) + \alpha \phi\left(\mathbf{x}, t\right) = g\left(\mathbf{x}, t\right) \qquad \text{on} \quad \Gamma_R, \tag{9.11}
$$

$$
\phi\left(\mathbf{x}, t\right) = l\left(\mathbf{x}, t\right) \qquad \text{on} \quad \Gamma_D, \tag{9.12}
$$

where

$$
\frac{\partial \phi}{\partial \mathbf{n}_A}\left(\mathbf{x}, t\right) \equiv \sum_{i,j=1}^{d} a_{ij}\left(\mathbf{x}, t\right) \frac{\partial \phi}{\partial x_j}\left(\mathbf{x}, t\right) n_i\left(\mathbf{x}\right) \tag{9.13}
$$

$$
= \mathbf{A}\left(\mathbf{x}, \mathbf{t}\right) \nabla \phi\left(\mathbf{x}, t\right) \cdot \mathbf{n}\left(\mathbf{x}\right),
$$

and $\mathbf{n} = (n_1, \ldots, n_d)$ denotes a unit outward normal vector to Γ. In equations (9.11) and (9.12), functions α, g, and l are data.

In general, $\Gamma_0 = \Gamma \backslash \{\Gamma_D \cup \Gamma_R\}$ is a nonempty set in which no boundary conditions are needed because the natural condition for the weak formulation is identically satisfied. Specifically, Γ_0 is the set where ${}^t\mathbf{A}\left(\mathbf{x}, t\right) \mathbf{n}\left(\mathbf{x}\right) = 0$ and, therefore, $\frac{\partial \phi}{\partial \mathbf{n}_A}\left(\mathbf{x}, t\right) = 0$ for any function ϕ.

The discussion on boundary conditions, sometimes ignored in financial literature, is often a complicated task and depends on the particular financial product.

REMARK 9.2.1 *In a d-factor model the computational or "localized" domain Ω is frequently a rectangle $[a_1, b_1] \times [a_2, b_2] \times \ldots [a_d, b_d]$. In such a case, the boundary Γ may be decomposed as:*

$$
\Gamma = \bigcup_{i=1}^{d} \left(\Gamma_{i+} \cup \Gamma_{i-}\right), \tag{9.14}
$$

where Γ_{i+} (respectively Γ_{i-}) is the part of the boundary characterized by the unit outward normal vector

$$\left(0,\ldots,1^{(i)},\ldots,0\right)$$

(respectively $\left(0,\ldots,-1^{(i)},\ldots,0\right)$).

9.2.3 Strong Formulation of the Nonlinear Problem: Partial Differential Inequalities

Early-exercise features, in American options or convertible bonds, for instance, may be included in the model by means of unilateral constraints applied to ϕ. Hence, partial differential inequalities, rather than partial differential equations, have to be considered.

If $\phi(\mathbf{x}, t)$ is the value of an American-or Bermudan-style option, extra constraints need to be added to Problem 1 in order to avoid arbitrage opportunities. Specifically, if the holder of the option has the right to exercise at time t and to receive an exercise value $R_1(\mathbf{x}, t)$, then we need

$$\phi(\mathbf{x}, t) \geq R_1(\mathbf{x}, t). \tag{9.15}$$

In this case, $\phi(\mathbf{x}, t)$ satisfies equation (9.10a) only if

$$\phi(\mathbf{x}, t) > R_1(\mathbf{x}, t).$$

If

$$\phi(\mathbf{x}, t) = R_1(\mathbf{x}, t),$$

then

$$\mathcal{L}[\phi(\mathbf{x}, t)] - f(\mathbf{x}, t) \leq 0. \tag{9.16}$$

Similarly, if the option may be exercised by the issuer[2] at time t for an exercise value $R_2(\mathbf{x}, t)$, we need

$$\phi(\mathbf{x}, t) \leq R_2(\mathbf{x}, t). \tag{9.17}$$

In that case $\phi(\mathbf{x}, t)$ solves equation (9.10a) only if

$$\phi(\mathbf{x}, t) < R_2(\mathbf{x}, t).$$

If

$$\phi(\mathbf{x}, t) = R_2(\mathbf{x}, t),$$

---

[2]For example the convertible bond call provision or any other issuer callable contract.

then

$$\mathcal{L}\left[\phi\left(\mathbf{x}, t\right)\right] - f\left(\mathbf{x}, t\right) \geq 0. \tag{9.18}$$

We refer to (9.16) and (9.18) as *partial differential inequalities* (PDIs), and we call (9.15) and (9.17) *unilateral conditions, restrictions* or *constraints*.

The general nonlinear problem will be:

PROBLEM 2 *Nonlinear Problem (Strong Primal Formulation)*
Find $\phi : \Omega \times [0, T] \to \mathbb{R}$, *satisfying boundary conditions (9.11) and (9.12), such that*

$$\begin{cases} \mathcal{L}\left[\phi\left(\mathbf{x}, t\right)\right] - f\left(\mathbf{x}, t\right) = 0 & \text{if} \quad R_1\left(\mathbf{x}, t\right) < \phi\left(\mathbf{x}, t\right) < R_2\left(\mathbf{x}, t\right) & \text{in} \quad \Omega \times (0, T) \\ \mathcal{L}\left[\phi\left(\mathbf{x}, t\right)\right] - f\left(\mathbf{x}, t\right) \geq 0 & \text{if} \quad \phi\left(\mathbf{x}, t\right) = R_2\left(\mathbf{x}, t\right) & \text{in} \quad \Omega \times (0, T) \\ \mathcal{L}\left[\phi\left(\mathbf{x}, t\right)\right] - f\left(\mathbf{x}, t\right) \leq 0 & \text{if} \quad \phi\left(\mathbf{x}, t\right) = R_1\left(\mathbf{x}, t\right) & \text{in} \quad \Omega \times (0, T) \\ \phi\left(\mathbf{x}, T\right) = \Lambda\left(\mathbf{x}\right) & \text{in} \quad \Omega. \end{cases} \tag{9.19}$$

The above is a so-called *primal formulation*, because it involves only the unknown ϕ. It is also called *linear complementary problem*. Problem (9.19) can be rewritten by introducing a Lagrange multiplier, leading to a so-called *mixed formulation*. Specifically, (9.19) is equivalent to:

PROBLEM 3 *Nonlinear Problem (Strong Mixed Formulation)*
Find functions $\phi, p : \Omega \times [0, T] \to \mathbb{R}$ *satisfying boundary conditions (9.11) and (9.12) such that*

$$\mathcal{L}\left[\phi\left(\mathbf{x}, t\right)\right] - f\left(\mathbf{x}, t\right) = p\left(\mathbf{x}, t\right) \qquad in \quad \Omega \times (0, T) \tag{9.20a}$$

$$\phi\left(\mathbf{x}, T\right) = \Lambda\left(\mathbf{x}\right) \qquad in \quad \Omega \tag{9.20b}$$

and furthermore

$$R_1\left(\mathbf{x}, t\right) \leq \phi\left(\mathbf{x}, t\right) \leq R_2\left(\mathbf{x}, t\right), \tag{9.21}$$

with

$$R_1\left(\mathbf{x}, t\right) < \phi\left(\mathbf{x}, t\right) < R_2\left(\mathbf{x}, t\right) \Longrightarrow p\left(\mathbf{x}, t\right) = 0 \quad in \quad \Omega \times (0, T) \tag{9.22}$$

$$\phi\left(\mathbf{x}, t\right) = R_1\left(\mathbf{x}, t\right) \Longrightarrow p\left(\mathbf{x}, t\right) \leq 0 \qquad in \quad \Omega \times (0, T) \tag{9.23}$$

$$\phi\left(\mathbf{x}, t\right) = R_2\left(\mathbf{x}, t\right) \Longrightarrow p\left(\mathbf{x}, t\right) \geq 0 \qquad in \quad \Omega \times (0, T). \tag{9.24}$$

Function p is a *Lagrange multiplier*, which adds or subtracts value in order to ensure that constraints in the solution are being met. Certainly, in the region where $p = 0$, the equality in (9.10a) holds. The surfaces separating the regions where $p < 0, p = 0$ and $p > 0$ are the so-called *free boundaries*.

Let us introduce the following family (indexed by $\mathbf{x}, t$) of set- (or multi-) valued graphs defined by

$$G(\mathbf{x}, t)(Y) = \begin{cases} \emptyset & \text{if} \quad Y < R_1(\mathbf{x}, t) \\ (-\infty, 0] & \text{if} \quad Y = R_1(\mathbf{x}, t) \\ 0 & \text{if} \quad R_1(\mathbf{x}, t) < Y < R_2(\mathbf{x}, t) \\ [0, \infty) & \text{if} \quad Y = R_2(\mathbf{x}, t) \\ \emptyset & \text{if} \quad Y > R_2(\mathbf{x}, t) \end{cases} \tag{9.25}$$

It is straightforward to show that inequalities (9.21)–(9.24) are equivalent to the relation

$$p(\mathbf{x}, t) \in G(\mathbf{x}, t)(\phi(\mathbf{x}, t)). \tag{9.26}$$

Hence, Problem 3 may be rewritten as

PROBLEM 4 *Nonlinear Problem (Strong Mixed Formulation)*
Find $\phi(t) \in \mathcal{V}$ satisfying boundary conditions (9.11) and (9.12) and $p(t) \in \mathcal{M}$ such that

$$\mathcal{L}[\phi(\mathbf{x}, t)] - f(\mathbf{x}, t) = p(\mathbf{x}, t) \quad in \quad \Omega \times (0, T)$$

$$\phi(\mathbf{x}, T) = \Lambda(\mathbf{x}) \quad in \quad \Omega$$

$$p(\mathbf{x}, t) \in G(\mathbf{x}, t)(\phi(\mathbf{x}, t)) \quad in \quad \Omega$$

where $\mathcal{V}$ and $\mathcal{M}$ are suitable X-dependent function spaces for ϕ and p, respectively.

9.2.4 Weak Formulation of the Nonlinear Problem: Variational Inequalities

In order to discretize in space using the finite element method we have to rewrite the problem in a variational (or weak) form. We recall that variational inequalities are not only the starting point for the finite element discretization, but also constitute a powerful tool to deal with theoretical issues, such as existence and uniqueness of the solution as well as numerical analysis.

In order to write a weak formulation of the valuation problem we multiply equation (9.20a) by a *test function* ψ defined in Ω. Then we integrate in Ω to get

$$\int_\Omega \dot{\phi}(\mathbf{x}, t) \, \psi(\mathbf{x}) \, d\mathbf{x}$$

$$- \sum_{i,j=1}^d \int_\Omega \frac{\partial}{\partial x_i} \left(a_{ij}(\mathbf{x}, t) \frac{\partial \phi}{\partial x_j}(\mathbf{x}, t) \right) \psi(\mathbf{x}) \, d\mathbf{x}$$

$$+ \int_\Omega a_0(\mathbf{x}, t) \phi(\mathbf{x}, t) \psi(\mathbf{x}) \, d\mathbf{x}$$

$$= \int_\Omega f(\mathbf{x}, t) \psi(\mathbf{x}) \, d\mathbf{x} + \int_\Omega p(\mathbf{x}, t) \psi(\mathbf{x}) \, d\mathbf{x}. \tag{9.28}$$

We use Green's formula to transform the second term on the left-hand side:

$$\sum_{i,j=1}^{d} \int_{\Omega} \frac{\partial}{\partial x_i} \left(a_{ij}(\mathbf{x}, t) \frac{\partial \phi}{\partial x_j}(\mathbf{x}, t) \right) \psi(\mathbf{x}) \, d\mathbf{x}$$

$$= -\sum_{i,j=1}^{d} \int_{\Omega} a_{ij}(\mathbf{x}, t) \frac{\partial \phi}{\partial x_j}(\mathbf{x}, t) \frac{\partial \psi}{\partial x_i}(\mathbf{x}) \, d\mathbf{x}$$

$$+ \sum_{i,j=1}^{d} \int_{\Gamma} a_{ij}(\mathbf{x}, t) \frac{\partial \phi}{\partial x_j}(\mathbf{x}, t) \psi(\mathbf{x}) n_i(\mathbf{x}) \, d\Gamma \qquad (9.29)$$

The boundary term in this equation is decomposed as (from 9.13):

$$\sum_{i,j=1}^{d} \int_{\Gamma} a_{ij}(\mathbf{x}, t) \frac{\partial \phi}{\partial x_j}(\mathbf{x}, t) \psi(\mathbf{x}) n_i(\mathbf{x}) \, d\Gamma$$

$$= \int_{\Gamma} \frac{\partial \phi}{\partial \mathbf{n}_A}(\mathbf{x}, t) \psi(\mathbf{x}) \, d\Gamma$$

$$= \int_{\Gamma_D} \frac{\partial \phi}{\partial \mathbf{n}_A}(\mathbf{x}, t) \psi(\mathbf{x}) \, d\Gamma + \int_{\Gamma_R} \frac{\partial \phi}{\partial \mathbf{n}_A}(\mathbf{x}, t) \psi(\mathbf{x}) \, d\Gamma$$

If we restrict the test functions to those vanishing on Γ_D and replace $\frac{\partial \phi}{\partial \mathbf{n}_A}$ on Γ_R using boundary condition (9.11), we get

$$\int_{\Gamma} \frac{\partial \phi}{\partial \mathbf{n}_A}(\mathbf{x}, t) \psi(\mathbf{x}) = \int_{\Gamma_R} (g(\mathbf{x}, t) - \alpha \phi(\mathbf{x}, t)) \psi(\mathbf{x}) \, d\Gamma. \qquad (9.30)$$

Substitution into (9.29), and then of (9.29) into (9.28), yields

$$\int_{\Omega} \dot{\phi}(\mathbf{x}, t) \psi(\mathbf{x}) \, d\mathbf{x} + \sum_{i,j=1}^{d} \int_{\Omega} a_{ij}(\mathbf{x}, t) \frac{\partial \phi}{\partial x_j}(\mathbf{x}, t) \frac{\partial \psi}{\partial x_i}(\mathbf{x}) \, d\mathbf{x}$$

$$+ \int_{\Omega} a_0(\mathbf{x}, t) \phi(\mathbf{x}, t) \psi(\mathbf{x}) \, d\mathbf{x} + \int_{\Gamma_R} \alpha \phi(\mathbf{x}, t) \psi(\mathbf{x}) \, d\Gamma$$

$$= \int_{\Omega} p(\mathbf{x}, t) \psi(\mathbf{x}) \, d\mathbf{x} + \int_{\Omega} f(\mathbf{x}, t) \psi(\mathbf{x}) \, d\mathbf{x} + \int_{\Gamma_R} g(\mathbf{x}, t) \psi(\mathbf{x}) \, d\Gamma. \qquad (9.31)$$

This is a so-called *weak mixed formulation* since both the primitive unknown ϕ and the Lagrange multiplier p are involved. In what follows, we will write another weak formulation that includes only the unknown ϕ.

Let us introduce the family of convex sets of functions defined, for each t in $[0, T]$, by

$$\mathcal{K}(t) = \{\psi \in \mathcal{V} : R_1(\mathbf{x}, t) \le \psi(\mathbf{x}) \le R_2(\mathbf{x}, t), \quad \text{a.e. in } \Omega\} \quad (9.32)$$

where $\mathcal{V}$ is a suitable space for ϕ.
Using (9.22), (9.23) and (9.24) it is straightforward to show that, for any $\psi \in \mathcal{K}(t)$ we have[3]

$$\int_\Omega p(\mathbf{x}, t)(\psi(\mathbf{x}) - \phi(\mathbf{x}, t)) \, d\mathbf{x} \le 0. \quad (9.33)$$

For each time t we replace the arbitrary test function ψ in (9.31) by $\kappa - \phi$, where κ is in $\mathcal{K}(t)$ such that $\kappa(\mathbf{x}) = l(\mathbf{x}, t)$ on Γ_D. We get

$$\int_\Omega \dot\phi(\kappa - \phi) \, d\mathbf{x} + \sum_{i,j=1}^d \int_\Omega a_{ij}(\mathbf{x}, t) \frac{\partial \phi}{\partial x_j} \frac{\partial(\kappa - \phi)}{\partial x_i} d\mathbf{x}$$

$$+ \int_\Omega a_0 \phi(\kappa - \phi) \, d\mathbf{x} + \int_{\Gamma_R} \alpha\phi(\kappa - \phi) \, d\Gamma$$

$$= \int_\Omega p(\mathbf{x}, t)(\kappa - \phi) \, d\mathbf{x} + \int_\Omega f(\kappa - \phi) \, d\mathbf{x} + \int_{\Gamma_R} g(\kappa - \phi) \, d\Gamma. \quad (9.34)$$

Finally, we use (9.33) in this equality and obtain the following *variational inequality of the first kind*:

$$\int_\Omega \dot\phi(\kappa - \phi) \, d\mathbf{x} + \sum_{i,j=1}^d \int_\Omega a_{ij}(\mathbf{x}, t) \frac{\partial \phi}{\partial x_j} \frac{\partial(\kappa - \phi)}{\partial x_i} d\mathbf{x}$$

$$+ \int_\Omega a_0 \phi(\kappa - \phi) \, d\mathbf{x} + \int_{\Gamma_R} \alpha\phi(\kappa - \phi) \, d\Gamma$$

$$\le \int_\Omega f(\kappa - \phi) \, d\mathbf{x} + \int_{\Gamma_R} g(\kappa - \phi) \, d\Gamma \quad (9.35)$$

This is a *weak primal formulation* in the sense that now ϕ is the only unknown.

---

[3] In fact, the pointwise inequality holds

$$p(\mathbf{x}, t)(\psi(\mathbf{x}) - \phi(\mathbf{x}, t)) \le 0.$$

In order to write the problem in a more compact way, we introduce the following notations: Let $a(t; \cdot, \cdot)$ be the family of *bilinear symmetric forms*

$$a(t; \phi, \psi) = \sum_{i,j=1}^{d} \int_{\Omega} a_{ij}(\mathbf{x}, t) \frac{\partial \phi}{\partial x_j}(\mathbf{x}, t) \frac{\partial \psi}{\partial x_i}(\mathbf{x}) \, d\mathbf{x}$$

$$+ \int_{\Omega} a_0(\mathbf{x}, t) \phi(\mathbf{x}, t) \psi(\mathbf{x}) \, d\mathbf{x}$$

$$+ \int_{\Gamma_R} \alpha(\mathbf{x}, t) \phi(\mathbf{x}, t) \psi(\mathbf{x}) \, d\Gamma, \tag{9.36}$$

and $L(t; \cdot)$ be the family of *linear forms*:

$$L(t; \psi) = \int_{\Omega} f(\mathbf{x}, t) \psi(\mathbf{x}) \, d\mathbf{x} + \int_{\Gamma_R} g(\mathbf{x}, t) \psi(\mathbf{x}) \, d\Gamma. \tag{9.37}$$

Then the problem can be written in the two equivalent forms:

PROBLEM 5 *Nonlinear Problem (Weak Primal Formulation)*
Find $\phi(t) \in \mathcal{K}(t)$ satisfying Dirichlet condition (9.12) and final condition (9.2) such that

$$\int_{\Omega} \dot{\phi}(t) (\kappa - \phi(t)) \, d\mathbf{x} + a(t; \phi(t), \kappa - \phi(t)) \geq L(t; \kappa - \phi(t))$$

$$\forall \kappa \in \mathcal{K}(t), \kappa(\mathbf{x}) = l(\mathbf{x}, t) \qquad on \quad \Gamma_D. \tag{9.38}$$

PROBLEM 6 *Nonlinear Problem (Weak Mixed Formulation)*
Find $\phi(t) \in \mathcal{V}$ and $p(t) \in \mathcal{M}$ satisfying unilateral conditions (9.21) – (9.24), Dirichlet boundary condition (9.12) and final condition (9.2) such that

$$\int_{\Omega} \dot{\phi}(t) \psi \, d\mathbf{x} + a(t; \phi(t), \psi) = L(t; \psi) + \int_{\Omega} p \psi \, d\mathbf{x} \qquad \forall \psi \in \mathcal{V}_0, \tag{9.39}$$

where

$$\mathcal{V}_0 = \left\{ \psi \in \mathcal{V} : \psi_{/\Gamma_D} = 0 \right\}, \tag{9.40}$$

and $\mathcal{V}$ and $\mathcal{M}$ are suitable spaces for ϕ and p, respectively.

9.3 NUMERICAL SOLUTION OF PARTIAL DIFFERENTIAL INEQUALITIES (VARIATIONAL INEQUALITIES)

As mentioned before, the most common method of handling the early exercise condition is simply to advance the discrete solution over a time step ignoring the restriction and then to make a projection on the set of constraints. This is easy to implement, but a discrete form of the linear complementary problem or the variational inequality is not satisfied.

In the case of a single-factor American put, the algebraic linear complementary problems are commonly solved using a projected iteration method (PSOR) (see Wilmott [163], Vázquez [141]).

Clarke and Parrot [164] suggested a multigrid method to accelerate convergence of the basic relaxation method. They showed that the algorithm, when applied to the valuation of American options with stochastic volatility, gives optimal numerical complexity and the performance is much better than for the PSOR.

On the other hand, Forsyth and Vetzal [165] proposed an implicit penalty method for valuing American options and showed that when a variable time step is used, quadratic convergence is achieved. They derived sufficient conditions to guarantee monotonic convergence of the nonlinear penalty iteration and also to ensure that the solution of the penalty problem is an approximate solution to the discrete linear complementary problem. They compared the efficiency and the accuracy of the method with the commonly used technique of handling the American constraint explicitly in the tree methodologies. Convergence rates as the time step and the mesh size tend to zero for the standard CRR tree are compared with convergence rates for an implicit finite volume method with Crank-Nicolson time stepping and the penalty method for handling the American constraint. They found that the PDE method is asymptotically superior to the binomial lattice method.

Barone-Adesi et al. [97], Bermúdez and Nogueiras [107], and Bermúdez et al. [152, 197] used a *Lagrange multiplier* (or *duality*) method to solve variational inequalities arising in the valuation of convertible bonds and Amerasian options. This method has been introduced in [142] for solving elliptic variational inequalities of the second kind (see also Parés et al. [166] for further analysis). It has not been applied much in finance but has been used extensively in other fields such as computational mechanics. As mentioned in Section 9.1, the algorithm can be used for any type of constraint to be imposed on the value function or its derivatives, which may depend on the spatial variables and on time. It is based on the mixed formulation and could be applied to either the weak or the strong problem; hence it could be combined with either finite difference or finite element discretizations.

In this section, we describe this general methodology to solve the nonlinear problems introduced in the previous section. The solution of the nonlinear problem is approximated by a sequence of solutions of linear problems. In the next section, we describe the numerical solution of the linear problem using a discretization in time with characteristics and a discretization in space with finite elements. Finally, the Lagrange multiplier method is applied to the fully discretized problem.

9.3.1 A Duality (or Lagrange Multiplier) Method

Recall that inequalities (9.21) – (9.24) establish a relationship between p and ϕ, which can be written in a more compact way as

$$p(\mathbf{x}, t) \in G(\mathbf{x}, t)(\phi(\mathbf{x}, t)), \qquad (9.41)$$

where $G(\mathbf{x}, t)$ is the family (indicated by $\mathbf{x}, t$) of set (or multi)-valued graphs introduced in (9.25).

Since $G(\mathbf{x}, t)$ is a multivalued function, equation (9.41) is not easy to implement. However, we have the following result (see Bermúdez and Moreno [142]):

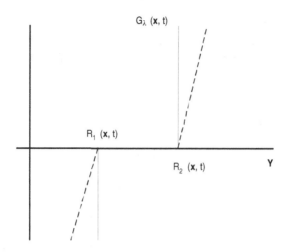

FIGURE 9.1 Yosida approximation.

LEMMA 9.3.1 *The following two statements are equivalent:*

$$\bullet \ U \in G\left(\mathbf{x}, t\right)\left(Y\right), \tag{9.42}$$

$$\bullet \ U = G_\lambda\left(\mathbf{x}, t\right)\left(Y + \lambda U\right) \ \forall\, \lambda > 0, \tag{9.43}$$

where $G_\lambda\left(\mathbf{x}, t\right)$ is the Yosida approximation of $G\left(\mathbf{x}, t\right)$ (see Figure 9.1) defined by

$$G_\lambda\left(\mathbf{x}, t\right)\left(Y\right) = \begin{cases} \frac{1}{\lambda}\left(Y - R_1\left(\mathbf{x}, t\right)\right) & \text{if } Y \le R_1\left(\mathbf{x}, t\right) \\ 0 & \text{if } R_1\left(\mathbf{x}, t\right) \le Y \le R_2\left(\mathbf{x}, t\right) \\ \frac{1}{\lambda}\left(Y - R_2\left(\mathbf{x}, t\right)\right) & \text{if } Y \ge R_2\left(\mathbf{x}, t\right). \end{cases}$$

We notice that, unlike G, G_λ is a Lipschitz-continuous (univalued) function.

In view of this lemma and the previous discussion, relations (9.21)–(9.24) are equivalent to the following equality:

$$p\left(\mathbf{x}, t\right) = G_\lambda\left(\mathbf{x}, t\right)\left(\phi\left(\mathbf{x}, t\right) + \lambda p\left(\mathbf{x}, t\right)\right), \tag{9.44}$$

where λ is a positive real number.

We are now in a position to introduce the following iterative algorithm:

(a) At the beginning, the function p_0 is given arbitrarily.
(b) At iteration m, an approximation of the Lagrange multiplier p_m is known and we proceed as follows:
First, we work out a new approximation of $\phi(t)$, ϕ_{m+1}, by solving the linear problem in either weak- or strong-form

PROBLEM 7 *Linearized Continuous Problem. Given $p_m \in \mathcal{V}$, find $\phi_{m+1} \in \mathcal{V}$ such that*

■ *Weak form*

$$\int_\Omega \dot{\phi}_{m+1} \psi \, d\mathbf{x} + a\left(t; \phi_{m+1}, \psi\right) = L\left(t, \psi\right) + \int_\Omega p_m \psi \, d\mathbf{x} \qquad \forall \psi \in \mathcal{V}_0,$$
(9.45)

or

■ *Strong form*

$$\mathcal{L}\left[\phi_{m+1}\right] = f + p_m \qquad\qquad (9.46)$$

together with boundary conditions (9.11), (9.12) *and final condition*

$$\phi_{m+1}\left(\mathbf{x}, T\right) = \Lambda\left(\mathbf{x}\right). \qquad\qquad (9.47)$$

Then, we update the Lagrange multiplier p by using equation (9.44). Precisely, p_{m+1} is defined as

$$p_{m+1}\left(\mathbf{x}, t\right) = G_\lambda\left(\mathbf{x}, t\right)\left(\phi_{m+1}\left(\mathbf{x}, t\right) + \lambda p_m\left(\mathbf{x}, t\right)\right), \qquad (9.48)$$

where, in order to achieve convergence, λ has to be greater than some positive value which depends on coefficients a_{ij}, a_0, and b_i (see Bermúdez and Moreno [142] for details).

9.4 NUMERICAL SOLUTION OF PARTIAL DIFFERENTIAL EQUATIONS (VARIATIONAL EQUALITIES): CLASSICAL LAGRANGE-GALERKIN METHOD

In the previous section we introduced an iterative algorithm to approximate the solution of the nonlinear problem by a sequence of solutions of linear problems. Note that equations (9.45) and (9.46) are linear because, although they include the Lagrange multiplier, it is known from the previous iteration. What remains is to solve the linear problem by discretizing in time an space. We approximate equation (9.45) with a semi-discretization in time using the method of characteristics and a spatial discretization using finite elements. Recall that spatial discretizations using finite differences start with the strong formulation (9.46), whereas spatial discretization using finite elements are applied to the weak formulation (9.45). Time discretization using characteristics could be combined with both finite differences and finite elements.

9.4.1 Semi-Lagrangian Time Discretization: Method of Characteristics

The pricing equation is simply the convection-diffusion equation together with a reaction term producing an exponentially decay due to the discounting. Accurate modeling of the interaction between convective and diffusive processes is one of the most challenging tasks in the numerical approximation of partial differential equations; the choice of the numerical method depends on whether the problem is diffusion dominated or convection dominated. Sometimes, in finance, the diffusion is quite small relative to the convection, leading to a so-called *convection-dominated problem*. The numerical solution of convection-dominated problems is more complex than the solution of fully elliptic or parabolic equations. Problems arise due to the lack of natural dissipation embedded in parabolic partial differential equations, which helps make numerical schemes stable. Moreover, the solution of linear hyperbolic problems will only be as smooth as the initial solution; hence, the regularizing effect of the fully parabolic equation could be lost. In all such circumstances, standard finite element and finite difference approximations may present difficulties. A large literature has been built up on a variety of techniques for analyzing and overcoming those difficulties; books like Morton [167] are entirely devoted to the subject. A summary of numerical methods for time-dependent convection-dominated PDEs can be found in Ewing and Wang [144]. They provide a historical review of classical numerical methods and a survey of the recent developments on the Eulerian and characteristics Lagrangian methods. *Eulerian methods* use the standard temporal discretization, while the main distinguishing feature of characteristic methods is the use of characteristics to carry out the discretization in time.

The *method of characteristics* (or *Lagrangian method*) for time discretization is a possible approach for dealing with convection-dominated problems. It is part of the more general family of upwinding methods, which take into account the local flow direction. This approach is based on the discretization of the total (or material) derivative, introduced in (9.7), which is the time derivative along the characteristic lines. In other words, it is the derivative in time for a particle moving with velocity $\mathbf{v}$ (see (9.5)). In a Lagrangian coordinate system, one would only see the effect of diffusion, reaction, and the right-hand-side terms but not the effect of convection. Often, the solutions of the convection-diffusion PDEs change less rapidly along the characteristics than they do in the time direction. This explains why characteristic methods usually allow large time steps while still maintaining stability and accuracy.

When combined with finite elements, the method of characteristics is referred to as the *characteristics finite element* (or the *Lagrange-Galerkin*) *method*. Its main advantages are that it is unconditionally stable and that it yields discrete symmetrical linear systems.

The classical semi-Lagrangian or characteristics method is first-order accurate in time. Applications in finance have been developed by Vázquez [141], to solve the one-factor model arising in the valuation of American options; Pironneau and Hetch [168], to solve the two-factor model arising in the valuation of an American put on the maximum of two assets; and by Barone-Adesi et al. [97], Bermúdez and Nogueiras [107], and Bermúdez et al. [152, 197] in the valuation of convertible bonds and American-Asian options.

Characteristic Curves For given $(\mathbf{x}, t) \in \overline{\Omega} \times (0, T)$, where $\overline{\Omega} = \Omega \sqcup \Gamma$, the characteristic line through $(\mathbf{x}, t)$ associated with vector field $\mathbf{v}$ is the vector function $X_e(\mathbf{x}, t; \cdot)$ solving the initial value problem

$$\frac{\partial X_e(\mathbf{x}, t; \tau)}{\partial \tau} = \mathbf{v}(X_e(\mathbf{x}, t; \tau), \tau), \quad X_e(\mathbf{x}, t; t) = \mathbf{x}. \tag{9.49}$$

It represents the trajectory described by the material point that occupies position $\mathbf{x}$ at time t and is driven by the velocity field $\mathbf{v}$ (see Figure 9.2). Under some regularity

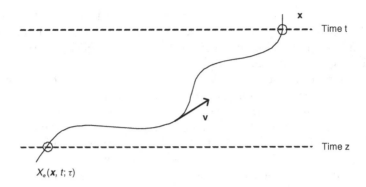

FIGURE 9.2   Characteristic line through $(\mathbf{x}, z)$ associated with vector field $\mathbf{v}$.

assumptions on $\mathbf{v}$, the characteristic line-solving problem (9.49) is well defined in $[0, T]$ and is unique for each initial condition $(\mathbf{x}, t)$.

From the definition of the characteristic curves and by using the chain rule, it follows that the material or total derivative, as defined in (9.7), satisfies

$$\dot{\phi}(X_e(\mathbf{x}, t; \tau), \tau) = \phi'(X_e(\mathbf{x}, t; \tau), \tau) + \mathbf{v}(X_e(\mathbf{x}, t; \tau), \tau) \cdot \nabla\phi(X_e(\mathbf{x}, t; \tau), \tau)$$

$$= \frac{d\phi}{d\tau}(X_e(\mathbf{x}, t; \tau), \tau), \tag{9.50}$$

where ϕ' denotes the partial derivative with respect to time and ∇ is the gradient.

Approximation of the Material Derivative: Time Discretization   In order to carry out a semidiscretization in time, we consider a partition of the time interval $[0, T]$ into N time steps of size $\Delta t = T/N$ that we will denote by $t_n = T - n\Delta t$ for $n = 0, 1, ..., N$. Then, equation (9.50) suggests the following first-order approximation of $\dot{\phi}$ at time t_{n+1}

$$\dot{\phi}(\mathbf{x}, t_{n+1}) = \frac{d\phi}{d\tau}(\mathbf{x}, t_{n+1}) \approx \frac{\phi(X_e(\mathbf{x}, t_{n+1}; t_n), t_n) - \phi(\mathbf{x}, t_{n+1})}{t_n - t_{n+1}}, \tag{9.51}$$

where we have used that $X_e(\mathbf{x}, t_{n+1}; t_{n+1}) = \mathbf{x}$.

The approximation (9.51) leads to the following implicit *semidiscretized scheme* for equation (9.45):

PROBLEM 8 *Semi-Discretized Scheme*
  Given $p_m^{n+1} \in \mathcal{V}$, find $\phi_{m+1}^{n+1} \in \mathcal{V}$ for $n = 0, \dots, N - 1$, satisfying Dirichlet boundary condition $\phi_{m+1}^{n+1}(\mathbf{x}) = l(\mathbf{x}, t_{n+1})$, such that

$$\int_\Omega \frac{\phi^n(X_e(\mathbf{x}, t_{n+1}; t_n)) - \phi_{m+1}^{n+1}(\mathbf{x})}{t_n - t_{n+1}} \psi(\mathbf{x}) d\mathbf{x} + a^{n+1}\left(\phi_{m+1}^{n+1}(\mathbf{x}), \psi\right)$$

$$= L^{n+1}(\psi) + \int_\Omega p_m^{n+1}(\mathbf{x})\psi(\mathbf{x}) d\mathbf{x} \qquad \forall \psi \in \mathcal{V}_0, \tag{9.52}$$

and

$$\phi_{m+1}^0(\mathbf{x}) = \Lambda(\mathbf{x}),$$

where $\phi^{n+1}(\mathbf{x}) = \phi(\mathbf{x}, t_{n+1})$, $p^{n+1}(\mathbf{x}) = p(\mathbf{x}, t_{n+1})$, $a^{n+1}(\phi, \psi) = a(t_{n+1}; \phi, \psi)$ *and* $L^{n+1}(\psi) = L(t_{n+1}; \psi)$.

In most cases, the Cauchy problem (9.49) is not easy to solve analytically. However, the $O(\Delta t)$ error of scheme (9.52) does not change if we replace $X_e(\mathbf{x}, t_{n+1}; t_n)$ by a first-order approximation given, for example, by an explicit *Euler scheme*

$$X_E(\mathbf{x}, t_{n+1}; t_n) = \mathbf{x} - \Delta t \, \mathbf{v}(\mathbf{x}, t_{n+1}). \tag{9.53}$$

9.4.2 Space Discretization: Galerkin Finite Element Method

Galerkin methods are obtained by restricting both the solution and the test functions involved in the variational formulation to be in a finite dimensional space. In *finite element methods*, this space is made up of globally continuous functions that are polynomials in each element of a polygonal mesh of the domain Ω. In Galerkin methods, the solution and the test functions are looked for in the same finite dimension space. The solution of the PDE is built as a sum of all these local approximating functions. Usually, only the spatial variables are treated in this way, while time is discretized with FD or other methods. With two spatial variables, the domain is partitioned into triangles and/or quadrangles. Three-dimensional spatial domains allow partitions into tetrahedrons, hexahedrons, or prisms.

The distinction between FE and FD is relevant at the theoretical level, when dealing with the numerical analysis. Once the discrete scheme is written and one is left with algebraic transformations of values at the grid points, the distinction vanishes. On structured meshes, finite differences and finite elements plus specific numerical integration (using, for example, vertices) can be shown to be equivalent. The contrast should be seen more as variational methods versus finite differences rather than finite elements versus finite differences.

However, as mentioned in section 9.1, FE are more flexible than FD in incorporating boundary conditions and in that they allow unstructured meshes. As shown by Zvan et al. [110], unstructured meshing can be applied to a wide variety of financial models. The idea is that an accurate solution of the pricing PDE requires on many occasions a fine-mesh spacing in certain regions of the domain, usually where the gradient is steep, whereas in regions where the gradient is flat, a coarser mesh can be used. Some studies have indicated, for example, the need for small-mesh spacing near barriers (Figlewski and Gao [169], Zvan et al. [170]). Pooley [171] proves that the finite element method with standard unstructured meshing techniques can lead to significant efficiency gains over structured meshes with a comparable number of vertices for pricing barrier options. Pironneau and Hetch [168] present and test an adaptive algorithm for a problem with a free boundary that arises in finance for the pricing of American options, leading to satisfactory results.[4]

FE has some other computational practicalities compared to FD (see Winkler et al. [172]):

- FE is very suitable for modular programming.

---

[4]They use a characteristics/FE method for the space discretisation and the Brennan Schwartz algorithm to deal with the American early exercised.

- A solution for the entire domain is computed instead of isolated nodes as with the FD method.
- FE provides accurate "greeks" as a byproduct.
- FE can easily deal with irregular domains, whereas this is difficultly in FD.

Finite elements, which are a widely used technique in areas such as computational mechanics, have become quite popular in financial engineering. A recent text book is Topper [196].

Fully Discretized Lagrange-Galerkin Scheme In order to solve the Problem 8 numerically, a discretization must be done; in other words, the problem must be replaced by a new one with a finite number of degrees of freedom or unknowns.

As mentioned previously, Galerkin methods, replaces the space of functions V by a finite dimensional space V_h, and defines a discrete counterpart of Problem 8 where the function ϕ is approximated by $\phi_h \in V_h$ and the Lagrange multiplier p is approximated by $p_h \in V_h$. In finite elements, the space V_h is made up of globally continuous functions that are polynomials in each element of a polygonal *mesh* of the domain Ω. Let us denote by $\mathcal{T}_h$ a family of polygonal meshes of the domain Ω, where the parameter h tends to zero and represents the size of the mesh. We assume that the mesh contains N_h *nodes* and that any function in V_h is uniquely defined by its values at the nodes. If $\psi \in V_h$ we call the values $\psi(q_i)_i, i = 1, \ldots, N_h$ the set of *degrees of freedom*. As in the continuous problem, we define

$$V_{0,h} = \left\{ \psi_h \in V_h : \psi_h(\mathbf{q}) = 0 \text{ for all nodes } \mathbf{q} \text{ on } \Gamma_D \right\}. \tag{9.54}$$

The discrete problem can be written as:

PROBLEM 9 *Fully Discretized Scheme*
   Given $p_{h,m}^{n+1} \in V_h$, find $\phi_{h,m+1}^{n+1} \in V_h$, for $n = 0, 1, \ldots, N-1$ such that

$$\phi_{h,m+1}^{n+1}(\mathbf{q}) = l(\mathbf{q}) \qquad \forall \mathbf{q} \text{ node on } \Gamma_D, \tag{9.55}$$

$$\int_\Omega \frac{\phi_h^n(X_e(\mathbf{x}, t_{n+1}; t_n)) - \phi_{h,m+1}^{n+1}}{t_n - t_{n+1}} \psi_h d\mathbf{x} + a^{n+1}\left(\phi_{h,m+1}^{n+1}, \psi_h\right)$$
$$= L^{n+1}(\psi_h) + \int_\Omega p_{h,m}^{n+1} \psi_h d\mathbf{x}, \qquad \text{for every } \psi_h \in V_{0,h}, \tag{9.56}$$

and

$$\phi_{h,m+1}^0(\mathbf{q}) = \Lambda_h(\mathbf{q}), \tag{9.57}$$

for all nodes $\mathbf{q}$ of the mesh $\mathcal{T}_h$, where Λ_h is the interpolated function of Λ in the space V_h.

Let us define the bilinear form

$$\tilde{a}^{n+1}\left(\phi_h^{n+1}, \psi_h\right) = a^{n+1}\left(\phi_h^{n+1}, \psi_h\right) - \frac{1}{\Delta t}\int_\Omega \phi_h^{n+1}\psi_h d\mathbf{x}, \qquad (9.58)$$

and the linear form

$$\tilde{L}_m^{n+1}\left(\psi_h\right) = L^{n+1}\left(\psi_h\right) - \frac{1}{\Delta t}\int_\Omega \phi_h^n\left(X_e\left(\mathbf{x}, t_{n+1}; t_n\right)\right)\psi_h d\mathbf{x}$$

$$+ \int_\Omega p_{h,m}^{n+1}\psi_h d\mathbf{x}. \qquad (9.59)$$

Then Problem 9 above can be rewritten as:

PROBLEM 10 *Given* $p_{h,m}^{n+1} \in P_h$, *find* $\phi_{h,m+1}^{n+1} \in V_h$ *satisfying Dirichlet boundary condition (9.55) such that*

$$\tilde{a}^{n+1}\left(\phi_{h,m+1}^{n+1}, \psi_h\right) = \tilde{L}_m^{n+1}\left(\psi_h\right) \qquad \forall \psi_h \in V_{0,h}. \qquad (9.60)$$

Let us ignore for the moment Dirichlet boundary condition (9.55), in other words, let us assume that $V_h = V_{0,h}$.

Let $B = \{\varphi_1, \varphi_2, ..., \varphi_{N_h}\}$ be a *basis* of V_h. Then the solution of (9.60) can be written (we omit indices for the sake of simplicity) in the form

$$\phi_{h,m+1}^{n+1} = \sum_{j=1}^{N_h} \xi_j \varphi_j, \qquad (9.61)$$

so that the discrete problem (9.60) is equivalent to finding N_h numbers $\left(\xi_1, \xi_2, ..., \xi_{N_h}\right)$ satisfying

$$\sum_{j=1}^{N_h} \tilde{a}^{n+1}\left(\varphi_j, \varphi_i\right)\xi_j = \tilde{L}_m^{n+1}\left(\varphi_i\right), \qquad i = 1, 2, ..., N_h. \qquad (9.62)$$

Equivalently:

PROBLEM 11 *Find* $\left(\xi_1, \xi_2, ..., \xi_{N_h}\right) \in \mathbb{R}^{N_h}$ *such that*

$$\mathcal{A}_h \xi = \mathbf{b}_h \qquad (9.63)$$

where

$$(\mathcal{A}_h)_{kl} = \tilde{a}^{n+1}(\varphi_l, \varphi_k) = -\frac{1}{\Delta t}\int_\Omega \varphi_l\varphi_k d\mathbf{x} + \sum_{i,j=1}^{d}\int_\Omega a_{ij}\frac{\partial\varphi_l}{\partial x_j}\frac{\partial\varphi_k}{\partial x_i}d\mathbf{x}$$

$$+ \int_\Omega a_0\varphi_l\varphi_k d\mathbf{x} + \int_{\Gamma_R}\alpha\varphi_l\varphi_k d\Gamma, \tag{9.64}$$

$$(\mathbf{b}_h)_k = \tilde{L}_m^{n+1}(\varphi_k) = \int_\Omega f\varphi_k d\mathbf{x} + \int_{\Gamma_R} g\varphi_k d\Gamma$$

$$-\frac{1}{\Delta t}\int_\Omega \phi_h^n(X_e(\mathbf{x},t_{n+1};t_n))\,\varphi_k d\mathbf{x} + \int_\Omega p_{h,m}^{n+1}\varphi_k d\mathbf{x}. \tag{9.65}$$

Since the matrix $\mathbf{A}$ is symmetric (see (9.4)), $\mathcal{A}_h$ is symmetric as well. If additionally $\mathcal{A}_h$ is positive definite, Cholesky's method can be used to solve the system (9.63). In the special case where coefficients a_{ij}, a_0, and α do not depend on time, the linear system has a matrix independent of both time step and iteration; therefore, it needs to be computed and factorized only once. Also, in expression (9.65) the first two terms on the right hand side are independent of time (if f and g are) and iteration, whereas the third term must be computed at every time step, and the fourth at every time step and iteration. Consequently, in order to solve these systems it is convenient to use Cholesky or, more generally, direct Gauss-like methods, because, since the factorization step needs to be done only once, at each iteration just two triangular systems have to be solved.

In Problem 11 we have not taken into account Dirichlet boundary conditions. More precisely, we have included test functions ϕ_i in the basis of $\mathcal{V}_h$ that do not satisfy the boundary condition $\psi_{i/\Gamma_D} = 0$. Eliminating these functions of the basis is equivalent to eliminate the corresponding unknowns and equations (degrees of freedom). This process turns out to be unpleasant from the programming point of view. A simpler procedure is to replace the i-th equation (assuming the node i belongs to Γ_D) by the equation

$$\xi_i = l(\mathbf{q}_i).$$

Actually the i-th equation is replaced by the "programming equivalent" obtained by substituting the diagonal term $(\mathcal{A}_h)_{ii}$ by a large number, say H, and the right-hand side by $Hl(\mathbf{q}_i)$. This process is called *blocking of the degrees of freedom*.

The problem arising now is how to choose the basis $B = \{\varphi_1, \varphi_2, ..., \varphi_{N_h}\}$. The elements of a suitable basis are functions that become zero in big regions of Ω so that many terms of the matrix $\mathcal{A}_h$ are zero; that is, $\mathcal{A}_h$ is a sparse matrix. We also need an efficient algorithm to work out the matrix of coefficients, $\mathcal{A}_h$, and the right-hand-side vector $\mathbf{b}_h$, since the calculation of $\mathcal{A}_h$ and $\mathbf{b}_h$ using formulas (9.64) and (9.65) is inefficient.

In the appendix, we consider *Lagrange triangular finite elements* in a d-dimensional domain Ω. We will show how to build the matrix of coefficients and the independent term in the particular case of Lagrange triangular finite elements of degree one in two space dimensions. This finite element space consists of continuous piecewise linear functions on a triangular mesh of the domain Ω. Specifically,

$$\mathcal{V}_h = \left\{ \psi_h \in C\left(\overline{\Omega}\right) : \psi_h|_K \in \mathcal{P}_1 \qquad \forall K \in \mathcal{T}_h \right\}, \tag{9.66}$$

where $C\left(\overline{\Omega}\right)$ denotes the space of continuous functions defined in $\overline{\Omega}$ and $\mathcal{P}_1$ represents the space of polynomials of degree less than or equal to one in two variables. In this case the basis function φ_i takes value 1 at the vertex i of the mesh of the domain and is zero at all other vertices. We refer to Ciarlet [180] and Zienkiewicz et al. [181] as reference textbooks in the finite element method.

The Iterative Algorithm   The algorithm we have introduced in section 9.3 to solve the continuous variational inequalities can now be written in summarized form for the fully discretized problem.

At time step $n + 1$ we start with $p_{h,0}^{n+1} = p_h^n$ and calculate sequences $p_{h,m}^{n+1}$ and $\phi_{h,m}^{n+1}$, indexed by m, and defined as follows:

(a) At iteration m, we know $p_{h,m}^{n+1}$.
(b) We first compute $\phi_{h,m+1}^{n+1}$ as the solution of the linear problem

$$\tilde{a}^{n+1}\left(\phi_{h,m+1}^{n+1}, \psi_h\right) = \tilde{L}_m^{n+1}(\psi_h) \qquad \forall \psi_h \in \mathcal{V}_{0,h}. \tag{9.127}$$

(c) Then we update the Lagrange multiplier using formula (9.48)

$$p_{h,m+1}^{n+1}\left(\mathbf{q}\right) = G_\lambda\left(\mathbf{q}, t_{n+1}\right)\left(\phi_{h,m+1}^{n+1}\left(\mathbf{q}\right) + \lambda p_{h,m}^{n+1}\left(\mathbf{q}\right)\right),$$

for all nodes $\mathbf{q}$ of the mesh $\mathcal{T}_h$ where

$$G_\lambda\left(\mathbf{q}, t_{n+1}\right)(Y) = \begin{cases} \frac{1}{\lambda}\left(Y - R_1\left(\mathbf{q}, t_{n+1}\right)\right) & \text{if} \quad Y \leq R_1\left(\mathbf{q}, t_{n+1}\right) \\ 0 & \text{if} \quad R_1\left(\mathbf{q}, t_{n+1}\right) \leq Y \leq R_2\left(\mathbf{q}, t_{n+1}\right) \\ \frac{1}{\lambda}\left(Y - R_2\left(\mathbf{q}, t_{n+1}\right)\right) & \text{if} \quad Y \geq R_2\left(\mathbf{q}, t_{n+1}\right) \end{cases} \tag{9.128}$$

By applying the results of convergence in Bermúdez-Moreno [142] we know that, for λ sufficiently large, the sequence $\left\{\phi_{h,m}^{n+1}\right\}$ converges to the solution ϕ_h^{n+1} as m goes to infinity.

Figure 9.3 shows a flow chart of the complete algorithm: Lagrange-Galerkin combined with the iterative procedure.

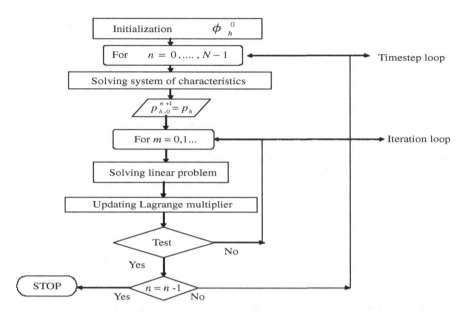

FIGURE 9.3 Iterative method combined with Lagrange-Galerkin discretization.

9.4.3 Order of Classical Lagrange-Galerkin Method

There is a broad literature analyzing the classical first-order characteristic method combined with finite elements applied to convection diffusion equations. Suli [182] showed error estimates of the form $O\left(h^k + \Delta t\right)$ in $l^\infty\left(L^2\left(\Omega\right)\right)$ norm, where Δt denotes the time step, h the spatial step, and k the degree of the finite element space.[5] Pironneau [145] stated error estimates of the form $O\left(h^k + \Delta t + h^{k+1}/\Delta t\right)$ in $l^\infty\left(L^2\left(\Omega\right)\right)$ norm under the assumption that the normal component of the velocity field vanishes on the boundary of the spatial domain and for an approximate discrete velocity field. In both cases, the constants depend on the norm of the solution. More recently, Bause and Knabner [183] proved convergence of order

---

[5]$L^2(\Omega)$ is the space of square-integrable $\mathbb{R}$-valued functions defined in Ω with the norm

$$\|f\|_{L^2} =: \left(\int_\Omega f(\mathbf{x})^2 dx\right)^{1/2}.$$

$l^\infty(L^2(\Omega))$ is the space of $\mathbb{R}$-valued functions, ψ, defined in $\{t_n\}_{n=0}^N \times \Omega$ such that $\psi(t_n) \in (\Omega)$ for all $n = 0, \ldots, N$. In this space we consider the norm

$$\|\psi\|_{l^\infty(L^2)} =: \max_{n=0,\ldots,N} \|\psi(t_n)\|_{L^2}$$

$$= \max_{n=0,\ldots,N} \left(\int_\Omega \psi(\mathbf{x}, t_n)^2 dx\right)^{1/2}.$$

$O\left(h^2 + \min\left(h, h^2/\Delta t\right) + \Delta t\right)$ for linear finite elements and zero velocity on the boundary, where the constants on the error estimates depend only on the data.

9.5   HIGHER-ORDER LAGRANGE-GALERKIN METHODS

In order to obtain a better accuracy in space, it is necessary to use finite element spaces of higher order. In order to achieve a better accuracy in time, it is necessary to use *higher-order characteristic methods*. The latter consists of higher-order schemes for the discretization of the total derivative (9.7). There are two main approaches: *multilevel schemes*, which use a multistep formula to approximate the total derivative, and *Crank-Nicolson schemes*, which use a centered formula. Specifically, for fixed $(\mathbf{x}, t) = (\mathbf{x}, t_{n+1})$ the following two second-order formulae could be used to approximate the material derivative:

$$\frac{d\phi}{d\tau}\left(X_e(\mathbf{x}, t_{n+1}; \tau), \tau\right),$$

- *Centered formula*

$$\frac{\phi\left(X_e(\mathbf{x}, t_{n+1}; \tau + \frac{\Delta t}{2}), \tau + \frac{\Delta t}{2}\right) - \phi\left(X_e(\mathbf{x}, t_{n+1}; \tau - \frac{\Delta t}{2}), \tau - \frac{\Delta t}{2}\right)}{\Delta t} \quad (9.67)$$

- *Three-level backward formula*

$$\frac{3\phi\left(X_e(\mathbf{x}, t_{n+1}; \tau), \tau\right) - 4\phi\left(X_e(\mathbf{x}, t_{n+1}; \tau - \Delta t), \tau - \Delta t\right) + \phi\left(X_e(\mathbf{x}, t_{n+1}; \tau - 2\Delta t), \tau - 2\Delta t\right)}{2\Delta t} \quad (9.68)$$

The exact characteristic lines can be replaced by second-order approximations keeping still the $O\left(\Delta t^2\right)$ error. Possible schemes are:

- *Runge-Kutta scheme*

$$X_{RK}\left(\mathbf{x}, t_{n+1}; t_n\right) := \mathbf{x} - \Delta t \mathbf{v}^{n+\frac{1}{2}}\left(\mathbf{x} - \frac{\Delta t}{2}\mathbf{v}^{n+1}(\mathbf{x})\right) \qquad \text{for} \quad n = 0, 1, ..., N - 1$$

$$(9.69)$$

- *Explicit two-step scheme*

$$X_{TS}\left(\mathbf{x}, t_{n+1}; t_n\right) := \mathbf{x} - \Delta t \left(2\mathbf{v}^n(\mathbf{x}) - \mathbf{v}^{n-1}(\mathbf{x})\right) \qquad \text{for} \quad n = 2, ..., N - 1$$

$$(9.70)$$

Ewing and Russel [184] introduced multistep Lagrange-Galerkin methods for the convection-diffusion equation with constant coefficients. Boukir et al. ([150], [185]) also used multistep characteristics combined with either mixed finite elements or spectral methods to solve the incompressible Navier-Stokes. They proved the stability of the method and obtained error estimates.

Rui and Tabata [151] proposed a second-order Crank-Nicolson characteristic method for the convection-diffusion equation with constant coefficients and Dirichlet boundary conditions, with the exact characteristics approximated using a Runge-Kutta scheme. Bermúdez et al. [152, 197] extended their work to variable coefficients, possibly degenerate diffusion, nondivergence-free velocity field, non-zero reaction, and more general Dirichlet-Robin boundary conditions.

9.5.1 Crank-Nicolson Characteristics/Finite Elements

In section 9.3 we showed how the solution of the nonlinear problem could be written as the limit of solution of linear problems. In section 9.4 those linear problems were discretized using first order Lagrange-Galerkin schemes. In this section, we describe the second-order Lagrange-Galerkin method proposed by Bermúdez et al. [152, 197] for solving the general linear problem (9.10) together with boundary conditions (9.11) and (9.12). First, we write the weak formulation and then the semi-Lagrangian time discretization using both exact and approximate characteristics. Finally, we write the fully discretized problem and address some of the results in Bermúdez et al. [152, 197].

Weak Formulation We proceed to write a weak formulation of equation (9.3). Given that we will carry out a semi-discretization in time using characteristics, we first write equation (9.3) at point $X_e(\mathbf{x}, t; \tau)$ and time τ giving (see (9.50)),

$$
\frac{d\phi}{d\tau}(X_e(\mathbf{x}, t; \tau), \tau) - \sum_{i,j=1}^{d} \frac{\partial}{\partial x_i}\left(a_{ij}(X_e(\mathbf{x}, t; \tau), \tau)\frac{\partial \phi}{\partial x_j}(X_e(\mathbf{x}, t; \tau), \tau)\right)
$$
$$
+ a_0(X_e(\mathbf{x}, t; \tau), \tau)\phi(X_e(\mathbf{x}, t; \tau), \tau) = f(X_e(\mathbf{x}, t; \tau), \tau). \tag{9.71}
$$

Equivalently, in vector notation

$$
\frac{d\phi}{d\tau}(X_e(\mathbf{x}, t; \tau), \tau) - \mathrm{div}\left(\mathbf{A}(X_e(\mathbf{x}, t; \tau), \tau)\nabla\phi(X_e(\mathbf{x}, t; \tau), \tau)\right)
$$
$$
+ a_0(X_e(\mathbf{x}, t; \tau), \tau)\phi(X_e(\mathbf{x}, t; \tau), \tau)
$$
$$
= f(X_e(\mathbf{x}, t; \tau), \tau). \tag{9.72}
$$

We will use the following notation:

$$
(\mathbf{F}_e)_{kl}(\mathbf{x}, t; \tau) := \frac{\partial (X_e)_k}{\partial x_l}(\mathbf{x}, t; \tau)
$$
$$
= (\nabla X_e)_{kl}(\mathbf{x}, t; \tau).
$$

In order to write a weak formulation, we need the following lemma.

LEMMA 9.5.1 *Let* $X : \overline{\Omega} \to \overline{X(\Omega)}$, $X \in C^1(\overline{\Omega})$, *be an invertible vector valued function. Let* $\mathbf{F} = \nabla X$ *and assume that* $\det \mathbf{F}(\mathbf{x}) \neq 0 \ \forall \mathbf{x} \in \overline{\Omega}$. *Then for smooth vector field* $\mathbf{w}$ *and scalar field* ψ, *we have:*

(a)

$$\int_\Omega \operatorname{div} \mathbf{w} \left(X \left(\mathbf{x} \right) \right) \psi \left(\mathbf{x} \right) d\mathbf{x}$$

$$= \int_\Gamma \mathbf{F}^{-t} \left(\mathbf{x} \right) \mathbf{n} \left(\mathbf{x} \right) \cdot \mathbf{w} \left(X \left(\mathbf{x} \right) \right) \psi \left(\mathbf{x} \right) d\Gamma$$

$$- \int_\Omega \mathbf{F}^{-1} \left(\mathbf{x} \right) \mathbf{w} \left(X \left(\mathbf{x} \right) \right) \cdot \nabla \psi \left(\mathbf{x} \right) d\mathbf{x}$$

$$- \int_\Omega \operatorname{div} \mathbf{F}^{-t} \left(\mathbf{x} \right) \cdot \mathbf{w} \left(X \left(\mathbf{x} \right) \right) \psi \left(\mathbf{x} \right) d\mathbf{x}. \qquad (9.73)$$

(b) If additionally $X \left(\mathbf{x} \right) = \mathbf{x} \ \forall \mathbf{x} \in \Gamma$,

$$\int_\Gamma \mathbf{F}^{-t} \left(\mathbf{x} \right) \mathbf{n} \left(\mathbf{x} \right) \cdot \mathbf{w} \left(X \left(\mathbf{x} \right) \right) \psi \left(\mathbf{x} \right) d\Gamma$$

$$= \int_\Gamma \mathbf{n} \left(\mathbf{x} \right) \cdot \mathbf{w} \left(X \left(\mathbf{x} \right) \right) \psi \left(\mathbf{x} \right) \ \det \mathbf{F}^{-1} \left(\mathbf{x} \right) d\Gamma, \qquad (9.74)$$

where $\mathbf{n}$ *is the outward unit normal vector to* Γ.

Proof: See Bermúdez et al. [152, 197]

Note that equation (9.73) can be considered a Green's formula. Also, substitution of (9.74) into (9.73) yields

$$\int_\Omega \operatorname{div} \mathbf{w} \left(X \left(\mathbf{x} \right) \right) \psi \left(\mathbf{x} \right) d\mathbf{x} = \int_\Gamma \mathbf{n} \left(\mathbf{x} \right) \cdot \mathbf{w} \left(X \left(\mathbf{x} \right) \right) \psi \left(\mathbf{x} \right) \det \mathbf{F}^{-1} \left(\mathbf{x} \right) d\Gamma$$

$$- \int_\Omega \mathbf{F}^{-1} \left(\mathbf{x} \right) \mathbf{w} \left(X \left(\mathbf{x} \right) \right) \cdot \nabla \psi \left(\mathbf{x} \right) d\mathbf{x} - \int_\Omega \operatorname{div} \mathbf{F}^{-t} \left(\mathbf{x} \right) \cdot \mathbf{w} \left(X \left(\mathbf{x} \right) \right) \psi \left(\mathbf{x} \right) d\mathbf{x}. \qquad (9.75)$$

To write a weak formulation we multiply equation (9.72) by a test function ψ satisfying $\psi = 0$ on Γ_D, integrate in Ω, and use the Green's formula (9.75) with $X \left(\mathbf{x} \right) = X_e \left(\mathbf{x}, t; \tau \right)$ and $\mathbf{w} = \mathbf{A} \nabla \phi$, obtaining

$$\int_\Omega \frac{d\phi}{d\tau} \left(X_e(\mathbf{x}, t; \tau), \tau \right) \psi \left(\mathbf{x} \right) d\mathbf{x}$$

$$+ \int_\Omega \mathbf{F}_e^{-1}(\mathbf{x}, t; \tau) \mathbf{A} \left(X_e(\mathbf{x}, t; \tau), \tau \right) \nabla \phi \left(X_e(\mathbf{x}, t; \tau), \tau \right) \cdot \nabla \psi \left(\mathbf{x} \right) d\mathbf{x}$$

$$+ \int_\Omega \operatorname{div} \mathbf{F}_e^{-t}(\mathbf{x}, t; \tau) \cdot \mathbf{A} \left(X_e(\mathbf{x}, t; \tau), \tau \right) \nabla \phi \left(X_e(\mathbf{x}, t; \tau), \tau \right) \psi \left(\mathbf{x} \right) d\mathbf{x}$$

$$+ \int_\Omega a_0 \left(X_e(\mathbf{x}, t; \tau), \tau \right) \phi \left(X_e(\mathbf{x}, t; \tau), \tau \right) \psi \left(\mathbf{x} \right) d\mathbf{x}$$

$$- \int_{\Gamma_R} \mathbf{n} \left(\mathbf{x} \right) \cdot \mathbf{A} \left(X_e(\mathbf{x}, t; \tau), \tau \right) \nabla \phi \left(X_e(\mathbf{x}, t; \tau), \tau \right) \psi \left(\mathbf{x} \right) \det \mathbf{F}_e^{-1}(\mathbf{x}, t; \tau) d\Gamma$$

$$= \int_\Omega f \left(X_e(\mathbf{x}, t; \tau), \tau \right) \psi \left(\mathbf{x} \right) d\mathbf{x}. \qquad (9.76)$$

Now, using Robin condition (9.11), the boundary term in the above formulation can be rewritten as

$$\int_{\Gamma_R} \mathbf{n}(\mathbf{x}) \cdot \mathbf{A}(X_e(\mathbf{x}, t; \tau), \tau) \nabla\phi(X_e(\mathbf{x}, t; \tau), \tau) \psi(\mathbf{x}) \det \mathbf{F}_e^{-1}(\mathbf{x}, t; \tau) d\Gamma$$

$$= \int_{\Gamma_R} (g(X_e(\mathbf{x}, t; \tau), \tau) - \alpha\phi(X_e(\mathbf{x}, t; \tau), \tau)) \psi(\mathbf{x}) \det \mathbf{F}_e^{-1}(\mathbf{x}, t; \tau) d\Gamma. \qquad (9.77)$$

Substitution of (9.77) into (9.76) yields

$$\int_\Omega \frac{d\phi}{d\tau}(X_e(\mathbf{x}, t; \tau), \tau) \psi(\mathbf{x}) \, dx$$

$$+ \int_\Omega \mathbf{F}_e^{-1}(\mathbf{x}, t; \tau) \mathbf{A}(X_e(\mathbf{x}, t; \tau), \tau) \nabla\phi(X_e(\mathbf{x}, t; \tau), \tau) \cdot \nabla\psi(\mathbf{x}) \, dx$$

$$+ \int_\Omega \operatorname{div} \mathbf{F}_e^{-t}(\mathbf{x}, t; \tau) \cdot \mathbf{A}(X_e(\mathbf{x}, t; \tau), \tau) \nabla\phi(X_e(\mathbf{x}, t; \tau), \tau) \psi(\mathbf{x}) \, dx$$

$$+ \int_\Omega a_0(X_e(\mathbf{x}, t; \tau), \tau) \phi(X_e(\mathbf{x}, t; \tau), \tau) \psi(\mathbf{x}) \, dx$$

$$+ \int_{\Gamma_R} \alpha\phi(X_e(\mathbf{x}, t; \tau), \tau) \psi(\mathbf{x}) \det \mathbf{F}_e^{-1}(\mathbf{x}, t; \tau) d\Gamma$$

$$= \int_\Omega f(X_e(\mathbf{x}, t; \tau), \tau) \psi(\mathbf{x}) \, dx$$

$$+ \int_{\Gamma_R} g(X_e(\mathbf{x}, t; \tau), \tau) \psi(\mathbf{x}) \det \mathbf{F}_e^{-1}(\mathbf{x}, t; \tau) dx. \qquad (9.78)$$

This is a weak formulation of equation (9.3). Note that if $\tau = t$ it reduces to the weak formulation in (9.31) with $p = 0$ (since we are solving the linear problem).

Second-Order Semidiscretized Scheme with Exact Characteristic Lines In order to carry out a semidiscretization in time, we consider a partition of the time interval $[0, T]$ into N time steps of size $\Delta t = T/N$ that we will denote by $t_n = T - n\Delta t$ for $n = 0, \frac{1}{2}, 1, \frac{3}{2}, ..., N$.
We introduce the following notation:

$$X_e^n(\mathbf{x}) := X_e(\mathbf{x}, t_{n+1}; t_n), \qquad \mathbf{F}_e^n(\mathbf{x}) := \mathbf{F}_e(\mathbf{x}, t_{n+1}; t_n),$$

$$X_e^{n+\frac{1}{2}}(\mathbf{x}) := X_e\left(\mathbf{x}, t_{n+1}; t_{n+\frac{1}{2}}\right), \qquad \mathbf{F}_e^{n+\frac{1}{2}}(\mathbf{x}) := \mathbf{F}_e\left(\mathbf{x}, t_{n+1}; t_{n+\frac{1}{2}}\right)$$

The method proposed in [152, 197] consists of fixing $t = t_{n+1}, n = 0, 1, ..., N - 1$ in the weak formulation (9.78) and applying a Crank-Nicholson scheme with respect to τ. We have

$$\int_\Omega \frac{\phi^n\left(X_e^n\left(\mathbf{x}\right)\right) - \phi^{n+1}\left(\mathbf{x}\right)}{\Delta t} \psi\left(\mathbf{x}\right) d\mathbf{x}$$

$$+ \tfrac{1}{2} \int_\Omega \mathbf{A}^{n+1}\left(\mathbf{x}\right) \nabla\phi^{n+1}\left(\mathbf{x}\right) \cdot \nabla\psi\left(\mathbf{x}\right) d\mathbf{x}$$

$$+ \tfrac{1}{2} \int_\Omega \left(\mathbf{F}_e^n\right)^{-1}\left(\mathbf{x}\right) \mathbf{A}^n\left(X_e^n\left(\mathbf{x}\right)\right) \nabla\phi^n\left(X_e^n\left(\mathbf{x}\right)\right) \cdot \nabla\psi\left(\mathbf{x}\right) d\mathbf{x}$$

$$+ \tfrac{1}{2} \int_\Omega \mathrm{div}\,\left(\mathbf{F}_e^n\right)^{-t}\left(\mathbf{x}\right) \cdot \mathbf{A}^n\left(X_e^n\left(\mathbf{x}\right)\right) \nabla\phi^n\left(X_e^n\left(\mathbf{x}\right)\right) \psi\left(\mathbf{x}\right) d\mathbf{x}$$

$$+ \tfrac{1}{2} \int_\Omega a_0^{n+1}\left(\mathbf{x}\right) \phi^{n+1}\left(\mathbf{x}\right) \psi\left(\mathbf{x}\right) d\mathbf{x}$$

$$+ \tfrac{1}{2} \int_\Omega a_0^n\left(X_e^n\left(\mathbf{x}\right)\right) \phi^n\left(X_e^n(\mathbf{x})\right) \psi\left(\mathbf{x}\right) d\mathbf{x}$$

$$+ \tfrac{1}{2} \int_{\Gamma_R} \alpha\phi^{n+1}\left(\mathbf{x}\right) \psi\left(\mathbf{x}\right) d\Gamma$$

$$+ \tfrac{1}{2} \int_{\Gamma_R} \alpha\phi^n\left(X_e^n\left(\mathbf{x}\right)\right) \psi\left(\mathbf{x}\right) \det\left(\mathbf{F}_e^n\right)^{-1}\left(\mathbf{x}\right) d\Gamma$$

$$= \tfrac{1}{2} \int_\Omega \left(f^{n+1}\left(\mathbf{x}\right) + f^n\left(X_e^n(\mathbf{x})\right)\right) \psi\left(\mathbf{x}\right) d\mathbf{x}$$

$$+ \tfrac{1}{2} \int_{\Gamma_R} g^{n+1}\left(\mathbf{x}\right) \psi\left(\mathbf{x}\right) d\mathbf{x}$$

$$+ \tfrac{1}{2} \int_{\Gamma_R} g^n\left(X_e^n\left(\mathbf{x}\right)\right) \psi\left(\mathbf{x}\right) \det\left(\mathbf{F}_e^n\right)^{-1}\left(\mathbf{x}\right) d\mathbf{x}, \tag{9.79}$$

where we have used that $X_e(\mathbf{x}, t_{n+1}; t_{n+1}) = \mathbf{x}$ and $\mathbf{F}_e(\mathbf{x}, t_{n+1}; t_{n+1}) = \mathbf{I}$, $\mathbf{I}$ being the identity matrix.

Bermúdez et al. [152, 197] proved that the scheme (9.79) is of order $O\left(\Delta t^2\right)$ at point $\left(X_e^{n+\frac{1}{2}}\left(\mathbf{x}\right), t_{n+\frac{1}{2}}\right)$.

Second-Order Semidiscretized Scheme with Approximate Characteristic Lines As mentioned before, in most cases the system of characteristics (9.49) cannot be solved exactly. Following Rui and Tabata [151], the exact characteristic lines, $X_e^n\left(\mathbf{x}\right)$, could be replaced in (9.79) by a numerical approximation using an explicit method, like the first-order Euler scheme (9.53), or second-order Runge-Kutta scheme (9.69). As before, we will denote this approximations by $X_E^n\left(\mathbf{x}\right)$ and $X_{RK}^n\left(\mathbf{x}\right)$, respectively.

Thus, we are left with the following second-order approximation to (9.79) in the case the characteristic lines are not known explicitly:

$$\int_\Omega \frac{\phi^n\left(X_{RK}^n\left(\mathbf{x}\right)\right) - \phi^{n+1}\left(\mathbf{x}\right)}{\Delta t} \psi\left(\mathbf{x}\right) d\mathbf{x}$$

$$+ \tfrac{1}{2} \int_\Omega \mathbf{A}^{n+1}\left(\mathbf{x}\right) \nabla\phi^{n+1}\left(\mathbf{x}\right) \cdot \nabla\psi\left(\mathbf{x}\right) d\mathbf{x}$$

$$+ \tfrac{1}{2} \int_\Omega \left(\mathbf{F}_E^n\right)^{-1}\left(\mathbf{x}\right) \mathbf{A}^n\left(X_E^n\left(\mathbf{x}\right)\right) \nabla\phi^n\left(X_E^n\left(\mathbf{x}\right)\right) \cdot \nabla\psi\left(\mathbf{x}\right) d\mathbf{x}$$

$$+ \tfrac{1}{2} \int_\Omega \mathrm{div}\,\left(\mathbf{F}_E^n\right)^{-t}\left(\mathbf{x}\right) \cdot \mathbf{A}^n\left(X_E^n\left(\mathbf{x}\right)\right) \nabla\phi^n\left(X_E^n\left(\mathbf{x}\right)\right) \psi\left(\mathbf{x}\right) d\mathbf{x}$$

$$+ \tfrac{1}{2} \int_\Omega a_0^{n+1}\left(\mathbf{x}\right) \phi^{n+1}\left(\mathbf{x}\right) \psi\left(\mathbf{x}\right) d\mathbf{x}$$

$$+ \tfrac{1}{2} \int_\Omega a_0^n\left(X_E^n\left(\mathbf{x}\right)\right) \phi^n\left(X_E^n(\mathbf{x})\right) \psi\left(\mathbf{x}\right) d\mathbf{x}$$

$$+ \tfrac{1}{2} \int_{\Gamma_R} \alpha\phi^{n+1}\left(\mathbf{x}\right) \psi\left(\mathbf{x}\right) d\Gamma$$

$$+ \tfrac{1}{2} \int_{\Gamma_R} \alpha \phi^n \left(X_E^n \left(\mathbf{x} \right) \right) \psi \left(\mathbf{x} \right) \det \left(\mathbf{F}_E^n \right)^{-1} (\mathbf{x}) d\Gamma$$

$$= \tfrac{1}{2} \int_{\Omega} \left(f^{n+1} \left(\mathbf{x} \right) + f^n \left(X_E^n(\mathbf{x}) \right) \right) \psi \left(\mathbf{x} \right) d\mathbf{x}$$

$$+ \tfrac{1}{2} \int_{\Gamma_R} g^{n+1} \left(\mathbf{x} \right) \psi \left(\mathbf{x} \right) d\mathbf{x}$$

$$+ \tfrac{1}{2} \int_{\Gamma_R} g^n \left(X_E^n \left(\mathbf{x} \right) \right) \psi \left(\mathbf{x} \right) \det \left(\mathbf{F}_E^n \right)^{-1} (\mathbf{x}) d\mathbf{x}. \qquad (9.80)$$

Note that, in order to preserve the $O \left(\Delta t^2 \right)$ error bounds, it is necessary to use a second-order approximation of the characteristics lines in one term only. Besides, similarly to the exact characteristic case, $\det \left(\mathbf{F}_E^n \right)^{-1}$, $\operatorname{div} \left(\mathbf{F}_E^n \right)^{-t} (\mathbf{x})$, and $\left(\mathbf{F}_E^n \right)^{-1}$ could be replaced by their $O \left(\Delta t^2 \right)$ approximations below, avoiding the inversion of matrix $\mathbf{F}_E^n$. Indeed, given

$$\mathbf{F}_E^n \left(\mathbf{x} \right) := \nabla X_E^n \left(\mathbf{x} \right) = \mathbf{I} \left(\mathbf{x} \right) - \Delta t \, \mathbf{L}^{n+1} \left(\mathbf{x} \right),$$

it can be shown (see [152, 197]) that

$$\left(\mathbf{F}_E^n \right)^{-1} \left(\mathbf{x} \right) \approx \mathbf{I} + \Delta t \, \mathbf{L}^{n+1} \left(\mathbf{x} \right) + \Delta t^2 \left(\mathbf{L}^{n+1} \left(\mathbf{x} \right) \right)^2$$

$$\det \left(\mathbf{F}_E^n \right)^{-1} \approx 1 + \Delta t \operatorname{div} \mathbf{v}^{n+1} \left(\mathbf{x} \right) \qquad (9.81)$$

$$\operatorname{div} \left(\mathbf{F}_E^n \right)^{-t} \left(\mathbf{x} \right) \approx \Delta t \, \nabla \operatorname{div} \mathbf{v}^n \left(X_E^n \left(\mathbf{x} \right) \right).$$

Bermúdez et al. [152, 197] proved stability in $l^\infty \left(L^2 \right)$ norm of scheme (9.80) under some hypothesis on the data and sufficiently small time step. Also, under further regularity assumptions on the data, they proved $l^\infty \left(L^2 \right)$ error estimates of order $O \left(\Delta t^2 \right)$ for the semidiscretized in time scheme.

Fully Discretized Lagrange-Galerkin Scheme In Bermúdez et al., [152, 197] a fully discretized Lagrange-Galerkin scheme is proposed for a wide class of finite element spaces. Let $\mathcal{V}_h^k$ be a family of finite element spaces, where h denotes the space parameter and k is the "approximation order" in the following sense:
"*There exists an interpolation operator* $\pi_h : C^0 \left(\overline{\Omega} \right) \to \mathcal{V}_h^k$ *satisfying*

$$\| \pi_h \psi - \psi \|_s \leq K h^{k+1-s} \| \psi \|_{k+1} \quad \forall \psi \in C^0 \left(\overline{\Omega} \right) \cap H^{k+1} \left(\Omega \right), \qquad s = 0, 1$$

for a positive constant K independent of h."[6]

---

[6] $H^{k+1}(\Omega)$ is the Sobolev space of order $k + 1$. This is the set of $\mathbb{R}$-valued functions defined in Ω which are square-integrable and have square-integrable derivatives up to order $k + 1$. In this space we consider the norm

$$\| \psi \|_{k+1} =: \left(\| \psi \|_{L^2}^2 + \sum_{\alpha=1}^{k+1} \| D^\alpha \psi \|_{L^2}^2 \right)^{\tfrac{1}{2}},$$

where D^α denotes the derivative of order α.

Notice that the finite element space (9.66) falls into this family for $k = 1$. The fully discretized scheme reads as follows:

PROBLEM 12 *Fully Discretized Second Order Scheme*

Given $\phi_h^0 \in \mathcal{V}_h^k$, find $\widehat{\phi}_h := \{\phi_h^n\}_{n=1}^N \in \left[\mathcal{V}_h^k\right]^N$ such that

$$\left\langle \mathcal{L}_{\Delta t}^{n+\frac{1}{2}} \widehat{\phi}_h, \psi_h \right\rangle = \left\langle \mathcal{F}_{\Delta t}^{n+\frac{1}{2}}, \psi_h \right\rangle \qquad \forall \psi_h \in \mathcal{V}_h^k \qquad for \quad n = 0, ..., N-1, \qquad (9.82)$$

where

$$\left\langle \mathcal{L}_{\Delta t}^{n+\frac{1}{2}} \phi_h, \psi_h \right\rangle := \int_\Omega \frac{\phi_h^n \circ X_{RK}^n - \phi_h^{n+1}}{\Delta t} \psi \, d\mathbf{x}$$

$$+ \int_\Omega \frac{\mathbf{A}^{n+1} \nabla \phi_h^{n+1} + \left(\mathbf{A}^n \nabla \phi_h^n\right) \circ X_E^n}{2} \cdot \nabla \psi_h \, d\mathbf{x}$$

$$+ \frac{\Delta t}{2} \int_\Omega \mathbf{L}^{n+1} \left(\mathbf{A}^n \nabla \phi_h^n\right) \circ X_E^n \cdot \nabla \psi_h \, d\mathbf{x}$$

$$+ \frac{\Delta t}{2} \int_\Omega \left(\nabla \operatorname{div} \mathbf{v}^n \cdot \mathbf{A}^n \nabla \phi_h^n\right) \circ X_E^n \, \psi_h \, d\mathbf{x}$$

$$+ \int_\Omega \frac{a_0^{n+1} \phi_h^{n+1} + \left(a_0^n \phi_h^n\right) \circ X_E^n}{2} \psi_h \, d\mathbf{x}$$

$$+ \int_{\Gamma_R} \alpha \frac{\phi_h^{n+1} + \left(1 + \Delta t \operatorname{div} \mathbf{v}^{n+1}\right) \phi_h^n \circ X_E^n}{2} \psi \, d\Gamma,$$

and

$$\left\langle \mathcal{F}_{\Delta t}^{n+\frac{1}{2}}, \psi_h \right\rangle := \int_\Omega \frac{f^{n+1} + f^n \circ X_E^n}{2} \psi_h \, d\mathbf{x}$$

$$+ \int_{\Gamma_R} \frac{g^{n+1} + \left(1 + \Delta t \operatorname{div} \mathbf{v}^{n+1}\right) g^n \circ X_E^n}{2} \psi \, d\Gamma.$$

In Bermúdez et al. [152, 197] stability results for the fully discretized scheme (9.82) and error estimates of order $O\left(\Delta t^2\right) + O\left(h^k\right)$ in $l^\infty\left(L^2\right)$ norm are proved. These results are under the hypothesis that all inner products in the Galerkin formulation are calculated exactly. However, in practice numerical integration has to be used to approximate these integrals. Quadrature formulae have to be carefully chosen in order to preserve stability and the above order in the error estimates.

Specifically, in [152, 197] the following finite element spaces are considered

- For a family of rectangular meshes of parameter h, $\mathcal{T}_h$

$$Q_h^k = \left\{ f \in C^0\left(\overline{\Omega}\right) : f|_K \in Q_k, \quad \forall K \in \mathcal{T}_h \right\},$$

where Q_k is the space of polynomials of degree less than or equal to k in each variable separately.

- For a family of triangular meshes of parameter h, $\mathcal{T}_h$

$$\mathcal{P}_h^k = \left\{ f \in C^0\left(\overline{\Omega}\right) : f|_K \in \mathcal{P}_k, \quad \forall K \in \mathcal{T}_h \right\},$$

where $\mathcal{P}_k$ is the space of polynomials of degree less than or equal to k.

They carried out some numerical tests in two space dimensions to illustrate the theoretical results regarding second-order Lagrange-Galerkin schemes combined with quadrature. It is well known that for the classical first-order-in-time Lagrange-Galerkin method, numerical integration may lead to conditional stability (see [184], [186], [187]). They did not find any sign of instability when using scheme (9.82) combined with either Q_h^2 and the tensor product of the Simpson rule in each coordinate or $\mathcal{P}_h^2$ with a seven-point quadrature formula. In both cases, an extra term of the form $O\left(1/\Delta t\right)$ appears in the estimates of the error for fixed h. This agrees with evidence found for the first-order Lagrange-Galerkin scheme ([145], [187]).

They also carried out a comparison between the second-order Lagrange-Galerkin and the classical first-order scheme. Some of their results are shown in Figures 9.4 through 9.7. Example 1 in Figures (9.4) through (9.6) shows specific numerical solutions obtained with first- and second-order discretization in space. Example 2 in figure (9.7) shows the first- and second-order convergence in the time discretization.

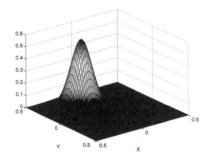

FIGURE 9.4   Exact solution of the rotating Gaussian hill problem with $T = 2$ (Source: Nogueiras [198]).

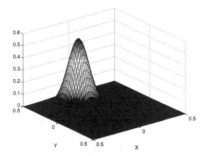

FIGURE 9.5   Second-order characteristics with second-order Q_h^2 FE. Numerical solution for the rotating Gaussian hill problem with $T = 2$. Mesh parameters are $h = 0.015625$ and $\Delta t = 0.01$. (Source: Nogueiras [98]).

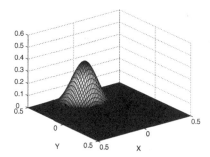

FIGURE 9.6 Second-order characteristics with first-order Q_h^1 FE. Numerical solution for the rotating Gaussian hill problem with $T = 2$. Mesh parameters are $h = 0.015625$ and $\Delta t = 0.01$. (Source: Nogueiras [98]).

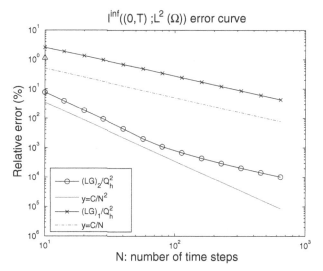

FIGURE 9.7 Second order Q_h^2 FE and different characteristics methods. $l^\infty (L^2)$ norm of numerical error in log-log scale for a convection-(strong degenerated)-diffusion-reaction problem with variable coefficients. (Source: Nogueiras [98]).

Overall, the second-order scheme outperforms the first-order scheme in terms of trade-off between the speed and the accuracy.

9.6 APPLICATION TO PRICING OF CONVERTIBLE BONDS

In this section, we apply the numerical methods described in this chapter to the valuation of convertible bonds. We consider the intensity-based framework for pricing convertible bonds described in section 4.4.

We study the convergence of the numerical method using the special case of a bond convertible only at expiry. Then we show prices for a real bond. Section 9.6.1 describes the numerical solution, and section 9.6.2 gives the numerical results.

9.6.1 Numerical Solution

The valuation of convertible bonds can be considered as a special case of the more general two-factor model presented in section 9.2. Moreover, the model in section 4.4.2 is a special case of the Problem 3 for the choices:

$$x_1 = r_t, \tag{9.83}$$

$$x_2 = S_t, \tag{9.84}$$

$$A_{11} = \frac{1}{2}\sigma_r^2, \quad A_{12} = A_{21} = \frac{1}{2}\rho S_t \sigma_S \sigma_r, \quad A_{22} = \frac{1}{2}\sigma_S^2 S_t^2, \tag{9.85}$$

$$B_1 = \mu_r, \quad B_2 = (r_t - d_t + q_t + \lambda_t \eta_t), \tag{9.86}$$

$$A_0 = r_t + \lambda_t, \quad F = \lambda_t V_t^*(S_t, t), \tag{9.87}$$

and

$$R_1(r_t, S_t, t) = \max\{nS_t, M_{P_t}\}, \tag{9.88}$$

$$R_2(r_t, S_t, t) = \max\{nS_t, M_{C_t}\}. \tag{9.89}$$

The Interest Rate Model We assume the interest rate follows the extended Vasicek model introduced in 3.1. This model combines tractability with the flexibility to calibrate to a prespecified initial term structure. We recall that the short-rate process under the EMM is

$$dr_t = (\theta_t - \kappa_t r_t)\,dt + \sigma_r dW_t, \tag{9.90}$$

where $\theta(t)$ can be chosen so that model spot rates coincide with market spot rates.

9.6.2 Numerical Results

In this section, we show numerical results obtained when using classical Lagrange-Galerkin methods to price an actual CB, the Adidas-Salomon issue maturing on October 8, 2018. The evaluation date is December 16, 2005; hence, the time to maturity of the convertible expressed in years is

$$T = 12.8192. \tag{9.91}$$

The bond has face value

$$F = 50000 \quad \text{EUR}, \tag{9.92}$$

and can be converted until September 20, 2018, at the rate (see table 9.1)

$$n = 440.1961. \tag{9.93}$$

TABLE 9.1 Conversion schedule for Adidas-Salomon convertible bond

From Date	To Date	Conversion Ratio
18-Nov-03	20-Sep-18	490.1961

TABLE 9.2 Call schedule for Adidas-Salomon convertible bond

From Date	To Date	Call Price (% Par)	Trigger Level
8-Oct-09	7-Oct-12	100	132.6
8-Oct-12	7-Oct-15	100	117.3
8-Oct-15	8-Oct-18	100	

TABLE 9.3 Put schedule for Adidas-Salomon convertible bond

Date	Put Price (% Par)
8-Oct-09	100
8-Oct-12	100
8-Oct-15	100

The Adidas-Salomon issue is continuously soft-callable, that is, the stock price has to be above the *trigger level* before the call can be exercised; the call schedule is in table 9.2.

It is also puttable at par at three-year intervals, as shown in table 9.3.

The bond pays a 2.5% coupon annually on July 12.[7]

We assume a constant volatility for the underlying stock of $\sigma_S = 23\%$, a continuous dividend yield $d = 1.5868\%$ and a repo rate $q = 0.4\%$. We obtain $\rho = -0.0188$ for the correlation between the short rate and the equity, using the one-month EUROLIBOR as a proxy for the instantaneous rate (see figures 9.8 and 9.9).[8]

The extended Vasicek model (9.90) has been calibrated to market data as of December 16, 2005 (see section 3.3.1). The following values were obtained for the

---

[7]This issue has a call announcement period of 45 days and a conversion announcement period of 14 days. It has also the so-called French dividend conversion, meaning that the shares received upon conversion do not pay those dividends paid by ordinary shares between the date of conversion and the end of the fiscal year in which conversion occurs. All those features have been ignored for the sake of simplicity.

[8]Both time series were obtained from Bloomberg.

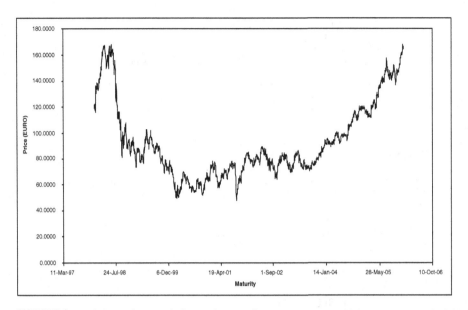

FIGURE 9.8 Adidas-Salomon daily stock price from January 1, 1998, to January 12, 2006.

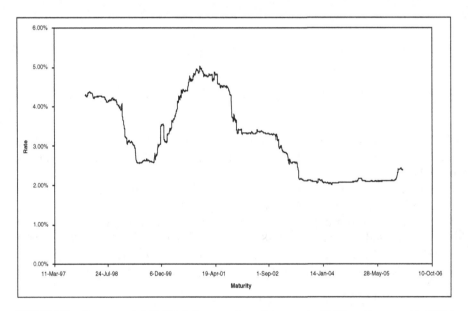

FIGURE 9.9 One-month LIBOR daily rates from January 1, 1998, to January 12, 2006.

interest rate volatility parameters:

$$\kappa = 0.0203, \tag{9.95}$$

$$\sigma_r = 0.6868\%. \tag{9.96}$$

We use for the default specification $\lambda = 0.0055$, $\eta = 1$ and $R = 40\%$.
The instantaneous interest rate is $r = 2.3804\%$ and the stock price $S = 157.54$.

Convergence test In order to test the numerical method, we consider the special case of bond convertible only at expiry, for which we have an analytical solution (see section 4.4.4) and therefore we can compute the errors.

We set

$$R_1\,(r_t, S_t, t) = 0, \tag{9.97}$$

$$R_2\,(r_t, S_t, t) = \infty, \tag{9.98}$$

given that there is no early-exercise embedded options.

Domain bounds are set to be $\Omega^r = [0, 1.5]$ and $\Omega^S = [9, 2077]$. Ω^S corresponds to roughly a 99.9% confidence interval on S_T. We give L^2 errors over both the entire domain Ω and also over a narrower region of interest $\widehat{\Omega} = \widehat{\Omega}^r \times \widehat{\Omega}^S$, where $\widehat{\Omega}^r = [0, 0.15]$ and $\widehat{\Omega}^S = [16, 1152]$. $\widehat{\Omega}^S$ is roughly a 99% confidence interval on S_T. $\widehat{\Omega}$ reflects a range of values of r and S likely to be observed in practice and so the error on $\widehat{\Omega}$ is likely to be more representative.

We present results obtained for successive grid refinements for the relative error in L^2. Mesh 1 is the coarsest with just 15 space steps in the interest rate dimension, 40 in the stock dimension, and 120 time steps up to time $T = 3.5$. Each successive mesh doubles both the number of space steps in each dimension and the number of time steps so that the finest mesh, mesh 4, has 120 interest rate steps, 320 equity steps, and 280 times steps. We use as a benchmarking measure the total relative error define as

$$\frac{\left[\int_0^T \| \text{error}_t \|_{L^2}^2 \, dt \right]^{\frac{1}{2}}}{\left[\int_0^T \| \text{exact solution}_t \|_{L^2}^2 \, dt \right]^{\frac{1}{2}}},$$

where

$$\| f \|_{L^2} =: \left(\int_\Omega f^2 d\Omega \right)^{\frac{1}{2}},$$

and

$$\text{error}_t = \text{exact solution}_t - \text{numerical solution}_t.$$

TABLE 9.4 Error and convergence

Mesh	ErrorTD	Convergence Factor	ErrorRI	Factor
1	$8.36E - 03$	–	$5.25E - 03$	–
2	$4.59E - 03$	1.82	$2.99E - 03$	1.76
3	$2.45E - 03$	1.88	$1.92E - 03$	1.56
4	$1.28E - 03$	1.91	$1.19E - 03$	1.61
5	$6.66E - 04$	1.92	$7.91E - 04$	1.51

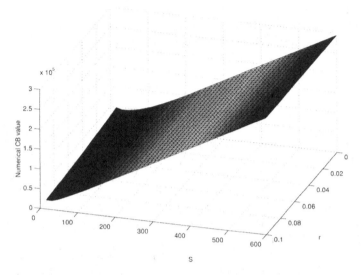

FIGURE 9.10   Numerical solution at evaluation date.

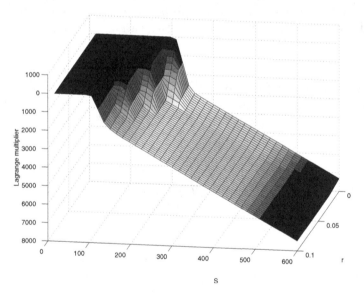

FIGURE 9.11   Lagrange multiplier at evaluation date.

The analytical formulae for the "exact solution" was given in (4.27); the value of the "exact solution" for the current level of the interest rate and the stock price is 79674.4525.

The numerical results are presented in table 9.4. On the boundaries we use the analytical solution. In each case two of the boundaries are Dirichlet and two are Neumann. "Error TD" is the error on the entire domain Ω; "Error RI" is the error on the region of interest, $\widehat{\Omega}$. "Factor" is the progressive error reduction factor in moving to a finer mesh level from the preceding mesh level.

As mentioned in section 9.4.3, the classical Lagrange-Galerkin method is unconditionally stable and has convergence order of $O\left(h\right) + O\left(\frac{h^2}{\Delta t}\right) + O\left(\Delta t\right)$ under suitable conditions for the coefficients of the equation. Although our models do not satisfy the required assumptions, the same error estimate has been obtained empirically. In table 9.4 it can be seen that the ratio between two consecutive errors tends to 2, which is consistent with the order of convergence given above.

Pricing of a real CB Finally, we show the numerical solution for the Adidas-Salomon issue maturing on October 8, 2018, as of December 16, 2005. Figure 9.10 shows the CB prices, and figure 9.11 the Lagrange multiplier. Results were computed with mesh 4.

9.7 APPENDIX: LAGRANGE TRIANGULAR FINITE ELEMENTS

9.7.1 Lagrange Triangular Finite Elements in $\mathbb{R}^d$

The domain $\Omega \subset \mathbb{R}^d$ is decomposed into simplices of dimension d (triangles if $d = 2$, tetrahedra if $d = 3$, etc.) and the space $\mathcal{V}_h$ is the space of continuous functions in $\overline{\Omega}$ that are polynomials of degree smaller than or equal to k over any single simplex.

A set of $d + 1$ points $\{c_1, ..., c_{d+1}\}$ not lying on the same hyperplane is considered, that is, such that the matrix

$$\begin{bmatrix} c_{11} & \cdots & c_{1d} & 1 \\ \vdots & & \vdots & \\ c_{d1} & & c_{dd} & 1 \\ c_{d+11} & \cdots & c_{d+1d} & 1 \end{bmatrix} \tag{9.99}$$

has a nonzero determinant.

The convex hull of these $d + 1$ points

$$K = \left\{ \mathbf{x} = \sum_{i=1}^{d+1} \lambda_i c_i \quad 0 \le \lambda_i \le 1, \quad 1 \le i \le d+1, \quad \sum_{i=1}^{d+1} \lambda_i = 1 \right\}, \tag{9.100}$$

is called a *d-dimensional simplex* in $\mathbb{R}^d$

If $\mathbf{x} \in K$ the corresponding $\lambda_i(\mathbf{x}) = \lambda_i$ are known as *barycentric coordinates* of $\mathbf{x}$. Notice that

$$\lambda_i(c_j) = \delta_{ij},$$

and that λ_i is an affine function (polynomial of degree one) in the variables x_j.

The subsets of K obtained when the following conditions are imposed

$$\lambda_{i_1} = \lambda_{i_2} = \ldots = \lambda_{i_r} = 0,$$

are called $d - r$ *dimensional faces* of K.[9]

The *barycenter* of K is the point that has all the barycentric coordinates equal,

$$\lambda_i = \frac{1}{d+1} \quad 1 \le i \le d+1.$$

Let K be a d-simplex and k a positive integer; the subset of points of K

$$\sum_K^{(k)} = \left\{ \mathbf{x} \in K : \lambda_j(x) \in \left\{ 0, \frac{1}{k}, \ldots, \frac{k-1}{k}, 1 \right\}, \quad 1 \le j \le d+1 \right\}, \quad (9.101)$$

is called a *lattice of order k* in K. Note that the lattice of order k in K has $\binom{d+k}{k}$ elements.

Let $\mathcal{P}_k$ be the space of polynomials of degree equal to or less than k. Since a homogeneous polynomial of d variables and degree j has $\binom{d+j-1}{j}$ terms, the dimension of $\mathcal{P}_k$ is

$$1 + \binom{d}{1} + \binom{d+1}{2} + \cdots + \binom{d+k-1}{k} = \binom{d+k}{k}. \quad (9.102)$$

It can be shown that any polynomial of degree k is uniquely determined by its values at the $\binom{d+k}{k}$ points of the lattice of order k in K.

With the triple $\left(K, \sum_K^{(k)}, \mathcal{P}_k \right)$ we will build spaces of approximation V_h.

Let $\mathcal{T}_h$ be a partition of $\overline{\Omega}$ into simplices such that every face of a simplex K_i of $\mathcal{T}_h$ is either:

- A subset of Γ_D,
- A subset of Γ_R,

or

- A face of another simplex K_j of $\mathcal{T}_h$; in such a case K_i and K_j are said to be adjacent.

The diameter of K is denoted by h_K and $h = \max\{h_K, K \in \mathcal{T}_h\}$.

For $k \ge 1$ the following functional spaces are built associated to $\mathcal{T}_h$

$$V_h^k = \left\{ \psi_h \in C^0(\overline{\Omega}) : \psi_h|_K \in \mathcal{P}_k(K) \quad \forall K \in \mathcal{T}_h \right\}. \quad (9.103)$$

Clearly,

$$V_h^k \subset \prod_{K \in \mathcal{T}_h} \mathcal{P}_k(K). \quad (9.104)$$

---

[9]For $d = 3$, those are edges, faces, and vertices.

This inclusion simply states that any function of $\mathcal{V}_h^k$ is a polynomial of degree equal to or less than k over each individual element. Conversely, what is the necessary and sufficient condition for an element of $\prod_{K\in\mathcal{T}_h} \mathcal{P}_k(K)$ to be in $\mathcal{V}_h^k$, that is, for the polynomial pieces to stick with continuity? The above will hold if and only if for every pair of adjacent elements K_i and K_j, the pieces defined on them agree on the points

$$\sum\nolimits_{K_i}^{(k)} \cap \sum\nolimits_{K_j}^{(k)}. \tag{9.105}$$

Therefore, any function in $\mathcal{V}_h^k$ is uniquely determined by its values at the points of the set

$$\sum\nolimits_h^{(k)} = \bigcup_{K\in\mathcal{T}_h} \sum\nolimits_K^{(k)}. \tag{9.106}$$

From now on, $\mathcal{T}_h$ will be called a *triangulation* of Ω (even if the dimension d is different from 2) and the elements of $\sum_h^{(k)}$ *nodes of the triangulation*. Notice that there can be nodes that are not vertices.

The dimension of space $\mathcal{V}_h^k$ is the same as the number of nodes. Also, it is possible to define a basis of $\mathcal{V}_h^k$ such that its elements are functions with support reduced to a few elements of $\mathcal{T}_h$. Let N_h be the number of nodes that we will assume to be numbered.

$$\sum\nolimits_h^{(k)} = \left\{ \mathbf{q}_i : i = 1, \dots, N_h \right\}. \tag{9.107}$$

Node $\mathbf{q}_i$ contributes to the basis with function $\varphi_i \in \mathcal{V}_h^k$ uniquely determined by

$$\varphi_i(\mathbf{q}_j) = \delta_{ij} \quad 1 \leq j \leq N_h. \tag{9.108}$$

9.7.2 Coefficients Matrix and Independent Term in Two Dimensions

We consider the problem in two dimensions ($d = 2$). Let us see how to organize the calculations to build $\mathcal{A}_h$ and $\mathbf{b}_h$ in (9.64) and (9.65), respectively, if we choose the space of Lagrange triangular finite elements of degree one,

$$\mathcal{V}_h^1 = \left\{ \psi_h \in C^0(\overline{\Omega}) : \psi_h|_K \in \mathcal{P}_1(K) \quad \forall K \in \mathcal{T}_h \right\}. \tag{9.109}$$

First, we consider the calculations ignoring the boundary condition on Γ_D.

Let $\sum_h^{(1)}$ be the set of nodes of the triangulation $\mathcal{T}_h$ that we will assume to be numbered

$$\sum\nolimits_h^{(1)} = \left\{ \mathbf{q}_i : i = 1, \dots, N_h \right\}. \tag{9.110}$$

Notice that the dimension of $\mathcal{V}_h^1$ equals N_h. Any node $\mathbf{q}_j$ defines an element in the basis $\varphi_i \in \mathcal{V}_h^1$ such that

$$\varphi_i(\mathbf{q}_j) = \delta_{ij} \quad 1 \leq i, j \leq N_h. \tag{9.111}$$

Then the solution ϕ_h can be written as

$$\phi_h = \sum_{j=1}^{N_h} \xi_j \varphi_j \quad \text{and} \quad \xi_j = \phi_h(\mathbf{q}_j).$$

Therefore, the column vector $\left(\phi_h(\mathbf{q}_1), \ldots, \phi_h(\mathbf{q}_{N_h})\right)^t$ is the solution of the linear system (9.63). The calculation of $\mathcal{A}_h$ and $\mathbf{b}_h$ using formulas (9.64) and (9.65) respectively, is inefficient because the same integrals are calculated several times over the same triangles. The method described below, which is the one used in practice, is based on the concepts of *elementary matrix* and *assembling*. The idea is that we will compute the contribution to the matrix and right-hand side vector over each individual element of the triangulation and then we will assemble them together in a systematic way to build the global approximation of the solution.

Let us recall that the discretized problem in two dimensions (ignoring Dirichlet boundary conditions) can be written as follows:

PROBLEM 13 *Find* $\mathbf{u}_h = \phi_{h,m+1}^{n+1} \in \mathcal{V}_h^{(1)}$ *such that*

$$\sum_{i,j=1}^{2} \int_{\Omega} a_{ij} \frac{\partial \mathbf{u}_h}{\partial x_j} \frac{\partial \mathbf{v}_h}{\partial x_i} d\mathbf{x}$$

$$+ \int_{\Omega} \tilde{a}_0 \mathbf{u}_h \mathbf{v}_h d\mathbf{x}$$

$$+ \int_{\Gamma_R} \alpha \mathbf{u}_h \mathbf{v}_h d\Gamma$$

$$= \int_{\Omega} \tilde{f} \mathbf{v}_h d\mathbf{x} + \int_{\Gamma_R} g \mathbf{v}_h d\Gamma \qquad \forall \mathbf{v}_h \in \mathcal{V}_h^{(1)}, \tag{9.112}$$

where

$$\tilde{a}_0 = a_0 - \frac{1}{\Delta t}$$

$$\tilde{f} = f - \frac{1}{\Delta t} \phi_h^n \circ X_e + p_{h,m}^{n+1}.$$

Let us consider the first term of the left-hand-side of this equality. We have that

$$\sum_{i,j=1}^{2} \int_{\Omega} a_{ij} \frac{\partial \mathbf{u}_h}{\partial x_j} \frac{\partial \mathbf{v}_h}{\partial x_i} d\mathbf{x} = \sum_{K \in \mathcal{T}_h} \int_{K} \begin{pmatrix} \frac{\partial \mathbf{v}_h}{\partial x_1} & \frac{\partial \mathbf{v}_h}{\partial x_2} \end{pmatrix} \begin{pmatrix} a_{11} & a_{12} \\ a_{21} & a_{22} \end{pmatrix} \begin{pmatrix} \frac{\partial \mathbf{u}_h}{\partial x_1} \\ \frac{\partial \mathbf{u}_h}{\partial x_2} \end{pmatrix} d\mathbf{x}. \tag{9.113}$$

Let $\mathbf{c}_1^K, \mathbf{c}_2^K, \mathbf{c}_3^K$ be the vertices of the triangle K and m_{1K}, m_{2K}, m_{3K} the corresponding indices in the numbering of $\mathcal{T}_h$, that is assume

$$\mathbf{c}_1^K = \mathbf{q}_{m_{1K}}; \quad \mathbf{c}_2^K = \mathbf{q}_{m_{2K}}; \quad \mathbf{c}_3^K = \mathbf{q}_{m_{3K}}. \tag{9.114}$$

Let $\mathbf{v}_h \in V_h^{(1)}$ then $\mathbf{v}_{h/K} = \sum_{i=1}^3 \mathbf{v}_h\left(\mathbf{c}_i^K\right) \pi_i^K$, where π_i^K is the only polynomial of degree equal to or less than one, such that

$$\pi_i^K(\mathbf{c}_j^K) = \delta_{ij}. \tag{9.115}$$

Equivalently,

$$\mathbf{v}_{h/K} = \begin{pmatrix} \pi_1^K & \pi_2^K & \pi_3^K \end{pmatrix} \begin{pmatrix} \mathbf{v}_h\left(\mathbf{c}_1^K\right) \\ \mathbf{v}_h\left(\mathbf{c}_2^K\right) \\ \mathbf{v}_h\left(\mathbf{c}_3^K\right) \end{pmatrix} = \left[\Pi^K\right](\mathbf{v}_{h/K}). \tag{9.116}$$

Therefore,

$$
\begin{pmatrix} \frac{\partial \mathbf{v}_h}{\partial x_1} \\ \frac{\partial \mathbf{v}_h}{\partial x_2} \end{pmatrix} = \begin{pmatrix} \sum_{i=1}^3 \mathbf{v}_h\left(\mathbf{c}_i^K\right) \frac{\partial \pi_i^K}{\partial x_1} \\ \sum_{i=1}^3 \mathbf{v}_h\left(\mathbf{c}_i^K\right) \frac{\partial \pi_i^K}{\partial x_2} \end{pmatrix}
$$

$$
= \begin{pmatrix} \frac{\partial \pi_1^K}{\partial x_1} & \frac{\partial \pi_2^K}{\partial x_1} & \frac{\partial \pi_3^K}{\partial x_1} \\ \frac{\partial \pi_1^K}{\partial x_2} & \frac{\partial \pi_2^K}{\partial x_2} & \frac{\partial \pi_3^K}{\partial x_2} \end{pmatrix} \begin{pmatrix} \mathbf{v}_h\left(\mathbf{c}_1^K\right) \\ \mathbf{v}_h\left(\mathbf{c}_2^K\right) \\ \mathbf{v}_h\left(\mathbf{c}_3^K\right) \end{pmatrix}
$$

$$
= \left[\mathrm{D}\Pi^K\right](\mathbf{v}_{h/K}). \tag{9.117}
$$

Substitution of (9.117) into (9.113) yields

$$\sum_{i,j=1}^2 \int_\Omega a_{ij} \frac{\partial \mathbf{u}_h}{\partial x_j} \frac{\partial \mathbf{v}_h}{\partial x_i} d\mathbf{x} = \sum_{K \in \mathcal{T}_h} \int_K (\mathbf{v}_{h/K})^t \left[\mathrm{D}\Pi^K\right]^t \mathbf{A} \left[\mathrm{D}\Pi^K\right] (\mathbf{u}_{h/K}) d\mathbf{x}. \tag{9.118}$$

A similar process for the other terms leads to the following formulation of Problem 13:

$$
\sum_{K \in \mathcal{T}_h} (\mathbf{v}_{h/K})^t \left[\int_K \left[\mathrm{D}\Pi^K\right]^t \mathbf{A} \left[\mathrm{D}\Pi^K\right] d\mathbf{x} \right.
$$

$$
\left. + \int_K \tilde{a}_0 \left[\Pi^K\right]^t \left[\Pi^K\right] d\mathbf{x} + \int_{\partial K \cap \Gamma_R} \alpha \left[\Pi^K\right]^t \left[\Pi^K\right] d\Gamma \right] (\mathbf{u}_{h/K})
$$

$$
= \sum_{K \in \mathcal{T}_h} (\mathbf{v}_{h/K})^t \left[\int_K \left[\Pi^K\right]^t \tilde{f} d\mathbf{x} + \int_{\partial K \cap \Gamma_R} \left[\Pi^K\right]^t g \, d\Gamma \right] \tag{9.119}
$$

We introduce the Boolean matrix

$$
\left[\mathbf{M}^K\right] =
\begin{bmatrix}
 & \overset{\overset{m_{1K}}{\downarrow}}{} & \overset{\overset{m_{2K}}{\downarrow}}{} & \overset{\overset{m_{3K}}{\downarrow}}{} & & \\
0 & \dots & 1 & 0 & \dots & 0 \\
0 & 1 & 0 & \dots & \dots & 0 \\
0 & \dots & \dots & 1 & \dots & 0
\end{bmatrix},
$$

such that, for any vector $\mathbf{v}$ of N_h components

$$
\left[\mathbf{M}^K\right] (\mathbf{v}) =
\begin{bmatrix}
v_{m_{1K}} \\
v_{m_{2K}} \\
v_{m_{3K}}
\end{bmatrix}
= (v/_K), \tag{9.120}
$$

that is, matrix $\left[\mathbf{M}^K\right]$ selects among the set of all degrees of freedom $\mathbf{v} \in \mathbb{R}^{N_h}$ the three that correspond to the element K.

In that way, Problem 13 can be written as

$$
(\mathbf{v}_h)^t \left[\sum_{K \in \mathcal{T}_h} \left[\mathbf{M}^K\right]^t \left(\int_K \left[\mathbf{D}\Pi^K\right]^t \mathbf{A} \left[\mathbf{D}\Pi^K\right] d\mathbf{x} \right. \right.
$$

$$
\left. \left. + \int_K \widetilde{a}_0 \left[\Pi^K\right]^t \left[\Pi^K\right] d\mathbf{x} + \int_{\partial K \cap \Gamma_R} \alpha \left[\Pi^K\right]^t \left[\Pi^K\right] d\Gamma \right) \left[\mathbf{M}^K\right] \right] (\mathbf{u}_h)
$$

$$
= (\mathbf{v}_h)^t \left[\sum_{K \in \mathcal{T}_h} \left[\mathbf{M}^K\right]^t \left(\int_K \left[\Pi^K\right]^t f d\mathbf{x} + \int_{\partial K \cap \Gamma_R} \left[\Pi^K\right]^t g d\Gamma \right) \right]. \tag{9.121}
$$

Notice that this equality must be satisfied for all $\mathbf{v}_h \in \mathbb{R}^{N_h}$; therefore,

$$
\mathcal{A}_h = \sum_{K \in \mathcal{T}_h} \left[\mathbf{M}^K\right]^t \left[\mathcal{A}_h^K\right] \left[\mathbf{M}^K\right] \quad \text{and} \quad \mathbf{b}_h = \sum_{K \in \mathcal{T}_h} \left[\mathbf{M}^K\right]^t \left[\mathbf{b}_h^K\right], \tag{9.122}
$$

where

$$
\left[\mathcal{A}_h^K\right] = \int_K \left[\mathbf{D}\Pi^K\right]^t \mathbf{A} \left[\mathbf{D}\Pi^K\right] d\mathbf{x}
$$

$$
+ \int_K \widetilde{a}_0 \left[\Pi^K\right]^t \left[\Pi^K\right] d\mathbf{x}
$$

$$
+ \int_{\partial K \cap \Gamma_R} \alpha \left[\Pi^K\right]^t \left[\Pi^K\right] d\Gamma, \tag{9.123}
$$

and

$$\left[\mathbf{b}_h^K\right] = \int_K \left[\Pi^K\right]^t f d\mathbf{x} + \int_{\partial K \cap \Gamma_R} \left[\Pi^K\right]^t g d\Gamma. \tag{9.124}$$

The 3×3 matrix $\mathcal{A}_h^K$ is often called the *elementary matrix*, and the three-component vector $\mathbf{b}_h^K$ is the *elementary right-hand side*, corresponding to the element K.

The operations in (9.122) are known with the name of *assembling* of the elementary matrix and the right-hand-side terms. Let us see how it works in practice. By definition,

$$\left[\mathbf{M}^K\right]_{ij} = \delta_{m_i K j}. \tag{9.125}$$

Hence,

$$\left(\left[\mathbf{M}^K\right]^t \left[\mathcal{A}_h^K\right] \left[\mathbf{M}^K\right]\right)_{ij} = \sum_{s=1}^3 \left(\left[\mathbf{M}^K\right]^t \left[\mathcal{A}_h^K\right]\right)_{is} \left[\mathbf{M}^K\right]_{sj}$$

$$= \sum_{s=1}^3 \sum_{r=1}^3 \left[\mathbf{M}^K\right]_{ri} \left[\mathcal{A}_h^K\right]_{rs} \left[\mathbf{M}^K\right]_{sj}$$

$$= \sum_{s=1}^3 \sum_{r=1}^3 \delta_{m_r K i} \left[\mathcal{A}_h^K\right]_{rs} \delta_{m_s K j},$$

and therefore,

$$\left(\left[\mathbf{M}^K\right]^t \left[\mathcal{A}_h^K\right] \left[\mathbf{M}^K\right]\right)_{ij} = \begin{cases} 0 & \text{if} \quad i \neq m_{rK} \quad \text{or} \quad j \neq m_{sK} \quad r,s = 1,2,3 \\ [\mathcal{A}_h^K]_{rs} & \text{if} \quad i = m_{rK} \quad \text{and} \quad j = m_{sK} \quad r,s = 1,2,3. \end{cases} \tag{9.126}$$

In that way, for the calculation of $\mathcal{A}_h$ and $\mathbf{b}_h$ the following algorithm can be used:

- Initialize $\mathcal{A}_h$ and $\mathbf{b}$ to zero.
- Do a loop over the elements of $\mathcal{T}_h$. For every $K \in \mathcal{T}_h$, compute $\mathcal{A}_h^K$ and $\mathbf{b}_h^K$ and then define

$$(\mathcal{A}_h)_{m_{\alpha K} m_{\beta K}} = (\mathcal{A}_h)_{m_{\alpha K} m_{\beta K}} + \left[\mathcal{A}_h^K\right]_{\alpha\beta}$$

$$\left[\mathbf{b}_h\right]_{m_{\alpha K}} = (\mathbf{b}_h)_{m_{\alpha K}} + \left[\mathbf{b}_h^K\right]_\alpha.$$

Change to the Reference Element   The integrals that appear in the calculation of $\mathcal{A}_h^K$ and $\mathbf{b}_h^K$ will be done through a change of variable to the reference element. Integrals on the boundary and on the interior have to be dealt with differently. Therefore, we will denote

$$\left[\mathcal{A}_h^K\right]^1 = \int_K \left[D\Pi^K\right]^t \mathbf{A} \left[D\Pi^K\right] d\mathbf{x}$$

$$+ \int_K \tilde{a}_0 \left[\Pi^K\right]^t \left[\Pi^K\right] d\mathbf{x} \tag{9.127}$$

$$\left[\mathcal{A}_h^K\right]^2 = \int_{\partial K \cap \Gamma_R} \alpha \left[\Pi^K\right]^t \left[\Pi^K\right] d\Gamma, \tag{9.128}$$

and

$$\left[\mathbf{b}_h^K\right]^1 = \int_K \left[\Pi^K\right]^t f d\mathbf{x} \tag{9.129}$$

$$\left[\mathbf{b}_h^K\right]^2 = \int_{\partial K \cap \Gamma_R} \left[\Pi^K\right]^t g d\Gamma. \tag{9.130}$$

Let $\widehat{K}$ be the triangle of vertices

$$\widehat{\mathbf{c}}_1 = \begin{pmatrix} 0 \\ 0 \end{pmatrix}, \quad \widehat{\mathbf{c}}_2 = \begin{pmatrix} 1 \\ 0 \end{pmatrix}, \quad \widehat{\mathbf{c}}_3 = \begin{pmatrix} 0 \\ 1 \end{pmatrix}, \tag{9.131}$$

that we will call the *reference triangle*. Let K be any element of $\mathcal{T}_h$. There exists a unique affine invertible mapping $F_K : \widehat{K} \to K$ such that $F_K(\widehat{\mathbf{c}}_i) = \mathbf{c}_i^K$ for $i = 1, 2, 3$. It is the mapping

$$F_K(\hat{\mathbf{x}}) = \mathbf{C}_K \hat{\mathbf{x}} + \mathbf{c}_1^K, \tag{9.132}$$

where $\mathbf{C}_K$ is the matrix

$$\mathbf{C}_K = (\mathbf{c}_2^K - \mathbf{c}_1^K, \mathbf{c}_3^K - \mathbf{c}_1^K). \tag{9.133}$$

It is easy to check that

$$\pi_i^K \circ F_K = \widehat{\pi}_i, \qquad i = 1, 2, 3, \tag{9.134}$$

where

$$\widehat{\pi}_1(\widehat{x}_1, \widehat{x}_2) = 1 - \widehat{x}_1 - \widehat{x}_2, \tag{9.135}$$

$$\widehat{\pi}_2(\widehat{x}_1, \widehat{x}_2) = \widehat{x}_1, \tag{9.136}$$

$$\widehat{\pi}_3(\widehat{x}_1, \widehat{x}_2) = \widehat{x}_2. \tag{9.137}$$

Indeed, $\pi_i^K \circ F_K \in \mathcal{P}_1(\hat{K})$ and also $\left(\pi_i^K \circ F_K\right)(\widehat{\mathbf{c}}_j) = \widehat{\pi}_i(\widehat{\mathbf{c}}_j) = \delta_{ij}$.

The formula of the change of variable is

$$\int_K \psi \, d\mathbf{x} = \int_{\widehat{K}} \psi \circ F_K \left| \det C_K \right| d\widehat{\mathbf{x}}. \tag{9.138}$$

On the other hand, by the chain rule, we have that

$$\begin{pmatrix} \frac{\partial \widehat{\pi}_\alpha}{\partial \widehat{x}_1}(\widehat{\mathbf{x}}) \\ \frac{\partial \widehat{\pi}_\alpha}{\partial \widehat{x}_2}(\widehat{\mathbf{x}}) \end{pmatrix} = \begin{pmatrix} \frac{\partial (F_K)_1}{\partial \widehat{x}_1}(\widehat{\mathbf{x}}) & \frac{\partial (F_K)_2}{\partial \widehat{x}_1}(\widehat{\mathbf{x}}) \\ \frac{\partial (F_K)_1}{\partial \widehat{x}_2}(\widehat{\mathbf{x}}) & \frac{\partial (F_K)_2}{\partial \widehat{x}_2}(\widehat{\mathbf{x}}) \end{pmatrix} \begin{pmatrix} \frac{\partial \pi_\alpha^K}{\partial x_1}(F_K(\widehat{\mathbf{x}})) \\ \frac{\partial \pi_\alpha^K}{\partial x_2}(F_K(\widehat{\mathbf{x}})) \end{pmatrix}. \tag{9.139}$$

Therefore,

$$\begin{pmatrix} \frac{\partial \pi_\alpha^K}{\partial x_1} \\ \frac{\partial \pi_\alpha^K}{\partial x_2} \end{pmatrix} = \left[C_K^{-1} \right]^t \begin{pmatrix} \frac{\partial \widehat{\pi}_\alpha}{\partial \widehat{x}_1} \\ \frac{\partial \widehat{\pi}_\alpha}{\partial \widehat{x}_2} \end{pmatrix}, \tag{9.140}$$

or, in summarized form,

$$\left[D\Pi^K \right] = \left[C_K^{-1} \right]^t \left[D\widehat{\Pi} \right]. \tag{9.141}$$

Substituting this expression for $[D\Pi^K]$ in (9.127) we obtain

$$\left[\mathcal{A}_b^K \right]^1 = \int_{\widehat{K}} \left[D\widehat{\Pi} \right]^t \left[C_K^{-1} \right] A \left[C_K^{-1} \right]^t \left[D\widehat{\Pi} \right] \left| \det C_K \right| d\widehat{\mathbf{x}}$$

$$+ \int_{\widehat{K}} \widetilde{a}_0 \left[\widehat{\Pi} \right]^t \left[\widehat{\Pi} \right] \left| \det C_K \right| d\widehat{\mathbf{x}}.$$

If we introduce the following notation:

$$[G_K] = \left[C_K^{-1} \right] A \left[C_K^{-1} \right]^t$$

$$\Delta_K = \left| \det C_K \right|,$$

we may write

$$\left[\mathcal{A}_b^K \right]^1 = \Delta_K \int_{\widehat{K}} \left[D\widehat{\Pi} \right]^t [G_K] \left[D\widehat{\Pi} \right] d\widehat{\mathbf{x}}$$

$$+ \Delta_K \int_{\widehat{K}} \widetilde{a}_0 \left[\widehat{\Pi} \right]^t \left[\widehat{\Pi} \right] d\widehat{\mathbf{x}}. \tag{9.142}$$

Therefore,

$$\left[\mathcal{A}_h^K\right]_{\alpha\beta}^1 = \Delta_K \sum_{\mu,\gamma=1}^{2} \int_{\widehat{K}} \left[\mathbf{D}\widehat{\Pi}\right]_{\alpha\mu}^t \left[\mathbf{G}_K\right]_{\mu\gamma} \left[\mathbf{D}\widehat{\Pi}\right]_{\gamma\beta} d\widehat{\mathbf{x}} + \Delta_K \int_{\widehat{K}} \widetilde{a}_0 \widehat{\pi}_\alpha \widehat{\pi}_\beta d\widehat{\mathbf{x}}$$

$$= \Delta_K \sum_{\mu,\gamma=1}^{2} \int_{\widehat{K}} \left[\mathbf{G}_K\right]_{\mu\gamma} \frac{\partial \widehat{\pi}_\alpha}{\partial \widehat{x}_\mu} \frac{\partial \widehat{\pi}_\beta}{\partial \widehat{x}_\gamma} d\widehat{\mathbf{x}} + \Delta_K \int_{\widehat{K}} \widetilde{a}_0 \widehat{\pi}_\alpha \widehat{\pi}_\beta d\widehat{\mathbf{x}}. \qquad (9.143)$$

If the coefficients $a_{ij}, \widetilde{a}_0$ are constant in K, then $[G_K]$ is constant in K and

$$\left[\mathcal{A}_h^K\right]_{\alpha\beta}^1 = \Delta_K \sum_{\mu,\gamma=1}^{2} \left[\mathbf{G}_K\right]_{\mu\gamma} \int_{\widehat{K}} \frac{\partial \widehat{\pi}_\alpha}{\partial \widehat{x}_\mu} \frac{\partial \widehat{\pi}_\beta}{\partial \widehat{x}_\gamma} d\widehat{\mathbf{x}} + \Delta_K \widetilde{a}_0 \int_{\widehat{K}} \widehat{\pi}_\alpha \widehat{\pi}_\beta d\widehat{\mathbf{x}}. \qquad (9.144)$$

The numbers

$$\mathbf{H}_{\alpha\beta\mu\gamma} = \int_{\widehat{K}} \frac{\partial \widehat{\pi}_\alpha}{\partial \widehat{x}_\mu} \frac{\partial \widehat{\pi}_\beta}{\partial \widehat{x}_\gamma} d\widehat{\mathbf{x}} \qquad \text{and} \quad \mathbf{J}_{\alpha\beta} = \int_{\widehat{K}} \widehat{\pi}_\alpha \widehat{\pi}_\beta d\widehat{\mathbf{x}}, \qquad (9.145)$$

do not depend on the element considered and are calculated just once. Also, notice that

$$\mathbf{H}_{\alpha\beta\mu\gamma} = \mathbf{H}_{\beta\alpha\gamma\mu}, \quad \mathbf{J}_{\alpha\beta} = \mathbf{J}_{\beta\alpha} \quad \text{and} \quad \int_{\widehat{K}} \widehat{\pi}_\alpha^r \widehat{\pi}_\beta^s \, d\widehat{\mathbf{x}} = \frac{r!s!}{(r+s+2)!}. \qquad (9.146)$$

In this way, just the matrix $[G_K]$ and $\widetilde{a}_0$ depend on the element. The matrix $[G_K]$ is worked out using the values of a_{ij} and the coordinates of vertex $\mathbf{c}_i^K$. Completing the calculations described, we obtain

$$\left[\mathcal{A}_h^K\right]_{\alpha\beta}^1 = \frac{\Delta_K}{2} \begin{bmatrix} g_{11} + 2g_{12} + g_{22} & -(g_{11} + g_{21}) & -(g_{12} + g_{22}) \\ -(g_{11} + g_{12}) & g_{11} & g_{12} \\ -(g_{21} + g_{22}) & g_{21} & g_{22} \end{bmatrix}$$

$$+ \frac{\widetilde{a}_0 \Delta_K}{12} \begin{bmatrix} 1 & 1/2 & 1 \\ 1/2 & 1 & 1/2 \\ 1/2 & 1/2 & 1 \end{bmatrix}, \qquad (9.147)$$

where

$$
g_{11} = \Delta_K^{-2} \left\{ a_{11} \left(c_{32}^K - c_{12}^K \right)^2 + (a_{12} + a_{21}) \left(c_{11}^K - c_{31}^K \right) \left(c_{32}^K - c_{12}^K \right) \right.
$$
$$
\left. + a_{22} \left(c_{11}^K - c_{31}^K \right)^2 \right\},
$$
$$
g_{12} = g_{21} = \Delta_K^{-2} \left\{ a_{11} \left(c_{12}^K - c_{22}^K \right) \left(c_{32}^K + c_{12}^K \right) + a_{12} \left(c_{21}^K - c_{11}^K \right) \left(c_{32}^K - c_{12}^K \right) \right.
$$
$$
\left. + a_{21} \left(c_{12}^K - c_{22}^K \right) \left(c_{11}^K - c_{31}^K \right) + a_{22} \left(c_{21}^K - c_{11}^K \right) \left(c_{11}^K - c_{31}^K \right) \right\},
$$
$$
g_{22} = \Delta_K^{-2} \left\{ a_{11} \left(c_{12}^K - c_{22}^K \right)^2 + (a_{12} + a_{21}) \left(c_{21}^K - c_{11}^K \right) \left(c_{12}^K - c_{22}^K \right) \right.
$$
$$
\left. + a_{22} \left(c_{21}^K - c_{11}^K \right)^2 \right\}.
$$

Similarly, for the right-hand-side term we have that

$$
\left[\mathbf{b}_h^K \right]^1 = \Delta_K \int_{\widehat{K}} \left[\widehat{\Pi}^K \right]^t \widetilde{f} \left(F_K \left(\widehat{\mathbf{x}} \right) \right) d\widehat{\mathbf{x}}. \tag{9.148}
$$

We proceed to compute the boundary integrals of the elementary matrix and the right-hand side by a change of variable to the reference element. In order to do so, we will define parameterizations of the edges of K

$$
\text{Edge 1: } \gamma_K^1(\hat{\sigma}) = F_K \left(\hat{\sigma}, 0 \right) = \left(\mathbf{c}_2^K - \mathbf{c}_1^K \right) \hat{\sigma} + \mathbf{c}_1^K
$$

$$
\text{Edge 2: } \gamma_K^2(\hat{\sigma}) = F_K \left(1 - \hat{\sigma}, \hat{\sigma} \right) = \left(\mathbf{c}_3^K - \mathbf{c}_2^K \right) \hat{\sigma} + \mathbf{c}_2^K
$$

$$
\text{Edge 3: } \gamma_K^3(\hat{\sigma}) = F_K \left(0, 1 - \hat{\sigma} \right) = \left(\mathbf{c}_1^K - \mathbf{c}_3^K \right) \hat{\sigma} + \mathbf{c}_3^K.
$$

Therefore,

$$
\int_{l \text{ edge}} \psi \, d\tau = \int_0^1 \psi \left(\gamma_K^l(\hat{\sigma}) \right) \left| \mathbf{c}_{l+1}^K - \mathbf{c}_l^K \right| d\hat{\sigma} \quad \left(\mathbf{c}_4^K = \mathbf{c}_1^K \right), \tag{9.149}
$$

and finally we have

$$
\left[A_h^K \right]_{\alpha\beta}^2 = \sum_{l=1}^3 \chi_K^l \left| \mathbf{c}_{l+1}^K - \mathbf{c}_l^K \right| \int_0^1 \alpha \left(\gamma_K^l(\hat{\sigma}) \right) \widehat{\pi}_\alpha \left(\widehat{\gamma}^l(\hat{\sigma}) \right) \widehat{\pi}_\beta \left(\widehat{\gamma}^l(\hat{\sigma}) \right) d\hat{\sigma},
$$

$$
\left[b_h^K \right]_{\alpha}^2 = \sum_{l=1}^3 \chi_K^l \left| \mathbf{c}_{l+1}^K - \mathbf{c}_l^K \right| \int_0^1 \widehat{\pi}_\alpha \left(\widehat{\gamma}^l(\hat{\sigma}) \right) g \left(\gamma_K^l(\hat{\sigma}) \right) d\hat{\sigma},
$$

where

$$
\widehat{\gamma}^1(\hat{\sigma}) = (\hat{\sigma}, 0), \quad \widehat{\gamma}^2(\hat{\sigma}) = (1 - \hat{\sigma}, \hat{\sigma}), \quad \widehat{\gamma}^3(\hat{\sigma}) = (0, 1 - \hat{\sigma}), \tag{9.150}
$$

and

$$\chi_K^l = \begin{cases} 1 & \text{if} \quad l \subset \Gamma_R \\ 0 & \text{otherwise.} \end{cases} \tag{9.151}$$

The calculation of the integrals that appear in $\left[\mathbf{b}_h^K\right]_\alpha$, as well as the ones that appear in the elementary matrix when the coefficients a_{ij}, and $\tilde{a}_0$ are not constant in the element K, are done via numerical integration. It can be shown ([180]) that the error does not increase if an appropriate formula, which depends on the finite element space, is used.

CHAPTER 10

American Monte Carlo

10.1   INTRODUCTION

Traditionally, the numerical techniques for pricing derivatives fall into two distinct categories: Monte Carlo simulation and backwards induction methods such as trees or PDE methods. The following table sums up the strengths of each type:

	Monte Carlo	Trees/PDEs
Early exercise	N	Y
Path dependent	Y	N
Many underlyings	Y	N

In the most general terms, a derivative consists of a series of payments that depend on decisions made by the two parties in the contract and the values of some quantities observable in the market: the underlyings, which we will model with some stochastic processes. The payments can depend on the values of the underlyings observed on the date of the payment or on some functional of the paths followed by the underlyings up to the payment date.

To price derivatives using PDE methods, we must be able to represent the price of the derivative at time t as a function of a small number of state variables. For path-dependent options, the number of state variables may be larger than the number of underlyings. For instance, were we pricing an Asian option, our state-space at time t would have to include the current stock price and the running average stock price.

If we assume that our stock price follows the Black-Scholes SDE, and that the average is defined as

$$A_t = \frac{\sum_{t_i \le t} S_{t_i}}{\sum_{t_i \le t} 1},$$

for some set of averaging dates t_i, then we have the following PDE for the price of the derivative in between averaging dates.

$$\frac{\partial V}{\partial t} = r_t V - r_t S \frac{\partial V}{\partial S} - \frac{1}{2}\sigma^2 S^2 \frac{\partial^2 V}{\partial S^2}. \tag{10.1}$$

Across averaging dates we have the condition

$$V(S_{t_i}, A_{t_i^-}, t_i^-) = V(S_{t_i}, A_{t_i^+}, t_i^+), \tag{10.2}$$

where

$$A_{t_i^+} = \frac{1}{i+1}\left(S_{t_i} + iA_{t_i}\right) \tag{10.3}$$

At the maturity of the option, we calculate the final payment as a function of both S and A, suitably discretized, then evolve it back to the previous averaging date using equation (10.1). At that date, we can calculate the value of the option as a function of S and A before the averaging using equations (10.2) and (10.3).

The computational time taken to price derivatives using PDE methods scales exponentially with the number of state variables. For this reason, PDEs are not generally used to price options that depend on more than a few underlyings, or path-dependent options more complicated than simple knock-in/out barriers. For these options, Monte Carlo methods have traditionally been used.

In Monte Carlo pricing, we exploit the fact that the value of a series of payments, C_i at times t_i, can be written as

$$V(0) = \mathbb{E}^{\mathbb{Q}}\left[\sum_i \frac{C_i}{B_{t_i}}\right],$$

where B_t is the money market account and $\mathbb{Q}$ is the risk-neutral measure. We generate sample paths for the underlying processes and calculate the value the derivative would have if each path were realized. We then average over the paths to get the value of the option. We can easily handle path-dependent options, as we have the entire path available to us. Additionally, the time taken to price multiunderlying deals scales linearly with the number of underlyings involved, rather than exponentially as in the PDE case.

However, this approach cannot always be used directly when pricing options where the holder/issuer must make some decision that does not depend in a trivial way on the market data. In the case of a simple European call option, the exercise decision directly depends on the values of market observables (the stock price) on the exercise date and so the choice is trivial (we exercise if the stock is worth more than the strike) and can be incorporated into a Monte Carlo pricing. However, when the option can be exercised before maturity (i.e., the holder has an early exercise decision) the decision depends only indirectly on the market observables, through the price of another option. For example, at the maturity date of a European call with strike K, we know that we will exercise if $S > K$ and receive an amount $S - K$. For a monthly Bermudan call, the decision at the maturity date is identical (assuming we have not already exercised). However, one month from maturity we must decide whether we would rather receive $S - K$ immediately or keep what is effectively a one-month European call. Two months from maturity, we can either receive $S - K$

or a two-month Bermudan call and so on. Traditional Monte Carlo methods fall down here, as we have no way of calculating the values of these suboptions.[1]

In this chapter, we present some methods for pricing these options using Monte Carlo simulation. Throughout the chapter, we will use *expected continuation value* to mean the expected value of the remaining payments in the option (i.e., the value of continuing to hold the option). We will use *exercise value* to mean the value we would get for exercising the option immediately and *realized continuation value* to mean the value of the remaining payments in the option along a particular path. Note that the exercise decision can never be based on the realized continuation value as this would imply that the exerciser could foretell the future.

10.2 BROADIE AND GLASSERMAN

The expected continuation value at any exercise date is just the price of an option, seen at the exercise date. Pricing options with many exercise dates can be thought of as pricing options on options on options, and so on. We can always use Monte Carlo to price these suboptions, by starting a new Monte Carlo simulation for each path as it hits each exercise date. This was first suggested by Broadie and Glasserman [88].

We will assume we have a derivative that can be exercised at a set of dates $T_1 \dots T_N$, and that the evaluation date is T_0. From T_0 to T_1, we simulate P paths. At T_1, we split each path into P more paths from T_1 to T_2, each starting where the original path left off. At T_2, we split each of these P^2 paths into P more paths, and so on until the maturity of the option. This is shown in figure 10.1.

We can treat each set of paths that are common up to the last early exercise date T_{N-1} as a separate Monte Carlo and average over them to get the expected continuation value at T_{N-1} given the path up to that point. We can use this to decide whether or not to exercise for those paths at T_{N-1} (assuming we have not exercised beforehand). We then take all the paths that are common up to T_{N-2} and average over those to give the expected continuation value at T_{N-2}, and so on. We repeat this procedure until we get back to the evaluation date.

The number of paths needed for the final section of the path is P^N, which makes the algorithm prohibitively slow if there are several exercise dates. In fact, we do not need the whole path up to T_{N-1} in order to do a Monte Carlo simulation for the last period and therefore find the expected continuation value at T_{N-1}. Since problems will often be Markovian in just a few factors, any paths with identical Markov factors at the branching date will have identical expected continuation values. We can use this information to come up with a more efficient algorithm.

10.3 REGULARLY SPACED RESTARTS

When pricing using PDEs, we discretize our state space into a finite set of states at each date and store the expected continuation value for each of these possible

---

[1]Pricing options with early exercise decisions is not a problem with backwards pricing methods since at any exercise date t, the contents of our PDE grid will be the value (at t) of the remaining payments in the option (assuming we have not already exercised) as a function of the state space at t. In the Bermudan option case, we simply replace the contents of our grid at each node with $S - K$ if this is larger.

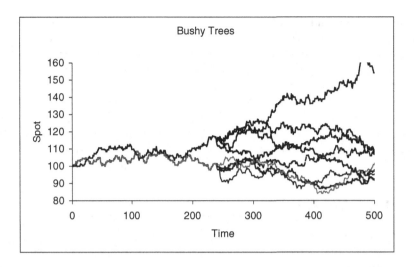

FIGURE 10.1 Broadie and Glasserman method. We simulate P paths up to the first exercise date, then divide each path into P new paths. At the second exercise date, we divide each of the P^2 paths into P new paths, and so on up until the maturity of the option.

states. We can do the same thing with Monte Carlo simulation. Starting at the last early-exercise date, we can discretize our state space in some way and start a Monte Carlo simulation at each point. For each point, we generate P paths running from time T_{N-1} to T_N and average over each set of paths to give the expected continuation value at each point in our discretized state-space at T_{N-1}.

We can now go back to the penultimate early-exercise date, T_{N-2}; again, we discretize the state-space and start a Monte Carlo simulation at each point, simulating P paths from T_{N-2} to T_{N-1}. For each path, we can decide whether the option would be exercised at T_{N-1} based on the exercise value at T_{N-1} and the expected continuation value there, which we estimate by interpolating between the points at which we started our first set of Monte Carlo simulations. For each new set of paths, we average over the paths to calculate the expected continuation value at time T_{N-2} as a function of the discretized state-space there. This is shown in figure 10.2.

We can iterate this until we get back to the evaluation date. This approach scales much more nicely with the number of early exercise dates and paths than the Broadie and Glasserman approach. However, it is still prohibitively slow, especially when we have to discretize in several dimensions at each fixing date. The time taken using P paths per starting point and M restart points per fixing in each of d directions is proportional to $M^d P$. Assuming the expected continuation value is a smooth function and we interpolate linearly, we will have a discretization error that scales as $1/M^2$. To get $1/\sqrt{P}$ convergence in our price, as we would expect from Monte Carlo, we therefore need $M \propto P^{1/4}$, making the CPU time scale as $P^{1+d/4}$.

In high-dimensional problems, this scaling can make the method completely impractical. No method based on calculating the expected continuation value at a discrete set of points across state space will be able to cope with very-high-dimensional problems as there is too much information to store or calculate. Take the example of an option on a basket of 20 stocks. If we try to estimate the expected continuation values on an M^{20} point mesh, even with $M = 3$, that is 3.5×10^9 values to store.

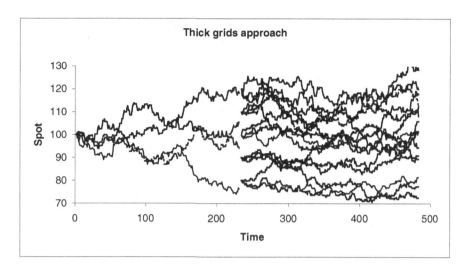

FIGURE 10.2 Regularly spaced restarts. At each early exercise date, we discretize the state space and for each point we simulate P paths up to the following exercise date and average to get the expected continuation value.

10.4 THE LONGSTAFF AND SCHWARTZ ALGORITHM

The Longstaff and Schwartz algorithm [189] is an algorithm for combining backwards induction and Monte Carlo simulation that overcomes the scaling of the previous two methods at the expense of introducing some bias into the answer. The algorithm is sometimes called least-squares American Monte Carlo.

As with the previous methods, we try to use Monte Carlo simulation to find the expected continuation value (CV^e) for each path at each early exercise date. As discussed in the previous section, we cannot hope to find CV^e as a function of all the Markov factors in a high-dimensional problem. In least-squares Monte Carlo, we instead try to reduce it to a function of a *few* relevant quantities: the *regression variables*. If we choose the regression variables well, this will drastically reduce the dimensionality of the problem of calculating CV^e. However, if we do not choose good regression variables, we will throw away useful information and find a bad exercise strategy and hence a biased price.

10.4.1 The Algorithm

The strategy is as follows. We simulate P complete paths up to the maturity of the option, then work backwards through the exercise dates. Assuming we have not exercised the option early, we calculate all of the payments made after the last early exercise date (T_{N-1}) and discount them to that date (for each path). We refer to this value as the realized continuation value, $CV_p^r(T_{N-1}^+)$, for each path p just after the early exercise date. For each path, we also calculate the values of some regression variables (observable at T_{N-1}), $\mathbf{r}_p^{N-1}$, on which we think the estimated continuation value will depend strongly. We then let the estimated continuation value, $CV^e(T_{N-1})$, be some parameterized functional form of the regression variables and try to find the parameters that gives the best fit (in a least-squares-error sense) to the realized continuation values. If our CV^e function has parameters $\mathbf{c}^{N-1}$, we can write

$$CV_p^e(T_{N-1}) = f^{N-1}(\mathbf{r}_p^{N-1}|\mathbf{c}^{N-1}).$$

We try to find the parameters $\mathbf{c}^{N-1}$ that minimize

$$\varepsilon(\mathbf{c}) = \sum_p \left[CV_p^r(T_{N-1}^+) - f^{N-1}(\mathbf{r}_p^{N-1}|\mathbf{c}^{N-1}) \right]^2. \tag{10.4}$$

Now that we have the function CV^e, we have an estimate of the expected continuation value for each path. We can use this to decide whether the option would be exercised for each path by comparing CV_p^e with the exercise value for the path at that exercise date: EV_p. If the holder of the option has the right to exercise, it will be exercised if $EV_p > CV_p^e$, whereas if the issuer has the right it will be exercised if $EV_p < CV_p^e$. According to this strategy, the realized continuation value for path p just before the exercise decision is made, $CV_p^r(T_{N-1}^-)$, is EV_p if we exercise and $CV_p^r(T_{N-1}^+)$ if we do not.

Note that although we use CV_p^e to determine whether or not we exercise, the value we get if we choose not to is $CV_p^r(T_{N-1}^+)$. This differs from the approach in the previous section where we set the realized value to CV_p^e (because CV_p^r was not available). This approach matches what would happen in real life and gives rise to a less biased result, as will be explained later.

Having calculated the realized continuation value just before the exercise date T_{N-1}, we discount these values back to date T_{N-2} where they become $CV_p^r(T_{N-2}^+)$. We repeat the above procedure to calculate $CV_p^+(T_{N-2}^-)$ and so $CV_p^r(T_{N-3}^+)$, and so on. We iterate this until we reach the evaluation date and have parameterized expected continuation values, CV^e, for each of the early exercise dates.

We could average over the realized continuation values for each path at the evaluation date ($CV_p^r(T_0)$) to give the price of the option. However, this gives rise to a slight bias (the *foresight bias*) as the exercise decision for each path will weakly depend on the realized continuation value for that path, through the regression coefficients. We discuss this bias in more detail in section 10.5. It is common practice to remove this bias by using a separate set of Monte Carlo paths to price the option.[2] We will refer to the two sets of paths as the regression paths and the pricing paths.

---

[2]There are practical reasons for using separate regression and pricing paths. In general, the computational time for one regression path will be more than that for one pricing path. Also, random errors in the functions CV^e only have a second-order effect on the overall price (see section 10.5), so we can afford to use fewer paths to estimate these functions than we need to use to find the final price. There is also an issue with the amount of memory used in the regression phase of the algorithm. Since we have to store all paths in the regression phase (or recalculate them, expensively), for some problems we can run out of memory trying to store too many paths. Instead, we can use a smaller number of paths in the regression phase, few enough to fit in the computer's memory, and then use a larger number of paths in a separate pricing phase, where we can calculate one path at a time and discard them after they have been processed.

With each of the pricing paths, we can repeat the above backwards-induction algorithm (but omitting the regression step and using the previously calculated regression coefficients) to find $CV_p^r(T_0)$. Alternatively, we can loop forward over the exercise dates until we find the date at which the option will be exercised; we then discount the exercise value at this date to the evaluation date to give $CV_p^r(T_0)$.

10.4.2   Example: A Call Option with Monthly Bermudan Exercise

To demonstrate the regression phase of the algorithm we will consider the simple example of a Bermudan option with monthly exercise dates and a maturity of two years. The strike of the option is set to 100, which is the current spot price.

If we price this with deterministic volatility, hazard, and interest rates, then the estimated continuation value at time T_{N-1} can only depend on the stock price at that time, so we choose this as our regression variable. The first two columns of the table below show the values of the stock at times T_{N-1} and T_N. If we choose not to exercise the option at T_{N-1}, we will eventually receive $\max(S_N - 100, 0)$ at T_N. Discounting this back to T_{N-1} (using the discount factor of 0.997) gives the realized continuation values shown in the third column.

S_{N-1}	S_N	$CV^r(T_{N-1}^+)$
112.07	114.67	14.62
86.19	95.53	0
106.74	90.20	0
109.77	113.82	13.78

Our decision on whether or not to exercise will be based on the estimated continuation value, which we will model as a cubic function of the regression variable (S_{N-1}):

$$CV_{N-1}^e(S_{N-1}) = a_{N-1} + b_{N-1}S_{N-1} + c_{N-1}S_{N-1}^2 + d_{N-1}S_{N-1}^3.$$

Taking all the paths into account, we try to find the regression coefficients, a, b, c and d, that minimize equation (10.4). (Details of how to do this are given in section 10.5.2.) We find the least-square error comes from the polynomial

$$CV_{N-1}^e(S_{N-1}) = 37.18 - 1.19S_{N-1} + 0.0098S_{N-1}^2 - 0.000011S_{N-1}^3. \qquad (10.5)$$

Figure 10.3 shows the results of fitting a cubic function to 2000 paths. The points are the realized continuation values, and the line is the above cubic function.

The table below shows the same four paths but we have added two extra columns. The fourth column shows the estimated continuation value found using equation (10.5), and the fifth column shows the value we get if we choose to exercise immediately.

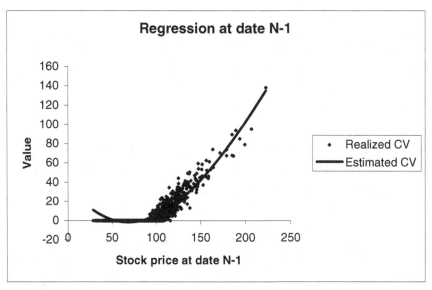

FIGURE 10.3 Result of fitting a cubic to the realized continuation values at the penultimate exercise date of a Bermudan call option.

S_{N-1}	S_N	$CV^r(T_{N-1}^+)$	$CV^e(T_{N-1})$	EV_{N-1}	$CV^r(T_{N-1}^-)$
112.07	114.67	14.62	11.62	12.07	12.07
86.19	95.53	0	0.60	0	0
106.74	90.20	0	8.65	6.74	0
109.77	113.82	13.78	10.30	9.77	13.78

For the first path, $CV^e < EV$, so we choose to exercise the option immediately. For the remaining three paths, $CV^e > EV$, so we choose not to exercise the option. The final column of the table shows the realized continuation value for each path just before the exercise decision. Note that for the third path, we decide not to exercise but the option ultimately expires worthless; not exercising was the best decision we could make with the information available at the exercise date.

For the next step in the regression phase, we take the realized values at date T_{N-1} and discount them back to date T_{N-2} where they become the realized continuation values, CV^r. The discount factor for T_{N-2} to T_{N-1} is 0.997, giving the following results.

S_{N-2}	S_{N-1}	$CV^r(T_{N-2}^+)$
110.95	112.07	12.03
92.11	86.19	0
109.18	106.74	0
119.21	109.77	13.74

We have included S_{N-1} only for comparison with earlier tables; it is not used in this step of the regression phase. Now we have a new set of regression variables (S_{N-2})

and corresponding realized continuation values, CV^r, so we repeat the above step to estimate CV^e at date T_{N-2}. We repeat this until we get back to the evaluation date.

10.5   ACCURACY AND BIAS

In the above algorithm, we have four main sources of error—three in the regression phase and one in the pricing phase.

Like any Monte Carlo price, both the regression and pricing phases suffer from random errors. If we use too few paths in the pricing phase, our result will not be very accurate. Similarly, if we use too few paths in the regression phase, the regression coefficients will not be very accurate, which in turn means our exercise strategy will not be optimal.

For options with a single regression variable, such as the one considered above, the error coming from the pricing phase is likely to be much bigger than the error coming from the regression phase, for the same number of paths. The only points where the accuracy of the regression coefficients matter are the points where CV^e and EV cross over and we move from a region where it is optimal to exercise to a region where it is optimal to hold on to the option—in other words, the exercise boundary.

If our function CV^e is slightly wrong, the position of the exercise boundaries (and therefore our exercise strategy) will also be slightly wrong. However, in the vicinity of the true exercise boundary, it makes little difference whether we exercise or hold on to the option as both choices result in very similar prices. Small errors in CV^e therefore have a much smaller effect on the overall pricing—in fact the error in the pricing scales as the square of the error in the exercise boundary.

A more important source of error comes from the fact we are modeling CV^e by some smooth parameterized function. This might not have enough freedom accurately to approximate the true expected continuation values. In figure 10.4, we show CV^e for the penultimate exercise date of the Bermudan call approximated with cubic and quintic functions, as well as the exact answer.

Clearly the cubic and quintic do not—indeed cannot—fit the real expected CV for all spots, although the quintic does a much better job than the cubic. These errors do not go away as we increase the number of paths used in the regression phase, which means that for this option, American Monte Carlo gives only a lower bound to the price. This is a general result: The Longstaff and Schwartz algorithm always gives a suboptimal exercise strategy and so if the holder has the right to exercise, the algorithm will always give a lower bound, whereas if only the issuer has the right to exercise, the algorithm will give an upper bound to the price.

Figure 10.4 also demonstrates why we use CV^r and not CV^e as the realized value of the option if we choose not to exercise. The inaccurate values of CV^e have only a small effect on the pricing when we use them only to determine the exercise strategy; were we to use them as the realized values for nonexercised paths, the errors in CV^e would become errors in our final price, potentially leading to very biased results. We would also have no guarantee that we had found a lower (or upper) bound to the price.

The polynomials in figure 10.4 do not agree closely with the more accurate piecewise-linear function. We show how to improve on this in section 10.5.1.

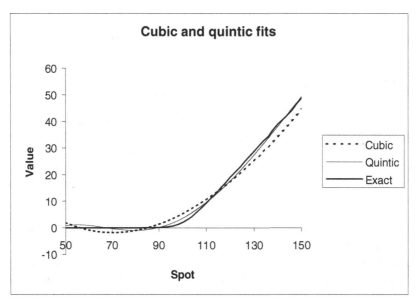

FIGURE 10.4   Fits to the expected continuation value at the penultimate exercise date of a Bermudan call option.

The final source of error is the foresight bias mentioned in section 10.4.1. In the regression phase, the exercise decision for each path depends on the regression coefficients, which in turn depend on the realized continuation value for that path. We therefore have a small foresight bias; for a low number of paths, our exercise strategy will be better (for those paths) than the real-world exercise strategy. In figure 10.5, we show the results of pricing an at-the-money call option, exercisable after 2y and 4y.

Generally, this foresight bias will be much smaller than the random error in the price, and can be reduced by using independent pricing and regression paths. However, for derivatives with many early exercise dates, this error may be compounded up until it is significant. See Fries [190] for more details.

10.5.1   Extension: Regressing on In-the-Money Paths

In the above example with the cubic function, CV^e becomes slightly negative for some out-of-the-money paths of the stock price when in reality we know it must be slightly positive. This is just an artifact of fitting a polynomial to the data. In the region where CV^e becomes negative, our strategy would tell us to exercise the option even though we receive nothing and give up the chance to receive a positive amount at the next exercise date. In reality, we would never consider exercising the option unless it were in-the-money. We can use this to improve our pricing.

Since we will consider exercising the option only when it is in-the-money, we also only need to know CV^e for the paths where the option is in-the-money. Instead of fitting a cubic to all the points in figure 10.3, we can just fit it to the in-the-money points (i.e., where the stock is above the strike at T_{N-1}). The result of doing this is shown in figure 10.6.

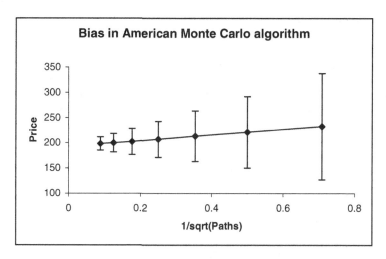

FIGURE 10.5 Foresight bias when pricing an in-the-money call, exercisable after 2y and 4y. The line shows the average price of the option from 10,000 independent pricings, each using P paths, against $P^{-0.5}$. The error bars are one standard deviation of the random errors in each individual pricing. Here the bias scales as $P^{-0.5}$, and is equivalent to approximately one third of a standard deviation.

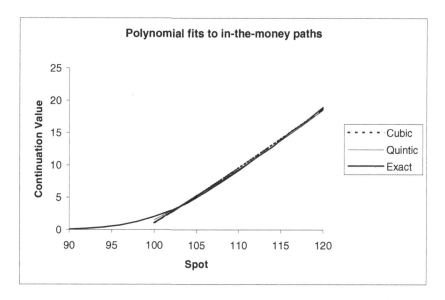

FIGURE 10.6 Cubic and quintic fits to the expected continuation value using only the in-the-money paths.

The fit to the in-the-money region is now much better than when we tried to fit all points at once. The fit to the region that's out-of-the-money is truly abysmal, but since we know we're not going to exercise there anyway, it doesn't matter.

For any option where we know we will not exercise if some condition does not hold, we can improve the performance of the algorithm by only regressing on paths that could potentially be exercised, and never exercising paths that can never be exercised (regardless of the estimated expected continuation value).

10.5.2 Linear Regression

We will now go into more detail on how to fit the CV^e functions.

Assuming we have a set of regression variables $\mathbf{r}_p$ and realized continuation values CV_p^r, how should we fit a function $CV^e(\mathbf{r}_p)$? Dropping the $N-1$ indices from equation (10.4), we want to minimize

$$\varepsilon(\mathbf{c}) = \sum_p \left[CV_p^r - f(\mathbf{r}_p|\mathbf{c}) \right]^2.$$

For a general nonlinear function of the coefficients, we would have to use some general minimization algorithm like the Newton-Raphson algorithm described in section 3.6.1. However, since we may have thousands or even millions of paths, this will be incredibly slow. For this reason, we restrict the allowed functions to linear functions of the coefficients. We write

$$CV_p^e = f(\mathbf{r}_p|\mathbf{c})$$

$$= \sum_{k=1}^{K} f_k(\mathbf{r}_p)c_k.$$

Letting

$$F_p^k = f_k(\mathbf{r}_p),$$

we have

$$\varepsilon(\mathbf{c}) = \sum_p \left[CV_p^r - \sum_k F_p^k c_k \right]^2$$

$$= A - 2\mathbf{R}^T \mathbf{c} + \mathbf{c}^T \mathbf{M} \mathbf{c} \qquad (10.6)$$

where

$$A = \sum_p (CV_p^r)^2,$$

$\mathbf{R}$ is the vector

$$R_i = \sum_p F_p^i CV_p^r,$$

and $\mathbf{M}$ is the symmetric matrix

$$M_{ij} = \sum_p F_p^i F_p^j.$$

Note that once we have computed A, $\mathbf{R}$, and $\mathbf{M}$, the computational time taken to calculate the mean-square error ε for a given trial set of parameters, $\mathbf{c}$, is independent of the number of paths. This makes linear regression much faster than fitting some nonlinear function.

Differentiating equation (10.6) with respect to c_k gives

$$\frac{\partial \varepsilon}{\partial c_k} = 2 \sum_{k'} c_{k'} M_{kk'} - 2 R_k.$$

To find the coefficients that minimize ε, we need to solve the simultaneous equations

$$\mathbf{Mc} = \mathbf{R}. \tag{10.7}$$

Since $\mathbf{M}$ is a symmetric matrix, we can invert equation (10.7) by finding the Cholesky decomposition of $\mathbf{M}$. However, it is possible that one or more of the regression coefficients has no effect on the solution or that some of the functions are linearly dependent, either through the choice of regression functions or through using an insufficient number of paths. There is also the possibility that if the real matrix $\mathbf{M}$ is close to singular, then numerical rounding/truncation errors may cause it to have negative eigenvalues and so according to equation (10.6) there will be no minimum of ε. Cholesky decomposition will fail if $\mathbf{M}$ has zero or negative eigenvalues, so instead we use singular value decomposition as a more robust way of solving equation (10.7).

In singular value decomposition (SVD), we decompose the matrix $\mathbf{M}$ as

$$\mathbf{M} = \mathbf{UDV}^T, \tag{10.8}$$

where $\mathbf{U}$ and $\mathbf{V}$ are orthogonal matrices and $\mathbf{D}$ is a diagonal matrix containing the singular values of $\mathbf{M}$ (i.e., the eigenvalues of $\mathbf{M}^2$). Since $\mathbf{M}$ is a real, symmetric $K \times K$ matrix, $\mathbf{U}$, $\mathbf{V}$ and $\mathbf{D}$ are also $K \times K$ matrices and we have

$$\mathbf{c} = \mathbf{VD}^{-1}\mathbf{U}^T\mathbf{R}. \tag{10.9}$$

Now if there exist any linear combinations of the regression coefficients that are zero for all paths (i.e., the regression functions are not linearly independent), there will be elements of $\mathbf{D}$ that are zero. The corresponding columns of $\mathbf{V}$ are called the nullspace of $\mathbf{M}$. If the vector $\mathbf{e}$ is in the nullspace, we have $\mathbf{Me} = 0$, and so any component of $\mathbf{c}$ in this direction has no effect on ε and so cannot be determined. We can therefore set the components of $\mathbf{c}$ in these directions to something arbitrary without affecting the result. To set the components to zero, we set the corresponding elements of $\mathbf{D}^{-1}$ to zero.

In fact, very small singular values may be the result of numerical rounding errors and so it is best to ignore all singular values below some threshold. *Numerical Recipes* [70] suggests ignoring all singular values which are less than ϵ of the largest singular value, where ϵ is machine precision (about 10^{-15} for double-precision numbers) by setting the corresponding elements of $\mathbf{D}^{-1}$ to zero.

10.5.3   Other Regression Schemes

If the expected continuation value we are trying to approximate is not a particularly smooth function of the regression variables, fitting it with a polynomial will smooth out features that we want to capture. A common alternative is to break the phase space up into smaller regions and fit either a constant or some other functional form in each region. If we split the domain of possible regression variables into groups A_i, we can write the expected continuation value as

$$CV^e(\mathbf{r}) = \sum_{ik} f_k^i(\mathbf{r}) 1_{\mathbf{r} \in A_i}.$$

One way of doing this is to perform a separate regression for each set of paths, the i'th set of paths being all the paths for which $\mathbf{r}_p \in A_i$. The limit of fitting just a constant for each group is Tilley's method [191].

An alternative method is just to treat

$$f_k^i(\mathbf{r}) 1_{\mathbf{r} \in A_i}$$

as separate regression functions and do a single regression but with many regression functions. The SVD method described in section 10.5.2 is robust enough to handle this. The "exact" lines in figures 10.4 and 10.6 were produced by fitting piecewise-linear functions in this way.

The drawback of this approach is that the more partitions are used, the fewer paths fall into each partition, so we must use a greater number of overall paths to guarantee a good accuracy of the estimated continuation value. We must also be careful how we choose the partitions, making sure that we are likely to get a reasonable number of paths in each. This approach can work well for low-dimensional problems where the phase space can easily be partitioned, but for higher-dimensional problems, the number of partitions (and consequently the number of paths we need to use) may make the algorithm too slow.

10.5.4   Upper Bounds

The Longstaff and Schwartz algorithm gives a lower bound for options where the holder has the right to exercise. Upper bounds to the price can be found using strategies proposed by Rogers [192] and Andersen and Broadie [193]. The value of an option can be expressed as

$$Q = \sup_{\tau} \mathbb{E} \left[\frac{h_\tau}{B_\tau} \right]$$

where τ is a stopping time and h_t is the value of exercising at time t. In other words the option is worth the expectation of the discounted cashflows from the optimal exercise strategy. The Longstaff and Schwartz algorithm effectively tried to find the optimal stopping strategy, but in reality would always find a less-than-optimal strategy and hence give a lower bound to the price.

In Rogers and the like, they express the price in terms of a dual formulation

$$Q = \inf_M \left(M_0 + \mathbb{E}\left[\max_{t \in T_i} \left(\frac{h_t}{B_t} - M_t \right) \right] \right),$$

where M is some martingale. The strategy then becomes to find the M that minimizes the above expression. The better the choice of M, the tighter the upper bound.

10.6 PARAMETERIZING THE EXERCISE BOUNDARY

In the previous section, we discussed the Longstaff and Schwartz algorithm, where the expected continuation value is parameterized as a function of some regression variables. The estimate of the expected continuation value was only used to decide the exercise strategy; all that mattered was whether it was greater or less than EV.

This gives rise to an alternative strategy suggested by Andersen [194]. Instead of parameterizing the expected continuation value, we can parameterize the exercise boundary itself. This strategy can only work if we already have some knowledge of the topology of the exercise regions (e.g., how many exercise boundaries we need to find). If we allow the strategy to find an arbitrary number of exercise regions, we will end up with an exercise region around each path where $CV^r < EV$ (i.e., perfect foresight).

As an example, consider the example of the Bermudan call option again. We know that we only exercise such an option before maturity in order to receive a dividend. We give up some optionality in exercising the option, but the value of this optionality decreases the more in the money the option becomes, so there is some stock price above which we will exercise the option and below which we will not. We can find the best exercise boundary for a set of paths by finding the path p' that minimizes

$$\mathbb{E}[(EV_p - CV_p^r)1_{S_p > S_{p'}}].$$

If we sort the paths by their stock prices, we just need to find $S_{p'}$ that minimizes

$$\frac{1}{P}\sum_{p=1}^{p'}[EV_p - CV_p^r].$$

As we increase the total number of paths used, $S_{p'}$ will converge to the correct exercise boundary. Note that this strategy is biased—the exercise strategy will always be better for those paths than we could hope for in real life, so this procedure will give an upper bound to the price. If we then price the option with a new set of paths but using the same exercise boundary, we can generate a lower bound to the price.

Bibliography

[1] Blanchet-Scalliet, C., and Jeanblanc, M. Hazard rate for credit risk and hedging defaultable contingent claims, Working Paper, 2002.

[2] Delbaen F., and Schachermayer, W. A general version of the fundamental theorem of asset pricing. *Mathematische Annalen* 300:463–520 (1994).

[3] Samuelson, P. Rational theory of warrant pricing. *Industrial Management Review* 6: 13–31 (1965).

[4] Merton, R.C. The theory of rational option pricing. *Bell Journal of Economics and Management Science* 4:141–183 (1973).

[5] Black, F., and Scholes, M. The pricing of options and corporate liabilities. *Journal of Political Economy*, 81: 637–59 (1973).

[6] Balland, P. Deterministic implied volatility models. *Quantitative Finance* 2: 31–44 (2002).

[7] Kellerer, H. Markov-komposition und eine anwendung auf martingale (in German). *Mathematische Annalen* 198: 217–229 (1972).

[8] Cox, J. The constant elasticity of variance option pricing model. *Journal of Portfolio Management* (December 1998).

[9] Föllmer, H., and Schied. *Stochastic Finance.* 2nd edition. Berlin: de Gruyter, 2004.

[10] Madan, D., and Yor, M. Making Markov martingales meet marginals: with explicit constructions. Working Paper 2002.

[11] Dupire, B. Pricing with a smile. *Risk* 7 (1):18–20, 1996.

[12] Gyöngy, I. Mimicking the one-dimensional marginal distributions of processes having an Ito differential". *Probability Theory and Related Field* 71:501–516, 1986.

[13] Revuz, D., and Yor, M. *Continuous Martingales and Brownian Motion,* 3rd ed. Heidelberg: Springer, 1999.

[14] Merton, R.C. Option pricing with discontinuous returns. *Bell Journal of Financial Economics* 3: 145–166 (1976).

[15] Protter, P. *Stochastic Integration and Differential Equations,* 2nd edition. Heidelberg: Springer, 2004.

[16] Buehler, H. Expensive martingales. *Quantitative Finance* (April 2006).

[17] Glasserman, P. *Monte Carlo Methods in Financial Engineering.* Heidelberg: Springer, 2004.

[18] Buehler, H. Volatility markets: Consistent modelling, hedging and practical implementation. PhD thesis, 2006.

[19] Heston, S. A closed-form solution for options with stochastic volatility with applications to bond and currency options. *Review of Financial Studies* (1993).

[20] Aït-Sahalia, Y., and Kimmel, R. Maximum likelihood estimation of stochastic volatility models. NBER Working Paper No. 10579, June 2004.

[21] Andersen, L., Piterbarg, V. Moment explosions in stochastic volatility models. Working Paper, April 15, 2004. http://ssrn.com/abstract=559481.

[22] Carr, P., and Madan, D. Towards a theory of volatility trading. In Robert Jarrow (ed.). *Volatility.* London: Risk, (2002), 417–427.

[23] Lewis, A. *Option Valuation under Stochastic Volatility*. Newport Beach, CA: Finance Press, 2000.

[24] Hagan, P., Kumar, D., Lesniewski, A., Woodward, D. "Managing smile risk," *Wilmott*, pp. 84–108 (September 2002).

[25] Jourdain, B. Loss of martingality in asset price models with lognormal stochastic volatility. Working Paper, 2004. http://cermics.enpc.fr/reports/CERMICS-2004/CERMICS-2004-267.pdf

[26] Hagan, P., Lesniewski, A., and Woodward, D. Probability distribution in the SABR model of stochastic volatility. Working Paper, March 22, 2005.

[27] Henry-Labordère, P. "A general asymptotic implied volatility for stochastic volatility models". April 2005 http://ssrn.com/abstract=698601

[28] Bourgade, P., Croissant, O. Heat kernel expansion for a family of stochastic volatility models: δ-geometry. Working Paper, 2005. http://arxiv.org/abs/cs.CE/0511024.

[29] Scott, L. Option pricing when the variance changes randomly: theory, estimation and an application. *Journal of Financial and Quantitative Analysis* 22:419–438 (1987).

[30] Fouque, J-P., Papanicolaou, G., and Sircar, K. *Derivatives in Financial Markets with Stochastic Volatility*. New York: Cambridge University Press: 2000.

[31] Overhaus, M., Ferraris, A., Knudsen, T., Milward, R., Nguyen-Ngoc, L., and Schindlmayr, G. *Equity Derivatives—Theory and Applications*. Hoboken, NJ: Wiley, 2002.

[32] Schoutens, W. *Levy Processes in Finance*. Hoboken, NJ: Wiley, 2003.

[33] Cont, R., and Tankov, P. *Financial Modelling with Jump Processes*. Boca Raton, FL: CRC Press, 2003.

[34] Schoebel, R., and Zhu, J. Stochastic volatility with an Ornstein-Uhlenbeck process: An Extension. *European Finance Review* 3:2346 (1999).

[35] Bates, D. Jumps and stochastic volatility: Exchange rate process implicit in deutschemark options. *Review of Financial Studies* 9:69–107 (1996).

[36] Brace, A., Goldys, B., Klebaner, F., and Womersley, R. Market model of stochastic implied volatility with application to the BGM model. Working Paper, 2001. http://www.maths.unsw.edu.au/~rsw/Finance/svol.pdf.

[37] Schönbucher, P.J. A market model for stochastic implied volatility. *Philosophical Transactions of the Royal Society A* 357:2071–2092 (1999).

[38] Cont, R., da Fonseca, J., and Durrleman, V. Stochastic models of implied volatility surfaces. *Economic Notes* 31(2): 361–377 (2002).

[39] Haffner, R. *Stochastic Implied Volatility*. Heidelberg: Springer, 2004.

[40] Derman, E., and Kani, I. Stochastic implied trees: Arbitrage pricing with stochastic term and strike structure of volatility/*International Journal of Theoretical and Applied Finance* 1(1):61–110 (1998).

[41] Barndorff-Nielsen, O., Graversen, S., Jacod, J., Podolskij, M., and Shephard, N. A central limit theorem for realised power and bipower variations of continuous semimartingales. Working Power 2004. http://www.nuff.ox.ac.uk/economics/papers/2004/W29/BN-G-J-P-S_fest.pdf.

[42] Demeterfi, K., Derman, E., Kamal, M., and Zou, J. More than you ever wanted to know about volatility swaps. *Journal of Derivatives* 6(4):9–32 (1999).

[43] Carr, P., and Madan, D. Towards a theory of volatility trading. In: Robert Jarrow, ed., *Volatility*. Risk Publications, pp. 417–427 (2002).

[44] Carr, P., and Lewis, K. Corridor variance swaps. *Risk* (February 2004).

[45] El Karoui, N., Jeanblanc-Picquè, M., and Shreve, S.E. Robustness of the Black and Scholes formula. *Mathematical Finance* 8:93 (April 1998).

[46] Carr, P., and Lee, R. Robust replication of volatility derivatives. Working Paper, April 2003. http://math.uchicago.edu/ rl/voltrading.pdf.

[47] Heath, D., Jarrow, R. and Morton, A. Bond pricing and the term structure of interest rates: A new methodology for contingent claims valuation. *Econometrica* 60(1992).

[48] Bergomi, L. Smile dynamics II. *Risk* (September 2005).

[49] Buehler, H. Consistent variance curves *Finance and Stochastics* (2006).

[50] Musiela, M. Stochastic PDEs and term structure models. *Journées Internationales de France*, IGR-AFFI, La Baule (1993).

[51] Björk, T., and Svensson, L. On the existence of finite dimensional realizations for nonlinear forward rate models. *Mathematical Finance*, 11(2): 205–243(2001).

[52] Filipovic, D. *Consistency Problems for Heath-Jarrow-Morton Interest Rate Models* (Lecture Notes in Mathematics 1760). Heidelberg: Springer, 2001

[53] Filipovic, D., and Teichmann, J. On the geometry of the term structure of interest rates. *Proceedings of the Royal Society London A* 460: 129–167 (2004).

[54] Buehler, H. Volatility markets: Consistent modeling, hedging and practical implementation. PhD thesis TU Berlin, to be submitted 2006.

[55] Björk, T., and Christensen, B.J. Interest rate dynamics and consistent forward curves. *Mathematical Finance* 9(4): 323–348 (1999).

[56] Duffie, D., Pan, J., and Singleton, K. "Transform analysis and asset pricing for affine jump-diffusions. *Econometrica* 68: 1343–1376 (2000).

[57] Dupire, B. Arbitrage pricing with stochastic volatility. In Carr, P., *Derivatives Pricing: The Classic Collection* pp. 197–215, London: Risk, 2004.

[58] Sin, C. Complications with stochastic volatility models. *Advances in Applied Probability* 30: 256–268 (1998).

[59] Brace, A., Gatarek, D., and Musiela, M. The market model of interest rate dynamics. *Mathematical Finance* 7: 127–154 (1997).

[60] Heath, D., Jarrow, R., and Morton, A. Bond pricing and the term structure of interest rates: A new methodology for contingent claims valuation. *Econometrica* 61(1): 77–105 (1992).

[61] Hull J., and White, A. One-factor interest-rate models and the valuation of interest rate derivatives. *Journal of Financial and Quantitative Analysis* 28: 235–254 (1993).

[62] Vasicek, O. An equilibrium charecterisation of the term structure. *Journal of Financial Economics* 5: 177–188 (1997).

[63] Black, F., and Karasinski P. Bond and option pricing when short rates are lognormal. *Financial Analysts Journal* (July–August 1991): 52–59.

[64] Cox, J.C., Ingersoll, J.E., and Ross, S.A., A theory of the term structure of interest rates. *Econometrica* 53: 385–407 (1985).

[65] Black, F., Derman, E., and Toy, W. A one-factor model of interest rates and its application to Treasury bond options. *Financial Analysts Journal* (July–August 1990): 52–59.

[66] Jamshidian, F. Forward induction and the construction of yield curve diffusion models. *Journal of Fixed Income* 1:62–74 (1991).

[67] Hull, J., and White, A. Numerical procedures for implementing term structure models I: Single-factor models. *Journal of Derivatives* 2: 7–16 (1994).

[68] Jamshidian, F. Bond and option evaluation in the Gaussian interest rate model. *Research in Finance* 9:131–70 (1991).

[69] Kloeden, P., and Platen, E. *Numerical Solution of Stochastic Differential Equations*, 3rd ed. Heidelberg: Springer, 1999.

[70] Press, W.H., Teukolsky, S.A., Vetterling, W.T., and Flannery, B.P. *Numerical Recipes in C*, 2nd ed., Cambridge: Cambridge University Press, 1993.

[71] Gill, P.E., Murray, W., and Wright, M.H., *Practical Optimization*. San Diego: Academic Press, 1981.

[72] Black, F., and Scholes, M. The pricing of options and corporate liabilities. *Journal of Political Economy* 81:637–654 (1973).

[73] Merton, R.C. Theory of rational option pricing. *Bell Journal of Economics and Management Science* 4:141–183 (Spring 1973).

[74] Black, F., and Cox, J. Valuing corporate securities: Some effects of bond indenture provisions. *Journal of Finance* 351–367 (1976).

[75] Merton, R.C. On the pricing of corporate debt: The risk structure of interest rates. *Journal of Finance* 29:449–470, 1974.

[76] Geske, R. The valuation of corporate liabilities as compound options. *Journal of Financial and Quantitative Analysis* 12:541–552 (1977).

[77] Hull, J., and White, A. The impact of default risk on the prices of options and other derivatives securities. *Journal of Banking and Finance* 19(2):299–322 (1995).

[78] Nielsen, L.T., Saa-Requejo, J., and Santa-Clara, P. Default risk and interest rate risk: The term structure of default spreads. Working Paper, INSEAD, 1993.

[79] Schonbucher, P.J. Valuation of securities subject to credit risk. Working paper, University of Bonn, February 1996.

[80] Zhou, C. A jump-diffusion approach to modeling credit risk and valuing defaultable securities. *Finance and Economics Discussion Series, Federal Reserve Board* 15 (1997).

[81] Longstaff, F.A., and Schwartz, E.S. A simple approach to valuing risky fixed and floating rate debt. *Journal of Finance* 29:789–819 (1995).

[82] Briys, E. and Varenne, F. Valuing risky fixed rate debt: An extension. *Journal of Financial and Quantitative Analysis* 32(2):239–248 (1997).

[83] Ramaswamy, K., and Sundaresan, S.M. The valuation of floating rate instruments, theory and evidence. *Journal of Financial Economics* 17:251–272 (1986).

[84] Jarrow, R.A., and Turnbull, S.M. Pricing derivatives on financial securities subject to credit risk. *Journal of Finance* 50:53–85, 1995.

[85] Duffie, D., and Singleton, K. Econometric modelling of term structures of defaultable bonds. Working Paper, Stanford University, 1994.

[86] Duffie, D., and Singleton, K. An econometric model of the term structure of interest rate swap yields. *Journal of Finance* 52(4):1287–1321 (1997).

[87] Duffie, D., and Singleton, K.J. Modeling term structure of defaultable bonds. *Review of Financial Studies* 12:687–720 (1999).

[88] Lando, D. On Cox processes and credit risky bonds. *Review of Derivatives Research* 2(2/3):99–120 (1998).

[89] Ingersoll, J.E. A contingent claim valuation of convertible securities. *Journal of Financial Economics* 4:289–322 (1977).

[90] Brennan, M.J., and Schwartz, E.S. Convertible bonds: Valuation and optimal strategies for call and conversion. *Journal of Finance* 32:1699–1715 (1977).

[91] Brennan, M.J., and Schwartz, E.S. Analysing convertible bonds. *Journal of Financial and Quantitative Analysis* 15(4):907–929 (1980).

[92] Nyborg, K.G. The use and pricing of convertible bonds. *Applied Mathematical Finance* 3:167–190 (1996).

[93] Carayannopoulos, P. Valuing convertible bonds under the assumption of stochastic interest rates: An empirical investigation. *Quarterly Journal of Business and Economics* 35(3):17–31 (summer 1996).

[94] Cox, J., Ingersoll, J., and Ross, S. A theory of the term structure of interest rates. *Econometrica* 53:385–467 (1985).

[95] Zhu, Y.-I., and Sun, Y. The singularity separating method for two factor convertible bonds. *Journal of Computational Finance* 3(1):91–110 (1999).

[96] Epstein, D., Haber, R., and Wilmott, P. Pricing and hedging convertible bonds under non-probabilistic interest rates. *Journal of Derivatives*, Summer 2000, 31–40 (2000).

[97] Barone-Adesi, G., Bermúdez, A., and Hatgioannides, J. Two-factor convertible bonds valuation using the method of characteristics/finite elements. *Journal of Economic Dynamics and Control* 27(10):1801–1831 (2003).

[98] Nogueiras, M.R. 2005. Numerical analysis of second order Lagrange-Galerkin schemes. Application to option pricing problems. Ph.D. thesis, Department of Applied Mathematics, Universidad de Santiago de Compostela, Spain.

[99] McConnell, J.J., and Schwartz, E.S. LYON taming. *The Journal of Finance* 41(3):561–577 (July 1986).

[100] Cheung, W., and Nelken, I. Costing the converts. *Risk* 7(7):47–49 (1994).

[101] Ho, T.S.Y., and Pfteffer, D.M. Convertible bonds: Model, value, attribution and analytics. *Financial Analyst Journal*, (September–October 1996):35–44.

[102] Schonbucher, P.J. *Credit Derivatives Pricing Models: Models, Pricing and Implementation.* Hoboken, NJ: Wiley, 2003.

[103] Arvanitis, A., and Gregory, J. *Credit: The Complete Guide to Pricing, Hedging and Risk Management.* London: Risk Books, 2001.

[104] Bermúdez, A., and Webber, N. An asset based model of defaultable convertible bonds with endogenised recovery. Working Paper, Cass Business School, London, 2004.

[105] Vasicek, O.A. An equilibrium characterisation of the term structure. *Journal of Financial Economics*, 5:177–188 (1977).

[106] Hull, J.C., and White, A. Pricing interest rate derivative securities. *Review of Financial Studies* 3:573–592 (1990).

[107] Bermúdez, A., and Nogueiras, M.R. Numerical solution of two-factor models for valuation of financial derivatives. *Mathematical Models and Methods in Applied Sciences* 14(2):295–327 (February 2004).

[108] Davis, M., and Lischka, F. Convertible bonds with market risk and credit risk. *Studies in Advanced Mathematics.* Somerville, MA: American Mathematical Society/International Press, 2002:45–58.

[109] Black, F. Derman, E., and Toy, W. A one factor model of interest rates and its application to Treasury bond options. *Financial Analyst Journal* 46:33–39 (1990).

[110] Zvan, R., Forsyth, P.A., and Vetzal, K.R. A general finite element approach for PDE option pricing model. *Proceedings of Quantitative Finance* 98, (1998).

[111] Yigitbasioglu, A.B. Pricing convertible bonds with interest rate, equity and FX risk. *ISMA Center Discussion Papers in Finance*, University of Reading (June 2002).

[112] Cheung, W., and Nelken, I. Costing the converts. In *Over the Rainbow*, vol. 46, London: Risk Publications, 1995: 313–317.

[113] Kalotay, A.J., Williams, G.O., and Fabozzi, F.J. A model for valuing bonds and embedded options. *Financial Analyst Journal* (May–June 1993): 35–46.

[114] Takahashi, A., Kobayahashi, T., and Nakagawa, N. Pricing convertible bonds with default risk: A Duffie-Singleton approach. *Journal of Fixed Income*, 11(3):20–29, (2001).

[115] Tseveriotis, K., and Fernandes, C. Valuing convertible bonds with credit risk. *Journal of Fixed Income*, 8(2):95–102 (September 1998).

[116] Ayache, E., Forsyth, P.A., and Vetzal, K.R. Next generation models for convertible bonds with credit risk. *Wilmott Magazine* 68–77 (December 2002).

[117] Ayache, E., Forsyth, P.A., and Vetzal, K.R. Valuation of convertible bonds with credit risk. *Journal of Derivatives* 11(1):9–29, (April 2003).

[118] Protter, P. *Stochastic Integration and Differential Equations*, vol. 21 of *Applications of Mathematics*, 3rd ed. Heidelberg: Springer-Verlag, 1995.

[119] Jacod, J., and Shiryaev, A.N. *Limit Theorems for Stochastic Processes.* Berlin: Springer, (1988).

[120] Olsen, L. Convertible bonds: A technical introduction. Research tutorial, Barclays Capital, 2002.

[121] Das, S.R., and Sundaram, R.K. A simple model for pricing securities with equity, interest-rate and default risk. Defaultrisk.com, 2004.

[122] Andersen, L., and Buffum, D. Calibration and implementation of convertible bond models. *Journal of Computational Finance* 7(2):1–34 (2003).

[123] Kiesel, R., Perraudin, W., and Taylor, A. Credit and interest rate risk. In M.H.A. Dempster, ed., *Risk Management: Value at Risk and Beyond.* New York: Cambridge University Press, 2002.

[124] Bielecki, T. and Rutkowski, M. *Credit Risk: Modeling, Valuation and Hedging.* Heidelberg: Springer Finance, 2002.

[125] Bakshi, G., Madan, D., and Zhang, F. Understanding the role of recovery in default risk models: Empirical comparisons and implied recovery rates. Working Paper, University of Maryland, November 2001.

[126] Unal, H., Madan, D., and Guntay, L. A simple approach to estimate recovery rates with APR violation from debt spreads. Working Paper, University of Maryland, February 2001.

[127] Hamilton, D.T., Gupton, G., and Berthault, A. Default and recovery rates of corporate bond issuers: 2000. Special comment, Moody's Investor Service, Global Credit Research, February 2000.

[128] Altman, E.I., Resti, A., and Sirone, A. Analysing and explaining default recovery rates. Report, ISDA, Stern School of Business, New York University, December 2001.

[129] Realdon, M. Convertible subordinated debt valuation and "conversion in distress." Working Paper, Department of Economics and Related Studies, University of York, 2003.

[130] Overhaus et al., *Modelling and Hedging Equity Derivatives*, Risk Books, 1999.

[131] JeanBlanc, M. Modelling of Default Risk. Mathematical Tools, 2000."

[132] Duffie Khan A yield factor model of interest rates, 1996.

[133] Nelson, R.B. An introduction to copulas. *Mathematical Tools*, 2000, p.91.

[134] Black, F., and Scholes, M. The pricing of options on corporate liabilities. *Journal of Political Economy* 81: 637–659 (1973).

[135] Heston, S.L. A closed-form solution for options with stochastic volatility with applications to bond and currency options. *Review of Financial Studies* 6: 327–343 (1993).

[136] Dupire, B. Pricing with a smile. *Risk* 7: 18–20 (January 1994).

[137] Revuz, D., and Yor, M. *Continuous Martingales and Brownian Motion*, 3rd ed. Heidelberg: Springer, 1998:375 (theorem (2.1)).

[138] Gyöngy, L. Mimicking the one-dimensional marginal distributions of processes having an Ito differential. *Probability Theory and Related Fields* 71: 501–516 (1986).

[139] Clewlow, L., and Strickland, C. *Implementing Derivative Models.* Hoboken, NJ: Wiley, 1998.

[140] Wilmott, P., Dewynne, J., and Howison, J. *Option Pricing: Mathematical Models and Computation.* New York: Oxford Financial Press, 1993.

[141] Vázquez, C. An upwind numerical approach for an American and European option pricing model. *Applied Mathematics and Computation* 273–286 (1998).

[142] Bermúdez, A., and Moreno, C. Duality methods for solving variational inequalities. *Computer Mathematics with Applications*, 7:43–58 (1981).

[143] Hull, J.C., and White, A. Efficient procedures for valuing European and American path dependent options. *Journal of Derivatives* 1:21–31 (Fall 1993).

[144] Ewing, R.E., and Wang, H. A summary of numerical methods for time-dependent advection-dominated partial differential equations. *Journal of Computational and Applied Mathematics* 128:423–445 (2001).

[145] Pironneau, O. On the transport-diffusion algorithm and its application to the navier-stokes equations. *Journal of Numerical Mathematics* 38(3):309–332 (1982).

[146] Douglas, J., and Russell, T. Numerical methods for convection dominated diffusion problems based on combining methods of characteristics with finite element methods or finite differences. *SIAM Journal on Numerical Analysis* 19(5):871 (1982).

[147] Baker, M.D., Suli, E., and Ware, A.F. Stability and convergence of the spectral Lagrange-Galerkin method for mixed periodic/non-periodic convection dominated diffusion problems. *IMA Journal of Numerical Analysis*, 19:637–663 (1999).

[148] Baranger, D., Esslaoui, D., and Machmoum, A. Error estimate for convection problem with characteristics method. *Numerical Algorithms*, 21:49–56 (1999).

[149] Baranger, J., and Machmoum, A. A "natural" norm for the method of charactersistics using discontinuous finite elements: 2d and 3d case. *Mathematical Modeling and Numerical Analysis* 33:1223–1240 (1999).

[150] Boukir, K., Maday, Y., Metivet, B., and Razanfindrakoto, E. A high order characteristics/finite element method for the incompressible Navier-Stokes equations. *International Journal for Numerical Methods in Fluids* 25:1421–1454 (1997).

[151] Rui, H., and Tabata, M. A second order characteristic finite element scheme for convection-diffusion problems. *Journal of Numerical Mathematics* 92:161–177 (2002).

[152] Bermúdez, A., Nogueiras, M.R., and Vázquez, C. 2006. Numerical analysis of convection-diffusion-reaction problems with higher order characteristics/finite elements. Part I: Time discretization. To appear in *Siam Journal on Numerical Analysis*.

[153] Ciarlet, P.G., and Lions, J.L. eds. *Handbook of Numerical Analysis*, vol. 1 of *North-Holland*. Amsterdam: Elsevier Science, 1989.

[154] Kangro, R., and Nicolaides, R. Far field boundary conditions for Black-Scholes equations. *SIAM Journal on Numerical Analysis* 38(4):1357–1368 (2000).

[155] Barles, G., and Souganidis, P.E. Convergence of approximation schemes for fully nonlinear second order equations. *Asymptotyc Analysis* 4(4):271–283 (1991).

[156] Duvaut, G., and Lions, J.L. Les inéquations en mécanique et en physique. In *Travaux et Recherches Mathématiques*, vol. 21. Paris: Dunod, 1972.

[157] Glowinski, R., Lions, J.L., and Trémolières, R. *Analyse Numérique Des Inéquations Variationnelles*. Paris: Dunod, 1973.

[158] Bensoussan, A. and Lions, J.L. *Applications Des Inéquations Variationneles En Contrôle Stochastique*. Paris: Dunod, 1978.

[159] Jaillet, J., Lamberton, D., and Lapeyre, B. Variational inequalities and the pricing of American options. *Acta Applicandae Mathematicae* 21:263–289 (1990).

[160] Crandall, M.G., Ishii, H., and Lions, P.L. User's guide to viscosity solutions of second order partial differential equations. *Bulletin of the American Mathematical Society* 27(1):1–67 (1992).

[161] Lions, P.L. Optimal control of diffusion processes and Hamilton-Jacobi-Bellman equations, part 2: Viscosity solutions and uniqueness. *Communications in Partial Differential Equations* 8(11):1229–1276 (1983).

[162] Barles, G., Daher, C.H., and Souganidis, P. Convergence of numerical schemes for parabolic equations arising in finance theory. *Mathematical Models and Methods in Applied Science* 5:125–143 (1995).

[163] Wilmott, P. *Derivatives: The Theory and Practice of Financial Engineering*. Hoboken, NJ: Wiley, 1998.

[164] Clarke, N., and Parrot, K. Multigrid American option pricing with stochastic volatility. *Applied Mathematical Finance* 6:177–195 (1999).

[165] Forsyth, P.A., and Vetzal, K. Quadratic convergence for valuing american options using a penalty method. *SIAM Journal on Scientific Computation* 23:2096–2123 (2002).

[166] Parés, C., Castro, M., and Macías, J. On the convergence of the Bermúdez-Moreno algorithm with constant parameters. *Numerische Mathematik* 92:113–128 (2002).

[167] Morton, K.W. *Numerical Solution of Convection-Diffusion Problems*. Boca Raton, FL: Chapman & Hall, 1996.

[168] Pironneau, O., and Hetch, F. Mesh adaptation for the Black and Scholes equations. *Journal of Numerical Mathematics*, 8(1):25–35 (2000).

[169] Figlewski, S., and Gao, B. The adaptive mesh model: A new approach to efficient option pricing. Working Paper, Stern School of Business, New York University, 1997.

[170] Zvan, R., Forsyth, P.A., and Vetzal, K.R. PDE methods for pricing barrier options. *Journal of Economic Dynamics and Control*, 24 (2000).

[171] Pooley, D.M., Forsyth, P.A., Vetzal, K.R., and Simpson, R.B. Unstructured meshing for two asset barrier options. *Applied Mathematical Finance* 7:33–60 (2000).

[172] Winkler, G., Apel, T., and Wystup, U. Valuation of options in heston's stochastic volatility model using finite element methods. In *Foreign Exchange Risk*. London: Risk Publications, 2001.

[173] Topper, J. Finite element modeling of exotic options. Discussion paper 216, Department of Economics, University of Hannover, December 1998.

[174] D'Halluin, Y., Forsyth, P., Vetzal, K., and Labahn, G. A numerical PDE approach for pricing callable bonds. *Applied Mathematical Finance*, 8:49–77 (2001).

[175] Zvan, R., Forsyth, P.A., and Vetzal, K.R. A finite volume approach for contingent claims valuation. *IMA Journal of Numerical Analysis* 21:703–721 (2001).

[176] Zvan, R., Forsyth, P.A., and Vetzal, K.R. Convergence of lattice and PDE methods valuing path dependent options with interpolation. *Review of Derivatives Research* 5:273–314, 2002.

[177] Zvan, R., Forsyth, P.A., and Vetzal, K.R. Robust numerical methods for PDE models of Asian options. *Journal of Computational Finance* 1:39–78 (1998).

[178] Zvan, R., Forsyth, P.A., and Vetzal, K.R. A finite element approach to the pricing of discrete lookbacks with stochastic volatility. *Applied Mathematical Finance* 6:87–106 (1999).

[179] Selmin, V., and Formaggia, L. Unified construction of finite element and finite volume discretisation for compressible flows. *International Journal for Numerical Methods in Engineering* 39:1–32, (1996).

[180] Ciarlet, P.G. *The Finite Element Method for Elliptic Problems*, vol. 4 of *Studies in Mathematics and its Applications*. Amsterdam: North-Holland, 1978.

[181] Zienkiewicz, O.C., Taylor, R.L., and Zhu, J.Z. *The Finite Element Method: Its Basis and Fundamentals*. Amsterdam: 6th ed., *Elsevier Butterworth-Heinemann*, 2005.

[182] Suli, E. Stability and convergence of the Lagrange-Galerkin method with nonexact integration. In J. R. Whiteman, ed. *The Proceedings of the Conference on the Mathematics of Finite Elements and Applications, MAFELAP VI*. Academic Press: London, 1998: 435–442.

[183] Bause, M., and Knabner, P. Uniform error analysis for Lagrange-Galerkin approximations of convection-dominated problems. *SIAM Journal of Numerical Analysis* 39:1954–1984 (2002).

[184] Ewing, R.E., and Russel, T.F. Multistep Galerkin methods along characteristics for convection-diffusion problems. In R. Vichtneveski and R.S. Stepleman, ed. *Advances in Computer Methods for Partial Differential Equations IV*. IMACS Publications, 1981: 28–36.

[185] Boukir, K., Maday, Y., Metivet, B., and Razafindrakoto, E. A high-order characteristics/finite element method for incompressible Navier-Stoke equations. *International Journal on Numerical Methods in Fluids* 25:1421–1454 (1997).

[186] Priestley, A. Exact projections and the Lagrange-Galerkin method: A realistic alternative to quadrature. *Journal of Computational Physics*, 112:316–333 (1994).

[187] Morton, K.W., Priestley, A., and Suli, E. Stability of the Lagrange-Galerkin method with nonexact integration. *Mathematical Modeling and Numerical Analysis* 22:625–653, 1988.

[188] Broadie, M., and Glasserman, P. (1973). Pricing American-style securities using simulation. *Journal of Economic Dynamics and Control* 21(8–9): 1323–1352 (1997).

[189] Longstaff, F., and Schwartz, E. Valuing American options by simulation: A simple least-squares approach. *Review Financial Studies* 14:113–148 (2001).

[190] Fries, Christian P. Foresight bias and suboptimality correction in Monte-Carlo pricing of options with early exercise: Classification, calculation and removal. http://www.christian-fries.de/finmath/foresightbias.

[191] Tilley, J.A. Valuing American options in a path simulation model. *Transactions of the Society of Actuaries* 45:83–104 (1993).

[192] Rogers, C. Monte Carlo valuation of American options. *Mathematical Finance* 12:271–286 (2002).

[193] Andersen, L., and Broadie, M. "A primal-dual simulation algorithm for pricing multidimensional American options. *Management Science* 50(9): 1222–1234 (2004).

[194] Andersen, L.B.G. A simple approach to the pricing of Bermudan swaptions in the multifactor LIBOR market model. (March 5, 1999). http://ssm.com/abstract=155208.

[195] Windcliff, H., Forsyth, P., and Vetzal, K. Asymptotic boundary conditions for the Black-Scholes equation. Working Paper, University of Waterloo, October 2001.

[196] Topper, J. 2005. *Financial Engineering with Finite Elements*. Hoboken, NJ: Wiley-Finance.

[197] Bermúdez, A., Nogueiras, M.R., and Vázquez, C. 2006 Numerical analysis of convection-diffusion-reaction problems with higher order characteristic/finite elements. Part II: Fully discretized scheme and quadrature formulas. To appear in *Siam Journal on Numerical Analysis*.

Index